An Empire of Small Places

Early American Places is a collaborative project of the
University of Georgia Press, New York University Press,
Northern Illinois University Press, and the University of
Nebraska Press. The series is supported by the Andrew
W. Mellon Foundation. For more information, please visit
www.earlyamericanplaces.org.

ADVISORY BOARD
Vincent Brown, *Duke University*
Stephanie M. H. Camp, *University of Washington*
Andrew Cayton, *Miami University*
Cornelia Hughes Dayton, *University of Connecticut*
Nicole Eustace, *New York University*
Amy S. Greenberg, *Pennsylvania State University*
Ramón A. Gutiérrez, *University of Chicago*
Peter Charles Hoffer, *University of Georgia*
Karen Ordahl Kupperman, *New York University*
Joshua Piker, *University of Oklahoma*
Mark M. Smith, *University of South Carolina*
Rosemarie Zagarri, *George Mason University*

AN EMPIRE OF SMALL PLACES

Mapping the Southeastern Anglo-Indian Trade, 1732–1795

ROBERT PAULETT

The University of Georgia Press
ATHENS AND LONDON

© 2012 by the University of Georgia Press
Athens, Georgia 30602
www.ugapress.org

All rights reserved

Printed digitally in the United States of America

LIBRARY OF CONGRESS CATALOGING-IN-PUBLICATION DATA

Paulett, Robert, 1976–
 An empire of small places : mapping the southeastern Anglo-Indian trade, 1732–1795 / Robert Paulett.
  p. cm. — (Early American places)
 Includes bibliographical references and index.
 ISBN 978-0-8203-4346-4 (hardcover : alk. paper)
 ISBN 0-8203-4346-3 (hardcover : alk. paper)
 ISBN 978-0-8203-4347-1 (pbk. : alk. paper)
 ISBN 0-8203-4347-1 (pbk. : alk. paper)
 1. Chickasaw Indians—Commerce. 2. Chickasaw Indians—Economic conditions. 3. Chickasaw Indians—History—18th century. 4. Southern States—Commerce—Great Britain. 5. Great Britain—Commerce—Great Britain. I. Title.
E99.C55P38 2012
976.004'97386—dc23

2012019929

British Library Cataloging-in-Publication Data available

Contents

List of Illustrations ix
Acknowledgments xi

Introduction. The View from the Bluffs: Envisioning the Spaces of the Anglo-Creek Deerskin Trade 1
1 Strung Together: Mapping the Colonial Southeast 12
2 The Life of the Region: The Many Meanings of the Savannah River 49
3 Keeping Company, Keeping Store: The Shaping of Colonial Augusta 78
4 To Make the Path White and Clear: Possibilities and Problems in Southeastern Travel 115
5 Breaking Houses: Trading Posts and Power in the Colonial Southeast 142
Conclusion. To Remove All Obstructions: Southeastern Geography after the American Revolution 173

Notes 199
Bibliography 237
Index 251

Illustrations

1   The engraved Thomas Nairne inset from Edward Crisp's
    1711 "A Compleat Description of the Province of Carolina."   14
2   Herman Moll, "A New Map of the North Parts of America
    Claimed by France," 1720.   17
3   The Barnwell-Hammerton manuscript map, ca. 1721.   18
4   Mingo Ouma-Alexandre de Batz, "Nations Amies et
    Enemies des Tchikachas," 1737.   25
5   Detail from the John Stuart-Joseph Purcell Manuscript
    Map. The highlighted areas show the locations of the (from
    west to east) Chickasaws, Upper Creeks, Lower Creeks, and
    Augusta, circa 1775. Some of the major trade paths are also
    visible between these areas.   26
6   Details from Henry Popple, "A Map of the British Empire
    in America," 1733.   33
7   Cartouche from Popple, "Map of the British Empire."   36
8   Detail from John Mitchell, "Map of the British and French
    Dominions in North America," 1755.   37
9   Cartouche from Mitchell, "Map of the British and French
    Dominions."   38
10 John Gerar William de Brahm, "Map of Carolina and
    Part of Georgia," 1757.   41

11	The Stuart-Purcell manuscript map, 1775.	46
12	A Savannah River trading boat as depicted in an untitled drawing by Philip Georg Friedrich Von Reck.	67
13	Detail from Archibald Campbell, "Sketch of the Northern Frontiers of Georgia," 1780.	82

Acknowledgments

It is somewhat odd to sit here and actually begin writing the acknowledgments that I had many times composed in my head. Frequently during the years of research and writing, I would distract myself with thoughts of the final product, whom I would thank, and in what order. Each time, the list grew a little longer, as I accumulated large favors and small on the path from abstract idea to finished product. A list in no way complete, I would like to take this opportunity to thank those who most directly made this work possible and enjoyable.

First and foremost, I thank the state of Virginia. Its obsession with its own past and its commitment to public higher education provided both the inclination and institutional support necessary for me to complete this project. I also thank the state of Illinois, whose dodgy financial situation after the meltdown of 2008 allowed for a steady paycheck and not much else—the ideal conditions for a young scholar to devote his energy to revising an already existing work.

On a more personal and serious note, I do need to thank the long chain of friends and mentors who made all of this work possible. The College of William and Mary is home to a remarkably creative and supportive community that has learned to adapt to living in a town of retirees and tourists. I cannot hope to list all those who made my Williamsburg years worthwhile, but a few require special mention. Gordon Barker, Evan Bennett, Seth Bruggeman, Dave Corlett, Phil Levy, Emily Moore, Catharine Dann Roeber, Mike Shumann, and James Spady deserve thanks for their constant reminders that life exists outside of libraries.

I have also benefited from the wisdom and insight of a remarkable series of scholars. At James Madison University, Michael Galgano first taught me what it meant to be a professional and dedicated historian and his example has served me well ever since. At William and Mary, James Axtell taught me the historian's art, and I owe him my greatest debts as a scholar and a writer. His patient effort to correct every one of my bad habits has almost completely succeeded. Kris Lane has provided a constant example of what it means to truly love history, and his perspective is always appreciated. Ed Crapol, Bob Gross, Leisa Meyer, and Carol Sheriff have all shaped my work more than they know, and I thank them at last. To James Whittenburg I owe my deepest gratitude. "Thank you" seems too small a repayment for all of his advice, assistance, and unwavering faith in me, but it is offered here with the greatest sincerity.

My lengthy tenure in Williamsburg has also indebted me to the town's two main institutions. The College of William and Mary obviously provided the bulk of the support for this current work. The staff at Earl Gregg Swem Library alone deserves their own page of acknowledgments. I thank the Lyon G. Tyler Department of History at the College of William and Mary for funding my research through its generous offers of stipends, writing preceptorships, summer travel grants, conference funding, fellowships, and awards. I also thank Louise Kale, Director of the Historic Campus, and Edward Chappell of the Colonial Williamsburg Foundation for a research assistantship given in 2005.

I am also greatly indebted to the other cornerstone of Williamsburg life, the Colonial Williamsburg Foundation. Their Department of Archaeological Research has provided me a second degree's-worth of education and much-appreciated employment over the years. Marley Brown deserves special recognition for giving a historian the chance to work as an archaeologist and providing me with an array of questions about past landscapes that I have brought to bear on the colonial Southeast. Andy Edwards, Dave Muraca, Bill Pittman, and Meredith Poole also deserve thanks for their guidance and instruction during my days in the field. I also thank the Colonial Williamsburg Department of Historical Research and Kevin Kelly in particular for their generous offer of a research assistantship during the 2005–2006 academic year.

This work would not have been possible without the help of numerous other institutions. I thank the Newberry Library in particular for their award of a short-term fellowship and a month among their wonderful map collection. It was there that both the first chapter and the outline of the whole project were born. I would also like to thank James Akerman for his ongoing support and encouragement. The William L. Clements Library at the University of Michigan, Ann Arbor, awarded me a Jacob Price Fellowship that proved crucial for the writing of the fourth and fifth chapters. For everything in between, I owe a debt of gratitude to the staff of the Southern Historical Collection at the University of North Carolina, Chapel Hill; the Georgia Historical Society; the Hargrett Library at the University of Georgia, and the Special Collections staff at the Reese Library at Augusta State University. This book could not have been written without their assistance. I also thank Christopher Newport University, Old Dominion University, and the University of Mary Washington (and Carter Hudgins in particular) for the introduction to the professional life that they provided for me.

I also owe a special debt of gratitude to my colleagues at Southern Illinois University Edwardsville who have made a new home for me in the middle of the country. I am grateful to them all, but I feel like I should single out Jason Stacy for his tireless efforts to smooth my transition from the East Coast to the Midwest.

Thanks, of course, to the University of Georgia Press for taking on this project and making it theirs. Derek Krissof has been honest and patient throughout the whole process,, and I am grateful for his work. The anonymous readers who provided their thoughtful (and thorough) comments improved this book greatly and will forever have my gratitude.

Two more personal debts must here be acknowledged. First, Bridget Reddick has lived with this project almost as long as I have. She knew this work would be finished, even when I myself had doubts. It will take a lifetime and a lengthy series of nice dinners to repay her patience. Finally, I owe my mother, Millie Paulett, my greatest thanks. It is to her that I dedicate this work and hope that she can find room for one more book on her already groaning shelves.

An Empire of Small Places

Introduction. The View from the Bluffs: Envisioning the Spaces of the Anglo-Creek Deerskin Trade

In March 1733, James Oglethorpe looked at the Savannah River and came up with an idea for a new town. Around him the original English settlers of Georgia had barely begun implementing his grand scheme for the town of Savannah, but Oglethorpe wanted Georgia to reach further into the American interior. Watching the river traffic from atop Savannah's bluff, Oglethorpe counted "12 Trading Boats" that had "passed by" in the first few weeks of Georgia's settlement.[1] These boats were not small craft; they were forty feet long, rowed by four-man crews, and filled with thousands of deerskins bound for the port of Charles Town. Seeking both an economic footing for Georgia and a diplomatic edge in the imperial contest with France, Oglethorpe eventually devised a plan to redirect the trading boats to Savannah. He would build a town at the falls of the river, encouraging Indian traders from Carolina to cross the Savannah and do business with the colony of Georgia. This new town, to be named Augusta, would dominate the Anglo-Creek trade and play a major role in southeastern Indian-white relations until the American Revolution. Looking down at the boatmen, Oglethorpe planned a new Southeast.[2]

But what of those who looked back? Here in this vignette were two different views of the landscape and what it represented. Oglethorpe's imperial gaze encompassed the Savannah River, and he imagined the river as a main artery for Georgia's commerce. But the boatmen saw the river differently. For European and African American boatmen alike the river was an ever-shifting place of eddies, snags, and other dangers. Looking out across thousands of dressed deerskins, the boatmen were more concerned with keeping the slim canoe upright and its cargo dry. The grand ambitions of bluff-top visionaries were not necessarily a part of their view. And, in reality, the boatmen's idea of space had more influence on the deerskin trade than Oglethorpe's elaborate scheming. After all, without them, the trade would not have been possible in the first place.

And what of the Indians whom Oglethorpe tried to encompass in his gaze? Missing from this vignette, obviously, are the numerous Indian views of what the Southeast was and should become. Oglethorpe's ambitions, after all, relied on Creek, Cherokee, Chickasaw, and possibly Choctaw cooperation. It included Yuchis and Yamacraws and numerous others, as well. They each had their own ideas of what the Southeast should look like, and they did not always match Oglethorpe's vision. The story at the bluffs was thus more than a story of Georgia's involvement in the deerskin trade. It was a story of differing visions of what the Southeast was and could be. Within the British Southeast, colonists, Indians, and the enslaved all competed to define the deerskin trade.

Although part of the same empire, Oglethorpe's view and the boatmen's was not the same view of landscape. The deerskin traders and their adjuncts experienced the Southeast in a very different way. They traveled a landscape of distinct but interconnected spaces that did not always conform to imperial expectations. Formed out of an ongoing contest between Europeans, Indians, and Africans, the trade's geography defined the slim but significant corridors of human interaction in the Southeast between 1732 and 1774. It was a human geography where Indians and Europeans found common concepts of space and created an improvised system of linked places that defined the shape of southeastern history.

As the main source of interaction between Indians and Europeans, the deerskin trade had a major influence over the course of southeastern history. Those who sought power and influence in the trade thus had to maintain control over a disparate set of spaces: river traffic, colonial towns and trading posts, paths, and storehouses in Indian villages. Controlling access to and exerting influence over these spaces occupied much of the effort of European administrators, merchants, and traders. It likewise occupied much of the effort of Indian headmen, warriors, and women. It also concerned the enslaved African Americans who moved through these spaces.

And while such a variety of players created numerous contests over and within the trade, they also created a surprisingly stable and durable system of places. The trade underwent numerous changes and upheavals after the arrival of the English in Carolina in 1670, and the establishment of Georgia in 1732 was one of these. But between 1732 and 1774, the trade's spaces settled into a channel that remained largely unaltered until the American Revolution. European goods arrived at Charles Town (and to a lesser extent, Savannah) and moved through major merchant houses, along the coast, and up the Savannah River to Augusta. At Augusta, the trade's leading merchants established their warehouses and main stores. From the town, goods traveled by packhorse train until arriving in Indian villages. Within or near the village, the local trader conducted the actual exchange of European goods for Indian deerskins. The skins then followed the reverse route back to Charles Town and out to the Atlantic.

As those employed in trading moved through these spaces, they created a geography that did not always sit well within British visions of empire. Formed at the intersection of European and Indian cultural ideas of space, the trade's geography seemed anarchic and dangerous to British administrators. Throughout the period from 1732 to 1774, the trade was an uneasy adjunct to British territorial goals in the Southeast. As Britain sought order within a knowable system of places, traders and Indian headmen defended the trade's uncertain geography of human interaction. At once unpredictable and reliable, traders and Indians found that their knowledge of these complex spaces served as a bolster to their authority in the region. Each group, of course, thought that it was completely in control of the trade, and neither group was entirely right.

The struggle to define space forced each participant to define the way they thought the world should be. Their efforts have provided modern readers with a window into the imperial process in the eighteenth century. What resulted was a multifaceted contest over the places and possibilities of the Southeast. These contests within the British Empire were themselves challenged by African American slaves and, later, by the new American Empire that emerged after the Revolution. Spaces were thus not just the settings for history; they were a problem that needed constant attention, required Europeans to adapt to Indian ideas, and, in that adaptation, define for themselves what the empire was and how it should function.

The outlines of this contest over space in the Southeast reflect the broad outlines of empire that Eric Hinderaker has described in the Ohio Valley. Like their northern counterparts, traders and Indians in the Southeast created a human "Empire of Commerce" that benefited local interests and proved very difficult to manage from imperial centers. In their efforts to organize the seemingly anarchic trade geography, imperial administrators articulated an "Empire of Land" in which Britain tried to better regulate the region. But in the Southeast, this "Empire" was defined more by administrative initiative than settlement and overlapped with the "Empire of Commerce." In the end, both of these British Empires were replaced by an American "Empire of Liberty" that grew out of white settlers seeking to define the region for themselves and to push out altogether the Anglo-Indian trade's ideas of human connection and space. In their stead rose an empire devoted to the exclusion of Indians and the promotion of agriculture as the defining contest of human history.[3]

Historians have long been concerned with the spaces of the southeastern deerskin trade. Ever since Frederick Jackson Turner's student Verner Crane coined the phrase "the southern frontier," studies of the region have carried an implicit spatial component. For Crane, the early Southeast was marked by failed Edenic schemes until the establishment of Georgia finally turned the British empire toward aggressive territorial expansion. Crane replicated his teacher's emphases on successive frontiers preparing the way for the triumph of an Anglo-American sense of space—a conquering agrarian empire.[4] While later historians have abandoned Crane's celebration of British expansion, they still echo his spatial conceptions in their readiness to employ the term "the southern frontier" and its implications of a spatial contest between Europeans and Indians.[5] For those following Crane, southeastern history happened across borders, as Indians responded to European aggression and adapted accordingly.

Historians of the southern backcountry have furthered deepened our understanding of agricultural spaces and their meanings in the eighteenth-century Southeast. These studies have generally followed in the wake of Robert Mitchell's work of historical geography *Commercialism and Frontier*. White settlers, primarily Scots-Irish and German, distributed themselves across the southern backcountry so that they might best take advantage of England's commercial empire. Rather than independent pioneers, these were enterprising farmers seeking the economic and political advantages of full membership in the Atlantic economy. In seeking that access, they rearranged the backcountry into a landscape of cleared fields, open roadways, market towns, and mills. And they organized quickly against any obstacle to that progress: coastal elites who monopolized governmental authority, bandits who threatened the system of property, and Indians who cut off access to fresh lands.[6] But Indians have had only a small role in this literature other than providing lands on which these settlers can imprint their ideals.

Recovering the Indian sense of space has been left to the creative energy of ethnohistorians. For them, the contest of space has also been crucial. Ethnohistorians have undone Turner's heroic narrative of triumphant white expansion and have rightly emphasized Indians' adaptability to colonialism and their efforts, ultimately unsuccessful, to shape the southeastern situation to their benefit. On the regional scale, historians such as James Merrell, Robbie Ethridge, and Steven Hahn have noted how Indians invented their own idea of a "national" space as a means of maintaining their autonomy in the face of British expansion.[7] Others such as Kathryn Braund and Claudio Saunt have focused on the crucial contest over smaller spaces such as fields and houses. In these places, a European spatial sensibility formed by ideas of private property and the accumulation of wealth transformed Indian, specifically Creek, territory from the ground up.[8]

But the Anglo-Creek trade, in addition to its importance in Indian society, was also influential in shaping the patterns of settlement and society in the English colony of Georgia. Not just a "first nature" to be replaced, the trade's landscapes were an ongoing creative force within English colonies, requiring both physical and intellectual adjustment. Following the trade from Indian villages to English seaports reveals the ways in which the deerskin trade helped shaped the colonial landscape and forced Europeans to adapt to its pressures. What most of these studies have neglected is a close examination of the spaces of the deerskin trade outside of Indian villages. The deerskin trade represented another idea of space (or, more accurately, numerous other ideas of spaces) within the English empire, one that did not sit easily with the plans of administrators or the farms of settlers. As a means of encountering the landscape, the deerskin trade required English adaptations that other southeastern endeavors did not, and those adaptations had major consequences on the whole of southeastern history.

This study is therefore more than a study of the British side of the deerskin trade. It is a study in the ideals and realities of colonialism in the Southeast. Colonial planners and governors had their ideal visions of how the process should unfold. They were confounded at every turn by traders who had their own ideals of how the trade should operate. Governors and traders alike were confounded by the power of Indians to shape the trade to suit their needs and the ability of enslaved African

Americans to exploit the trade for their own uses. Indians and African Americans, however, also had to negotiate their place within an increasingly unequal system of colonization. Settlers moving into the area had to reconcile the ideas they brought from northern colonies with the unfamiliar rhythms and patterns of the trade system.

Given the range of human relationships that defined its key spaces, the deerskin trade itself was therefore defined by a certain predictable uncertainty. There were few guarantees that peace would subsist and that trade would continue. Even when Anglo-Indian relations were peaceful, traders had to contend with difficult rivers, unpredictable weather, vindictive competitors, and the near-constant presence of hostile Indians from outside the Southeast. To help reduce the uncertainty involved, the trade's participants directed the whole system through a set series of places. Threats to any of these places threatened the stability of the whole. The trade allowed freedom to negotiate the terms of the trade within these spaces, but could not bear any threats from outside.

Studying the deerskin trade requires that some account be made of this central tension between uncertainty and the desire for stability. These tensions require a different narrative form that replaces the assured progress of white settlement with a more complicated and uncertain future. D. W. Meinig has proposed a way of mapping the Atlantic World's geographic and social spaces that captures this complexity. In the first volume of his *The Shaping of America* series, Meinig noted the traditional divisions of colonial American studies into the familiar oppositions of "homeland and colonies," "metropolis and frontier," and "center and periphery." Meinig believed such "crude bipartite structures provide no real basis for geographical analysis."[9] In their place, Meinig offered an elaborate diagram, in which a "transect" from London to the Creek village of Cowcta, for example, passed through ten distinct zones, each marked by variations in social, political, and economic makeup. To fully understand the geography of the eighteenth-century British Atlantic empire, one had to allow for the great variety of power relationships that lay along Meinig's "transects."[10]

Meinig's approach bears fruit in southeastern studies. The closer one comes to the ground, the less uniform and the less certain the geography of the colonial Southeast becomes. The assured progress of white settlement into the interior suddenly seems less so, and the frontier narrative becomes less applicable to the experiences of everyday life in the deerskin trade.[11] Even on eighteenth-century maps, the documents that most clearly celebrated the British fantasy of continental control, the future of the Southeast seems wholly dependent on the trade's spatial and social relationships.

More important, a focus on the creation of space leads to a better accounting of human actions in the Southeast. Rivers did not "naturally" lead to interior commerce. They functioned as highways only when people put boats in the water. Towns did not accidentally form at fall lines; their location depended on both the boats and the inhabitants who settled them. Paths did not automatically transmit goods from place to place; using them required a lot of effort and a lot of horses. To study spaces thus requires de-naturalizing the landscape and understanding the Southeast as a place built by thousands of discrete human interactions.

In the interests of clarity, I have focused on just one segment of the Anglo-Indian deerskin trade within a specific set of years. This book is concerned with those spaces linked by the Anglo-Creek-Chickasaw trading route running from Charles Town up the Savannah River, through Augusta, through the Creeks, and finally reaching the Chickasaws in present-day northern Mississippi and western Tennessee. To follow the traders everywhere they went would expand this study into unmanageable lengths, as would trying to account for all the numerous permutations of Anglo-Indian trade between 1670 and 1795. I have therefore devoted the bulk of this study (Chapters 2 through 5) to the relatively stable period between Georgia's founding in 1732 and the American Revolution in 1774. Chapters 1 and 6 will provide the reader with an overview of major developments before and after this time period.

Constraining the study to this period in the history of the trade allows for all the yearly movements to build into something of a composite picture of the trade's spaces. Georgia's entry into Anglo-Creek relations required some revision of the trade as it had developed in the wake of the Yamasee War, especially in the development of Augusta. Georgia's entry also marked a series of sustained scrutiny of the southeastern Anglo-Indian deerskin trade between 1735 and 1776. The Georgia Trustees' efforts to create an ideal colony cast light on the workings of the deerskin trade and how its participants failed to live up to the trustees' standards. The events of the War of Austrian Succession between 1744 and 1748 and the Seven Years' War between 1754 and 1763 brought forth flurries of village diplomacy that required careful supervision of the deerskin traders, Britain's main diplomats. The years between 1763 and 1776 brought even more attention as Britain's royal and colonial governments sought to reform a trade they blamed for the previous two wars' evils.

The scrutiny revealed a set of places somewhat unique in British North America. While none of the trade's spaces was without parallel in the eighteenth century, few matched the Anglo-Creek corridor's particular set of circumstances. The Southeast was a region with no clear boundary, either legal or physical, between Indians, English, Spanish, and French. The traders who moved through the region moved farther and more frequently than the average colonist. And, unlike the traders in the Ohio Valley or more northern regions, the southern trade was heavily reliant on African American slaves from an early date. The unique circumstances of the Southeast therefore created a unique regional trade that nonetheless bore the marks of the global cultures that shaped it: European, Indian, and African.

These spaces all influenced each other in an interlocked system, even if the influence was indirect. While boatmen on the Savannah River did not daily interact with traders from Indian villages, the work of the two places was obviously connected. For example, the boats represented a transfer of work from the Indian porters of the late 1600s to the enslaved African Americans of the 1700s. As another example, the rise of slavery on Augusta plantations removed a labor burden from Indian women when Europeans used slaves to tan deerskin leather beginning in the middle of the eighteenth century.

The commonalities between cultures allowed for the creation of shared spaces, but the fit was never perfect. English ideas of rivers, towns, and houses never quite matched up with Indian or African ones. The similarities and superficial resemblances thus made the trade possible but ensured an ongoing pattern of conflict and misunderstanding. This work thus joins that of more recent scholars of Anglo-Indian relations who have begun emphasizing similarity as a crucial factor in cultural conflict.[12]

As a study of spatial conceptions, this book begins with a consideration of how Indians and Europeans conceived the space of the Southeast. The deerskin trade stretched across a large area, and its participants could think in grand terms. Chapter 1 thus focuses on two different regional spatial concepts: the European map and the point-to-point geography of the deerskin trade. Imperial administrators planned out their visions on the increasingly technocratic maps of the eighteenth century as a means of knowing and controlling the Southeast. The Indians and traders who traveled the paths, however, conceived of the region as a set of discrete but interconnected places. Travel through the Southeast required the proper negotiation of these spaces in the proper order.

Finding advantages in this processional geography, the trade's European and Indian participants defended their landscape in the face of imperial efforts to regulate the trade, as the point-to-point network served their ends better and afforded traders and Indians alike a sense of control over the trade.

Chapter 2 focuses on the Savannah River as both a conceptual space and a living space in the trade and demonstrates the ways in which southeasterners differed in their idea of landscape. A key connector in the Anglo-Creek trade, the Savannah posed a number of challenges to European ideas of rivers. Rivers like the Savannah proved an uneasy fit in the English imperial vision. In the eighteenth century, the English spent a great deal of time trying to turn England's rivers into empty spaces: open, smooth-flowing highways freed of the vestiges of medieval river use. An "unoccupied" river like the Savannah seemed a perfect example of this ideal, but the river itself proved a much more disorderly and unmanageable space. Failing to adapt their vision to the reality of the Southeast, the English largely "abandoned" the Savannah as a living space and turned it over to the enslaved boatmen who piloted American dugout canoes and made the whole trade possible. In doing so, these boatmen helped create a distinctly African American space within the larger world of the deerskin trade.

Chapter 3 focuses on the town of Augusta and how the trade encouraged British traders to adapt their idea of town planning to suit the needs of the trade. The exchange of deerskins required an open and constant movement between Augusta and the Creeks. Rather than close themselves off in a typical backcountry, fortified town, Augusta's merchant-traders settled in a much more open and dispersed manner. But rather than abandon the idea of community, Augustans organized their town around the basic institution of the trading company and its main built environment—the fortified trading compound. The Augusta companies thus manifested themselves as a physical, social, and economic presence in Augusta, shaping the town to suit the needs of their business and, much like they did with rivers, encouraging the development of race-based slavery as an important component of the deerskin trade.

Movement was a key aspect of life for traders and other sojourners, and the path (the subject of Chapter 4) was a living space every bit a much as the Savannah River. Indian headmen and warriors, traders, packhorsemen, servants, slaves, and fugitives all made temporary homes on the paths. The act of traveling the path required numerous adjustments from the primarily Scottish and Irish traders. Their lives defined by the balance sheets of European ledgers, traders nonetheless had to adapt to places where ideas of personal property held the greatest sway. This pressure shaped the traders' lives on the trails. As important was the presence of horses. The trade's demand for horses required Europeans and Indians alike to adapt to the needs of their four-legged friends.

Following the journey to its destination, Chapter 5 focuses on the trading houses located in Indian villages. Most of the trade occurred in these spaces, and they thus attained a symbolic importance in British ideas of the trade's meanings. English ideas of the house in particular invested these structures with meaning far beyond their function, as traders built a self-image of themselves as a civilizing force in native America. All of their mythmaking, however, had to confront the fact that they were living in Indian-built houses and sharing space with Indian women who had their own claims to primacy in the household. Out of these local contests over houses, however, emerged a particular vision of the trade that would remain influential even after the American Revolution.

The book ends with the American Revolution and the rise of a new set of spatial ideas in the southeastern interior. The war severed the links between Georgia and the Creeks. While the trade simply redirected itself toward the Gulf Coast during the war and the basic arrangement of spaces was restored, the occupants of the Georgia-Creek corridor had new visions for what the Southeast should become. The Savannah River, Augusta, even the old trading paths were absorbed into a new idea of empire being articulated by a new generation of southeastern leadership. The farmers and planters who came to occupy Augusta after the war had little use for Indians and indeed strongly disliked the human geography of the trade and its attendant conflicts. What these new leaders proposed was a simpler imperial space whereby land would be mapped and occupied by whites. Indians would be cast to the margins, if not removed altogether. This familiar form drew from the particular circumstances of the 1780s and 1790s and contested the older trade geography, now represented by the United States government's "Plan for Civilization."

To effect this course, post-Revolutionary Americans relied on words. While modern cartography was quickly charting the Southeast, it was in their newspapers and speeches that postwar Augustans formed their new understanding of their region. Relying on the trope of "neighborhood," Georgians quickly established a set of geographic terms that excluded Indians from their vision of North America and made them an obstacle to be eliminated. Newspapers in particular became an important new medium of geographic representation in the southeastern interior, with their emphasis on conflict along borders. Thus did newsprint help Georgia's new leaders craft a language of exclusion, removal, and even annihilation.

But the old trade geography still endured in a number of forms. That it took a revolution to undo the Augusta-Creek trade and even that did not completely erase the old geography should serve as testament to the trade's remarkable durability. It had taken the combined efforts of hundreds of people from three different continents to create the southeastern deerskin trade. It took a similarly massive reorganization of the Southeast to redirect the trade southward to the Gulf Coast, but it endured there for decades more. The trade's geography also remained as an echo in the Washington administration's "Plan for Civilization." Even though the American sense of space did eventually prevail, the trade's human geography defined relations for almost half a century. Therefore, it is worth taking a look at the colonial Southeast through the eyes of a boatman.

1 / Strung Together: Mapping the Colonial Southeast

More than most North American colonies, Georgia was founded to serve the interests of British imperial maps. In the 1700s, a cartographic contest began heating up between Britain and France as the two empires sought to expand in southeastern North America. Encountering new European rivals and increasingly involved in the native Southeast, British colonists in South Carolina in particular urged the home country to be ever more ambitious in its plans for the region. On numerous maps in the 1700s, Britain's imperial planners drew ambitious plans for future colonies, eventually resulting in the founding of Georgia in 1732. Empires created maps, and maps helped create the idea of empire; imperial and cartographic power helped define and reinforce each other throughout the 1700s.[1]

But, as these planners called for and created more and more maps, they actually helped reinforce a colonial sense of space that contradicted and counteracted the grandest ambitions of British imperialists, because making the maps required the incorporation of geographic information from Indians and traders in the Southeast. Based as they were on the information of Indians and traders, British maps necessarily reveal something of the colonial sense of space that defined the economic, political, and personal relationships of the Southeast. Rather than an empty, Enlightenment sense of cartographic truth, Southeasterners inhabited a world and constructed an idea of space based on the complex connections and interactions between the people who inhabited the Southeast.

Instead of a landscape of physical features and lines of longitude, Southeasterners defined their place in the world by their position in relation to other peoples. It was a complex, dynamic sense of order that, to imperial eyes, looked suspiciously like disorder. To that end, Britain sought new ways to describe the Southeast that were independent of the trade, even crafting new methods of mapping the Southeast. But the geography of people and paths proved a durable and lasting imprint throughout the eighteenth century, even becoming a central feature of Britain's imperial maps.

To look at British maps of the Southeast, then, is to see a heretofore unexplored contest between different ideas of colonial space. Beyond contests between Britain and France, beyond even contests between Europeans and Indians, imperial maps reveal contests between different ideas of the relations between people, space, and time. On the one hand was the imperial desire to create a knowable (and governable) terrain by asserting governments' authority over all physical and human features of the region. On the other was a colonial improvisation: an idea of spatial relationships centered on the complex interactions between peoples that resisted imperial control. Created and defended by Indians and traders alike, this other geography proved to be the dominant feature on British maps of the southeastern interior throughout the eighteenth century. Rather than a contest between Britain and France, this cartographic conflict was between different "empires" within the British realm—between royal ambition and local preference.[2]

Reading eighteenth-century maps of the Southeast reveals a more complex contest over the region than that of competing European and Indian claims on the land. Some colonizers may have preferred an empty continent to remake as they saw fit, allowing plantations to grow inland without fear of European rivals or aboriginal occupants. Yet no such conditions existed in the Southeast, for France and Spain had their own claims to the territory and thousands of Indians made it their home. No formal boundaries separated European settlements from one another, and none recognized the others' claims as legitimate. Britain, would-be possessor of the interior, could not fall back on treaty lines and political boundaries to secure its claims against its French rivals. Security and legitimacy could come only through Indian allies, whose hearts were to be won or lost on the everyday exchanges of the Anglo-Indian deerskin trade. If the contest of maps was to be won, it would be through the successful negotiation of a complicated Indian geography.

FIGURE 1. The engraved Thomas Nairne inset from Edward Crisp's 1711 "A Compleat Description of the Province of Carolina." Courtesy of the Library of Congress, Geography and Map Division.

The history of Georgia in general and Augusta in particular began, perhaps appropriately, on a map drawn in the Charles Town jail. In July 1708, Thomas Nairne, South Carolina's recently appointed Indian agent, sat imprisoned on a charge fabricated by his political rivals. Having recently returned from a journey through the Southeast, Nairne composed a letter and drew a map (fig. 1) that would have profound influence on southeastern history. Nairne's main objective was to persuade English officials of the supposed threat posed to South Carolina by the aggrandizing intentions of the French, who sought to link their settlements from Canada to Louisiana and to drive the English out of North America. Written in the middle of the War of Spanish Succession, Nairne laid out a plan for the future defense of South Carolina and for the future of English expansion in the Southeast.[3]

From Nairne's memorial onward, the history of southeastern maps and empires would be linked with the Indian trade. Nairne's 1708 memorial emphasized the potential threat of French encroachment and offered southeastern Indians as a catchall solution. He included the map so that English leaders might "at one view perceive what part of the Continent we are now persest [possessed] off, and what not, and procure the Articles of peace, to be formed in such a mannr. that the English American Empire may not be unreasonably Crampt up." Nairne feared that the French, though few in number, might avail themselves of a loose claim to the Carolina coast and use Indian allies to drive English settlers out of America. To frustrate these efforts, Nairne proposed securing Indian allies, in particular the Cherokees, through the "trade for Cloath [which] always atracts and maintains the obedience and friendship of the Indians."[4] The loyalty of the Indians would give the English a check on potential French attacks and protection for future English settlements. Nairne's memorial first united the two relationships that would govern life for much of the eighteenth-century Southeast: the imperial rivalries of Britain, France, and Spain and the trade relationships between Englishmen and Indians. The former would lead ultimately to the founding of Georgia, and the latter would persuade James Oglethorpe to settle a town at the headwaters of the Savannah River in order to annex the Indian trade to the young colony. From 1708 on, the lines of empire would follow the winding trading paths of the Southeast, laying claim to the continent.

Nairne's plan did not become official policy, but his memorial and map found a receptive audience among British mapmakers, most notably Herman Moll. The Treaty of Utrecht, which ended the War of Spanish Succession in 1713, had failed to specify any boundaries between French and English colonies in the Southeast. Moll, England's most prolific cartographer in the first quarter of the eighteenth century, worried about the lack of clear borders and the opportunities they provided French ambition. He used his maps to express outrage over the situation. In his 1715 "A New and Exact Map of the Dominions of the King of Great Britain on ye Continent of North America," Moll devoted a special inset to southeastern North America, crediting his information to "Capt. T. Nearn and others."[5] Another inset in the maps' lower right echoed Nairne's concern over French aggression by portraying English settlements as a thin sliver surrounded by an extensive French interior. As with Nairne, Moll saw the map as the place to create an imperial vision.

Moll's imperialist visions were matched by French maps of the Southeast, particularly those coming from the Delisle mapping house. Guillaume Delisle's 1718 "Map of Louisiana and the Course of the Mississippi" confirmed his fears. Delisle earned a reputation as one of the first "modern" cartographers, basing his charts on careful survey, astronomical observation, and thorough scrutiny of all written accounts.[6] However, his maps of North America also relied heavily on the information networks of the Franco-Indian trade.[7] His 1718 map was a bold assertion of French claims on the Southeast. French territories included all of North America west of the Appalachians and south of Virginia, including Carolina, except for Spanish Florida (the boundary of which Delisle based on his attempted tracing of Soto's 1540 route through the Southeast). Delisle claimed the Carolina coast for France, noting that the colony had originally been "named in honor of Charles IX by the French who discovered it in taking possession and establishing themselves in 15 ... [Delisle did not include the last two digits of the year]."[8]

Delisle's aggression prompted Moll to publish more maps and to incorporate more information from southeastern trade networks. In 1720 he published "A New Map of the North Parts of America claimed by France" (fig. 2). Moll mostly reprinted Delisle's map, though adding information from the Nairne map, as well as a map provided by "the Ingenious Mr. Berisford," a reference to Richard Beresford, Nairne's former correspondent and South Carolina's agent in London.[9] Moll traced Delisle's offending boundary claims against Carolina so that "those Noblemen, Gentlemen, Merchants &c. who are interested in our Plantations in those Parts, may observe whether they ... do not justly deserve ye Name of Incroachments." As outrageous as Delisle's paper claims against Charles Town were, Moll pointed to a more immediate threat from the French claiming the allegiance of "ye Cherakeys and Iroquois, by much ye most powerfull of all ye Neighbouring Indian Nations, the old Friends and Allies of the English."[10] Into this situation, Moll began projecting aggressive English expansion, as represented by the slice of territory labeled "Azilia"—a reference to a planned English colony that did not exist in 1720, nor would it ever.[11] As Moll demonstrates, the escalating war of maps between Britain and France increased British mapmakers' dependence on the information of those connected with the Indian trade.

Moll's map also indicates that those connected with the trade were likewise becoming increasingly dependent on maps. Beresford had journeyed to London in the aftermath of the Yamasee War of 1715–16 to promote Carolina's security and to secure a fortified frontier to protect the emerging rice colony of Carolina. Beresford and his friend John Barnwell had come from a Carolina that had recently experienced a real-life demonstration of how threatened it was. The war devastated the colony and had awakened Carolinians to the dangers of a united Indian war and the need for a stable Indian policy. Abuses in the trade and Indian anger over English encroachments had sparked a war that united the coastal and Piedmont Indians of Carolina with the Creek Indians of the interior. The aftermath of the war would dramatically reshape the southeastern

FIGURE 2. Herman Moll, "A New Map of the North Parts of America Claimed by France," 1720. Courtesy of the Hargrett Rare Book and Manuscript Library, University of Georgia Libraries.

interior, as the Yamasees and other small bands of coastal Indians left for the protection of Spanish Florida and the Creek Indians living south of the Savannah River moved westward and resettled along the Chattahoochee River. Indians recently allied against Carolina were moving farther away from English influence, politically and physically. Worse still, the war had allowed the French to situate the small garrison of Fort Toulouse among the Alabama Creeks, giving them a secure foothold and influence among the Indians. Suddenly, the fear of a French-led Indian invasion of South Carolina seemed all too real and posed a threat to British settlement in southeastern North America.

To further their cause, Beresford and Barnwell made a map. Despite the Yamasee War, or perhaps because of it, Beresford and Barnwell again believed that the Indian trade was the best means of securing Britain's colonial empire in the Southeast. Like Nairne, Barnwell had drawn a manuscript map (fig. 3) to illustrate his plans for the region. Along with South Carolina's other agent in London, Joseph Boone, Barnwell met with the Board of Trade in August 1720. The two men again proclaimed the French threat to the Southeast and proposed a program similar to Nairne's but with an emphasis on fortifications among the Indians, essentially adopting the strategy the French had employed with Fort Toulouse.[12]

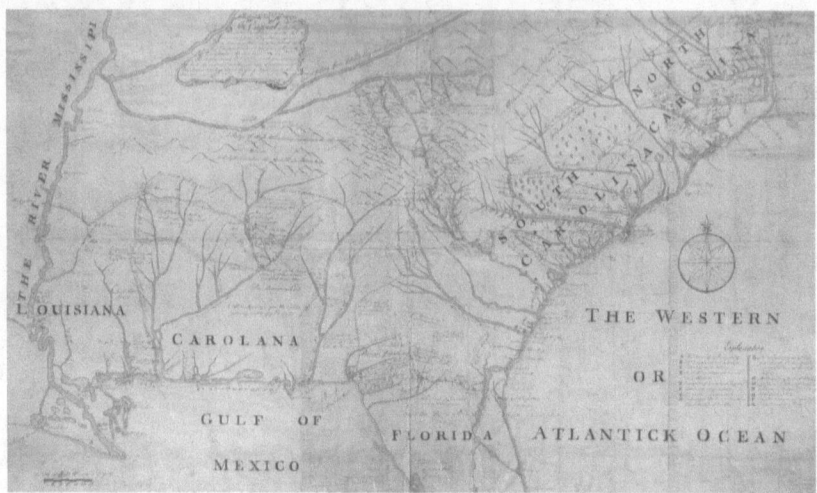

FIGURE 3. The Barnwell-Hammerton manuscript map, ca. 1721. Courtesy of the Hargrett Rare Book and Manuscript Library, University of Georgia Libraries.

Barnwell's forts would strengthen the Indian trade and provide defense against attack as well as nodes for future English settlement. Indian alliances would secure British claims in the Southeast and provide a defense against the French. British trade would secure that alliance, but imperial oversight of the trade would be necessary. A series of six or seven British forts, located at strategic points throughout the Southeast, would be necessary to provide protection for the traders and give distant Indians easy recourse to British redress should the French attack or try to persuade them to turn against their British allies.

Barnwell's plan was never fully realized. One of his proposed forts was approved, Fort King George at the mouth of the Altamaha River, but none of the others were built. The Board of Trade had heartily approved of his plan, but the Privy Council rejected it due to the enormous expense required to build and maintain forts at such great distances from British settlements. However, Barnwell did succeed in turning the British government's attention southward, and his emphasis on securing the Atlantic coast south of Carolina persisted in imperial minds. Ten years later, when the Trustees for Establishing the Colony of Georgia sought a charter in America, it was to this region that they looked, and it was Barnwell's fortified frontier barrier that provided the foundation for the new venture.[13]

However, as men like Moll and Barnwell drew and redrew their lines and their plans, the foundation of their visions was shifting. The Anglo-Indian deerskin trade had undergone a number of transformations in the wake of the Yamasee War. The Carolina legislature, fearing another Indian War and wanting its own oversight of the trade, at first experimented with a public trade monopoly in 1716. Based in frontier forts along the Carolina Piedmont, the public trade operated at fixed prices and discouraged potentially threatening Indians from traveling among the settlements. The trade quickly failed—undermined by private traders, its own cost to the public, and the official veto of the Privy Council. By 1718, the public trade had been abandoned, but a somewhat unofficial trade system had emerged. Private traders, recognizing their need to ingratiate themselves with their Indian clients, began taking up residence in Indian towns, marrying into local families, and trading from their own storehouses. The Carolina government claimed nominal oversight of the trade and appointed a single Agent for Indian Affairs, whose commission required traveling to Indian towns and redressing any abuses, thus stemming any potential French influence. The agent also oversaw the granting of licenses, which restricted traders to a single town and required them to travel to Charles Town every year for renewal. By the 1720s, this basic system governed the trade, and it would continue to do so until the American Revolution. Britain would rely on this trade network for its Indian diplomacy throughout the eighteenth century, using private traders living in Indian towns to spread British influence throughout the Southeast and to secure Indian dependence, and ostensibly friendship. Georgia's founding only deepened the relationship between the Indian trade and the cartographic ambitions of Britain. James Oglethorpe, seeking a role for Georgia in southeastern politics, likewise hoped the trade would secure Georgia's claims to the interior.[14]

Oglethorpe was himself a man preoccupied with geography, and the colony of Georgia was largely founded for the service of maps. In July 1732, Oglethorpe, out of his personal effects, donated items to the trustees' office in London. In addition to twelve cushioned chairs, Oglethorpe donated maps of the world, of England and Wales, two maps of North America, one of South America, a map of Pennsylvania, as well as "Two Globes mounted on Frames with Covers."[15] Something of an amateur surveyor and cartographer himself, Oglethorpe also made significant contributions to one of the major British imperial maps of the eighteenth century, Henry Popple's 1733 "A Map of the British Empire in America." Oglethorpe has been credited as the major source for Sheet 10 of that large, multipart map, which showed the colony of South Carolina and the coast between the Savannah River and Spanish Florida. Historians also believe Oglethorpe may have even exaggerated certain features to Georgia's advantage.[16] Thus when Oglethorpe made his plans for the security and future of Georgia, he kept in mind the large-scale perspective of one who commanded the information of maps.

The founding of Augusta was part of Oglethorpe's plan for the future of the young colony. In 1736, Oglethorpe designated two locations for Georgia's frontier defense: Fort Frederica along the southern coast of Georgia to guard against any invasion from Spanish Florida; and Fort Augusta, at the headwaters of the Savannah River, to protect against any incursions of the French and with the added benefit of diverting the lucrative Indian trade and control of its allegiances to Savannah.[17] As South Carolina already had established the frontier township of New Windsor and Fort Moore at the same location (albeit on the northern side of the river), Oglethorpe believed that stealing control of the Indian trade would, at once, bring trade to Savannah and also take the trade away from self-serving Carolina traders who had, after all, brought on the Yamasee War. Oglethorpe succeeded to a degree, and for the next forty years the Anglo-Indian deerskin trade would pass through the town of Augusta, albeit on its way to the old trade port of Charles Town. Through two major European wars, Augusta traders and merchants would pass English trade goods to Indian towns in exchange for deerskin leather and would act as intermediaries between British imperial officials and headmen of the Creek, Chickasaw, Cherokee, and Choctaw Indian towns.[18]

From the pinpoint of Augusta, Oglethorpe hoped to remake the map of the Southeast by extending Georgia's influence well into the interior and securing its claims against French interlopers and Carolina traders. Georgia's colonial charter included all territory between the Atlantic Ocean and the Mississippi River, between the heads of the Savannah and Altamaha Rivers. Oglethorpe recognized that this jurisdiction included the powerful Creek and Choctaw Indian confederacies, as well as the smaller but influential Chickasaw confederacy. Oglethorpe refused to let Carolina traders hold sway over such a powerful collection of neighbors and used his influence in Parliament to pass the 1735 "Act for Maintaining the Peace with the Indians," which forbade any trader not licensed in Georgia to trade with any Indians within the bounds of the colony. Augusta's role was partly to help enforce this law by monitoring the river crossing from Carolina into Georgia. Commissioners from Georgia would likewise enforce the act in Indian towns, breaking open Carolina traders' stores, seizing their goods, and even searching trade boats along the Savannah River. As might be expected, Georgia's actions won few friends in Carolina, but they underscored how important Augusta was for Oglethorpe and the trustees, who sought to improve on Carolina's shaky history of Indian relations.

In their ambitious efforts to redraw the Southeast, British planners from Nairne to Oglethorpe engaged in the kinds of cartographic imperialism that historians have been analyzing for the last quarter of a century. In this formulation, maps were active agents in the creation and promotion of imperial designs upon foreign lands and indigenous peoples. The development of professional cartography served as a means of delegitimizing indigenous concepts of space and replacing them with a more "accurate" Western definition that, not coincidentally, justified European appropriation of indigenous resources. In the Southeast, planners such as Oglethorpe and the trustees imposed "straight lines and stability" on the Indian interior and encouraged a myth of empty lands awaiting European cultivation. British imperialism thus engaged in more than the cartographic sleight-of-hand that Oglethorpe employed in the Popple map: the emergence of maps as the only valid form of geographic representation formed a first step in the dispossession of Indian peoples. These historians have often presumed a monolithic British or European geography contesting an indigenous American concept of land and space, which was not necessarily the case for all Americans.[19]

Maps were more than imperial fantasies, however. Empires certainly used maps to claim space and project an image of current and future power over the landscape, and the maps of the Southeast certainly reflected the various imperial powers' territorial ambitions. But southeastern maps reveal more than that. They were themselves contested spaces within which various geographic discourses competed. The imperial fantasy of control and order contested with the relentlessly unpredictable and point-to-point geography of the deerskin traders, whose concept of space was itself shaped by a contest between European and Indian ideas. Maps were thus colonial artifacts reflecting the methods by which they were produced. Studying the maps of the Southeast reveals the various visions of landscape and space that shaped the deerskin trade and the region as a whole.[20]

Southeastern maps are thus a window into southeasterners' notions of space; they are not total representations of those notions. The majority of the people who lived and moved through the Southeast, after all, lacked the "overhead" perspective afforded by maps. Maps were elite documents, the possession of wealthy men in London and Charles Town. The traders who sojourned among Indians had little recourse to such maps and probably less use for them. And it was their geography that shaped social relations in southeastern North America and even dictated the form of the overarching perspective of imperial maps. A persistent and obvious geography of the trading path characterized even the most large-scale colonial maps, and it necessarily owed more to Indian conceptions of space than European ones. Relational and processional, the traders' geography provided the information for the large-scale maps that shaped colonial policy. This geography was not one of exclusion or dispossession, but of interconnected points, whose importance lay not in their position along axes of latitude and longitude, but in their placement along the communication networks that crossed the Southeast.

The persistence of the trade geography owed much to the persistent techniques of British cartography throughout the eighteenth century. As J. B. Harley has noted, the methods of map production greatly affected the forms that maps took and the features they emphasized.[21] In the colonial Southeast and the British Empire in general, survey work and mapmaking were largely the province of nominally trained private individuals. There was no centralized, state-sponsored cartographic enterprise such as existed in France from the end of the seventeenth century. Likewise, the map trade was an adjunct of the print trade that also sold engravings, pamphlets, and books, though print shops sold maps to an elite audience, not the population at large.

The conditions that governed the production of geographic knowledge extended to Georgia and South Carolina, in which maps were valued as private wealth rather than public use. Georgia's surveyor general, for example, could complain that his map, "the Product of the Memorialist's own Industry and Labour," had been lost by the colonial assembly, "to the great Detriment of the Memorialist, who is deprived of those Benefits he expected to reap from the Publication of that his industrious Performance."[22] A colonial governor could hesitate to turn over his maps of the Indian nations to his British superiors because "these Draughts were made at my private expense, and are my property as much as my books."[23] Even a surveyor's widow, recognizing the potential value of her late husband's charts, could defy colonial authorities for fear of losing "any Benefit of printing it."[24] Maps were valued possessions, not commonplace objects, a way of negotiating with people of higher rank. The overhead view of the world was an alien concept, useful more for its monetary value than for understanding one's place in the world.

When colonial mapmakers sent maps back to London, they thus retained a sense of the way they were made. No trained surveyors ventured into the southeastern interior until well after the Seven Years' War. Maps constructed before then were the product of travelers' accounts—letters and rough sketches provided by traders and Indian agents, reflecting less a planimetric certainty than a remembered procession along trails. These mapmakers gathered their information not from transits and chains, but from their travels along the paths and the verbal accounts of geography gained from Indian knowledge. The maps of Thomas Nairne and John Barnwell, the two most important English "base maps" for the eighteenth-century Southeast, were compiled in this manner—verbal descriptions made for the purpose of furthering British claims, but at the same time almost entirely dependent upon Indian notions of geography.

The history of the trade between 1732 and 1774 played out on a "map" created by the ongoing negotiations between Indians, traders, and colonial officials. By the 1730s, Indians and traders had both adopted a spatial language of interconnected points as the primary means of describing and understanding their relationship in the Southeast. Indian-authored maps, speeches, and strings of beads (as transcribed, translated, and interpreted by Europeans) described the Southeast as points on a string: towns and peoples connected by rivers and paths, which all had to be experienced in a particular sequence. British traders necessarily adopted this same processional geography in their letters and reports. They did, after all, make their living on Indian terms and on Indian terrain. But this processional geography also supported traders' own pretensions to power and influence in the Southeast, as they believed they could act as gatekeepers to the interior.

Indians and traders thus created a sort of "pidgin" geography that helped shaped southeasterners' understanding of their world. Mapping traditions do not easily translate between cultures save at the most superficial level, but Indians and traders managed to forge a common geographic language based on the superficial features of waterways, paths, and towns.[25] Its seeming superficiality did not, however, indicate insignificance. In fact, it became the predominant means by which Indians and traders described their relationship throughout the period of the Georgia trade.

It is difficult to know exactly when this spatial language first developed, given that no precontact indigenous maps have yet been discovered. It was likely based on indigenous mapping traditions, given the readiness with which Indians could produce maps when asked by European colonizers in the 1700s. Indians, for example, readily produced "path maps," maps of local terrain and rivers, and even sociopolitical maps on occasion. These maps frequently consisted of a series of places connected by trails and trade relationships; some paths were friendly and some were hostile, but all fit into a processional geography that moved from place to place. Indian maps also made no distinction between rivers and overland trails, but rather conceived of the whole as one large path of communication, an indication that topography was less a concern than knowing who one's friends and enemies were and what peoples lay between oneself and them.[26] Requested and translated by Europeans, existing maps and texts should be seen as colonial artifacts rather than indigenous ones, but they do provide a window into how Indians conceptualized and articulated the relationships of the colonial Southeast.[27]

As an example, a Chickasaw deerskin map created in the same year as Augusta's founding demonstrated Indians' ability to map the colonial situation. In 1737, Mingo Ouma, a Chickasaw headman, presented a map of the Southeast to French officials at New Orleans. The map (fig. 4) depicts Indian nations as well as English and French colonies as a series of circles connected by lines either of trade or of war. At the center was the Chickasaw nation, fortified and threatened by a band of circles representing the entirety of Indian North America from the Choctaws in the south to the Indians of Canada. Paths of trade and friendship connected the Chickasaws separately to the Upper Creeks and Cherokees, and from them onward through the Lower Creeks to Carolina. The map made no effort to record precise distances or directions between these peoples, but one could easily read the complex relationships of trade and war that a Chickasaw Indian had to navigate in the eighteenth century.[28] Likewise, the traveler was not free to traverse the countryside at random, but had to follow the well-worn paths that connected Indians and Europeans physically, economically, and politically. The British received similar maps from both the Chicaksaws and Catawbas, indicating that these cartographic conventions were fairly widespread in native America during the contact period.[29]

The Creek Indians likewise indicated that they shared this language of points and places with the Chickasaws and Catawbas. Though no colonial map exists detailing Creek notions of geography, their methods of representing the southeastern landscape closely resembled that of their Chickasaw neighbors. In Creek negotiations with the British, the visual

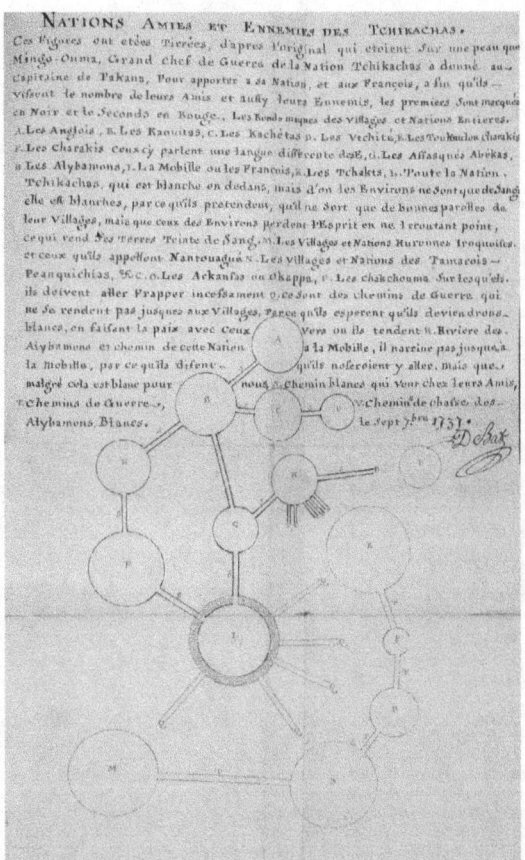

FIGURE 4. Mingo Ouma–Alexandre de Batz, "Nations Amies et Enemies des Tchikachas," 1737. Courtesy of the Archives Nationales d'Outre Mer, Aix-en-Provence, France.

symbol of trade relationships was the string of beads. In the midst of continental renegotiation after the Seven Years' War, for example, an Upper Creek headman, the Mortar of Okchai, traveled to Charles Town to reaffirm the long-standing friendship between the Upper Creeks and the British. He presented the governor of South Carolina with a string of white beads, symbolizing at once the linear shape of the friends' trading path and the peace and harmony that existed between them. He also sent another string south to Pensacola, composed of white and red beads, questioning whether the newer southern trading path was to be friendly

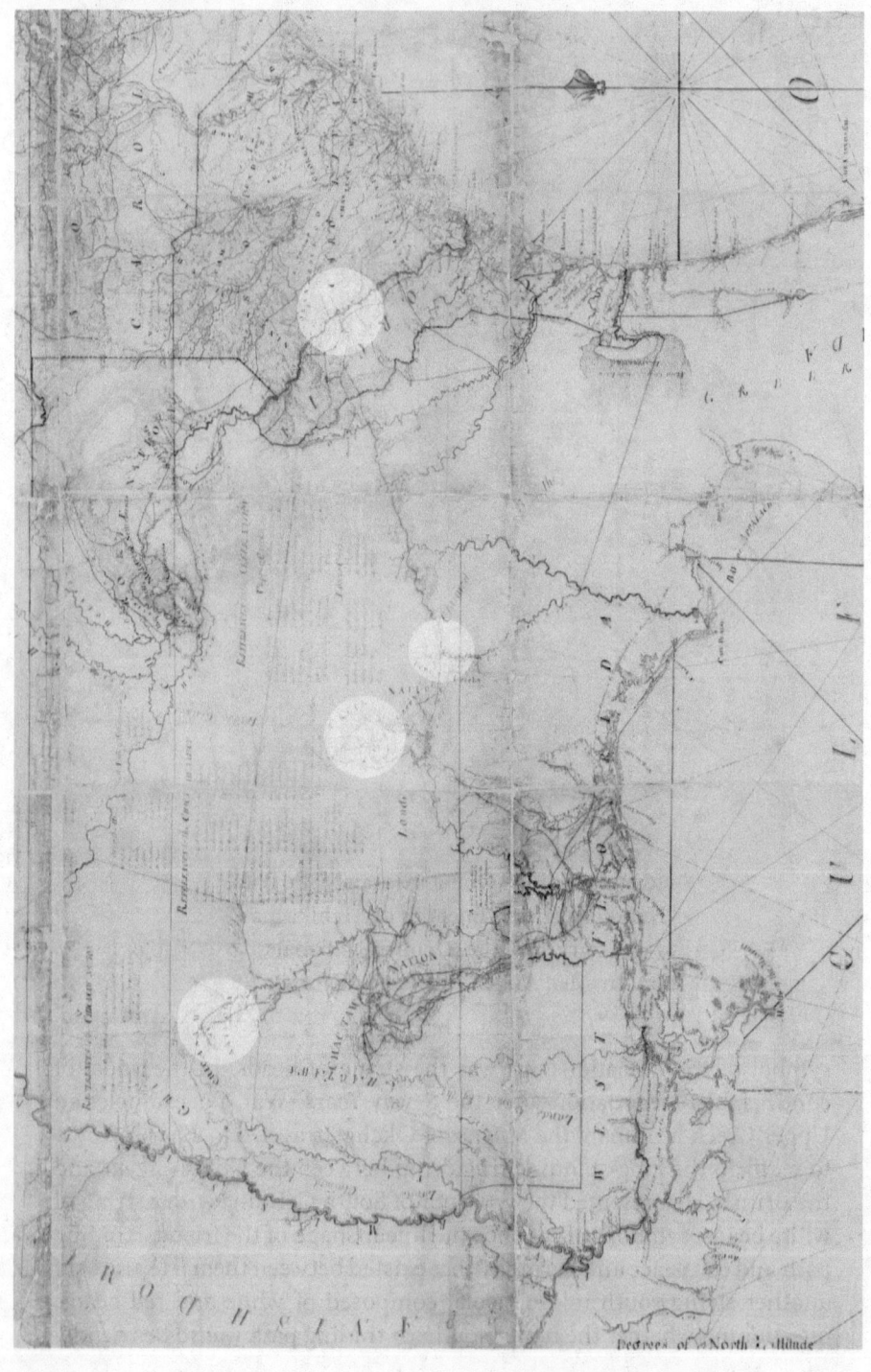

or hostile.[30] In verbal descriptions of the path, another Creek headman presented a verbal string of places: "the Old White Path ... Comes from Charles Town to the Couaties, from thence to ye Taukabatchees, from thence to the Abicouches and from thence to the Chickasaws."[31] To travel the Southeast was to travel between places in a set order. The fact that this headman changed the traditional route to favor his more southern towns very much upset his northern Upper Creek counterparts, emphasizing the importance of proper channels for communication and trade in Indian eyes.[32]

Nor were Indians the only southeasterners to adopt this language. Traders found a real benefit in this processional geography. If the Southeast were a connected series of points, then power and influence flowed to those who could control access to the trade's networks. Indians understood this and competed for control over the paths.[33] Traders themselves willingly appropriated Indians' idea of the Southeast. It was both a necessary part of their business and a politically useful language that traders could employ in their contest with imperial administrators.

Traders thus eagerly adopted this perspective of connected and related spaces. Their world was not composed so much of grand imperial ambitions but of individual Indian towns, linked together not by region but by a series of well-known and respected paths (fig. 5). To move westward from Augusta required taking the necessary twists and turns to follow the paths from place to place, in an ordered succession of towns. Beginning in Augusta, the trader moved westerly toward the crossing on the Ogeechee River. From there, travelers to the Lower Creeks turned southwest toward the Creek town of Coweta at the falls of the Chattahoochee River. Travelers to the Upper Creeks, Chickasaws, and Choctaws stayed a westerly course to the Upper Creek town of Okfuskee, and from thence northwestward to the Creek town of Coosa, and from thence to the Chickasaw towns near the Mississippi River, and from the Chickasaws southward to the Choctaw towns. For forty years, traders followed these routes, rarely varying course, for to do so risked getting lost in the vast interior of southeastern North America.[34]

FIGURE 5. Detail from the John Stuart–Joseph Purcell manuscript map. The highlighted areas show the locations of the (from west to east) Chickasaws, Upper Creeks, Lower Creeks, and Augusta, circa 1775. Some of the major trade paths are also visible between these areas. Photo courtesy of the Newberry Library, Chicago, Illinois. Call # Vault Oversize Ayer MS Map 228. Highlights made by author.

This was not travel that conveyed a sense of mastery of the landscape. For most of the journey, the path kept a narrow course through high woods on all sides. Each point of the journey brought its own challenges—horses running away from a campsite, the chance encounter with a friend or relation, the more harrowing encounter with an enemy. A town that had been friendly on the outward trek could very easily cease to be on the trip home. At each stop, the trader could receive word of a burgled home or of dead relatives and servants. Each turn in the path could bring about a new direction in one's own life. And yet these ambiguities were in a sense constant, for the travel and events along the paths formed a community and a mind-set that governed the geography of the Southeast.

Traders' description of their travel indicated that they shared with Indians an idea of the Southeast as a linked series of places. The imprint of this geography on the mental world of Indian traders was apparent in the basic narrative forms that their letters and journals took. Disruption along the trail was unknowable ahead of time and could mean the loss of one's property, one's family, or one's own life. Numerous letters and accounts follow the trail, but the following is a clear example of the form:

> I left Savana Town October 16, and arrived at the Oakfus-kees the 29th where I heard that one of my Hirelings had been killed by one of the Chickasaw Indians at the Breed Camp at my House. . . . Upon hearing this I made what Heast I could to get Home while Mr. Bosomworth [the Indian agent] was there, and left my Horses and Things at the Oakfuskes. When I arrived at the Abukutchees I saw Mr. Bosomworth and understood that the Checkesaws mostly had gone to the Woods, and most of them who stayed behind slept in the Woods for Fear of the Creeks coming to cut them off. . . . When I arrived here [the Breed Camp?] I had Accounts by Way of the Albama Fort that the Chickesaws had cut off several Boats in the Mississippi.[35]

This trader followed the same route in 1752 that Nairne had in 1708, but the path could change roles without the traveler's control. Traders, after all, traveled between Indian towns and confederacies that were often at war with each other or divided within themselves. But one should not confuse unpredictability with chaos. The patterns of behavior and rhythms of life along the paths and in the towns remained remarkably coherent and consistent from the founding of Augusta until the American Revolution.[36] Though any individual might find something quite surprising at any given moment, the overall shape and cycle of the Indian trade remained intact.

By narrating their travels in this way, traders were also making a claim on the Southeast. Traders claimed authority by emphasizing both the Southeast's uncertainty and their deep familiarity with its numerous places and peoples. In so doing they engaged in a form of "narrative mapping" that echoed the efforts of other colonists in the Americas in the eighteenth century. While few traders were American-born, their statements reflected a desire to assert their authority over the region in the face of increasing British regulation. Through their narratives, traders appropriated parts of the Indian conception of space (place-to-place travel and human geography) to assert their preeminence in the Southeast.[37]

Traders thus turned this geography of places to their advantage. Controlling key access points in the string of places assured traders a great deal of influence in southeastern affairs, as they were the most important links between imperial planners and Indian headmen. Augusta traders thus assumed a mastery of the complexities of the paths that convinced them of their superiority over other Europeans who might trespass. As Thomas Bosomworth, an Indian agent from South Carolina, complained, "The powerful Company at Augusta seem to look upon the whole Trade of the Creek Nation as their undoubted Right and whatever Part they are deprived of they are apt to imagine an Encroachment upon their Property."[38] The traders themselves defended their influence in Indian affairs, saying it was they "who have risqued our all in the Colony, & have been no Small Benefactors to it, for we must say (& without Vanity) that our House is the best Acquainted with Indian Affairs of any in this Colony, & that it is us who by our Endeavours, have in great Measure kept the Indians on good Terms ... for some Years past."[39] It was not against Indians that the traders defined themselves so much as against other Europeans who sought to control the trade from the distance of imperial capitals. Traders jealously guarded their position as intermediaries between Europeans and Indians, which meant that imperial officials would continue to rely on these voyageurs until a different source of geographic information could be obtained.

Given Indians' and traders' preferences for this relational and processional geography, it is small wonder that the geography of the trade proved such an enduring imprint on British maps of the Southeast. In large part the product of Indian agents and travelers along the path, the place-to-place relations along the trail emerged in print as a distinctive set of features and messages in eighteenth-century British mapmaking from Nairne's first map until the eve of the American Revolution. The contest between imperial control and trader autonomy on these maps echoed the intra-imperial tensions between traders and British officials. The traders' dual role as both promoters and competitors of British imperial aims created an uncertain geography, one that would remain the basis for mapmaking until a new language of scientific cartography began replacing it after the Seven Years' War. This new language, and its attendant message of dispossession, would eventually lead to the myth of empty lands that would characterize United States–Indian relations in the nineteenth-century Southeast.

The maps of Thomas Nairne and John Barnwell, though made with the intent of promoting British mastery of the interior, reflect more of this relational geography than one might at first suppose. Made not from formal survey but from memories of the trail, these eighteenth-century maps reflected the method by which they were produced. And the tension within these maps—claiming mastery while at the same time depicting an Anglo-Indian geography in which neither side held complete authority—would reverberate in the large-scale eighteenth-century maps produced by Henry Popple and John Mitchell.

Nairne's map of the Southeast set the pattern of cartographic relations that would follow. Nairne had a grand vision for the future of the Southeast, hoping to use the Indian trade to change the face of a continent. But, to formulate his plan and sketch out his vision, he needed to draw a map. To draw a map, he needed to travel the paths of the interior and rely on his native and trader guides for information. Therefore, Nairne's plan for the Southeast re-created the spatial conceptions of his sources: engraving the point-to-point geography of the Southeast on all of the continental maps that followed.

Nairne's 1708 map reflected the travels that produced it. In October 1707, rumors reached Charles Town that the French at Mobile were planning to raise an Indian army to attack Carolina. In January 1708, Nairne accompanied the Chickasaw trader Thomas Welch on a six-month diplomatic mission to preserve Chickasaw allegiance to the English and to try to disrupt the Franco-Choctaw alliance. Nairne succeeded in his mission but returned to imprisonment in Charles Town at the instigation of his political rival, proprietary governor Nathaniel Johnson. It was here that Nairne composed his 1708 memorial and drafted his manuscript map. The map would first appear as an inset on Edward Crisp's 1711 map of South Carolina and would also act as the model for Herman Moll's

1715 map.[40] It was also upon Nairne's map that the Georgia Trustees first outlined their designs for America.[41]

Nairne believed that English control of the path that linked them to the Indians would secure the interior for English expansion. The trading path therefore formed the centerpiece of Nairne's map, which introduced a wealth of detail about the Southeast. Indian towns suddenly appeared, and the trading path south of the Appalachian Mountains appeared for the first time, connecting Carolina to the Mississippi and promoting the ease of trade. The map and Nairne's accompanying letters revealed clearly the way Nairne experienced the landscape. Nairne's account of his trip followed the typical travel narrative: "Designing for the Chicasaws I set out from the Ochesses ... crossed over Cusa or the main branch of Mobile river ... we went the streightest road."[42]

Nairne mapped the path in the same way that he described it. The trail on Nairne's map ran in an almost perfect east-west course from Charles Town all the way to the Mississippi. Extending from the "Savanna" Indians in the East (who lived near present-day Augusta), Nairne's path continued due west through the "Okesee" villages to the "Chatahuches" and straight on to the "Talapoossie" villages. Nairne spaced these clusters of villages out in order to indicate distance. In reality, he would have most likely traveled south-by-southwest to reach the Ochese Creeks, west from there to reach the Muscogulge villages along the Chattahoochee, and then northwest from there to reach the Muscogulge villages along the Coosa and Tallapoosa Rivers.[43] The various twists and turns that the path followed in reality were not recorded. The Appalachian Mountains were safely brushed to the top of the map, giving Charles Town traders a straight and easy path of influence throughout the Southeast. Nairne apparently did not pay particular attention to the directions in which he traveled, and his account of the journey likewise revealed a memory less of space than of points and distance between them.

The path on the Barnwell-Hammerton map was similar to Nairne's.[44] The manuscript map, produced around 1721, filled in many details that the small Nairne map lacked and showed a greater number of individual Indian villages. However, Barnwell still showed the trading path from the Savannahs running in a due east-west course and placed Indian villages accordingly. Barnwell moved the former Ochese settlements to the headwaters of the Altamaha River so that they lay due west of the Savannahs. The path bypassed the numerous Muscogulge settlements on the Chattahoochee and ran straight west to a single village labeled "Chattahoochee." Barnwell probably did this to make his map better match that of Nairne (or he used Nairne as a base map when drafting his own). In either case, Barnwell's map reiterated Nairne's east-west linearity, even to the point of making the Southeast's rivers run from west to east, rather from northwest to southeast.[45]

Reliance on the trade's geography led to an image of disorder in the Barnwell-Hammerton map. The Southeast was a jumble of Indian towns, legends, annotations, and suggestions. At the time Barnwell composed the map, the southeastern interior was still in the process of recovering from the Yamasee War. The large Indian confederacies that would form the basis of eighteenth-century Anglo-Indian relations did not appear on the Barnwell map save as a number of towns scattered along river systems and trading paths, interspersed with mountains and notations of violence.

Echoing his map, the measures proposed by Barnwell and later adopted by the Lords of Trade would prove difficult to implement at best. Though Barnwell himself held great hope for the ease with which trade would reduce the Indians to alliance and dependence on the English, his map in many ways foreshadowed the numerous conflicts and difficulties that the Anglo-Indian trade alliance would bring about. While English trade goods secured Indian alliances (and dependence) for much of the eighteenth century and prevented any number of wars between Englishmen and Indians, the traders themselves were likewise dependent on the good will of Indians. This "mutual obligation, mutual dependence" characterized trade relationships for the eighteenth century.[46] The traders themselves opposed threats to their presumed independence from British authorities, ensuring the persistence of the tradeways.

The Barnwell map, made in the spirit of the greatest optimism, revealed a central tension of the Indian trade: the trade was both agent for and obstacle to imperial aims. Not simply a matter of British versus Indian or British versus French, the realities of life in the Southeast involved conflicts between trader and official, between trader and Indian, between Indian and official, and between trader and trader. The closer one moved to the ground, the more complicated the rules and worlds of the Indian trade became.

The confusing message of the Barnwell map led to two very different images of the Southeast. The complexity and ambiguity of Barnwell's jumbled landscape reverberated in Henry Popple's 1733 glorious mess of a large-scale imperial map (fig. 6). Popple mostly copied Barnwell's difficult interior topography and removed the triumphant legends. Taking the opposite route, John Mitchell's 1755 map selected those elements of

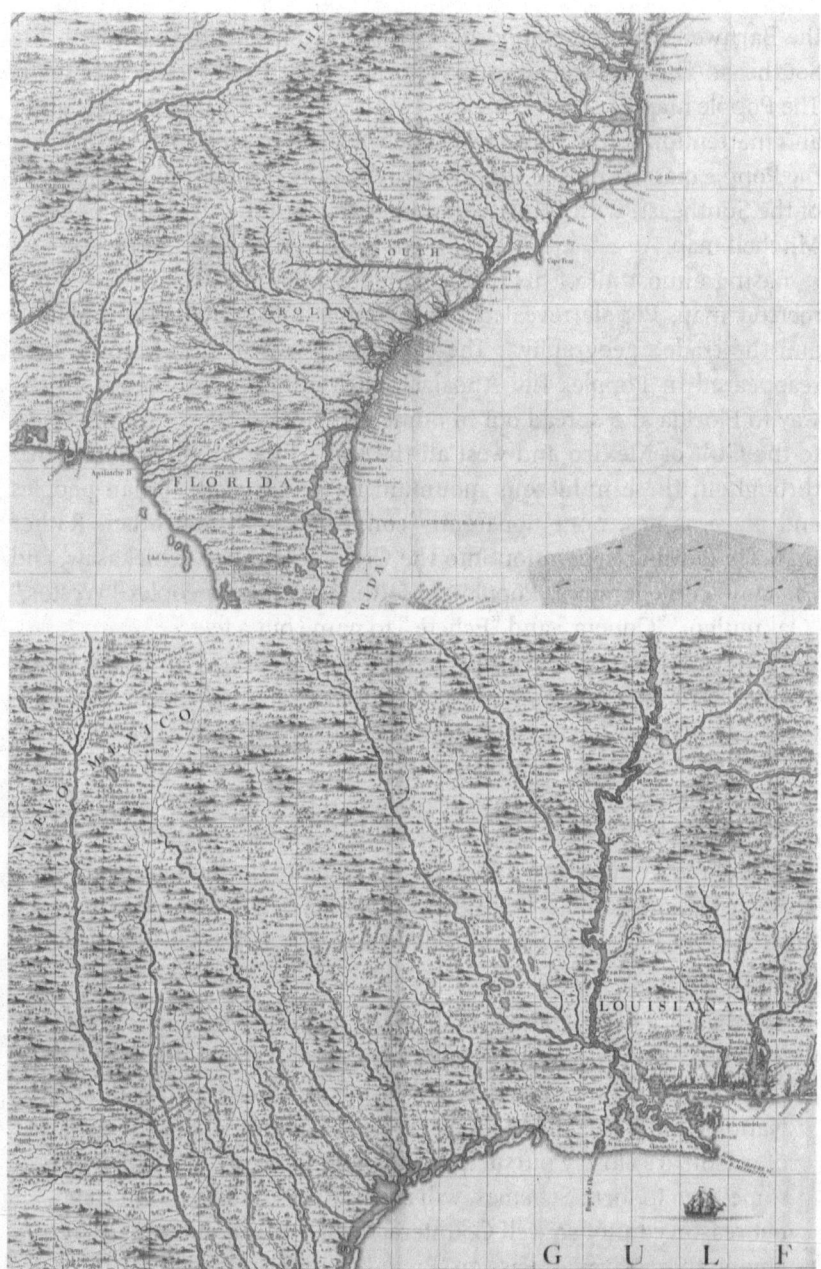

FIGURE 6. Details from Henry Popple, "A Map of the British Empire in America," 1733. Courtesy of the David Rumsey Map Collection, davidrumsey.com.

the Barnwell map that supported British pretensions to mastery in the Southeast. Thus the legends and victories of Barnwell took center stage. The Popple map has been criticized by historians for its flawed execution and inattention to the valuable legends of the Barnwell map.[47] However, the Popple map far more elegantly expresses the Indian trader geography of the Southeast, with subtlety and nuance, than the stridently political Mitchell map.

Basing almost all of his interior topography on the Barnwell-Hammerton map, Popple revealed the incompatibility of British ambition and the trade's geography.[48] The east-west rivers of the Barnwell map reappeared in Popple. The Appalachian Mountains ran south all the way to Florida and spread out in numerous small ranges running south to the Gulf of Mexico and west all the way to the Mississippi. Nestled throughout these numerous mountain fortresses were Indian peoples and place-names, none apparently connected with any other. Rather than the familiar separation into the Creek, Cherokee, Chickasaw, and Choctaw confederacies, Popple chose to label these peoples "Westos," "Oakmulgo," "Coueta," and "Echete," to name but a few.[49]

However, if Popple's map displayed little "accuracy" in its depiction of southeastern topography, Popple perhaps far more accurately captured the realities of the Southeast that awaited British expansion into the region. As British administrators would learn over and over again, Indian towns remained independent, even if they did form part of larger confederacies.[50] Popple's map revealed this sensibility that negotiations with Indians would prove difficult, unpredictable, almost impenetrable. This frustration would echo in the complaints of British governors, even those such as James Glen who prided themselves on their knowledge of Indian affairs.

> The distance betwixt the Indian Countreys and England is great and the conveyance is uncertain, but above all the Politicks of these People if I may use that expression, is different from all other Nations under the Sun, Among civilized Nations where the dictates of reason are closely pursued the same humane prudence that aids some Men to form Schemes, will assist others to disappoint them, but reason cannot so well Counteract what reason does not direct; among these Savages, Passion, Prejudice, Caprice usurp the place of reason, and Revenge is sometimes exercised in so wild a manner, that one who has made their manners his study for seven years is often at a stand, I truely think they are not to be learned by reading,

nor in any other way, but by an attentive and intimate observation, by occular inspection.[51]

The stubborn refusal of Indians to organize themselves into a more European system of governance frustrated those who hoped to treat Indians as nations rather than as people. Popple's map certainly offered nothing to those seeking a simplistic Indian landscape. Numerous Indian groups appeared barricaded in a series of mountains that did not actually exist, and to reach any of these mountain villages the traveler would have to ford numerous streams and travel through any number of independent Indian towns.

The confusion and ambiguity of Popple's geography was readily apparent in the message of his cartouche (fig. 7). In a familiar trope of New World maps, Indians in feathered headdresses and carrying bows flanked the map title. In the background Popple placed a bustling scene of English waterside commerce: men hoeing fields; others loading hogsheads onto a vessel waiting at anchor; and a group of well-dressed gentlemen discussing business as a white servant poured them wine.[52]

Yet the comfort of this familiar scene stood in marked contrast to the potential danger of the Indians resting in the foreground. To the right of the map's title a young warrior stared off into the distance, his bow ready at his side. Above the title, a female rested with a quiver full of arrows slung across her shoulder. Her left foot rested comfortably on a grinning alligator. In her right hand, an arrow pointed to the trophy resting under her right foot: the severed head of a bearded European, pierced with an arrow. Popple's prediction for the future of the Southeast was thus unclear. On the one hand, Popple celebrated the success and harmony of British commerce. On the other, he warned all who would spread that commerce into southeastern North America that numerous and unpredictable Indian foes could either help (by killing European rivals) or hinder (by killing the English themselves) the expansion of British America.

Popple's map proved unacceptable to British imperial planners, who wanted more certainty. This was made clear in 1755, when British diplomats negotiated with their French counterparts over a border. When the French delegation noted that Popple's map had been composed with the approbation of the British Board of Trade, the British negotiators responded that only Popple's undertaking had been approved; the final map had not received official recognition. The British diplomats' disavowal of Popple apparently stemmed from features on Popple's map

FIGURE 7. Cartouche from Popple, "Map of the British Empire." Courtesy of the David Rumsey Map Collection, davidrumsey.com.

that told against their claims.[53] A more favorable map was needed, and one was provided in that same year.

In 1755, John Mitchell published a map that more stridently asserted British claims in the Southeast, taking the most optimistic elements of the Barnwell map and using them to promote British dominion across North America (fig. 8). Mitchell's map bore the seal of imperial approval. Whereas Popple's 1733 map had carried the endorsement of Edmund Halley, famed astonomer and cartographer, John Pownall, secretary for the British Board of Trade, endorsed the Mitchell map as being "Undertaken with the Approbation and at the request of the Lords Commissioners."[54] A simple glance at the Mitchell map reveals why it would hang proudly in Whitehall.

Mitchell used the same source as Popple, yet to radically different effect. Though engraved two decades after Popple, the 1755 map drew its information on the southeastern interior from the same 1721 Barnwell map. The difference between Mitchell and Popple was one of emphasis rather than source. Mitchell borrowed heavily from the Barnwell map, but more as a document of imperial triumph than as an accurate representation of southeastern geography. The confusing jumble of mountains was reduced to thin chains of single ridges. The numerous Indian

FIGURE 8. Detail from John Mitchell, "Map of the British and French Dominions in North America," 1755. Courtesy of the Library of Congress, Geography and Map Division.

towns were grouped into more manageable confederacies. And, most prominently, Mitchell made British imperial claims the dominant feature of his map, extending English colonial borders all the way across the continent in bold swaths of color with English names in large typeface dominating the smaller script of Indian villages.

Over and above British domination of their French rivals, Mitchell's map broadcast a triumphant victory over Indians. In stark contrast to the ambiguous pose of the Indians in Popple's cartouche, those that flanked Mitchell's map title knew who the true masters of North America were (fig. 9). Mitchell's Indians bowed before English authority in a pose of submission and fear. Mitchell seemingly drew his cartouche as a response to Popple's. He featured Indians dressed in the same feathered headdresses and skirts as Popple, but their pose was far less defiant and far more pliant. Their bows and arrows lay at their sides, harmless. An Indian man knelt on the ground, his hands clasped before him in submission. His female companion clasped her hand to her breast and joined his skyward gaze. Above their heads flew a Union Jack and the British royal coat of arms, both held aloft by white cherubs. To emphasize how docile and harmless his Indians were, Mitchell allowed two small, white children to play right

FIGURE 9. Cartouche from Mitchell, "Map of the British and French Dominions." Courtesy of the Library of Congress, Geography and Map Division.

next to them, perfectly oblivious to the supposedly "fearsome" Indians that had stared defiantly out from Popple's cartouche.

The roots of Mitchell's dominant Britannia lay in the presumption of royal charter, but Mitchell, like Barnwell, also emphasized that British claims were secured by right of trade. Mitchell boasted that "the English have Factories and Settlements in all the Towns of the Creek Indians of any note except the Albama." Traders' houses thus became "settlements" and could be used to justify English claims. It was by this logic that Mitchell proclaimed the Chickasaws "in Alliance and Subjection to the English" because the trade stores among them acted as "the Extent of English Settlemts." Thus, despite Mitchell's triumphalist geography, his claims could be made only in reference to the trade geography. The emphasis had shifted between Popple and Mitchell as to which group, Indians or Britons, held the greatest sway over the interior, but the essential geography remained the same.

Mitchell's map tried to reassert the claims of control first made by Nairne but could no more effectively create imperial control than its predecessors. Mitchell's geography certainly proved much more popular than Popple's, not only with British imperial planners but also with the general public. His map was reprinted many times and sold throughout Europe. The attachment to Mitchell's geography was so great that at the end of the American Revolution, the new United States plotted its borders with British North America on a copy of the Mitchell map.[55] But events after 1755 proved that the Indians were not nearly as tractable as Mitchell hoped. In particular, the Cherokee War of 1760–61 devastated the South Carolina countryside and proved that Indians were still willing to deal harshly with their British neighbors.

The Mitchell map continued to prove inadequate to those who sought to reshape the Southeast in the years after the Seven Years' War. Following the Treaty of Paris in 1763, Britain knew no imperial rivals in the region. The war had gained them east and west Florida from the Spanish, and the French had ceded all claims to lands east of the Mississippi River. In essence, the war had settled the cartographic rivalries that had marked most of the eighteenth century. And yet, the British still faced constant issues with the deerskin trade and the Indians of the Southeast. Clearly the Mitchell map's conceit of a purely British Southeast had been made reality, yet the map showed a decades-old Indian interior and failed to depict Florida at all.

As Britain sought greater oversight of the deerskin trade after 1763, royal officials began seeking a new cartographic language to replace the old trade geography. They turned to the Enlightenment mapmaking that had become increasingly professionalized over the course of the 1700s. The need for more accurate maps and greater imperial regulation of the interior created the Stuart-Purcell manuscript map of 1775. This unpublished map introduced a new cartographic language into the southeastern interior, one composed simultaneously of Enlightenment ideals of mapmaking and British ideals of effective regulation. John Stuart, Superintendent of Indian Affairs in the Southern District, was himself something of an amateur cartographer, having made a map of the Cherokee territories in 1760 following his capture and escape to Virginia during the Cherokee War. Joseph Purcell was surveyor general of Georgia, a trained cartographer and a deputy of the Southeast's first modern mapmaker, John Gerar William De Brahm, who had been appointed surveyor general of the Southern District of North America in 1764—a sign of how seriously Britain took the accurate mapping of the Southeast.[56]

De Brahm's appointment signaled a new emphasis in southeastern cartography, one that tied effective imperial administration to accurate mapping of the Southeast. Beginning in late seventeenth-century France, cartographers began to abandon their old reliance on verbal accounts and sea-born "dead reckoning" and to insist on precise astronomical observation as the only true basis for latitudinal and longitudinal placement. All conjectural information would, ideally, be abandoned. Unlike France, which had early established a royal survey office, Britain lacked any royally commissioned cartographers until the end of the eighteenth century, but the royal appointment of two surveyors general for North America can perhaps be viewed as a step toward a national map office.[57]

De Brahm's mapmaking reflected this sensibility that a map was best left blank in places where no formal survey had been conducted. His 1757 map (fig. 10), for all its detail of the coastline, remained mostly blank. Rivers and roads vanished only a few miles into the interior, and the remarkable soil map that appeared along the South Carolina/North Carolina boundary was only "discovered by a N.W. Line run 40 Miles from the Mouth of Little River."[58] His great map of Florida, composed in the 1770s, mapped the peninsula's coast in painstaking detail, but left most of the interior virtually blank, which De Brahm himself attributed to his "exact representation of what I personally and faithfully examined on the spot of what is surveyed by my deputies and that I shall never attempt to make any return or insertment in General Maps of any other characteristick."[59] The new language of Enlightenment mapmaking boded ill for the Indians of the Southeast, for the preference for blank spaces over a "relict Indian geography" led to the mapping of a *vacuum domicilium* in the Southeast, "a blank space which is easily divided and ruled."[60] The new maps' foreshadowing of dispossession should not be overstated, however. De Brahm himself would later disavow the corruptions that empire had brought into Indian societies.[61] Even the great imperialist John Stuart's introduction of Enlightenment cartography into the interior was aimed not

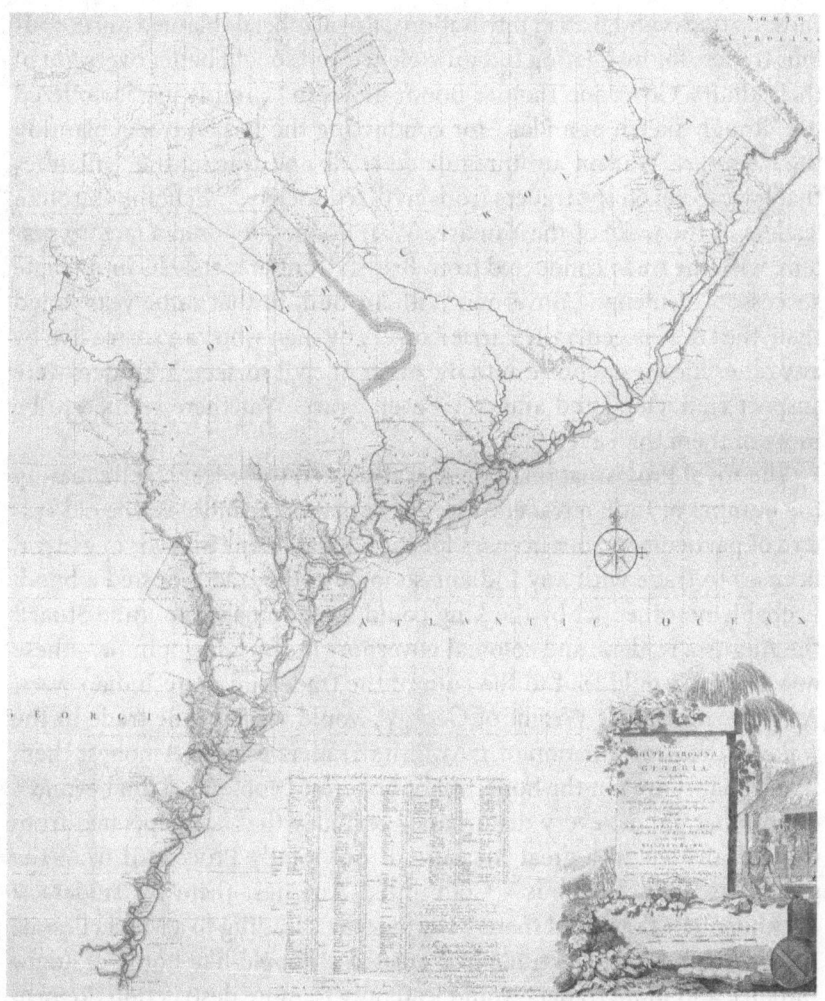

FIGURE 10. John Gerar William de Brahm, "Map of Carolina and Part of Georgia," 1757. Photo courtesy of the Newberry Library, Chicago, Illinois. Call # Ayer 133 D28 1757.

at dispossessing Indians of their lands, but at dispossessing Indian traders of their influence in southeastern affairs.

Following the Seven Years' War, management of the southeastern Indian trade became a principal concern of royal officials. The Cherokee War, though brief, had devastated the Carolina countryside. Indian as well as English settlements lay ruined and many had died in a series of

Indian attacks and British retributions. Royal officials blamed unscrupulous traders for instigating Indian violence and sought better oversight of their affairs. Governor Thomas Boone of South Carolina in 1764 offered his "Rough Sketch of a Plan" for conducting the Indian trade, blaming the Cherokee War on an unregulated trade and fearing the "villainies that have expelled the traders from civilized society."[62] Echoing Carolina leaders in the wake of the Yamasee War, Boone proposed a factory system, with the trade conducted from British frontier forts. His immediate successor, Lieutenant Governor William Bull, in that same year noted that "the trade is generally carried on . . . by men who can scarce live by any other means or conform to the order of civil society."[63] Traders were suspect characters, and after the Seven Years' War there seemed to be more of them than ever.

The royal Proclamation of 1763 exacerbated these fears by increasing the number of Indian traders. The proclamation abandoned the old system of particular trader licenses for individual towns in favor of general licenses to trade with any Indians so long as the trader posted a bond. Probably no other act by the king could have managed to unite Stuart, the Augusta traders, and colonial governors in the same opinion—these new traders would lead to the ruin of the trade and more Indian wars. As Governor James Wright of Georgia would write of the trade in the wake of the Proclamation of 1763, "The Traders who go Amongst them [the Indians] are not the honestest or Soberest People. . . . I am beyond a doubt, that almost every disturbance & injury that has happened from the Indians has in a great Measure, if not totally Proceeded from the great Misconduct & abuses Committed Amongst them by Traders & Packhorsmen Employed there."[64] Rather than leading to a Mitchellesque Indian submission, the trade had created a Popple-like horde of angry Indians, and more traders would lead only to more destruction. Reform was needed, and Stuart's major policy was to remove control of Indian affairs from private traders.

John Stuart, though in many ways a rival of imperial governors, echoed Wright's fear of an unregulated trade and blamed Anglo-Indian conflicts on white traders. Stuart characterized the traders as men who "dread the introduction of order, regularity and laws, by which their enormities may be punished and restrained."[65] For him, only a reduction of private influence in Indian affairs could preserve order in the Southeast. Appointing deputies to live among the Indians, Stuart would make his office the one to which Indians addressed their grievances, thereby increasing imperial oversight of the traders' conduct.[66]

Stuart also regretted the lack of imperial control over the trade networks of the Southeast. He wanted to oversee the licensing of traders himself, removing governors' decades-old privilege, and increasing his personal oversight over those who sought access to Indian towns.[67] Stuart fretted that the traders licensed separately by Virginia, South Carolina, and North Carolina were not "subjected to any general jurisdiction the consequences of which are the greatest disorder and confusions."[68] Without formal jurisdiction, the traders were free to "wander where they please to every nation and through every village."[69] Even a flood of new traders had to follow the paths through Indian towns. Stuart himself did not wish to abandon the old trader geography, but he did believe that imperial surveillance of the paths and restriction on traders' movement was necessary to the continuance of the trade. Stuart wanted to make certain that he and his deputies controlled access to Indian villages. Indeed, he hoped to reorient the trade south to Pensacola and thus to subvert Augusta's influence over the older eastern trading path.[70]

The Stuart-Purcell map was in many ways the fulfillment of John Stuart's commission as superintendent, symbolically as well as practically. The Proclamation of 1763 had forbidden British settlements west of a line running along the Appalachian Mountains. However, the line, based as it was on numerous treaties and talks between various British governors and Indian leaders, was fragmentary and difficult to trace. Stuart was thus ordered to have a skilled surveyor piece together the precise boundaries of the Proclamation line so that imperial administrators could better enforce the regulation. As a temporary measure to satisfy his superiors, Stuart forwarded a copy of Mitchell's 1755 printed map with a rough line inked on it. However, Stuart believed that the printed maps of the Southeast were wholly unreliable for his purposes. He complained in 1771 of "the impossibility" of mapping the Proclamation Line "with such a degree of accuracy as to convey a just idea of our boundaries upon any of the printed maps that I have seen, in all of which the natural boundaries specified in the different treaties are either erroneously laid down or entirely left out."[71] Mitchell's map, reliant on the old trade geography that Stuart hoped to supplant, was unsuitable.

Stuart's efforts to craft a better map were aided by new travelers along the paths. Following the Seven Years' War, packhorse trains began carrying more than the goods of the Indian trade. Now appearing alongside the traders were professional surveyors, men whose job it was to accurately map both the boundaries of various Indian land cessions as well as the trails and placement of Indian towns. William Bartram described one such survey party who journeyed from Augusta in 1773. The caravan consisted of "surveyors, astronomers, artisans, chain-carriers, markers, guides and hunters."[72] The 1773 survey party's goal was to map the boundaries of an enormous cession of land, dubbed the "New Purchase," by the Cherokees to the colony of Georgia in exchange for absolution of their standing debts.

Stuart, a party to the conference, was undoubtedly a part of this packhorse train, as were Joseph Purcell and Philip Yonge. All three names were listed in the map resulting from the survey, Philip Yonge's 1773 "A Map of the Lands Ceded to His Majesty by the Creek and Cherokee Indians."[73] However, Stuart was a fervent opponent of the New Purchase, which had been brokered by private traders at Augusta and threatened Anglo-Creek relations. The Creek Indians claimed part of the ceded lands and were angry that the Cherokees had given it away. Stuart opposed any private dealings for Indian land, since they reinforced the influence of traders among the Indians and threatened stability in the Southeast. In this way, Stuart was an opponent of dispossession, and his efforts to craft a precise map were in some ways a means to protect Indian lands.[74]

However, Stuart's own mapmaking projects were aimed at securing Indian land cessions. The survey works of Stuart's deputy, David Taitt, a contributor to the Stuart-Purcell map, were part of Taitt's 1772 commission to secure land cessions. In 1772, Stuart appointed Taitt as a delegate to journey among the Creek towns, to dissuade Creeks from negotiating with private traders and to seek the Indians' approval for a British land purchase along the Scambia River. Stuart appointed Taitt because he was both "a good surveyor and a man of prudence."[75] Stuart instructed Taitt, while on this diplomatic mission, to "Ride thro' all the Indian Villages of the Upper Creek as well as the Lower Creek Nation, and take particular Notice of their Situation and make such observations as may enable you to draw a Plan of the Country and of the Rivers etca."[76]

Taitt's journal reveals the attempts to superimpose a new cartographic language over the older contours of the trade geography. The narrative form of his journal reveals that place-to-place travel was now movement between invisible lines of latitude and longitude, rather than movement between peoples. Taitt set out along the Indian trading paths with his transit, a timepiece, and measuring chain. The level of precision in his verbal account is remarkable:

> Febry 2d. We set out this morning fourteen minutes after Eight and Continued our Course NW b[y] W about Eight miles, and then

NNE Nine Miles and Sixty Eight Chains further.... Febry 3d. This morning... we set out Seven minutes after Eight and Arrived at the little Scambia or Weoka Twenty minutes past ten being six miles and sixty Chains NE from last Camp... Febry 4th... we went along the path NNE one mile and a Quarter... here we Stoped at the side of a run (being the same where we were Encamped last night) to Dry the venison and wait for an Observation which I took at twelve Oclock and found to be in Latitude 31° 14 minutes North; being 43 miles to the Northward of Pensacola Answering to 49 3/4 English Statue miles.[77]

The meaning of place along the trail had changed. No longer paths between peoples, trails were merely one more feature to be plotted onto Stuart's intended large-scale map of the Southeast. Geography was now an assistant to imperial administration, a way of guiding the future rather than a description of present social relations.

Relying on De Brahm's former deputy Joseph Purcell, Stuart produced an ambitious and remarkably complete map of the Southeast, titled "A Map of the Southern Indian District of North America" (fig. 11).[78] Though never published, this 1775 manuscript map presented greater detail and planimetric certainty than any map that preceded it. For the first time, Indian towns were recorded not as places along a trail, but as points on a grid of latitude and longitude. The trails linking towns twisted and turned in ways that no previous map had captured. The Appalachian Mountains, so long the bane of southeastern mapmakers, now appeared in relief through a careful hachuring.[79] Stuart even attempted to define the boundaries of Indian hunting lands, a goal that presumed that Indians recognized some invisible and arbitrary division between their hunting grounds. Purcell painstakingly inked in the Proclamation Line, which in less than two years would become irrelevant as the American Revolution tore asunder the imperial framework that Stuart sought to build.

Although the map's "accuracy" was striking, the map also served Stuart's political purposes. The colonies that had stretched across the entirety of the Mitchell map now kept themselves confined east of the Proclamation Line. Georgia, in particular, suffered the greatest diminution. The colony that had dominated Mitchell's Indian interior now appeared as a thin strip of land on the south side of the Savannah River (to be fair, the actual bounds of the colony as determined by Indian treaty). However, Stuart, who had so strenuously asserted his preeminence over the Indian

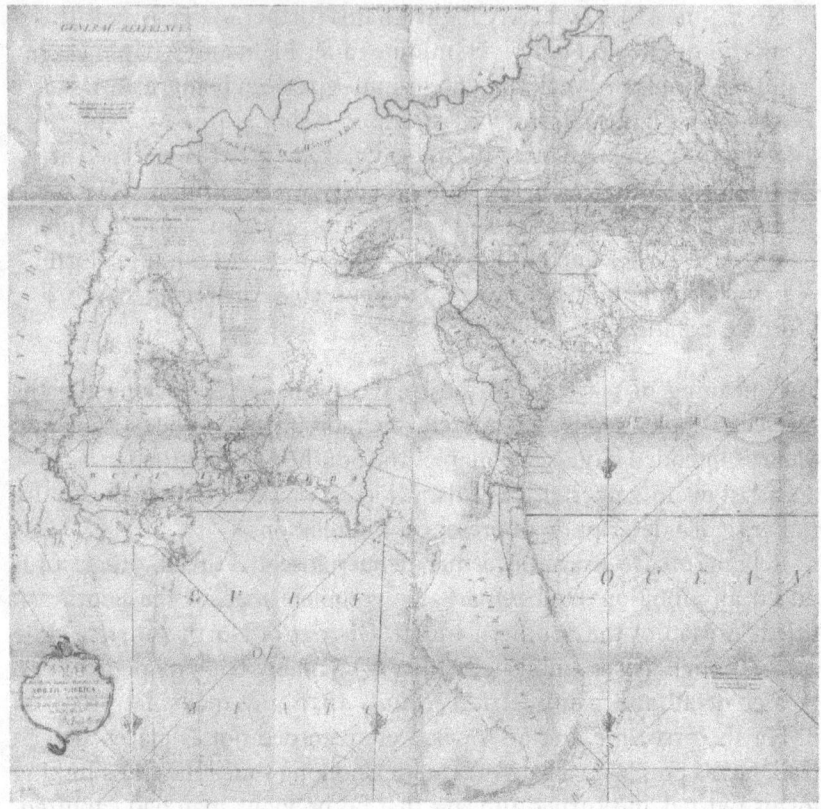

FIGURE 11. The Stuart-Purcell manuscript map, 1775. Photo courtesy of the Newberry Library, Chicago, Illinois. Call # Vault Oversize Ayer MS Map 228.

territories, must have felt some satisfaction in constraining Georgia's jurisdiction solely to its official boundaries. Likewise, Stuart emphasized the southern trading paths from each of these Indian nations. While numerous paths intersected each other and reached southward to Pensacola and West Florida, only a single road, stretched across a vast expanse of empty area, represented the "Great Old Path" from the Cowetas and Okfuskees to Augusta.

Despite his best efforts, though, Stuart could not free himself from that great old path of the Indian trade geography, either politically or cartographically. Stuart did not succeed in removing the influence of Indian traders in the Southeast; on the contrary he met near-constant resistance from those whose power and influence rested on the continuation of the old trade networks: colonial governors, the Indian traders at Augusta, and Indian headmen whose towns' placement along the old path had accorded them greater influence and prestige.[80] His map likewise revealed the stubborn persistence of the old routes. For all of his surveyors' attention to detail, Stuart's map remained entirely blank except for the immediate area surrounding the Indian trading paths. Even in 1775, these remained the limits of geographic knowledge in the Southeast.

Despite the removal of the French and Spanish, the increase of traders resulting from the Proclamation of 1763, the increasing number of land purchases from Indians, and John Stuart's best efforts, the Indian trade did not completely fall apart in the wake of the Seven Years' War. Historians, citing the impassioned pleas of Indian traders as well as the complaints of men such as Taitt and Stuart, have characterized the post-1763 trade as one of "decline and conflict."[81] However, a table included in Bernard Romans's *A Concise Natural History of East and West Florida* shows deerskin exports from Georgia increasing in the years after 1763. Though stopping at 1772, the table showed no marked decrease in the volume of trade, and a comparison with a chart Stuart made of deerskin exports from Charles Town reveals that the trade in the supposed period of decline compared favorably with any nine-year period during the supposed "golden age" of the deerskin trade.[82]

Clearly, the years 1763 to 1775 represented new challenges to the old trade geography: increasing imperial oversight, movement of trade south to West Florida, and increasing white settlement in the Piedmont. But not even Stuart, in his redrawing of the Southeast, could deny the traders' persistence, explaining why the store of James Germany, an old Augusta hand, appeared nestled safely among the Upper Creek Towns. Rather than as a period of decline and conflict, it is perhaps better to characterize the years between 1763 and 1775 as one of renegotiation in the Southeast. The removal of the French likewise removed the trade's "official" justification, but the culture and society of the trade did not disappear as quickly. Though a plantation economy and white settlements would eventually emerge victorious in the Southeast, that ending was but one of many possible outcomes envisioned during the interwar years.

The numerous possibilities that still existed after the Seven Years' War became polarized during the American Revolution. It was this event that suddenly and forcefully unmade the great old path and turned the numerous small-scale battles for influence in the Southeast into a cataclysmic winner-take-all proposition. The Revolutionary movement in Georgia owed part of its origin to a series of small skirmishes between Lower Creek Indians angered over the 1773 New Purchase and the increasing number of white settlers pushing against the eastern edges of the Creeks' hunting grounds. As events in New England and elsewhere grew more heated during 1775–76, Georgia became increasingly divided. On one side stood Governor Wright, John Stuart, and the Indians of the Southeast; on the other stood coastal merchants and an emerging backcountry planter elite with their agrarian base of support.[83] This new elite's victory would result in the dispossession of the Augusta traders and the sad history of Indian removal in the southeastern United States.[84]

Few of those involved in the deerskin trade foresaw such an outcome. From the perspective of the pre-Revolutionary Southeast, the trade seemed a durable and stable system of commercial and human relationships. Certainly the trade involved uncertainty and sometimes violence. But it endured for almost sixty years between the Yamasee War and the American Revolution. It survived the numerous Anglo-French contests for North America and even on occasion helped maintain peace when war broke out elsewhere. The British in particular attempted to use the trade to further imperial aims in the Southeast, laying grand plans for Indian alliances and united military actions. As the frustrated letters of men like Glen and Stuart attested, the deerskin trade proved only partly reliable as a handmaiden to the British empire.

As Britain's maps showed, the trade had a stubborn tendency to follow its own course. The trade's participants engaged in a volatile and unpredictable business. Boatmen faced the tricky currents of southeastern waterways and the fickle administration of colonial governments. Traders journeyed through a knotty series of paths and trails inhabited by friend and enemy alike. The political circumstances surrounding any given journey could change very quickly. Yet Southeasterners mitigated potential hazards by directing the trade through a series of relatively stable points such as the trading companies of Augusta or the village stores in Indian country. Alternating between uncertainty and stability, the deerskin trade created a series of unique places, each requiring its own set of rules and behaviors. The trade's position between unpredictability and dependability was clear from the moment one set out from Charles Town for Augusta. The boatmen could have told anyone how much the trade relied on unsteady vehicles to create a stable system.

2 /   The Life of the Region: The Many Meanings of the Savannah River

In May 1740, John Rae pushed off from the Charles Town docks. His cargo of Indian trade goods secured, Rae directed his slim canoe across the Charles Town bar. He would steer the boat around the sea islands of South Carolina and Georgia, and then make the two-week trip up the Savannah River to Augusta. His was an important charge. The goods fastened in the boat's bottom would supply entire villages of Indians and at the same time help maintain the continued friendship of the powerful Creek, Chickasaw, and Cherokee nations. Standing at the stern he kept an eye on the winds and currents that might easily tip the slim craft or drive it onto any of a number of sandbars or oyster rakes that lay just beneath the coastal waters. Rae would stop at Savannah and deliver the packet of letters from the Georgia Trustees, perhaps stay a couple of days and enjoy the company at the small town's taverns.

From Savannah, his four-man crew (most likely enslaved African Americans) would bend to the oars, forcing the boat upstream along the Savannah River's banks. Their only rest would come at nighttime camps in the woods or perhaps a stay at the occasional plantation home. At Augusta the trade goods would be turned into deerskins for the return trip downriver; Rae and his crew knew the traders were then coming into town, their packhorses straining under the weight of the previous winter's hunts. The trading boat would be back in Charles Town in just a few months, this trip just one of several Rae made between 1739 and 1742.[1]

By 1750, Rae had given up the boatman's life. Most boatmen vanished into obscurity, but Rae managed to become one of Augusta's wealthiest and most influential citizens. A partner in the powerful "Augusta Company" that dominated the Anglo-Creek deerskin trade, Rae also became a justice of the peace and a member of the Georgia assembly. His career would earn him wealth and prestige as one of the leading "gentlemen of Augusta" and would eventually secure him a large plantation on the river near Savannah. A slaveholder, a man of property, and one of the biggest beneficiaries of the deerskin trade, Rae's life began as "patroon" of one of the numerous trading boats that made hundreds of trips between Charles Town and Augusta in the years between 1737 and 1775.[2] It is fitting to begin the story of Augusta with him, since his life paralleled the rise of the town itself.

The Savannah River has assumed a prominent place in every account of Augusta, be it eighteenth- or twentieth-century. The river allowed relatively easy navigation from the Atlantic coast to the rocky uplands of the southern Piedmont, and Europeans seeking a link to the resources of a vast Indian interior sent their boats up to the falls to facilitate this trade. Seeking easy transportation for goods and capital into the interior, colonization naturally followed the ready-made river courses. Only when the white population and agricultural production increased did European expansion move from its small riverside footholds into the rest of the southern backcountry. Augusta was in many ways but one example of this basic process of settlement, which included such early interior towns as Albany, New York; Richmond, Virginia; and Camden, South Carolina. Certainly this process was commonplace by the eighteenth century and goes far in explaining why white settlers chose the places they did for their new homes in a New World.[3]

But the river itself remained active in the history of the Southeast, both as an idea and as a physical presence. For Indians, Europeans, and African Americans, the Savannah was both a boundary and a connector—a dual role that shaped much of the history of the deerskin trade. Creeks relied on the Savannah to mark the separation between themselves and an increasingly aggressive English empire. English imperialists, in contrast, saw the river as both a lifeline to colonial expansion and a means of asserting their control over the region. The idea of control, however, proved illusory when Englishmen actually encountered the Savannah. For Indian traders, the river was a useful tool for building both their wealth and their early dependence on slave labor. And for those enslaved boatmen who made the river functional, the Savannah was a tricky and dangerous workplace but one that connected the region's slave populations. The river, so obvious a feature of the southeastern landscape, was still fragmented into different meanings by its different users. And all of these uses combined to give shape to the trade.

Although few lived on the Savannah during the colonial period, southeastern Indians did have a very close connection to the region's numerous rivers. The waterways that crossed the Southeast were in fact crucial to native life in the eighteenth century. Rivers determined town location and provided the necessaries of life for much of an Indian's year. Given that native societies strung themselves along riverbanks, waterways were also important connectors between villages and to colonies. Given their centrality, it is not surprising that Indian cosmology accorded rivers special places and special powers. Rivers were also useful boundaries between Creek and English lands.

Village life in the native Southeast centered on rivers. Creek Indian towns in particular were almost always placed near running water and frequently named after some feature of the local stream. The river floodplains offered fertile fields and access to freshwater fish. But the river fall zones that Indians preferred also offered access to a dizzying array of environments—cane breaks, coniferous and deciduous forests, and swamps—each with its own internal variations and different species of plants. An Indian's year required the cultivation of river valleys as well as the harvesting of the various products of their variegated environment found only on the river.[4]

Given the central roles rivers played in Indian lives, it is small wonder that rivers featured prominently in southeastern Indians' cosmography. Southeastern Indians believed that rivers (along with other waterways and lakes) were entrances into the Under World. The Under World was associated with future time, and therefore the province of both good and bad things. Fertility and longevity were associated with waterways but so were monsters, chaos, and death. Rivers thus had special places in Indian rituals and religions. Indians bathed in the pure waters of rivers in order to cleanse themselves and prolong life (associating it with the snake's shedding of its skin). Indian priests could also look to rivers to divine the future.[5]

However, if southeastern Indians attached such deep meanings to the Savannah River, they did so only briefly. The Savannah Valley during the contact era was a place of ongoing native migration. When Hernando de Soto moved through the Savannah Valley in the 1540s, his men described it as an abandoned place, with neither habitations nor humans for a great distance.[6] By the time the English settled South Carolina in the 1670s, the valley had become home to numerous migrants, most of whom stayed for only a few decades. The Westos, dislocated from the Lake Erie area, had settled along the Savannah, but were displaced by the Second Westo War in 1680. The Savannahs, for whom the river was named, were themselves Shawnees relocating from the Ohio Valley and moved into the region during the Westos' heyday, but supplanted them in the region after the war. The Savannahs themselves relocated after the Yamasee War in 1715–16. The Yuchis, who lived along the Savannah River below the Savannahs, moved to the region sometime in the late 1600s and began moving westward after the Yamasee War, although some still lived in Georgia during the Trustee Period. The Indians who remained longest during the contact period were the eastern Chickasaws. Invited by the Carolinians, they moved to the area the Savannahs abandoned in 1723 and remained there until after the American Revolution.[7] While the Savannah was no doubt central to all of these groups, they were never very large populations. In truth, relatively few southeastern Indians lived alongside the Savannah during the colonial era, but many, perhaps most, southeastern Indians still knew the river, albeit in a more abstract way.

In the years after the Yamasee War, the Creeks' primary use for the Savannah was as a convenient boundary between themselves and South Carolina. Rivers were an important way in which Creeks conceived of their territory. Rivers were unmistakable features, more permanent and enduring than notches on trees, and the Creeks, like other Indians, used rivers as convenient, obvious boundaries that separated hunting and fishing grounds within and between indigenous polities. Creeks also reserved certain fishing grounds along rivers for a village's exclusive use, challenging others who might use it.[8]

In the contact era, the Creeks easily adapted the idea of boundary rivers to their dealings with the English. In the aftermath of the Yamasee War, when the Creeks and English both realized that more clearly defined territories might be a good idea, the two parties established the Savannah River as the limits of English settlement in the Southeast. The English were to keep to the river's northern/eastern banks and the Creeks retained for themselves the use of all territory south/west of the Savannah. It was this political division that governed much of Georgia's early relationships with the Creeks, as all of Georgia was planned for territory that even English treaties recognized as Creeks'. Oglethorpe's early diplomacy, for example, sought to secure Creek permission for Georgia settlers on the Savannah's southern banks.[9]

But if the Creeks used rivers as boundaries, they likewise recognized rivers' poor suitability to act as barriers. While rivers were difficult to move, they were easy to cross, which is why the Creeks relied on them to mark administrative districts but did not put much faith in rivers' ability to keep out unwanted intruders. Southeastern rivers could be ferocious and dangerous at times, but they were not so formidable as to prevent crossing. The Creeks crossed rivers all the time, and they knew that the English did as well. More important, they recognized that English livestock could cross a river just as easily as deer and bison did. This was why, by the 1800s, the Creeks were reminding Thomas Jefferson that rivers did not ensure peaceful relations because rivers made for very permeable boundaries.[10]

In Creek thinking, however, rivers also served to connect as much as they served to separate. The Savannah's other main function in Creek ideology was as a connector between themselves and the English colonies of Georgia and South Carolina. It was an abstract route, in other words. The river carried trade and diplomacy between the English coast and the native interior. While the Savannah bordered Creek hunting grounds and many Creeks likely had seen the river, few actually traveled along its route during the colonial era and then mostly when they journeyed down its stream for talks in the cities of Savannah or Charles Town. And while these processions could occasionally number in the hundreds, they were a relatively rare occurrence. Usually only a select few headmen made the downstream journey. Sadly, none of them left any known record of their impressions of the Savannah.

For most southeastern Indians, those whose villages and hunting grounds did not border the Savannah, the river probably existed simply as part of the connection between themselves and the English. The Chickasaw deerskin maps blend the Savannah and the trading path into one single link between themselves and the English colonies. Indian maps did not distinguish water and land carriage when depicting paths between places. How one traveled was less important than noting the lines of communication and trade, regardless of the mode of transport.[11] Thus, for those Indians who actually considered it, the Savannah was simply part of a larger connection, significant only as part of the pathways that led to the English colonies.

Like that of most Creeks, the English concept of the Savannah was abstract. The river formed an important jurisdictional boundary between South Carolina and Georgia. It also figured prominently in English accounts of the Southeast, serving as an important resource for future settlements. But mostly it was a connector, a route by which commerce and culture could flow easily from the Atlantic to the interior. The only English to frequently travel the river were the Augusta traders, and they took full advantage of the river's abstract purposes. As a connector, the river secured their status in the Southeast and made possible their business. As a boundary, the river allowed the traders to skirt Georgia law by taking advantage of the Savannah's easy crossings at Augusta. By establishing themselves on both sides of the river, the traders at Augusta established themselves as slave owners in the Georgia upcountry.

The English attachment to rivers was a relatively new development in the 1700s, compared to that of the southeastern Indians. Whereas river improvements had been important in places such as the Netherlands, the English simply had not had a particularly deep relationship with rivers prior to 1600. Although rivers were used for local transportation, most commerce in the British Isles went by way of coastal vessels. Rivers were not particularly useful for moving people or goods during medieval and early modern English history. In fact, the English considered rivers to be public only as far as tides flowed. Above tidal zones, rivers were accounted private property and therefore segmented by numerous millworks and fishing weirs, each of which provided physical and financial obstacles to river traffic (weir owners could charge boats for passage). These private interests remained an obstacle to river navigation well into the eighteenth century.[12]

But beginning in the 1600s, English thinkers began reimagining rivers as necessary conduits of commerce. Coinciding with England's modernizing and industrializing tendencies in the seventeenth and eighteenth centuries, river navigation became necessary to move goods from one part of the realm to another. The era of the South Seas speculation that ultimately led to Georgia's founding was also an age of river improvements.[13] Advocates for easier navigation pushed for the state to exert a greater influence over inland rivers, converting them from private domains into royal highways. As one member of Parliament put it in 1655, "Cosmographers agree that this Island is incomparably furnished with pleasant Rivers, like Veins in the Natural Body, which conveys Blood into all the Parts, whereby the whole is nourished, and made useful."[14] As England formed itself into a modern nation, rivers were seen as crucial conveyors within the body politic, carrying goods and commerce from one part to another. But this idea was contested in England, even in the 1700s, as private owners resisted Parliamentary efforts to break up their weirs in the service of national commerce.[15] But as England's waterborne empire developed in the 1600s and 1700s, the cosmographers' opinion was quickly becoming accepted as truth.

In the discourse of colonization in colonial Georgia and the Southeast, rivers were the source of a colony's health. Early southeastern promotional literature by Sir Robert Montgomery, Jean-Pierre Purry and the Trustees for Establishing the Colony of Georgia emphasized the utility and fertility that rivers provided new settlements. The future colony was "well water'd, with noble Rivers."[16] Colonial promoters emphasized that southeastern soil was "very rich ... that it abounds in game, deer, and wild bulls." The "numerous beautiful rivers teeming everywhere with excellent fishes" offered sustenance for a new colony.[17] The woods along riverbanks, "where the enlivening influence of the Sun prepares the Trees," would allow for pot-ash production and thus a marketable commodity.[18] From the beginning, Georgia's planners believed that the colony would grow along the banks of the Savannah and Altamaha Rivers, drawing from their fluid fertility and using them to increase its trade.[19] The rivers' long inland courses also provided Georgia with easy access to interior Indians, as John Barnwell himself wrote to Montgomery: "This Trade must, of Necessity, center with *you*, as not only being nearer to the *Indians*, who deal most, but also having Water-Carriage to within a little of their Towns."[20]

Europeans also associated southeastern rivers with fertility and future potential. The correlation between rivers and productive human endeavor continued as Georgia grew older. In the 1760s, as southeasteners began to turn their gaze westward for expansion, the numerous rivers of the Southeast offered the same advantages for profit and productivity. John Gerar William De Brahm emphasized in his "Report on the General Survey" that Georgia yet had future riches to reveal, "altho' only equal with South carolina as to Planting, yet being watered preferably to South carolina, cannot but have the Preference in the Capacity and Conveniences for Trade and Navigation ... in respect to the great Number of Streams, and Rivers, which are navigable."[21] The valleys of the Appalachian country were "of the richest Soil equal to Manure itself ... (besides being well watered with Rivulets)."[22] James Adair, changing careers from Indian trader to colonial promoter, advertised the potential of the Southeast's hilly interior, abounding as it was "with inexhaustible mines of iron ore" and lying "convenient to navigable rivers."[23] But it was not the Savannah River itself that inspired the founding of Augusta so much as a steady stream of small trading boats that caught Oglethorpe's eye.

Rather than divining the future from rivers, as Indians did, Europeans hoped to use rivers as agents to shape the future. Augusta's founding at the head of the Savannah's navigation became a key part in Oglethorpe's plans for Georgia. He believed that the falls of the river were militarily important but also hoped the lucrative Indian trade would underwrite the fledgling colony's economic viability. Augusta was to become "the Key of all the Indian Countrey."[24] The idea first occurred to him in March 1733, only a few weeks after his first landing at Savannah. Oglethorpe noticed the frequent traffic of boats from New Windsor, a small Carolina trading town at the falls of the Savannah. He reported back to the trustees that the Savannah River "has a very long course and a great Trade is carried on by it to the Indians, there having [been] above 12 Trading Boats passed by since I have been here."[25] Oglethorpe hoped to use the river's connections to enhance the wealth of his colony, but he also hoped to use it as a means of spreading his benevolent imperialism inland.

The English analogy of the river as a vein in a living body guided their approach to southeastern waterways. For the trustees and Oglethorpe, rivers did not contain any spirits or powers themselves; they were empty vessels capable of communicating any force that happened to need transport. Augusta would help Georgia spread its positive influences upriver, but the Savannah had to be guarded lest it be allowed to carry pernicious influences inland. The river was simply too open for the trustees' tastes and was allowing the infections of rum and slavery to spread from the West Indies and Carolina into Georgia. In particular, the trustees were worried about the ill health and immorality that prevailed in the British West Indies. The prohibition on rum had been enacted because Georgia's founders had noticed that rum had been "particularly hurtfull and pernicious to Man's Body and ... attended with dangerous Maladies and fatal distempers and if not timely prevented will in all likelyhood ruin the said Colony."[26] Slavery likewise harmed white men's bodies and colonies as a whole by obstructing "the Increase of English and Christian Inhabitants therein who alone can in case of War be relyed on for the Defence and Security of the same."[27] Slavery was also bad for the individual because "the white man, by having a Negro Slave, would be less disposed to labour himself; and that his whole time must by employed in keeping the Negro to Work."[28] Slaves also threatened white family life: "The Planter's Wife and Children would by the Death, or even the Absence of the Planter, be in a manner at the mercy of the Negro."[29]

The trustees considered the combination of rum and slavery a kind of disease that threatened the health of the fledgling colony. These were the plagues that ruined the health of Carolina and West Indian plantations. Oglethorpe reported happily in 1739 that "Georgia has been very healthy this year, the fatal Rum Fever of Charles Town hath not extended to us."[30]

But the colony did not remain immune for long. In 1740, responding to recent clamors among Georgia's Malcontents for rum and slaves, Thomas Jones, the trustees' storekeeper, bewailed, "That so much Ingratitude, (as well as other Vices) prevails in Georgia, whether besides the common Depravedness of human Nature; The Latitude 32, or the Evil Example of our Carolina Neighbours, may be infectious, I will not determine."[31] Another Georgian, in conversation with the earl of Egmont, blamed the infections of rum and slavery on the West Indies, saying, "tis a mistake to think the Inhabitants of Savannah have rum, what they have is a poisonous spirit from the Islands."[32] Where the trustees saw a river poisoned by rum and slavery, the traders at New Windsor and Augusta saw an economic lifeline that ensured their place in society.

The traders at the Savannah's falls also recognized that the river made for a very permeable boundary. According to the trustees' rhetoric, these "diseases" had entered Georgia through waterborne communication with South Carolina and Georgia, but in reality the "disease" of slavery came from just across the river. Taking advantage of the Savannah's easy crossings at the fall line, Augusta's early traders avoided the ban on slavery by owning land and slaves on the South Carolina side of the river but employing them on the Georgia side.[33] The trustees themselves recognized the traders' actions, but felt that if Georgia could control the river properly, they could eliminate these vices.

The trustees were determined that these vices would not spread up the Savannah River to the Indians. Therefore, one of Oglethorpe's first attempts to reform the Carolina trade was to attack their trading boats. To do this, Oglethorpe took advantage of the legalistic language of Georgia's charter, which granted the colony all the land lying between the Savannah and Altamaha Rivers. Likewise the colony was to include the entirety of both rivers, its jurisdiction extending "from the most Northern Stream of a River there commonly called the Savannah all along the Sea Coast to the Southward unto the most Southern Stream of a certain other great water or River called the Altamaha and Westward from the heads of the said Rivers respectively in Direct Lines to the South Seas."[34] Oglethorpe and the trustees interpreted this language to mean that Georgia had jurisdiction over the entire Savannah River, including the right of navigation. South Carolina, however, interpreted the charter to mean only the solid land between these two bounds and open communication along the river itself. From this language, Georgia and South Carolina would continue to dispute their shared boundary for the next two and a half centuries.[35]

Oglethorpe and his agents' attempts to purge the Savannah of rum and slaves set South Carolina and Georgia on an uneasy footing for decades. Echoing debates ongoing in England, the intercolonial squabble centered on who could claim jurisdiction over a river. During the debate, the two sides articulated an ideal of what rivers represented in the colonial mind-set. The ideal river was empty and passive, nothing more than a way of spreading commerce and increasing wealth. The founding of Georgia and Oglethorpe's attempts to gain a share of the Indian trade quickly transformed the Savannah River from an open highway into contested ground. For decades, South Carolina traders had enjoyed an unfettered river communication between Charles Town and the falls of the Savannah. There Carolina had planted a township, first known as Savannah Town but renamed New Windsor in 1730, that served as an entrepôt for Carolina traders moving goods back and forth between the coast and interior Indian villages. Oglethorpe's planned town of Augusta threatened a trade route that Carolinians had come to regard as a birthright. Unsurprisingly, his project received a chilly reception in Charles Town merchant houses. The debate revealed how closely tied to water the British empire had become and how oriented British colonists were to their waterways.

The uncertainty over river navigation had profound implications for the deerskin trade because the colony of Georgia had passed three laws that were anathema to any New Windsor trader. On January 9, 1734, the Georgia Trustees had simultaneously banned rum and slavery in the colony, and prohibited any Indian traders not licensed in Georgia from trading with any Indians living within Georgia's chartered boundaries. The possession of rum or slaves in any part of Georgia was forbidden, and should Georgia authorities find any person in possession of either, the rum kegs would be staved and the slaves would be seized. If one included the Savannah River as a part of Georgia, as Oglethorpe and his deputies did, then Georgia authorities had the right to stop any trading boat and seize any contraband rum or slaves onboard. And in May 1736 the constable in Savannah, Thomas Causton, exercised that right and stopped two trading boats bound for New Windsor. He "ordered the Boats ashore, opened their Packs, took out the rum and stav'd the heads of 3 hhds. and 10 Caggs, and confin'd the Patrons under a Pretence of a Fine of 5 l. sterl."[36]

Causton's actions provoked an uproar in Charles Town. The newspaper account of the staving reported that all of Charles Town was "allarmed with the unexpected Proceedings of our Neighbours the Georgians, in respect to our Trade."[37] The Council and Assembly of

South Carolina were shocked that "a People so lately Settled in America and so little acquainted with the Customs and manners of the Indians" would be so bold as to commit "such Violence" on boats that carried rum from one Carolina town to another.[38] The staved rum, they argued, was not intended for Georgia, "but was bound up the said River with other Goods and Merchandizes to the said Savannah Old Town and Fort Moore."[39] The council and assembly also recognized that cutting Charles Town commerce off from inland townships would destroy the lifeline to interior settlements. The Savannah was "the only Water Passage to the said Savannah Garrison and the Town of Purrysburgh."[40] They argued that "the Navigation of that River is so absolutely necessary to the well being of all the Southern parts of this Your [Majesty's] Province."[41] South Carolina's governor Thomas Broughton feared what Georgia's actions would mean for the recently settled townships: "A Commerce with these Settlements cannot be conveniently carried on, without the use and Navigation of the Savanna River."[42]

Carolina's traders resented Georgia's attempts to claim a river as its own and instead made the claim that rivers should be open highways that served the public at large. Carolinians were outraged that they should have to seek permission from another colony for traffic between towns within their own province. The council and assembly begged the king whether his intention in granting the Georgia charter was "that the River Savannah should be the Natural Boundary between the Two Provinces without ever intending to debar our Majesty's Subjects of this Your Ancient Colony from the free and open Navigation thereof into all Ports and Places within this Province."[43] Governor Broughton noted that "the Subjects of this Province whilst they are passing from One part of the Province to another think they have no need of a Particular Permission."[44] He also asked the Lords of Trade "whether there is not a known distinction between the Property and Passage of a Navigable River and whether all Navigable Rivers within His Majesty's Dominions are not free and open to the Passage of all His Subjects in the same manner as are the King's Highways altho' the soil may be the Property of a Private Person?"[45] In the Carolinians' view, the river was an empty space, an avenue for trade; it was not a landscape that could be possessed or transferred. Georgia had overstepped its bounds and, given the open-river sentiments of the English royal government, it is unsurprising that South Carolina's argument held up in London.

But while governments argued over the Savannah's role in the shaping of colonies, other Europeans formed more personal connections along the river. For the merchants of Augusta, the Savannah was significant more as a connector than as an experienced landscape. It allowed them to retain regular contact between the two poles that shaped their identities: the busy seaport of Charles Town and their busy trading stores in Indian villages. The river was a means to wealth and status. When in Augusta, they could remain connected to European culture and society and maintain their identity as Europeans even at their remote location. When traders visited lowcountry towns, the boats kept them connected to the Indian trade and to the information that offered them access to the elite ranks of lowcountry society. Colonial administrators and planners tended to speak abstractly of rivers. Traders, despite their constant movement up and down the river, never bothered to record their impressions of it. For them, as for most Europeans, the river was simply an empty vessel that carried traders' wealth and prestige back and forth.

For the Augusta merchants, the Savannah River provided them access to the European world. The downriver voyage was a legal requirement for the gentlemen of Augusta, but it also served to maintain social links with their lowcountry patrons. Law required that every trader renew his license annually during the summer months, but Charles Town was also a bustling social scene for the Indian traders. Charles Town was the Southeast's main port throughout the colonial era, and its merchants exported the traders' deerskins to Britain and imported the numerous trade goods that the traders carried back to Indian villages. The summertime journey from Augusta to Charles Town was a time to settle debts, visit with colonial governors and Indian commissioners, and partake of the amusements of European society. The small trade boats, having wound their way down the Savannah River, and up the coast along the inland waterway, made for the wharves and warehouses first.

Whether attending the governor or at dinner, Augusta traders felt a need to look presentable in lowcountry settings, and often it was river communication that allowed a respectable appearance in Savannah or Charles Town parlors. Rather than the contentious court days of the 1740s, the trader's life in Savannah by the 1770s was one of sociability and hobnobbing with lowcountry merchants. In 1775 the Augusta storekeepers Robert Mackay and Andrew MacLean journeyed downriver to settle their accounts with the General Assembly and Savannah merchants. Rather than suing each other, they enjoyed an evening of "claret and Punch." MacLean, in particular, hoped to make a good show with the Savannah merchant Thomas Netherclift, and indulged his vanity in town. "A French barber attends him twice a day," wrote the bemused Mackay, "and makes him the most complete Macaroni in Town." The reason for MacLean's meticulous grooming was his engagement "to dance with Mrs. Netherclift at the Assembly, but unless the Boat appears he'll not make the formidable show that's expected."[46] MacLean was awaiting his trading boat from Augusta to bring him proper gentleman's attire, evidence that, in addition to bringing finery up to Augusta, the boats also kept traders connected to the sources of their authority when traveling downriver.

Augusta residents, however, probably made few river trips themselves. Even Augusta merchants and traders only made the trip once or twice a year. Aside from the occasional trip to renew licenses or grievances, the Augusta merchants and traders spent relatively little time on the river. Certainly they did not mention it in their letters. Although it is possible that river trips were so common as to be unremarkable, it seems likelier that few Augustans spent much time on the Savannah. The river was probably not a central part of their lives unless they fished in it or crossed it to visit plantations on the Carolina side of the river. For them, as for most Indians and Europeans, the Savannah probably seemed most important for the connections it allowed to the larger Atlantic and Indian worlds.

On those few occasions when Europeans did comment on river spaces, it was apparent that the river challenged their notions of smooth and orderly progress. Much of that probably had to do with the spaces encountered along the way. For the first twenty years of Augusta's existence, the passage down the Savannah River was an odd tour through an unevenly settled continent. After leaving the Augusta riverfront, boats passed farms and plantations that quickly gave way to woods. Downriver, a sojourn through the Yuchi habitations above Mount Pleasant preceded a tour of the small farms of Purrysburg and Ebenezer and the town of Savannah. Taking a turn up the coast, the boats finally passed the lowcountry plantations of South Carolina before emerging in the metropolis of Charles Town. Spaced throughout these varying landscapes were the remnants of an Indian past: earthen mounds built by precontact peoples and the abandoned villages of post-Yamasee dislocations. By the time of the Revolution, these had all been usurped by a growing European plantation economy along Savannah River. But for much of the colonial period, Savannah boatmen set a course that was hardly the simplistic "wilderness to civilization" one might suspect. For all their variety, boatmen and river travelers called none of these places home and experienced them all as visitors staying for the night and then pushing off in the morning.

As it had been at least since Soto's time, the Savannah River remained a landscape marked unevenly by both disappearance and development. The years following the Yamasee War had seen a profound rearrangement of the Indian interior. Coastal Indians had either perished or fled to Florida. Creek Indians living in Georgia's coastal plains had retreated westward. Small bands of Indians such as the Yuchis had remained below Georgia's fall line, but the banks of the Savannah were littered with abandoned Indian fields and towns. The erosion of river bluffs revealed deposits of prehistoric oyster shells. The river spaces provoked in the Savannah's travelers a profound sense of ancient history and the romance of forgotten times. William Bartram, the great romantic, noted along the river near Augusta "very magnificent monuments of the power and industry of the ancient inhabitants of these lands... traces of a large Indian town, the work of a powerful nation, whose period of grandeur perhaps long preceded the discovery of this continent."[47] The river's waters had revealed at the high banks of Silver Bluff petrified wood, sharks' teeth, "as well as remains or traces of European military architects, and are supposed to be ancient camps of the Spaniards who formerly fixed themselves at this place in hopes of finding silver."[48] The river proved a mighty force in carving the landscape and had eaten human history, as at Fort Moore Bluff, where "the river hath so much encroached upon the Carolina shore, that its bed now lies where the site of the fort then was; indeed some told me that the opposite Georgia shore, where there is now a fine house and corn field, occupies the place."[49] The Savannah still evoked ruminations on ancient mysteries in the nineteenth century, as Harry Hammond rhapsodized about rivers as "the oldest features of all countries. Older are they than the everlasting hill, for their floods have given to mountain, hill and plain their shape and bounds, and while hourly molding these anew, bear in their currents the life of the region."[50] Rather than Oglethorpe's vision of orderly progress, the Savannah revealed human beings' more complicated routes through history.

And despite all the flattery, the Savannah River itself proved a difficult highway. The river was hazardous "because of the stumps and floating trees in the river and because of the danger of overturning the canoe, and sometimes because of the ebb and flood, which can be detected as far as Purrysburg."[51] William De Brahm described an even more violent river: "great Currents yearly wheeling down a Distance of 290 miles, especially at the time of great Freshes, by which great Trees with their Roots, and many Shrubs are grubbed up, which, and along with them great Quantity of Ground, Sand and Gravel is hurried down."[52] And the river was also home to the fearsome and mysterious alligator, which "from far away, you might think you see a fallen tree. It will not very likely attack a person unless it is in the river, a few cases of which we have had."[53] In England, where river floods and obstacles tended to be human-made, American rivers such as the Savannah and Altamaha must have seemed quite wild indeed.[54]

The Savannah punished inexperienced travelers. On even the best day, boatmen had to contend with snags, bars, and alligators. There were also frequent thunderstorms, as Philip Von Reck experienced firsthand. "A strong wind and cloudburst with thunder and lightning overtook us before we could reach land and safety, and the wind drove us into a rushing current where there were many cypress trees and where we were put in a very great danger of our lives.... Yet God saved us by means of a boat that met us in this desolate and deserted region."[55] In 1742 a woman named Langford and her son likewise experienced the caprices of Savannah River travel, "being on their Passage to Augusta [they] were Oversett, whereby they Remained many Hours in the River & were taken up by a Boat passing by."[56] The widow later died, but in both cases, novice travelers owed their escape from the river to more experienced hands, whose timely appearances testified to the frequency of Savannah River traffic.

Exposed to the whims of fast currents and fierce storms, it is small wonder that Europeans felt themselves helpless on the river. Unused to sleeping in open air on damp riverbanks, unprotected travelers quickly turned to contemplation of the Almighty. The Reverend Benjamin Ingham, while on a trip from Carolina south along the Atlantic coast, found it remarkable that his party "laid down to Sleep on the cold ground, without either bed or board, having no other covering besides our cloathes, but a Single blanket each, and the Canopy of Heaven."[57] Ingham was not alone in his sentiments. Boat travelers frequently moved from complaints about the uncomfortable conditions to sermons on the goodness of God. Boat travel inspired in Europeans a sense of powerlessness in "this wild land," as Von Reck testified, yet he assured his readers that one "can nevertheless rest safely under the protection of the Highest and under the shadow of the Almighty.... He preserveth them and hath commanded His angels to guard them on all their ways."[58]

William Bartram, traveling almost forty years after Von Reck, expressed a similar sentiment. On a canoe trip up the Altamaha River, Bartram became tired of fighting "the impetuous current," and thus "I resigned my bark to the friendly current, reserving to myself the control of the helm."[59] Grasping for some sense of mastery over the river, Bartram held the rudder while the course of the river directed him to his campsite. His small accomplishment in river navigation was quickly overshadowed by a sudden thunderstorm. The storm threw Bartram into speculation on the ultimate power of God. Wrote Bartram, "A gloomy cloud pervades the understanding, and when we see our progress retarded, and our best intentions frustrated, we are apt to deviate from the admonitions and convictions of virtue, to shut out eyes upon our guide and protector, doubt of his power, and despair of his assistance. But let us wait and rely on our God, who in due time will shine forth in brightness, dissipate the envious cloud, and reveal to us how finite and circumscribed is human power, when assuming to itself independent wisdom."[60] Mastery of the land was a well-established colonial ideal, yet river travel frustrated such fantasies, dependent as voyagers were on the whims of currents and tides, floods and ebbs, and the exposed nature of waterside campgrounds. Small wonder that the pious traveler would seek solace in divine grace.

The Savannah River and other southeastern rivers confounded European ideas of what a river should be and therefore required adaptation. English river barges in particular did not succeed on the Savannah River. Traditional English barges came in numerous sizes and shapes, but all were generally shallow-draft vessels, presumably designed to move over the numerous obstacles in English rivers.[61] They were designed to be sailed when wind was available and dragged by horses or men when the wind was not. In Georgia, Thomas Causton attempted to build an English barge, which was quickly overmatched by the fast-flowing Savannah. As Philip Von Reck described it to the trustees, "Mr. Causton caused a flat bateau to be made so heavy and unsuitable for the Savannah River.... You see that it is flat and that the prow is not sharp, so that it stops the water. The oars and the rudder avail nothing.... The thing is an invention of Mr. Causton, since one never sees such a thing on the Savannah River."[62] Von Reck contrasted Causton's unsuitable invention with a better-adapted vessel—the Indian trading boat.

The Indian trading boat was an American adaptation that made navigation of the Savannah possible. Truly creole watercraft, these narrow, fast, and delicate boats carried commerce from Charles Town to Augusta throughout the colonial period. These were dugout canoes similar to those adopted throughout the Southeast, but much larger. They were typically carved out of a single large cypress tree, taking advantage of old-growth cypress swamps in the Southeast. The wood, easily worked only with European-made iron tools, made the boats light and rot-resistant. Upwards of thirty feet in length, the canoes would average only two to three feet in breadth. A flattened bottom would allow for greater maneuverability and easier passage over the numerous bars and banks of the Savannah River and the coastal waterways between the Savannah and Charles Town. The narrow boats, pointed at the ends, also allowed for easier rowing upstream on the return trip, using European oars rather than Indian paddles. The slim boats, though, could easily tip and spill crew and cargo into the water. Boatmen traveling between Augusta and Charles Town thus required an extreme level of skill and mastery to avoid losses of an entire town's hunt or a trader's future prospects.[63]

It took three continents to create the Savannah River trade boats. The dugout canoe had both American and African ancestry. Indians, though, preferred pine or poplar for canoe construction.[64] Pine was more easily carved by fire, while poplar was a much lighter wood, facilitating overland carriage. Europeans, possessing the iron tools necessary for felling and working cypress trees, preferred the rot-resistant wood more readily available in the coastal swamps and marshes they first encountered. Africans had their own long-standing tradition of dugout vessels, and the "periagos" of West African coastal trade made possible European commerce on that continent.[65] However, by the eighteenth century, Anglo-Americans in the Southeast had learned and adapted the techniques of dugout construction to the point that the President and Assistants of Georgia in Savannah could complain of "several People at Work upon the River in cutting down Cypress trees and making Canoes of the Same without Leave or Licence for so doing."[66] Clearly, the dugout proved a successful innovation in southeastern waters.

And, despite travelers' shock at wild rivers, many European southeasterners learned to build and pilot boats on the Savannah. Some even earned the title of "patroon," meaning they supervised a crew opeating a larger boat. In the early years of Georgia, a number of Europeans found ready work as patroons, especially between Augusta and Charles Town. John Rae, for example, earned his way into Augusta's elite by beginning as a boatman. He was joined in William Stephens's journal by Peter Shepherd, another boatman who operated between Augusta and Charles Town. They were no doubt joined by the numerous farmers and planters who relied on canoes to move between settlements and carry their goods to market, as they did in South Carolina.

But despite the presence of white boatmen in the eighteenth century, it seems that most boatmen were in fact African American and most likely enslaved. Ferrying furs and skins down the Savannah, trading boats relied heavily on black hands to set their course. The typical trading-boat crew, at least in Augusta's early years, consisted of four African American oarsmen overseen by a white patroon at the rudder. The slave labor that moved Augusta's commerce was widely acknowledged, even by Georgia's original antislavery governors. William Stephens himself acknowledged that "their trading boats... commonly go with only 4 Negroes to row."[67] When Philip Von Reck sketched an Indian trading boat in the 1730s, he clearly placed four African American men at the boat's oars, with a white man at the rudder (fig. 12). Indeed, so closely were boatmen and Africans associated that in July 1740, as a boat rowed from Frederica to Savannah, the two-man crew was immediately assumed "not to be natural-born subjects, being of black and swarthy Complexion, somewhat of the Mulatto Kind."[68] The two men were in fact whites, but this was only discovered after they had been taken to "the Mulatto's landing" in Savannah.[69] That Savannahians had created a separate landing for mulattoes further implies the prevalence of nonwhite boatmen from an early date.

Although crucial to the successful navigation of the Indian trading boat, oarsmen were not credited with much of that success. Perhaps a reaction to their dependence on nonwhite boatmen, colonists typically believed watercraft to be merely the extension of a patroon's will, and it was his ability that led to the success or failure of every voyage. This attitude was perhaps best expressed in a trip made along the Atlantic coast in 1736. James Oglethorpe commanded a canoe voyage southward from Savannah to Frederica. At the mouth of the Ogeechee River, the wind rose and the water became "rough, almost every wave drove over the Side of the boat.... If Mr. Oglethorpe had not roused himself, and Struck life into the Rowers," the lives of all on board might have been lost.[70] In 1739 William Stephens reported that a pettiagua (a small vessel that could be rowed or sailed), bound for Augusta with supplies and settlers, overturned at the mouth of the Savannah River. The boat's crew "found themselves at a Loss for Want of a Patroon to govern the Vessel, who understood it better than him they had.... The two Negroes who belonged to the Pettyagua were also lost."[71] Had the crew only had a proper master, Stephens believed, then sixteen souls might have been saved.

The presence of enslaved oarsmen would have lent itself well to the patroon's assumed identity as master of the vessel. One of the crucial

FIGURE 12. A Savannah River trading boat as depicted in an untitled drawing by Philip Georg Friedrich Von Reck. From Philipp Georg Friederich Von Reck drawing book held in the Royal Library of Copenhagen, Call # NKS 565 kvart. Courtesy of the Royal Library, Copenhagen, Denmark.

underpinnings of slavery as a legal and formal institution in the South was the definition of the slave's body as an extension of the master's will.[72] The arrangement of the crew in the Indian trading boat certainly would have underscored this division between the "mind" of the patroon and the "body" of the slave rowers. As depicted in Von Reck's illustration, the patroon stood at the back of the boat, his gaze fixed forward and his hand on the rudder. His was the only pair of eyes able to scan ahead, looking for snags, bars, and rapids; determination of the boat's course was his alone. The rowers, by contrast, bent their backs to the labor, their gaze fixed backwards, with the patroon standing in the foreground of whatever view may have presented itself. Should an oarsman try to subvert this system, punishment could be swift and brutal, as Peter Shepherd proved in 1741. Shepherd, patroon of an Indian trading boat bound for New Windsor, "having catch'd one of his Negroes in a Piece of Thievery on board . . . tied him up, and lashed him very severely, *secundum usum Carolinoe.*"[73]

The white patroons, however, earned little respect from their fellow colonists, and it is probably not surprising that they soon vanished from the Southeast. Despite the importance of their services to the functioning of Georgia, contemporaries regarded them with a mixture of contempt and indifference. William Stephens considered them to be "Idle Fellows."[74] Stephens deplored idleness and those who found "one Day's Pay sufficient to maintain him two or three" and who would "work no more."[75] Such was the case of Peter Emery, a patroon based in Savannah who was "always fully employed, and might have saved Money; but it was squandered away as fast as got."[76] So low was the status of boatmen in the colony that a description of Oglethorpe's campaign to Saint Augustine listed the company in the following order: Oglethorpe's regiment, the Carolina troops, Indians, volunteers, as well as "several Stragglers and Boatmen from other parts of the Province and elsewhere."[77] This derogation of watermen should not be surprising given their general image in England.[78] Given their lack of status and the strain of the work, white patroons slowly vanished from the historical record. Only John Rae went on to attain the rank of gentleman; the rest disappeared.

Patroons earned little standing in society because they had little control over their own lives. Even within the confines of the river they supposedly mastered, boatmen lived on the indulgence of others. Whites trafficking the Savannah River had to accept whatever they were given in terms of weather, housing, and trade. The abandoned villages and small farms dotting the Savannah riverbanks became temporary homes, but the only space that a white boatman could claim as his own was his craft. Whereas the trip downriver could take only four or five days from Augusta to Savannah, the return trip could take four or five weeks. If a boat crew made five or six trips in any given year, this amounted to almost half the year spent either on the river or sheltered in its banks. While Georgia's settlement quickly snaked up the Savannah River as far as Mount Pleasant, long stretches remained unsettled, by either Indians or Europeans. The profound sense of isolation echoed even in mundane accounts such as William Stephens's journal of a trip to New Windsor: "Proceeded early and saw nothing all the day, but high close woods, with here and there a little opening where Some Indians had formerly lived.... At night lodged in Some old Indian hutts which had been forsaken Some time."[79] De Brahm's 1757 map of Georgia recorded these places along the Savannah, noting the locations of an "Indian Camp" or "Indian Cornhouse."[80]

Between these convenient abodes, the boatmen camped in the woods along the riverbanks. References to boatmen carrying kettles indicate that the trading boats certainly carried some provision with them, probably cornmeal from Augusta or perhaps rice from lowcountry South Carolina. The river itself probably provided much of a boatman's protein, being filled with "sturgeon, eels and cat fish, a most delicious fish without scales, bream, &c., terrapins, crocodiles, which some of the Indians also eat."[81] Hunting land-borne game was almost certainly part of the boatman's diet, as deer, bear, and perhaps even buffalo still roamed the woods along the Savannah's banks. If provisions ran short or took an unfortunate spill into the water, sustenance was indeed dependent on nature's providence. As one canoe party had to make do in 1734: "We made shift to shoot some crows and woodpeckers, which we lived on that day.... [The next day] met with a wolf in full chase after a deer, and had the good fortune to kill them both; so that we then had provisions sufficient for two days longer."[82] Indeed, hunting probably eased some of the monotony of the long river voyage. A canoe-based William Bartram described a hunter in south Georgia who stalked and killed an on-shore bear without ever leaving the boat.[83]

Boatmen could not even count on their presumed mastery of their own crewmen. Once on land and out of sight, white patroons found it difficult to maintain strict oversight of their oarsmen. In 1743, William Stephens received a report of "a foul Murder... committed by a Negroe belonging to a trading Boat, Stabbing his Comrade with a Knife," while camping in an abandoned Indian village along the Savannah. Before turning in for the night, the two men had come to blows, the victim having initiated the conflict by beating the accused. He then "followed him into his Hutt [and] renewd his Blows, when he received the wound of which he died." However, the Savannah court ruled the case manslaughter, "no proof was made of the Prisoner stabbing him, nor was any White man with them in the Hutt."[84] The patroon, apparently sleeping in another hut, lost a crewman when two of his oarsmen came to blows during the night. Despite being a man short, they finished the trip to Augusta, where the murderer was apprehended.

Given the difficulties involved and Europeans' general disdain for life on the river, it is perhaps unsurprising that the occupation of patroon itself soon became the province of African Americans. By the eve of the American Revolution, trading boats seem to have become operated mainly by enslaved African Americans with little white supervision. The river trade had become so well established that Augusta traders felt perfectly comfortable in leaving it entirely in black hands. The white patroons of the trustee period had mostly retired or relocated. By the late 1750s, black patroons had apparently become common and were still the norm at the time of Mackay and MacLean's 1775 Savannah jaunt. In 1759 the commander at Fort Augusta wrote to Governor William Henry Lyttelton of South Carolina by way of "Mr. [Martin] Campbles negro."[85] A year later, Edmond Atkin, British superintendent of Indian affairs, awaited "the Return of Mr [Francis] Macartan's Peter every Moment from Charlestown."[86] A man named Caesar controlled Mackay's boat, and MacLean's found its way upriver under the guidance of a man named Pompey, both names indicating that these patroons were enslaved.[87]

Alongside European cultural preferences, the increasing scale of the deerskin trade also likely played a large part in the Africanization of the Savannah River. In 1738, when patroons such as Rae and Shepherd were piloting the river, Charles Town merchants shipped 220,000 pounds of deerskins. Conservatively, one might estimate that half of that total came down the Savannah River from the Creeks and Chickasaws while the other half came down the overland routes from the Cherokees. Indian trade boats could hold roughly two thousand pounds of deerskins, so Augusta boats would have had to make approximately fifty six-week trips that year to carry that total. If a boat could make a maximum of nine trips per year, six boats employing twenty-five men would be the minimum needed to sustain Augusta's trade. By the 1750s, Charles Town's exports had reached 355,000 per year. Using the same formula, Augusta boatmen would have to make eighty-nine trips downriver, requiring ten boats employing fifty people for the entire year. In a region where slavery was already well established as the dominant labor system, it is unsurprising that Augusta traders would employ enslaved African Americans as year-round crews, especially as the trade itself became more of a year-round business with skins arriving at different times throughout the year.[88]

Given the difficulties of navigating the Savannah, it is all the more remarkable that very few of the Indian trading boats capsized, a testament both to the skills of the patroons and their boatmen. Colonists, for their part, recognized the skills of their enslaved boat crews. A Charles Town woman in 1749 advertised for sale a slave who was "a very good boatman, having been used to go in *Indian* trading Boats."[89] A 1764 advertisement in the *Georgia Gazette* included boatmen among "a large Parcel of Valuable Negroes."⁹⁰ Owners easily converted the skill of slave watermen into currency, as expressed in a runaway notice posted in 1748, when a planter in St. Thomas Parish, South Carolina, offered ten pounds reward for the return of his boatmen, but only forty shillings for their nonskilled companion.⁹¹ And while no slave owner ever accorded his boatmen much social prestige, some evidence indicates that white Carolinians did recognize and take advantage of West Africans' boating experience and ability in choosing whom to place in a boat.⁹²

However, most white southeasterners believed that slave boatmen were made, not born. Boatmen may have had a particular set of skills, they believed, but they could be learned by just about anyone. A 1769 advertisement in Georgia listed thirty slaves for sale, "17 of them are fit for field or boat work."⁹³ In this planter's mind, at least, skills on land and water were more or less equal, and they could be taught. The idea of "raising" African Americans to labor on boats was expressed perhaps most chillingly by Henry Laurens in 1767 when he commented that a Mister Oswald "will have a fine stock in a few Years from his Nursery of Negroes at Muskito . . . & I should think if half a dozen were distributed to learn to row in Canoes & to manage small Boats for two or three Years it would be further improvement."⁹⁴ Given the usual methods of transferring boating skill, whether it be from Africa to America or from Indians to African Americans, it is perhaps not surprising that white owners preferred to think that skilled watermen came from their own tutelage and oversight.⁹⁵

African American boatmen in the Southeast may have had their own contrasting notions of the importance of their skills on the river. Certainly rivers and water occupied important places in West African cosmography. The Bambaras of Senegambia credited the water spirit Faro with purifying souls after death so that they might be reborn into the family. Ibos from the Bight of Benin held similar beliefs. For Kongolese Africans, the watery barrier of Kalunga separated the realm of the living from the realm of spirits. Archaeological evidence from South Carolina has suggested a continuing association between rivers and communication with the spirits of ancestors. Colonoware bowls, incised with African cosmograms, have been recovered mostly from river contexts, indicating that enslaved Africans in the lower South translated African spiritual beliefs to American waterways.⁹⁶ In the context of slavery, beliefs in the power of waterways also translated into freedom from bondage, either in the next life or in this.

Southeastern slaves, regardless of their origins or spiritual beliefs, recognized water as a passage from bondage to freedom. The Savannah River, in particular, early marked an important boundary between slavery and freedom. In times of Anglo-Spanish war, the Spanish at St. Augustine offered freedom to those slaves who escaped from Carolina masters and made their way to Florida. This offer was a major reason for establishing Georgia, since it was understood "that the Spaniards at St. Augustine, would be continualy inticing away the Negroes, or encouraging them to Insurrection." Likewise, slave flight to Florida "might easily be accomplished, since a single Negro could run away thither without Companions, and would have only a River or two to swim over."[97] Coastal waters also connected Carolina slaves to freedom at St. Augustine, where a number of runaways "fled in Perriaguas and little Boats to the Spaniards, and [had] been protected."[98] The magistrates of Charles Town recognized this potential route of escape and sent a chilling warning. They executed a captured runaway named Caeasar and then had him "hung in Chains at *Hang-Man's* Point opposite to this Town, in sight of all the Negroes passing and repassing by Water."[99]

The Savannah River boatmen were connected to a much larger world of African and African American maritime culture. In the eighteenth and nineteenth centuries, these waterborne men, slave and free, acted as crucial links between blacks in all parts of the Atlantic world. From the earliest days of the slave trade in Western Africa, black canoemen acted as middlemen between European slavers and the interior of the continent, and the information they gleaned about New World slavery they passed to fellow Africans awaiting the Middle Passage. This exchange of news between black sailors, black canoemen, and black captives formed what one historian has dubbed a "constantly humming human telegraph" between the Americas and Africa.[100] Many of these canoemen were themselves seized and shipped to the Southeast, where plantation Carolina valued their boating skills to ferry goods from plantation to Charles Town and back. Manning small canoes and larger pettiaguas, fishing and ferrying, these lowcountry slaves enjoyed a greater freedom of movement and autonomy than most American slaves could claim. Often working without white supervision, they made possible the plantation trade. Black watermen also carried information from country to town, extending African American communication networks throughout the region, between field slaves and urban slaves. In Charles Town, they also received seaborne information brought from the West Indies, northern colonies, and Africa.[101]

Throughout the history of slavery, enslaved watermen played central roles in resistance to slavery. Beginning in the eighteenth century, Carolina slaves found boats handy for removing themselves from the colony. The links between slaves along waterways also provided a means of channeling goods stolen from owners in a hidden exchange among African Americans. By the end of the eighteenth century, black watermen were providing southern African Americans with news of the Haitian Revolution. In the nineteenth century black sailors on northern ships were carrying abolitionist tracts and sentiments to southern ports and spreading them from there into the interior.[102] As David Cecelski has noted, it is small wonder that black boatmen could be found at the center of some of the most famous slave conspiracies, such as Gabriel's Rebellion in 1800 and the Denmark Vesey conspiracy in 1822.[103]

The Savannah River boatmen were not revolutionaries, but they did act in small ways against the southeastern slave regime. Some engaged in the most common form of slave resistance—running away. In May 1748, a slave named Sambo, who "was used to row in one of the Indian-trading Boats," ran away from John Lloyd.[104] In 1737, Kennedy O'Brien, an Indian trader at New Windsor, advertised the loss of a slave named Peter, "born in Mrs. Kerr's Family, did afterwards belong to Mr. John Coleman the Indian Trader, and after that to Mr. Jordan Roche. He is well known in Charlestown, and has been lately seen with the fishing Negroes, at the Markett place."[105] While Peter was not necessarily a boatman, he was certainly connected with black watermen. Such notices were few and far between, however, indicating that these boatmen did not frequently challenge their lot in life.

However, slaves in Augusta and Charles Town likely benefited in both small and large ways from the connections that enslaved boatmen provided. It seems that few Savannah River boatmen directly challenged the institution of slavery, but it also seems likely that they did assist others in so doing. As frequent travelers between Augusta, Savannah, and Charles Town, these men would have been able to pass word of loved ones between these towns, especially given the communication links of lowcountry South Carolina. They thus likely formed part of a more pervasive and perhaps important form of slave resistance—the simple ability to maintain kinship ties throughout the region. The majority of runaways in Carolina did not flee to St. Augustine or sign on with oceangoing vessels in an attempt to quit the colony. Running away in the Southeast most often took the form of visiting friends and family members on other plantations, more possible in the dense slave communities of lowcountry Carolina than in, say, the Chesapeake.[106] Slaves removed themselves to visit friends and family, asserting their status as human beings in the face of a slave-owning regime that tried to deny them such simple markers of their humanity.[107]

A part of this network may have been formed under the noses of Georgia's early planners. Beginning in the 1740s, African American boatmen on the Savannah River had made a home for themselves along the riverbanks. The town of Savannah provided the most convenient space for boatmen beyond their masters' eyesight. The town, perched high on a bluff above Savannah River, included a small sandy strip of land on the riverbank. By the 1760s the bank had been overrun with wharves and warehouses, but in the 1740s and 1750s, slave boatmen used the land below the Savannah bluff as their own temporary home, assisted by lax oversight from the formerly vigilant Savannah constables. After the initial controversy with South Carolina over the Savannah River, the trustees decided that to preserve the Indian trade, enforcement of the bans on slavery and rum should be laxly enforced. Such was implied when the trustees commanded William Stephens in 1742 "that he should wink at the Importion of Rum, and discourage seizures thereof."[108] This "winking" also applied to the slave boatmen who rowed the rum upstream.

By 1742, Georgia's constables had improvised an "out of sight, out of mind" attitude toward the enslaved boatmen who stopped in Savannah. So long as the rowers remained below the bluff and did not enter the town of Savannah, they would be ignored and unmolested. Stephens interpreted the trustees' "winking" rule to be that "whenever any Vessel arrives here with Negroes, during their Stay, the Slaves are permitted to come ashore on the Strand by the Water-Side, to boil their Kettle; but in case they come up into Town, they are liable to be seized."[109] Of all the numerous times that Indian trading boats stopped in Savannah during his tenure, Stephens recorded but one instance of a slave seizure. Peter Shepherd violated the code when he brought one of his slaves into his lodgings and whipped the man for stealing, "which occasioned a great uproar among the Neighbourhood."[110] As many as four or five boats might be in Savannah at a time, providing their crews a small community in which to swap stories, compare experiences, and connect with each other outside of the patroons' eyesight. Even after the 1760s, when the Savannah waterfront was built into wharves and warehouses, an important African American community remained below the bluffs near Savannah, composed of as many as two to three hundred free blacks and slaves by 1770.[111]

The slave connections along the river may also explain why a number of runaways made their way inland to New Windsor and Augusta. While many runaway slaves stayed near the coast, a number made their way up the Savannah River. As early as 1738, runaway notices in the *South Carolina Gazette* advertised slaves heading that way. Samuel Montagut, a planter in Purrysburg, South Carolina, about twelve miles upriver from Savannah, lost three slaves. Robin, Tony, and "Rogue" or Miller. "*Tony* was taken last Year about *Savannah*-Town [New Windsor's original name], and is supposed to be travelling that Way again with his Companions."[112] In October of that year, William Walter, another planter on the Savannah River, advertised "two *Gambia* Negroes, about 5 feet 6 inches high, the one his Name is *Walley*, the other's *Bocarrey*, they were some time ago seen near *New Windsor*."[113] Placing advertisements in a Charlestown paper likewise indicated that these men hoped that the trading boats would either carry the notices upriver, or that some trader on the way down would have seen them.

In some cases, these men were making their way to a former home. Despite Georgia's ban between 1735 and 1750, slavery was early established and recognized at New Windsor and Augusta. Sold to coastal owners, many of these slaves escaped to upriver plantations where they had left friends and family. Joseph Gibbons, a planter near Savannah, lost two slaves in 1768, and supposed both of them headed toward Augusta. The first, Limus, had "some relations who may harbour him" at John Rae's plantation. He also "belonged formerly to the estate of the late John Fitch at Augusta, where he may probably attempt to go."[114] Gibbons's other lost servant, "a mulatto slave named John," had formerly "belonged to the Rev. Mr. Frink and formerly to Edward Barnard, Esq. of Augusta." John's relations spanned across Georgia, for he had "a wife living with Mr. Douglass"—presumably David Douglass, a former resident of Augusta then living in the Savannah area, but Gibbons also feared that he might "attempt to make his escape to Augusta and the Indian nation, where he formerly lived."[115] These slaves' connections to life in Augusta and along the trading paths were strong enough to pull them hundreds of miles upriver, in an attempt to maintain their former personal connections.

Other slaves saw the trip upriver as a more immediate means of preserving their lowcountry families. In 1769 William Coachman of South Carolina lost two slaves, a man named "York, or Yorkshire" and a Guinea woman named Sarah, who had been "lately seen in Georgia, taken up by the Creek Indians."[116] That same year, a slave family made its way from "the salt water" all the way to Augusta. Edward Barnard of Augusta advertised that he had taken up "A Negro Fellow, and A Wench, with A Child about two months old. The fellow... says his name is Sampson, and his wife's name Molly... says his master lives near the salt water... and his name is Jacob Middow."[117] Whether fear of sale or some other separation sent these families upriver, clearly they hoped that the voyage to Augusta would in some way allow them to remain together.

There is yet no evidence to directly connect the Savannah boatmen to these runaways, but the fact that large Indian traders such as Douglass, Barnard, and Rae were connected to many of these notices indicates a likely link. Augusta plantations were not so big that a worker on one would have been entirely separated from the boatmen who lived there. Although speculative, some connection seems reasonable even though the boatmen's actual role played in the these networks remains, for the moment, hidden. But, given their frequent trips between Augusta and Charles Town and given their connections to the larger slave communication networks of the Southeast, it seems within the realm of possibility that these boatmen played some role in the exchange of news and information between slaves living in Augusta and their relatives living in the lowcountry. Their "invisibility" in the colonial mind-set makes investigation difficult.

Their "invisibility" was also a testament to their necessity in the deerskin trade. After the trustees' efforts to police the river ended in the 1740s, very little attention was paid to the Savannah River traffic. So long as the boats carried skins to Charles Town and goods to Augusta with their crews and cargoes intact, there was little reason for whites to concern themselves with their enslaved watermen. Dozens of trading boats passed Georgia's riverfront plantations each year without either comment or incident. Yet each of these vessels likely carried news and information that helped slaves in some small way shape the Southeast to suit their own needs.

For all those attached to the Indian trade, the Savannah was thus a crucial space. Its multiple meanings of boundary, connector, and waterway defined life in the deerskin trade. When John Rae gave up the boatman's life in the 1740s, he remained attached to the river that provided his warehouses with goods and allowed him to ship leather to Charles Town, all thanks to the enslaved oarsmen who made the Savannah a productive space for Augusta's residents and made the trade possible for thousands of Indian hunters farther in the southeastern interior. Like Rae, Augusta's founding depended in a great measure upon the river, but it is really more accurate to say that the town's founding depended on enslaved boatmen's ability to move people and goods from coast to the falls of the Savannah. While large traders (except Rae) rarely traveled the rivers, the traders' power and presence in southeastern affairs depended on their water links to the Charles Town. That dependence also meant a dependence on the enslavement of African Americans and full participation in lowcountry's system of race-based enslavement. These characteristics of the river also transferred to the town of Augusta itself.

3 / Keeping Company, Keeping Store: The Shaping of Colonial Augusta

The packhorse train was ready. In September 1759, John Ross prepared to return along the well-traveled Upper Creek path to the town of the Okfuskees. The trip was routine for Ross, a regular part of his trade, but recent tensions between Creeks and British settlers presented new hazards on the old path. The Seven Years' War had given the French new impetus in winning over parties of Creek warriors in the town, and South Carolina and the Cherokees were on the brink of war. Ross had made some enemies in his town, partly due to his refusal to lower his prices and partly due to his reputation as "surly and ill-natured."[1] In a prescient move, Ross drew up his last will and testament as he prepared to leave Augusta. "I am in a short time to depart from this place for the Upper Creek Country," Ross wrote, and "considering the dangers I am daily exposed to," he granted Lachlan McGillivray all power to administer his estate in case of his death.[2] In May 1760, Ross died at the hands of angry Okfuskee warriors, in the same series of attacks that killed John Rae's son, William.[3]

It is difficult to define exactly what it was Ross was leaving. Certainly it was a community, but it was not much of a town. By the 1750s, Augusta had taken on a shape perhaps unique in Anglo-America: it was a town that grew to fit the deerskin trade in the Southeast. Dominating the landscape were the wealthy merchants' fortified trading houses, built along the path toward the Creeks in a line running a dozen or more miles long. Between these stood the homes and farms of Augusta's other residents, with a small town nucleus barely discernible among the scattering of homes and farms. Among these stood two large tracts of land belonging to the Lower Chickasaw Indians, numbering about forty families, who had moved to the area the 1720s. And, interspersed in every facet of Augusta life were the hundreds of enslaved African Americans who made possible the work of the deerskin trade.

Motley as it seemed, this assemblage was not random or the result of any "natural" process. Although Augusta did not conform to the idealized plans of the Georgia Trustees, the town had a distinct structure that served the needs of its inhabitants. Formed in large measure as a corrective to the trustees' intrusion into the deerskin trade, the great houses of Augusta served as poles for the community and governed the shape of everyday life in the community. For example, the rapidly increasing slave population began dressing deerskins and removing labor burdens from Indian women. But, central as the trading houses were to the community around the falls of the Savannah, their political power did not reach as far they imagined and could not survive the severing of the Augusta-Creek trade during the American Revolution. Ross thus perceived something of Augusta's colonial nature: a seeming center of power and authority that was only as strong as its connection to Indian villages.

Envisioned originally as an orderly Georgia town, Augusta was modeled on the spacious grid pattern of Savannah. Augustans, however, refused to settle according to this plan, much to the irritation and concern of Georgia's early governors. The original grid plan quickly became an afterthought as the merchant-traders at Augusta ranged themselves along the trading paths that led to Indian villages. The community of Augusta thus followed older contours and reached beyond trustee visions. Historians have noted Augustans' unwillingness to accommodate the Georgia Trustees' utopian and communal planning at every step and their particular disregard for the bans on rum and slavery. Augusta has thus emerged in historiography as the exception to early Georgia's development. Its early history has been described as "more 'natural' than that of much of the rest of Georgia."[4] Its dispersed population resulted from an animating "independent spirit" common to the American frontier where there were "lands to be settled, dangers to be faced, adventures to be had, goods to be traded, soil to be tilled, and fortunes to be made." The history of colonial Augusta as written has been the story of its transformation from unsettled frontier to a "true town," with churches, schools, and a developed social hierarchy.[5] However, Augusta's development and social life depended more on its particular circumstances as a central location in the Anglo-Creek deerskin trade than any "natural" inclination of its residents.

The trustees conceived Augusta as one of the model towns of Georgia. Their ideal town, as expressed in the design of Savannah, combined the moralistic zeal of an age of reform with the spacious and orderly squares of post-Restoration London. The trustees ordered Augusta laid out according to this plan: a central square composed of forty one-acre lots, surrounded by larger farm lots of fifty acres each.[6] Originating in the anti-Walpole factions of Parliament, Oglethorpe and the Georgia Trustees envisioned what one historian has termed an "American Zion" where the sins of materialism and the dissipation of alcoholism would be purged from London's middling and laboring classes. Given equal shares of land and freed from stockjobbing and the corrupting influence of slavery, the trustees' model colony would shine as an example to the rest of the British empire and effect in America what the reformers could not accomplish in London.[7] Form followed function in the trustees' town plan, in which uniform individual lots opened onto a healthful square that provided both proper air circulation and an exercise ground for Savannah's inhabitants.[8]

But the trustees also provided Augustans an easy means to subvert this plan of settlement by granting five-hundred-acre lots to the largest traders and merchants. Settlement at Augusta followed an irregular pattern due to the size of lots granted to merchants in the Indian trade. Oglethorpe lured these men to the town through the generous grant of a one-acre town lot in Augusta as well as with a five-hundred-acre plantation in the surrounding countryside. In Trustee Georgia, where most settlers enjoyed only a modest fifty-acre tract for their families, the five-hundred-acre "gentleman's lot" was a rarity.[9] The large plantations would become the trade-merchants' main residences and businesses, and their lots in town seemingly remained unused (or at least unmentioned). The immediate neighborhood surrounding the town was divided into large estates, making expansion of the town center difficult even if the motivation existed. Thus, during Augusta's forty-year existence before the American Revolution, only four new one-acre lots were added to the original forty, and it was not until after the Revolution that landowners began dividing up the large plantations and creating new urban landscapes such as Harrisburg.[10] In contrast to Oglethorpe's elaborate town planning, Augustans developed a neighborhood of plantations, each serving a number of economic, social, and military functions.

Augusta developed from Oglethorpe's orders but not his ideals. Less than a year after the town's founding, William Stephens received a report that "the Inhabitants were settling in a very irregular Manner, by building Stores on five hundred Acre Lotts some Miles distant from each other up the Path toward the Creeks."[11] The dispersed nature of Augusta's settlement became something of a defining characteristic of the town. Robert Mackay, son and namesake of the Augusta storekeeper Robert Mackay, remembered his birthplace as a town where "the houses stood far apart from each other."[12]

Even decades of development in Augusta could not settle the question of its quality. In 1763, the governors of Virginia, North Carolina, South Carolina, and Georgia convened a congress at Augusta to meet with headmen from the Catawba, Cherokee, Creek, Chickasaw, and Choctaw confederacies. Though they eventually settled on Augusta as the meeting-place, the governors from Virginia and the Carolinas were reluctant to meet "in so straggling and ill-settled a place as Augusta."[13] Governor James Wright of Georgia disagreed with the gentlemen's assessment, assuring them that "the place affords sufficient houses, plenty of provisions, and accommodations of every kind" even if they were "not so elegant as in Charles Town."[14] By the date of Wright's letter, the wealthiest Indian traders had amassed small fortunes and established commodious homes in the town, but Augusta still carried the stigmas of roughness and incivility.

The "straggling" settlement pattern was still evident even in 1780, as depicted on Archibald Campbell's "Sketch of the Northern Frontiers of Georgia," the only surviving map of the colonial town. On Campbell's map, Augusta appears as a small collection of buildings around Augusta's central crossroads surrounded by numerous named plantations standing apart from each other along the town's winding roads (fig. 13).[15] As Campbell himself described the town in 1779, "Augusta consisted of a Number of straggling houses, arranged in a long Street lying parallel to the River."[16]

Augusta did not seem to be much of a town at all. Rather than organizing themselves into a dense, nucleated settlement, Augustans strung themselves across the landscape. The population also changed seasonally: while wealthy merchant-traders and other town inhabitants occupied Augusta year-round, the population swelled by hundreds during the spring and summer months when sojourners arrived. It was a difficult community to place, and no two observers could agree on Augusta's early appearance. This disagreement stemmed, in large part, from the fact that Augusta did not easily conform to English models of township.

Two portraits of Augusta emerged shortly after the town's founding, each emphasizing the prosperity of the town. William Stephens, the trustees' secretary in Georgia, described a town succeeding on the

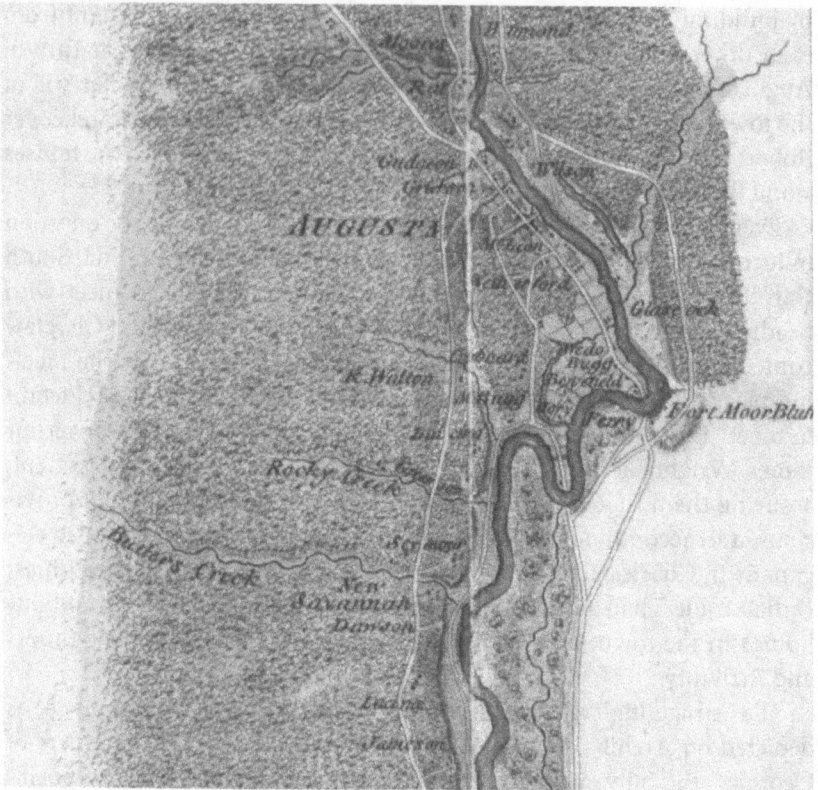

FIGURE 13. Detail from Archibald Campbell, "Sketch of the Northern Frontiers of Georgia," 1780. Courtesy of the Hargrett Rare Book and Manuscript Library, University of Georgia Libraries.

industry of its Indian trader inhabitants and the fertility of its soil. To him, the town was proof that the trustees' plan for Georgia could provide comfort and prosperity to its inhabitants. Augusta, he proclaimed, "has thriven prodigiously; there are several large Warehouses thoroughly well furnished with Goods for the *Indian* Trade." The residents of Augusta, including those who lived part of the year in Indian towns and all others "depending upon that Business, are moderately computed to be six Hundred white Men," and "live by their Trade."[17] The Malcontents, frustrated at Georgia's bans on slavery and rum, saw Augusta's prosperity as proof of their arguments. The town, they argued, succeeded because its inhabitants were "indulged and connived at in the Use of Negroes, by whom they execute all the laborious Parts of Culture." The town's "considerable

Quantity of Corn" had been raised not by the thirty white men computed to live in the town, but by the "upwards of *eighty* Negroes ... now in the Settlements belonging to that Place."[18] That Augusta alone succeeded in Trustee Georgia proved to the Malcontents that Augusta alone enjoyed the labor of slaves, a labor "so necessary for their Well-being."[19]

However, not all shared this vision of Augusta as a thriving town on the Georgia frontier. Soon after Stephens and the Malcontents painted their respective portraits of a successful Augusta, Stephens's son Thomas went to London to argue that the town actually struggled a great deal. The younger Stephens noted that, for a town of six hundred souls, Augusta lacked any civil government. "If they [the Trustees' agents in Savannah] really believed this Town to be so populous, why was it without even one civil Magistrate?"[20] Stephens referred his readers to the damning accounts he had appended to his treatise—affidavits from two Augusta residents, Kennedy O'Brien and John Gardner. Gardner's affidavit challenged William Stephens's numbers for Augusta inhabitants. O'Brien's Augusta barely clung to life: a place with barely forty white inhabitants, whose corn was primarily raised by slaves in South Carolina and imported across the river. Even the Indian trade, a supposed boon to Augusta's early settlement, had provided the town with "but *three trading Houses*, and those in a State of *Decay* and languishing Condition; and that through the *ill Regulation of the Indian Trade*."[21]

Much of this disagreement likely stemmed from competing political agendas, but another contributing factor was Georgians' seeming inability to define who, exactly, counted as a resident of Augusta. William Stephens's account, either to inflate the numbers or because traders in Indian towns counted as part of the town's economy, counted both those living in Augusta and traders residing primarily in Indian towns as residents. Those numbers struck some as fantasy. Thomas Stephens quoted Sir Richard Everard's conversation with Samuel Mercer on the subject. Everard had visited Augusta and knew the elder Stephens's population numbers to be too high. Mercer told Everard that he had been mistaken in counting "only the *exact Number* of Men and Horses said to be there, which would not amount to near the Numbers mentioned in the Representation." Had Everard "counted every Man and Horse, as *often* as ever they *went* from, or *came* to *Augusta*," Mercer continued, he would have arrived at "the Numbers mentioned in the Representation." Everard scoffed at such methods, and replied that Savannah magistrates "might have taken a shorter Method of counting, and not wait the Trouble of the Traders coming down from the Nation; that they had nothing more to do, but to make Capt. *Kent, Commander* of the Fort at *Augusta*, to march his Men in and out, as often as they pleased to count them, and they might make what Numbers they thought necessary for the Service of their Cause at any Time."[22] Though Everard scoffed at the phantom Augustans, the method underscored a deeper understanding of Augusta that made its definition as a town hard to specify; Augustans, or at least those who carried on the principal business of the town, moved constantly from place to place. Even those who resided in Augusta rarely settled within the town's limits.

Augusta's odd settlement posed larger problems for the trustees than just inaccurate census taking. The trustees' agents in Savannah, in their less boosterish moments, believed that Augusta's irregular settlement pattern caused the unsavory reports that occasionally drifted in from that quarter. In Trustee Georgia, distance equaled degeneracy. As Stephens reported, the distance between trading houses at Augusta had resulted from an individualistic and competitive spirit. The reason they settled so far apart was that "the Out-parts have the Advantage and Chance of intercepting the Customers of those who live in or near the Town of Augusta."[23] The traders' desire to cheat their fellows out of their rightful business would foster danger and violence if left unchecked. The dispersed settlements "lie under greater Danger of being cut off by Enemies of any sort," Stephens worried. Likewise, dishonesty would breed more dishonesty, because it would "be in the power of such Indian Traders as run in debt with the settled Storekeepers, to go to one of those outlying Stores, and be supplied, and then to return to the Indian nation, thereby defrauding their former Creditors, who cannot bring them to regular Justice."[24]

In Stephens's worldview, where health was dependent on hard work and strict morality, Augusta's scheming ways led to the decline in the physical bodies of its residents. Despite the good face he put on Augusta in his reports to the Trustees, Stephens believed that the town was suffering from its "irregular" settlement. In his journal, accounts of disease, violence, and wickedness usually followed descriptions of the town's dispersed settlement pattern. In the entry that contained John Miller's description of Indian traders settling along the paths, Stephens included the account from Samuel Brown, an Indian trader and "a Settler also at that Place," who reported that "they were grown extream sickly thereabouts; that it came through Carolina by Degrees to their Settlement at New-Windsor, and thence on crossed to Augusta."[25] Brown was almost certainly reporting on the common diseases and poxes that swept through eighteenth-century North America. However, Stephens's description of a "Carolina" infection that had ruined the health of Augusta carried a deeper meaning. The town had also been infected with the "Carolina" diseases of rum and slavery and suffered greatly for it. The weak town body, spread out along the trails, was particularly susceptible to these fevers, since no supervision existed to halt the spread of these infections.

Augustans' lifestyle ruined their health, Stephens concluded. The rapid deterioration of his clerk, Joseph Harrison, confirmed Stephens in this belief. Harrison had clerked in an Augusta store and in 1740 hired himself to Stephens to write copies of the latter's correspondence and lengthy journal. Almost as soon as the man started work, though, he proved unreliable. Soon after hiring Harrison, Stephens was frustrated "by Means of my Clerk being taken ill for two or three Days past, whom I had taken a little While since, upon the Recommendation of one who keeps Stores at *Augusta*, from whence he came."[26] By June of the next year, Harrison had again fallen sick, an illness that Stephens ascribed to "his dealing too free . . . when he lived up in the Nations, employ'd by some of our Keepers of Stores there."[27] A few days later the man died at the Bethesda orphanage, his "Nature was so far spent, that it was not to be restored."[28] A little more than a week after witnessing his clerk's failing health, Stephens again condemned Augustans as "a lawless, wild Crew of People," among whom "no Man's Property, or even personal Safety would be secure."[29]

The town's inability to conform to Stephens's ideal of an orderly Savannah-like grid would continue to bring it ill fortune and wicked ways in Stephens's accounts. An incident in October 1741 proved how far Augustans had allowed themselves to fall from civil, orderly English society. Here was proof positive that a straggling settlement such as Augusta was inherently depraved. Two African Americans had been held in the Savannah jail for several months during 1741, but escaped in October of that year. Stephens took this occasion to report their crimes and to indict their masters upriver. The story as Stephens told it was a nightmare scenario in which white servants had been placed at the merciless hands of black slaves, and had suffered greatly as a result.

> The Cause of their Commitment was, for that they had been guilty of many foul Crimes, under the Connivance (or rather Approbation) of their Master at *Augusta*, who once had a good Character; but of late the Reverse, and had been allowed the Use of a Boy and a Girl, *Dutch* Servants . . . but they were cruelly treated by him, not allowed competent Food and Cloathing, and sent far off to a Plantation of his, where they were tasked at the Discretion of these

Negroes... one of which attempted to commit a Rape upon the Girl, had he not been prevented by some Person, who hearing her Shrieks, came to her Relief; of which when she made Complaint to her Master, he first beat her with his Cane, and then ordered her to be stript stark naked, haul'd up to a Beam by her Arms tied, in the Presence of these two Negroes, and afterwards to be terribly whipped.[30]

The depths to which formerly honorable men had sunk appalled Stephens. Georgia, based on an ideal of industry and reform, could not tolerate such corruption among its populace.

For Stephens, the incident was a direct result of Augusta's dispersed settlement. The slaves' mere presence was due to Augustans "having Plantations on the *Carolina* Side of the river, as well as in *Georgia*, where they find it more advantageous to settle, and carry on the Trade with the *Indians*." Such a situation allowed them "an Opportunity of sliding two or three Negroes now and then at a Pinch into their Plantations, where during their skulking a while (which is not hard to conceive, considering the great Extent of the Township of *Augusta*, by reason of large Tracts of Land) they are not presently to be discovered."[31] Ignoring the fact that a nearby neighbor had heard the girl's screams, Stephens chose to blame the dispersed settlement of Augusta for the crime. The distance between Augusta plantations, he believed, allowed them to easily hide their slaves, and the corruption of the moral order went unnoticed, to the point where one planter allowed enslaved African Americans to hold power over a white European girl, an outrage that Stephens could hardly bear.

However, the violence and moral degeneracy that Stephens reported may have resulted more from the trustees' own actions, in particular those of their Indian agent Patrick Mackay, than to any "natural" inclination toward fisticuffs among Augusta's early residents. Contrary to the opinions of men like William Stephens, Augusta's supposedly "irregular" settlement pattern likely solved the problems of violence caused by the trustees' own agents. Oglethorpe's plans for the backcountry required an orderly and regulated trade, one that would not threaten the Southeast with another war like the Yamasee. Asserting Georgia's authority over the trade, Oglethorpe dispatched his agents into Indian villages to harass established Carolina traders who would not recognize Georgia's authority and abide by its rules. The actions of agents like Patrick Mackay created a lot of tension within the Indian trade in the 1730s. But by the 1740s, the trade had stabilized, as merchant-traders from the most powerful South Carolina firms began occupying the "gentlemen's grants" around Augusta and creating a stable political order attuned to the needs of the trade and capable of defending itself from interlopers such as Mackay.

Augusta's formation was a violent affair, as Georgia's Indian agents asserted their authority over Carolina's licensed traders. In the early spring of 1735, Patrick Mackay traveled through Creek villages to carry out his commission as the trustees' agent for Indian affairs. In late March, Mackay called a meeting of all the traders in the Lower Creek towns. The agent suspended the licenses of many of those assembled, "discharging whom he thought fit," and formed a new company of eleven traders licensed out of Georgia.[32] Mackay's selection was apparently arbitrary, and all those who were excluded from his company had to "depart the Nation with ... Goods and Horses with all convenient Diligence."[33] Mackay threatened others who continued to trade with a Carolina license that "he would seize their Horses and Effects."[34] Understandably surprised and upset at Mackay's new power over them, Carolina traders quickly argued their case. A dispute soon arose between the trader William Edwards and Patrick Mackay's "Doctor." Edwards was "brought to the Chunco or May Pole in the middle of the Square [at the Great Okfuskees] there stripped bare backed and tyed to the said Post or Pole by Order of the said Patrick Mackay and Thirty five Hickory Switches were cut and brought to the said Place."[35] The One-Handed King of the Okfuskees spared Edwards his whipping by shielding him with his own body and admonishing Mackay that "he had never seen such doings from the white People before."[36]

Many of Augusta's early residents were connected to Mackay's company, which perhaps explained why there was so much ill will in the early town. While the exact membership of Patrick Mackay's company is unknown, the few members named by their contemporaries appeared on a list of early traders and inhabitants of Augusta. Thomas Goodale, James Cossons, and John Facey all appeared as Mackay's accomplices or favorites in a lengthy petition from the leading merchants and traders of Charles Town.[37] Of those who made complaints of the Georgia agent's interference were many belonging to Archibald McGillivray and Company, the leading firm in the Creek trade in the 1730s and 1740s.[38] McGillivray's partners, Jeremiah Knott and George Cussings, both made depositions against Mackay, and William Edwards was a servant to Alexander Wood, who joined the firm in 1741. All three of these men appeared on Thomas Stephens's early census of Augusta, along with their partners

Daniel Clark, Patrick Brown, Archibald McGillivray, and William Sludders. None of McGillivray's partners were listed as residents of Augusta, only as "Traders ... as come from other Parts, and only pass through or by Augusta in their Way."[39] However, these men would shortly come to dominate Augusta, while Mackay and his associates rapidly lost any real influence in town life or the Indian trade in general.

Old grudges from Mackay's brief but violent sojourn among Creek towns probably spilled over into later Augusta interactions. In March 1738, less than a year after the town's founding, the Cherokee trader Samuel Brown came to Savannah "principally to take some Advice about a Wound which he got in his Head among his Fellow Traders."[40] Lieutenant Richard Kent, commander at Fort Augusta, complained in 1740 that the uncertain nature of his civil authority had caused him "frequent Embarrassment how to put it in Execution."[41] The uncertainty had caused much "Jangling among the Traders, and often Attempts of Violence with one another, to decide Controversies by Force, rather than submit to any Judicature."[42] This violence carried over into Indian towns, where in July of the same year "a Riot lately happened in the Lower Creek Nation, by several unlicensed Traders insulting some of those legally appointed, wounded, assaulting, and binding up two or three, and threatening immediate Death to them."[43]

Within a decade, however, accounts of violence at Augusta had subsided, replaced with new complaints about a monopolizing company. It was perhaps as a way of correcting the Georgia interlopers that Charles Town–connected traders such as McGillivray and Company or the partnership of Francis Macartan and Martin Campbell began moving their business from New Windsor to Augusta, and trying to cut off whatever business the original Augusta traders might have developed. It was this development that most likely led Mackay's former ally Thomas Goodale to try his luck with a "publick Victualling House" in 1745.[44] By 1754, Goodale had moved to the Little Ogeechee River after selling his Augusta plantation and town lot to Macartan and Campbell for four hundred pounds currency.[45]

Despite the trustees' plans, a new structure had emerged at Augusta, one that would serve as the basic political, social, and economic institution throughout the colonial period—the trading company. Unlike in most of British North America, where one might look to the family or household as the bedrock of society, the formal relationships between the gentlemen of Augusta mediated personal conflicts, forecast future economic prospects, and generally knit the inhabitants together.

Partnerships were fluid, but they created friendships and personal loyalties that stretched across lifetimes and generations. The most famous and most formidable of the Augusta co-partnerships was the firm of Brown, Rae, and Company. Formed in the 1740s out of the dissolution of Archibald McGillivray and Company, the Augusta firm boasted an unmatched influence in the Anglo-Creek deerskin trade, and its partners would emerge as very influential men in the southeastern backcountry. Patrick Brown, John Rae, George Galphin, Lachlan McGillivray, Daniel Clark, and William Sludders formed the company by merging their own smaller partnerships. Their names would continue to appear in colonial documents as interpreters, correspondents, monopolizers, justices of the peace, and members of the Georgia assembly as well as in virtually any other record relating to life in Augusta or southeastern Indian diplomacy in the eighteenth century.[46]

Descriptions of Augusta as "straggling" seem to have missed how these trading houses formed the deeper structure of Augusta settlement. Augusta was not centered on the traditional features of other English towns: courthouses, churches, or occasionally forts. Life in Augusta was centered on a series of large trading compounds formed and inhabited by the most prominent merchant-traders in the community. The "straggling" appearance of Augusta stemmed from the fact that these compounds stretched in a line running west of the town center, following the path that led to the Creeks. Occupying the five-hundred-acre grants given by the trustees, these compounds stood at some distance from each other but collectively provided the basic foundation of life in Augusta.

Spreading their businesses across the landscape probably offered a number of advantages to the Augusta merchants. Practically speaking, the trade relied on hundreds of pack animals, whose care and outfitting would have been difficult in town. Likewise, during threatening times, it was almost certainly easier to fortify a handful of relatively confined compounds than the entire town of Augusta. Given the secrecy with which merchant-traders preferred to operate, it is also likely that they enjoyed the fact that their operations were so easily shielded from public view.

Whatever reasons they may have had, the fortified trading houses became the most prominent features in the Augusta community. Visitors to Augusta in the 1760s remarked on the centrality of the fortified trading house to the town. As William Stephens had noted as early as 1738, settlement in Augusta followed the path toward the Creeks, and this pattern held more than two decades later. Edmund Atkin, superintendent of Indian affairs, noted the "Multitude of Little private Forts" in Augusta.[47] Dispatched in 1764 to improve the fortifications at Augusta, Gavin Cochrane echoed the unique appearance of Augusta.

> The Situation of Fort Augusta is rather odd; that part of the country is most thickly inhabited beyond the Fort. Their Church is half a Mile or more beyond it; half a Mile beyond the Church is Mr Macartan's house, fortified, wth a ditch, &c, & ten pieces of canon: a mile & half beyond this is Lt Barnard of the Rangers his house, well fortified with a plank wall 12 feet high, & 8 or 9 pieces of cannon; & a Garrison consisting of the Lt, the QuarterMr, and thirty Rangers. Both Mr Macartan's & this Fort are very well provided with great plenty of small arms. Two Miles farther up is Mr Raes house, stockaded.[48]

When Cochrane arrived at Augusta, the most noticeable public buildings were the run-down fort, the church, and three private forts belonging to Indian traders Francis Macartan, Edward Barnard, and John Rae. While these were certainly key to the military preparations Cochrane was there to inspect, they were much more than that.

What these observers described were the true town "centers" of Augusta. Each trading house represented a particular "node" on the path between Indian towns and Atlantic markets. Their location at the falls of the Savannah afforded them access to both the Indian trails that crossed the river at that point and to the boat traffic of the Savannah River. Each house also required economic connection to the merchants of Charles Town who exported Indian manufactures and imported European ones. Likewise, each house required the economic and personal connections that tied them to specific Indian villages.[49] A trading compound could only exist at the intersection of these myriad links and also required land enough to grow food and supplies for residents and traders alike. Meeting these requirements resulted in the trading compounds' isolated and independent appearance and provided Augusta with its unique shape.

Augusta's foundation in the deerskin trade distinguished it from other towns in the Southeast and even from other trading towns reliant on Indian trade. Stretching southward from the Shenandoah Valley in Virginia, a line of small settlements followed the migration of English, Scots-Irish, and German settlers from Pennsylvania along the southern Piedmont. These settlements developed first as small centers for local exchange and then grew into market towns with close connections to eastern ports. The history of these towns followed a familiar pattern, one well developed by historians. The newcomers spread across the land, developing only a household-based subsistence economy of small farms. As population grew, enterprising men from wealthier eastern settlements set up shops and mills to facilitate local exchange and develop a commercial export link with large ports such as Philadelphia, Baltimore, or Charles Town. The little villages provided planters in the neighborhood with available credit to expand their production and to purchase more luxuries, thereby inspiring a rise in commercial agriculture, which in turn created more wealth in the town and allowed for the diversification and elaboration of local hierarchies and services within the towns. From these forces grew such places as Winchester, Virginia; Salisbury, North Carolina; and Camden, South Carolina.[50]

Augusta did not fit this pattern. Its foundation in the Indian trade allowed it to bypass the agricultural base that influenced the settlement of these other towns. Its connections ensured that Augustans would have early access to lowcountry shipping and credit, and its settlers amassed small fortunes long before the wave of subsistence farmers ever reached the southern Piedmont. Moreover, its economic base was dependent not on the slow accumulation of wealth through generations of settled farmers but on the constant personal interactions between whites and Indians hundreds of miles away. Augusta's need for open communication with Indians explained why the town's primary institution was not a fort, church, or courthouse.

As an example of Augusta's uniqueness, the town lacked the walls common to other settlements in the Southeast. Augusta was a remarkably open place, owing to its dispersed population. American cities were largely devoid of the military embankments and fortified walls of Europe. However, it is striking how many of the few American walled cities were either familiar to Augustans or occupied similar places in the Anglo-Indian fur trade. Charles Town and Savannah both developed walled defenses surrounding the town core, mostly as a response to a naval invasion from the nearby Spanish colonies. Two of Augusta's northern counterparts, the Indian-trading town of Albany and the frontier outpost of Schenectady, both had walls surrounding them.[51] Augusta's nearest neighbors, the frontier settlements of Camden and Ninety-Six, resting so close to the Cherokee Indians, both had centralized settlement and palisades surrounding the early towns.[52] Augusta did not develop such elaborate defenses, due no doubt to the difficulty of erecting a palisade around a settlement that spread out for miles.

But Augusta also needed to remain open. Its existence depended on near-constant contact with the rest of the Southeast and Indians in particular. If fear of Indian attacks motivated Camden and Ninety-Six's plans, open contact with Indians motivated Augusta's. The town included the Lower Chickasaws as permanent residents, and Creek, Cherokee, and Upper Chickasaw visitors were an everyday occurrence during the colonial period. When Indian delegations made their way to Charles Town or Savannah, they passed through Augusta. When Indian hunters ranged eastward, they frequently traded in town. Augusta lacked a clear sense of separation between itself and the rest of the Southeast, and this fact was mirrored in its town plan.

It is also remarkable that no one seems to have commented much on the Indian presence at Augusta. Despite the everyday interactions that took place, there is not yet evidence of what these exchanges were like, where they were conducted, or what any of the participants thought of them. Much of this has to do with the nature of historical sources. Traders' reports mentioned the Augusta Chickasaws frequently, but in the same way that they mentioned the Creeks: as sources of diplomatic knowledge or assistants in military actions. Military descriptions tended to come during times of war, obviously, and likely did not witness much peaceful interaction within the community. And later observers—travelers' accounts and residents' letters—tended to come in the 1760s and 1770s, years when the British government was actively discouraging Indian trade within British settlements. But, even if their days in town went unreported, it was true that Indians were frequent visitors to the town.

Even when peace turned to war, Augustans did not alter their basic arrangement of space. Primarily, Augustans relied on Indians for their protection, specifically the Eastern or Lower Chickasaws who resided within the community. Provided with the relatively useless Fort Augusta, the merchant-traders and other residents of the town depended on the Lower Chickasaws to defend the town during the occasional threats from the Creeks or Cherokees. Much like the traders who lived in Indian villages, Augustans at numerous points in their history owed their security to Indian assistance, in this case Lower Chickasaw scouts and warriors.[53]

When attacks came, Augustans sheltered inside their fortified trading houses. During tensions with the Creeks in 1756 and attacks from the Cherokees in 1761–62, Augustans flocked to the trading houses (as well as Fort Augusta) and waited until peace was restored. By providing defense from these separate posts and relying on Indian rangers to fill the space between, Augustans allowed their town to retain a remarkably open appearance that was unlike that of many of its nearest neighboring communities and that kept the community connected to the surrounding countryside.

Augusta thus did not depend on a fixed definition of space. Its physical borders remained unclear, but this is not to say that the community was ill-defined. In some ways, Augusta mirrored the conceptions of township favored by their Creek clients. The Creeks understood towns to be not just people living in proximity, but more extended networks of personal connections. Creek "townships" or *talwas*, centered on central sources of authority, like any English town. In the Creek case, the centers were the political and ceremonial centers of the square, which contained buildings for the township's councils and spaces for religious and social occasions. But Creek townships also followed their inhabitants. When Creeks moved away to establish satellite towns, they remained part of the central community and were expected to participate in town life. Thus, Creeks remained part of the town even when they physically moved away.[54]

Augustans probably did not think much about it, but their community likewise required a fixed definition of membership that allowed for a flexible conception of space. Membership in the Augusta community depended on connection to the central trading companies that defined the "town." Those connections defined "Augustans" who lived close to the town's centers and those who traveled hundreds of miles away, and they took myriad forms: the business of the trade and its continuing links of debts and ledger sheets, the very real ties of kinship that linked traders and merchants together, and the ideologies of the traders that created a sense of community within greater Augusta. Although only superficially similar to Creek notions of township, the trading community of Augusta was not entirely a traditional English town.

But the merchant-traders of Augusta tried to wield power in traditionally English ways. The power of Augusta's trading houses has been noted before, but the mechanisms by which they created and exerted that power have not. The trading houses created a remarkably enduring and yet delicate system of power relations in Augusta. They governed individual, communal, political, and economic relationships, but only for so long as the Indian trade continued. The "house" was both a legal partnership of individuals and also a real physical structure in the case of the largest firms. And, in both senses, the Augusta trading houses dominated the local landscape. Although not every partner in an Augusta firm had his own fortified compound, it seems that the major partnerships all at least had one within their ranks, as Gavin Cochrane's description indicated: John Rae and George Galphin both representing the constellation of partners in the "Augusta Company," Francis Macartan for the Macartan and Campbell partners, and Edward Barnard for his own shifting set of partners inherited from his father-in-law, James Fraser.

Those partners living on their own, unfortified plantations still likely inhabited imposing spaces. The most detailed description of an Augusta plantation came in the form of an advertisement in the *Georgia Gazette* in the spring of 1769. The plantation was almost a town unto itself. The unknown planter advertised a five-hundred-acre plantation "As Compleat and Well found . . . as any in this province." The main house, "newly glazed and painted," contained two chambers, a dining room, hall, and "four very good shed rooms, and three fire places." Flanking the dwelling were two identical thirty-by-twenty-foot buildings: a "very good Store" and a kitchen building. The plantation also boasted a smokehouse, a dairy, a large barn, three corncribs capable of holding a thousand bushels each, a poultry house with a livery attached, as well as a "strong and well framed Stable for six or eight horses." There were also a house for an overseer, a garden, and an orchard containing peach, apple, mulberry, and plum trees, "from which a great quantity of peach brandy, cyder, and silk, may be made" as well as a "lagoon" and convenient indigo works. The plantation came complete with a workforce of thirty slaves, which included "a very good Bricklayer, a Driver, and two Sawyers." If the ideal plantation was a little village of its own, then this one Augustan, at least, had gone far.[55]

Although the town center failed to develop, the large plantations surrounding Augusta presented an almost urban landscape. George Galphin's plantation at Silver Bluff made for "a pleasant villa."[56] James Fraser built a "Brickhouse" on his five hundred acres in Augusta.[57] Robert Mackay's house had to be at least two stories.[58] Though none may have earned favorable comparisons with lowcountry mansions, they towered above humbler cabins such as William Mylne's across the river in South Carolina, which was "built of pine trees laid a top of one the other . . . covered with what they call clap boards . . . the contents inside sixteen feet by twelve." Mylne's cabin lacked the luxury of floorboard, so his single chair and mattress rested on the "clay floor."[59] The traders' substantial homes set them far above their neighbors, and provided Augusta's storekeepers with their social and economic authority in the community. Adding palisades and cannons to these structures served only to make an obvious point unmistakable—the owners considered themselves central to every possible town function.

Within the partnership symbolized by these houses, the key relationship was that between the partners themselves. Partnerships were formal and public associations, analogous to marriage in terms of their involvement in property and inheritance. The formation and dissolution of trade partnerships required public announcement, since partners could draw on each other's accounts and credit. The large firm of Archibald McGillivray and Company, for example went through some form of internal dispute in the summer of 1741. An advertisement placed in the *South Carolina Gazette* that year warned "any Person or Persons whatever not to trust or credit any of the said Company on the Company Accounts, except *Archibald McGillivray*, who is appointed sole Manager and Director."[60] McGillivray, the head of the trading house, had to assert his authority. The public form of this admonishment echoed advertisements that occasionally appeared from estranged husbands in southeastern newspapers. Take, for example, the following notice that appeared in the *Georgia Gazette* in 1768: "Whereas Susannah the wife of John Gotier staymaker has absented herself from him, this is therefore to caution all persons from crediting her on his account, as he will not pay any debts of her contracting."[61]

Involving the division of property and the maintenance of reputation, the dissolution of partnerships resembled a bitter divorce. The properties involved were often extensive and varied, as suggested by the end of the partnership between John Francis Williams and Robert Mackay. When they parted ways, joint property included "Their Trading House in Augusta ... Plantation, Negroes, Boats, Stock in Trade, Pack Horses, Indian Debts, &c."[62] The two men's disputes and separation were particularly bitter. Even four years later, as Williams lay on his death bed, Mackay spat, "When [I] am sure the Wretch is dying I will call and see him" but still felt compelled to have him "decently put in the Ground and his papers secured, for I suppose there is some of them not fit to appear in the world."[63] Williams apparently engaged in some dishonorable business practices, and Mackay feared that his public association with Williams would taint his own reputation. "Several glaring Frauds were intended" in Williams's account books and Mackay regretted that his name "should be joined with his in any claim or matter whatever."[64] Mackay's anger at his former partner demonstrated that partnerships were much deeper than business relations.

It is not surprising, then, that partnerships also became family relationships. When the Augusta traders handed down property, for example, it often went to their partners or their partners' children. Isaac Barksdale, who had no children, remembered his partner John Rae's progeny in his will, leaving 1000 pounds South Carolina currency and a slave named Tom to Rae's daughter Jane, 250 acres of his property and a slave named Ned to John Rae, Jr., and a slave named Sambo to William Rae. William Sludders divided his estate between his siblings and his business partners, giving his brother and sister one-third each and the remaining third to his partners Patrick Brown, Lachlan McGillivray, and Daniel Clark. Even more frequently, the traders served as executors for each others' estates—John Rae was Barksdale's executor; Patrick Brown, Lachlan McGillivray, and Daniel Clark were Sludders's; McGillivray oversaw Daniel Clark's bequests. Perhaps more significantly, members of different firms also shared responsibility for their fellow traders' property. John Rae shared his executor duties with both Francis Macartan and Martin Campbell when John Pettygrew died in 1761.[65]

The terms that these men used to describe each other likewise revealed a connection that went deeper than a mere business relationship. John Ross, as noted, considered Lachlan McGillivray to be his only friend. McGillivray and Galphin referred to each other as "sworn brothers."[66] In a letter posted in the *Georgia Gazette*, McGillivray twice in the same sentence referred to Galphin as "my friend" and painted them as fellow travelers—"neither would my friend or myself chuse to throw away money lavishly; we have suffered many hardships to acquire a small competency."[67] Partnerships supported a sense of family and friendship among the traders, exemplified in Brown, Rae, and Company's decision to refer to themselves as a household composed of smaller households: "there are Seven of us in Company ... we were formerly three Separate Houses in this place [Augusta] but for the more effectual carrying on the Trade and Supplying the Indians with goods, we thought it proper to join in one Company ... our House is the best Acquainted with Indian Affairs of any in this Colony."[68] It is important to note, however, that very little is known about the internal dynamics of partnerships. Traders had every reason to present a united front, as their partnerships were the basis for their power and influence in the region.

The Augusta trading houses also had connections between each other. The largest stores frequently did business with each other, creating an economic and trading community within the town. Given that the different firms were connected to different Indian towns by law and by license, there likely was little direct competition between firms for Indian business, allowing such ledger-sheet cooperation to exist. The preserved ledgers of Macartan and Campbell's Augusta store demonstrated the ongoing traffic between large firms. Between 1763 and 1766, most of the major firms in Augusta did business with Macartan's store at some point. The sojourner partnership of John Buckles and Co. used Macartan's store to settle a debt with George Galphin in 1763. The always fashionable Andrew McLean purchased his silk handkerchiefs and cotton lace from Macartan in 1764. In 1765, Trewin, Sludders, and McGillivray paid Macartan to ship their deerskins, and in 1766 Macartan used their boats to ship his.[69] Thus did the trading companies do more than bind together traders within their walls; they also knit together the space between compounds.

But the openness of partners and houses to each other did not extend to those outside of the houses. Those who attempted to regulate the trade frequently found themselves looking in from outside the compound walls. Those who tried to compete with the large houses for a share of the trade quickly found how powerfully connected the Augusta merchants were. Even those who simply wanted to live in the town of Augusta found their fortunes rose or fell depending on their ability to form meaningful connection to the great traders. So long as the connections between Atlantic ships and Indian stores remained, the Augusta houses shaped the political, economic, social, and racial dynamics of Augusta and its environs.

From an early date, no dispute in Augusta could find formal settlement without the consultation of the local storekeepers. Although the trustees initially appointed the commander of Fort Augusta to serve as the justice of the peace in the town, he was soon joined by a committee of three "assistants" to help the community settle its small claims. By 1751 it had proven beneficial to have such a system, with the justice "desiding little Controversies among his Neighbours ... with the Assistance of three creditable neighbour Freeholders, as is now practised at Augusta."[70] It was no accident that the men chosen to settle local disputes should come from the leading trading houses, since they were the men who held the most influence over the town and its traders. The first three "assistants" were James Fraser, John Rae, and James Campbell. The President and Assistants of Georgia, either in ignorance or in resignation, nominated the latter two men in the same letter in which they voiced their complaints about the "monopolizing Company" at Augusta and "Cabals and Quarrels of the Traders in different Interests" that would arise from the firm's tactics.[71]

Indeed, Georgia's governors may have even deliberately created this system whereby the justices were from different firms, a pattern that, either by luck or design, would persist throughout the colonial period and that may have helped ensure the decline in reports of violence and discord coming from Augusta. Although trading partners could be found acting jointly as commissioners for the peace, no one firm dominated the ranks of local justices. John Rae and David Douglass served nearly continuously from 1750 until 1770, but other traders rotated in and out. In 1760, Augusta's jurisprudence was divided among Rae, Douglass, Martin Campbell, Edward Barnard, Lachlan McGillivray, John Francis Williams, and Francis Macartan. Four years later, the task belonged to Rae, Barnard, Edmund Cartlidge, James Jackson, and William Trewin. In 1768, Rae, Barnard, and Williams had resumed their posts along with newcomers Leonard Claiborne, Edward Keaton, and John Walton. The presence of these last three on the magistrate lists indicated that nontraders had begun to find a role in town governance, mostly owing to older traders' tendency to move downriver, as did Rae and McGillivray, or simply to die. But for most of Augusta's colonial life, the basic administration of law flowed from the trading house.

Given the close-knit and powerful community of merchants in Augusta, it is not surprising that outsiders were continually stymied by the clandestine nature of negotiations between Augusta's traders. Edmund Atkin, the first British superintendent of Indian affairs in the southern colonies, often found himself on the outside looking in. At his first arrival in Augusta in 1758, he called the traders together and announced his intentions for his mission to the Creeks. "They put a good Face upon it," he muttered, "& declared a Readiness to accompany me; tho nothing was further from the Inclinations of most. . . . There is nothing they dread so much as the looking into the true State of the Trade."[72] When John Spencer defied Atkin's authority, he called down the wrath of Patrick Brown's heir, a merchant in Charlestown. Brown's heir, "in the Hearing of many publickly in Augusta," declared "that he would ruin Spencer, and would stop him from going into the Nation . . . would expose him & make him knuckle to the Agent."[73] If Spencer would defy colonial authority, then Brown would correct him. The man was calmed, though: "Thro' McGillivray's means, the Difference was made up by Spencer's asking Pardon of Brown."[74] The need to protect each others' businesses and reputations provided future historians with Robert Mackay's tantalizing, yet frustrating, admission that "The papers of J.F.W. [John Francis Williams] relative to the differences with his wife and us were committed to the flames unread the evening he was put in the ground."[75] More to protect his own reputation than his former partner's, Mackay quietly concealed the business of a fellow trader and prevented any outsiders from learning about his possibly illicit activities.

Even for those who simply wanted to be a part of Augusta life, the trading houses stood as barriers to entry in the town's social circles. For those outsiders who traveled to Augusta, the company of traders proved difficult to enter, which colored their experiences of the town. Two such outsiders came to Augusta in the 1770s, one man and one woman. Both fell in love with the area quickly and almost as quickly grew tired of the place. Mary Chilcott of Newport, Rhode Island, found company only through her marriage to the Augusta merchant Robert Mackay. From then on, Augusta became her home. For William Mylne, entrance into Augusta society proved formidable, despite his education. He simply could not keep up with the endless series of dinners and entertainments that could easily bankrupt any pretenders to Augusta's social elite.

Both Mylne and Chilcott quickly became enchanted with the Georgia upcountry's people and climate. Chilcott, a widow when she arrived in Augusta, had accompanied her daughter Catherine to Augusta after the latter married John Francis Williams. In May 1770 Chilcott sang the town's praises: "Here in Augusta we are all Health & serenity, such a succession of fine weather never did I before experience, so moderate, so pleasant, & so charming 'tis almost impossible to be dull or low spirited."[76] Though she missed her family dearly, Chilcott found much to praise about the locality. As she wrote her brother back in Rhode Island, "I wish you had some of the green pease that we wallow in every day—or the fine strawberrys, ten times better than ours, they seem to be of the wild kind, but quite as big as the largest hautboys."[77]

Mylne likewise found Augusta to be agreeable enough at first. Mylne had been an architect in Edinburgh, Scotland, and had built the North Bridge there, but questions over the bridge's soundness and delays in its construction had bankrupted him. He found his way to Charles Town and from there to Augusta to try to start anew and rebuild his ruined fortunes. Mylne began to feel better almost immediately: "My health thank God is perfectly reestablished, I do not think I was ever so well. Although it now begins to be hot yet I have felt it as hot as in Scotland, they tell me it will be warmer still but the mornings and evenings are cool and it lasts but for three months."[78] After a few months' stay at his "Hermitage" on Stephens's Creek in South Carolina, Mylne felt himself renewed and energized. "God Almighty has planted in our breasts an active principal for wise purposes.... I want again to be in action now the machine is repaired."[79] Mylne saw his future as that of an agrarian:

"The life of a planter is that I should like, in it I could lay by money; I have learnt the methods to cultivate the different articles of produce in this country."[80] He estimated that three or four hundred pounds would be enough to set himself up in planting and that every year would return enough for him to lay by money and answer his creditors, particularly his brother Robert.

Both Chilcott and Mylne, however, quickly found that life in Augusta proved frustrating for those on the margins of the Indian trade. Only a few months after her flattering portrait of the town, Chilcott complained that she was done "boasting of the climate, for it seems the fine moderate summer, & delightful showers we had every hot afternoon, occasions this mighty sickly Fall ... for I don't know a person in Augusta, except Mr. Williams, that hasn't been sick."[81] She herself had been "seiz'd with a fever & ague" and could not tell "the quantity of bark I've swallowed at 6s sterling an ounce ... the tho'ts of the expence didn't contribute at all to my cure I can tell you."[82] Mylne suffered his own bout of sickness, at the exact time of year that Chilcott did. In October of his first year, he had fallen into "a very severe fit of sickness, the fever and ague ... I was twice reduced to skin and bone and so weak that I could scarce walk across the room."[83] However, by the time that Mylne wrote these words, Mary Chilcott had become Mary Mackay and was a fixture of Augusta society. As he wrote in the same letter, Mary Mackay and her husband, Robert, "are extremely well bred and very civil and polite to strangers, their house is the great resort of the best people."[84] Mylne could not hope to enter this society, and within a year had left Carolina to find his fortunes in more northern colonies.

Although she found a position within Augusta society, Mary Chilcott Mackay's life was still circumscribed by her gender. Predictably, a woman in Augusta did not have the same freedom of association as a man. Traders, like colonists in other parts of America, based their power in part on controlling access to white women's bodies, and used their houses as means of controlling this access.[85] Augusta's ranks swelled every spring with the arrival of packhorse caravans from Indian towns. As Mackay wrote to her brother in May 1770, "The Indian Country People will be coming down, and the Gent[leme]n think as we are not used to them, it will be rather disagreeable to us to have them about the House."[86] Shortly after the death of Mackay's son-in-law, John Francis Williams, in January 1775, his young widow Catherine became an object of affection of the single gentlemen in Augusta. Her marriage had been the subject of local gossip for quite some time, as even William Mylne wrote to Scotland that Williams was "a rascal of this country... he used her extremely ill which has ruined her health and she was forced to leave him."[87] She moved in with her mother and stepfather, Williams's former partner Robert Mackay. When Williams finally died and the marriage officially ended, "Katy" as her mother called her, found willing beaus at the front door. None of these gentlemen could see her, though, as Catherine sat "up-stairs which disturbs Peter mightily as he cant get an opportunity to pop the question."[88] Catherine's mother Mary knew that sequestering the widow was necessary for the protection of her reputation; she would not allow the local ladies to say "that Mrs. W[illiams] stayed home till she heard of her Husband's death, then went gadding abroad as soon as the news came."[89] For the traders at Augusta, at least those who had lived in Indian towns and had been the ones protected, often by Indian women from Indian men, this was something of a role reversal from their earlier lives, one more suitable, perhaps, to European gender roles.

What drove Mylne away from Augusta and bound Mary Chilcott Mackay to the town was the cost of sociability among the town's leading families. Linked to eastern credit by their trading boats and Indian clients alike, Augustans lived in the English world of goods and spent a great deal of their wealth to keep up appearances. Mackay's letters to her husband revealed how closely knit Augusta society was and were filled with community news that Robert Mackay had missed while on business in Savannah. The size and frequency of social visits in Augusta took a toll, particularly on the Mackays' dishes. The loss of plates could prove embarrassing for the mistress of the household. "I hardly know how to ask you Mr. Mackay to bring some more plates, but I assure you the old ones have disappeared so all at once, that I find it difficult to make them go round for the present family."[90] Maintaining a respectful and deferential attitude toward her husband, she assured Robert that the loss was "not from my carelessness." Nonetheless, an Augusta household had to be well supplied with plates, for "two dozen and a half will by no means do when we have company."[91]

Mylne could not hope to maintain an equality with the people of Augusta. The architect who had traveled Europe, Mylne was good company in Augusta, having "several friends... at whose houses and tables I am always welcome."[92] But the cost of that welcome was prohibitive. Mylne could not make a proper visit without "a blue or black corderoe silk waistcoat" to wear "among the gentles, for they dress gayly both men and women."[93] Eventually, though he much adored his neighbors and his situation, Mylne simply could not afford the lifestyle at Augusta. As he conceded only a few months after arriving at Augusta, the "money required to settle a plantation so as to be comfortable is considerable and one must live on an equality with one's friends, this would be expensive," for "the principal people lives handsomely, these would visit me in their turn."[94] Nor could he find camaraderie among his poorer neighbors, for they were "very ignorant of the world and know little more than raising their crops and carrying it to the store." They also thought Mylne "a strange man, to live as I do by myself."[95] So Mylne decided to try the northern towns, "where money is a thousand times plentier than here and where I stand little chance of competitors."[96]

Unlike Mylne, however, other newcomers to the area chose to challenge the trading community rather than enter it. In the 1750s, the Indian trade became more democratized, as white newcomers and Indian migrants began seeking new connections outside of traditional trade centers. The lands north and west of Augusta became home to more frequent and casual interaction between whites and Creeks, and thus became home to more frequent conflicts and violence. Creek hunters in the 1750s began moving eastward from older towns such as Okfuskee in search of game and increased opportunities for a cheaper trade in Georgia's white settlements, where prices were lower than back home. Whites, too, had begun seeking out lands in this region, partly for agriculture, but also for the economic advantages of opening a direct trade with Indians and siphoning off a few Creek deerskins for their private profit, creating a more open "frontier exchange economy" in the British Southeast.[97]

Some Creeks, for their part, enjoyed the advantages of having a secondary source of trade. Unlike the established traders in Indian towns, settlement traders could offer fairer prices for deerskins. Traders in the nations typically weighed skins one at a time, and did not credit Indians for fractions of a pound. Settlement traders such as John Smith, in contrast, had "an unusual manner in which he takes their Leather, by putting a considerable number of Skins in the scale at once, and allowing for the broken weight which often makes a difference of 50 pr. ct."[98] The Indians were "quick enough in discovering what is most for their benefit, hence they must be a good deal surprized and offended at the practice of the Traders in the Nation, so different from that of those in the Settlements."[99] Though laws forbid trading in the settlement, Ellis recognized that enforcement was almost impossible, "from the difficulty of proving who are, or are not of that [Creek] Nation."[100] For the settler-traders near Augusta, the inability of their neighbors to identify different Indian ethnicities was a profitable advantage.

As the case of some settlements on the Ogeechee River shows, the Augusta traders did not take kindly to economic competition and used whatever influence they could to drive out competitors. By the late summer of 1756, a party of settlers had taken up residence along the Ogeechee, near the Augusta-Creek trading path. Merchant-traders and Creeks alike had noticed the settlement "at Hogatechy" which seemed to appear overnight. The Indians reported that "they are in such a haste in comeing that they travell in the Night with Waggons," and the trader James Germany feared that "if there is not a Stop put to the settling of Ogatechy it will prove the Ruin of the whole Country without any Dispute."[101] Some Creeks, already alarmed at the British building forts among the Cherokee towns, saw the rush to settle Ogeechee as another step toward British military aggression. These "Virginia Men," as the Creeks termed them, were but the advance guard of a massive British assault on their towns, a rumor that seemed likely once the Ogeechee settlers and the Creeks came to blows in 1756.[102]

The Ogeechee settlement represented an incursion into the traders' sense of control. The settlers' houses stood along the path between Augusta and the Lower Creek towns. In many ways, the settlements followed the pattern early established at Augusta of settling farther along the path. Having done it themselves, the Augusta traders likely recognized what the Ogeechee settlers were up to. They offered an alternate source of trade outside Augustans' control. And if it caused problems, the Ogeechee trade did not have the proper diplomatic experience to smooth over bad feelings, experience that had served the Augusta traders well for decades.

Part of the traders' concern about the Ogeechee settlers was likely that they offered other sources of trade for the Creeks. One Andrew Lambert apparently had invited the Indians into his house, likely for trade since he "entertained them in a friendly manner, but they got up very early in the morning, and stole off with several Blanketts & Horses."[103] The Creeks' complaints about the Ogeechee settlement likewise included both the familiar complaint that "their living so high up spoils our hunting Ground and frightens away the Deer" but also the revealing addition that "there is two Men who trade away back in the Woods, One is Ephraim Alexander, and the other is a Dutch Man, name unknown."[104] The real complaint against the Ogeechee settlers became clear the year after the attack, when Governor Henry Ellis reported that those most likely to carry on a clandestine trade with Indians "have lately come from the northward, and are settled between A[u]gusta, and the River Ogeeche, precisely where the difference with the Indians happened, the last year."[105] These people had "furnished themselves with dry Goods, and Rum, [and] carry on a Trade with the Creeks."[106]

Augustans complained about the Ogeechee settlement because it threatened their position in the Indian trade in addition to threatening war with the Creeks. The Ogeechee settlement had caused concern in Augusta even before the situation led to blows. Less than two weeks before the Ogeechee attack, the leading traders had expressed their wish that "there had been no Settlement made on Ogechee [sic] as yet for if ever the Creek Indians should break out a War with us ... we are Assured they will make that Settlement one Pretence" for the attack.[107] Should war come, the traders feared for their storehouses, "for in all Probability they would for the sake of those Stores ... be Attacked."[108] The Ogeechee attacks nearly realized these, and Augustans felt the immediate need for fortification. John Rae, David Douglass, and Martin Campbell, Augusta's three trader-justices of the peace, informed the governor that "the Fort cannot contain all the Inhabitants so that we will be obliged to Fortify some other Places."[109] Here was the first indication of the fortified trading compound in the Augusta landscape. The store was the merchant-traders' most prized possession, after all. And, when the settlement sparked violence, Augusta's merchant-traders happily let the Ogeechee settlers shelter in their fortified houses, demonstrating their power directly for their new competitors.

The Ogeechee incident revealed a crucial link in the thinking of Augusta's merchants: peace could be maintained only so long as they remained in control of the trade. Settlements of competitors, like the Ogeechee residents, threatened loss of control, and Augustans quickly responded with panicked declamations and warnings about imminent violence. Augusta's Indian traders were more familiar than most with Indian practices and customs. Nonetheless, they shared a sense of fear as to what might befall them should anything sour Anglo-Indian relations. Rae, along with two other Augusta storekeepers, James Fraser and David Douglass, in their petition for a church at Augusta, noted that "Indian Friendship is sometimes precarious."[110] In 1756, only a few weeks before the Ogeechee incident, Rae, Douglass, Isaac Barksdale, and Lachlan McGillivray all signed a petition to Governor John Reynolds pleading the case for improved defenses in Augusta. They feared that Augusta and its environs, "being not only frontiers but places where the Stores and Trading Goods for all the Chickesaws Creek and Part of the Cherokees are kept, are of the greatest Consequence.... That in our Present defenceless Condition those Places and Stores we are Morally certain wou'd fall too Easy a Prey to 'em." They feared that Fort Augusta, then in a "ruinous and untenantable Condition," no longer offered the town "an Asylum for their Women and Children and a Place of Security for their Effects in Case of Danger."[111] By fortifying their stores, Augusta's merchants reasserted their authority in the neighborhood and reclaimed their centrality in the economy of the community.

The Augusta merchant-traders also maintained their economic influence over the neighborhood in less dramatic ways. While the trade flowed back and forth primarily from Indian towns to British merchants, it created small local exchanges that tied storekeepers' neighbors to the Indian trade. Galphin's Silver Bluff trading house took in shirts and shoes made locally, some of which found their way up the trails to Indian villages. For example, a widow named Stewart made "ruffled shirts" which she then sold to Galphin for seven shillings, six pence each. She also sewed "Tra[de] Shirts," which earned her five shillings credit each and "C[ambric] Stock[ings]," which fetched forty shillings a pair. In exchange, the Widow Stewart bought from Galphin the materials she needed—cambric (at fifty shillings a yard) and gartering (at twenty-four shillings, six pence a yard) for stockings and possibly shirt ruffles, as well as osnaburg (at seven shillings, six pence a yard) for the trading shirts.[112] She also received other small necessaries—flowered ribbon, sleeve buttons, and needles as well as saltpetre and salt. She also sold her goods to local men, earning 2 pounds credit on Richard Brown's account for making him a pair of stockings. All in all, Stewart did not get rich through her handiwork. From the surviving entries dating between December 1767 and January 1769, Stewart did not appear to fare too well at Galphin's—her total debts amounted to £44.16s, while her labor earned her only £23.17.6 in credit.[113]

Stewart's cottage industry, though, helped supply the Indian trade and earned Galphin some extraordinary profits. Some of her shirts probably formed part of a shipment sent up the trails with Timothy Barnard. In the same period that Galphin took in Stewart's sewing, he credited Barnard for "4 White Rufled Shirts" and "6 Doz. Tra[de] Shirts" along with vermilion, trading knives, gun flints, and other traditional Indian trade goods. While Galphin apparently exercised some charity toward the widow, selling the trade shirts at loss for only 4s. 7d. apiece, the ruffled shirts now carried a value of forty shillings each (a more than 400 percent markup). By the rates going at Galphin's store, a trader would have to bring in three dressed deerskins (worth fourteen shillings each) or four raw skins (at ten shillings each) to repay Galphin for one ruffled shirt.

The Indian who bought that shirt paid more dearly still, as the trader almost certainly charged his Indian clients one or two skins more.[114]

Augusta's economy thus rose and fell with the deerskin trade. The traders' stores remained the primary centers for trade and credit in Augusta until the end of the colonial period. These stores, with their profitable export of deerskins, provided needed capital and credit for Augusta's local planters in the absence of a deerskin-independent economy. They relied on them for tools and goods, as well as for food in more difficult times. Galphin's complex at Silver Bluff provided the neighborhood with metal goods such as pots, kettles, hoes, and nails. It provided livery in the form of saddles, bridles, and bells for livestock. Cloth, shoes, furniture, paper, and ink all found their way to Silver Bluff before making their way into upcountry homes. Foodstuffs also made up part of planters' debts: staples such as wheat and corn from Galphin's mills, as well as dried beef, peas, and bacon were sold alongside luxury items such as coffee, tea, sugar, and "English Chester Cheese."[115] To make up these debts, Galphin traded extensively in local produce, as well as animal skins. His store accounts list hogs and horses, rice and tobacco—everything from heavy chests to candle wicks crossed Galphin's counter.

The merchant-traders also provided other services for Augusta's residents. Their economic endeavors presented a microcosm of British North American enterprise. Patrick Brown raised indigo; Galphin and McGillivray both owned mills; Rae and Galphin held large stocks of cattle, and a number of their cowpens dotted the landscape and served as landmarks on Georgia maps and in headright petitions. Other local planters raised tobacco and rice, though not to the extent one would expect in other colonies such as Virginia and South Carolina.

The stores exchanged services in addition to material goods. In December 1764, Macartan and Campbell's store ledgers mediated the exchange of various deeds in the community. Andrew Marr, a jack-of-all-trades, earned over one hundred pounds currency for various tasks: "binding Smolet's history" for one customer; "mending two Watches" for another; "imprisoning Sam, a Negroe;" and "for cash paid lawyers."[116] That same month another Augustan used his store account to make a donation for the church organ. Two other men drew on their accounts to settle a debt of money "Lost at a Race."[117]

As the case of Mrs. Stewart suggested, however, locals' balances often ran into the red. According to Mylne, new planters in the region were "generally in debt to the storekeeper who gives them his own price for their produce and that in goods not money."[118] Their indebtedness caused resentment toward the local merchants, and they complained of "the extravagant rates they are obliged to give for goods."[119] The cost of this indebtedness could be great: in 1758 William Irvin sold seven horses, eight head of cattle, twenty six hogs, and "all his household furniture and utensils" to Macartan and Campbell for seventy-one pounds currency.[120] Macartan and Campbell likewise received human property for debts, as when Dugald Campbell, a "victualler," sold them his slave Philis for 136 pounds currency. Nehemiah Wade, Jr. mortgaged his only two slaves, a "woman named Hegg and her child named Sam" to Lachlan McGillivray for 203 pounds currency.[121] As these latter two example show, Augusta stores provided more than the necessaries of life, they also provided upcountry Georgia with a darker legacy of human bondage.

The trading compounds were Augusta's main entry point for the institution of slavery. African Americans were a common sight in Augusta from the earliest days of its settlement, but their lives have largely been forgotten in the historic record. Slaveholding was fairly widespread in the area, in the town itself, in the neighboring community of Halifax some twenty miles downriver, and along the Little River some twenty miles farther north.[122] Based on petitions for headright land grants, where each inhabitant testified to the number of people in his household, one can gain a rough sense of how prevalent slavery was in early Augusta. By 1760, the governor and council had heard petitions from 103 heads of household, 34 of which (33 percent) had at least one slave. By 1770, the numbers had grown: 323 heads of household, with 116 (36 percent) claiming at least one slave. Although Augusta probably did not have a black majority, African Americans were a major presence in the neighborhood, as indicated by one minister's 1766 statement that his parishioners included 540 Europeans and 501 African Americans. The local population was clearly involved in the institution, such that one could only dream of wealth if one simultaneously dreamed of owning slaves.[123]

Although Augusta's slaveholders did not rival their lowcountry counterparts for the size of their estates, many did hold large numbers of slaves from a very early period. The wealthiest merchant-traders held many men, women, and children in bondage. By 1760, the surviving members of Brown, Rae, and Company claimed ownership of dozens of African Americans: John Rae claimed thirty-six; George Galphin claimed upwards of forty; and Lachlan McGillivray, fifty slaves. McGillivray and his partner Daniel Clark as co-partners claimed another forty-two. A decade later, their holdings had increased. Rae, Galphin, and

McGillivray each claimed more than eighty slaves in their households. Edward Barnard, the son-in-law and heir of the Augusta merchant James Fraser, owned eight slaves in 1760, but more than sixty ten years later. Although it was certain that many, or possibly most, of these bondsmen and bondswomen worked on Augustans' lowcountry plantations, many provided the labor for the neighborhood as well.

Traders' stores were a major access point for slavery's extension inland. The slave trade in Augusta ran, at least in part, through these buildings. Macartan and Campbell used their store accounts to purchase and hire slaves for their plantations.[124] Their store also facillitated the slave trade between Augusta and the lowcountry. For example, in 1762, Macartan and Campbell purchased two slaves from a local man and sent them to Charles Town to take the place of two lowcountry slaves acquired by their firm.[125] Their trading boats also carried others' slaves up the Savannah, as in 1765 when Edward Barnard paid Macartan and Campbell ten pounds "For Passage of 2 Negroes."[126] As slavery became more and more prominent in the Augusta area, it further tied the community to the business of the deerskin trade houses.

All of the merchant-traders' varied economic activities relied on slave labor. Enslaved boatmen, field hands, mill workers, cowboys, and sawyers made the business of Augusta possible. They even served in the defense of Augusta during the Cherokee War. In 1760 Edmond Atkin hoped to equip African Americans at Fort Moore in New Windsor, "of whom 14 are able to use [arms] but they have none, nor even Axes or Hatchets."[127] Unsurprisingly, African Americans in and around Augusta played the same roles in that developing settlement that an earlier generation of "black pioneers" had played in the formation of the South Carolina lowcountry.[128]

The growth of slavery in Augusta also helps partly explain a major shift in the deerskin trade. Historians have noted that the trade after the 1750s increasingly focused on "undressed" or "raw" skins, which had not been tanned. Due to increasing pressures on Creek hunters and especially Creek women, the Creeks preferred to trade the labor-saving raw skins. They were obliged by an influx of traders following deregulation of trading licenses after 1763. While this shift has been attributed to the pressures in Creek country and the unscrupulous new traders, the rise of slavery in Augusta helped make it possible, especially among larger trading firms such as the Augusta Company or Macartan and Campbell.[129]

While the burden of drying and stretching the raw skins had traditionally fallen on Indian women, there is evidence that Augusta's leading merchants began shifting the burden to enslaved African Americans after 1760. George Galphin's slave David George "mended deer skins" while living in Indian towns.[130] Numerous raw skins coming into stores such as Macartan and Campbell's were processed by enslaved labor before being shipped down to Charles Town, as evidenced by Macartan and Campbell's 1766 expenditure for the hire of two local slaves "for 25 days dressing skins." As with the boatmen, colonialism in the Southeast had once again required the transfer of knowledge from Indians to enslaved African Americans.[131]

At first glance, it might seem that Augusta slaveholders were more benevolent toward African Americans than one might expect. Involvement in the deerskin trade led to intimate associations between whites and Africans. Indian trader John Spencer's gift to the young Thomas Millen hinted at the trade's more intimate contacts. The young man received from Spencer "a mulatto fellow named Catoe, his wife Emelia, and her son Dick; a Negro woman named Memba and her daughter, a mulatto named Sapphoe" as well as "a Negro fellow named Jamie and his wife, Penda."[132] It was quite possible that Spencer had in fact fathered Memba's mulatto daughter. Racial boundaries were not as rigid among Indian traders as in the post-Stono Carolina lowcountry. In Indian towns, relations between white and black men and Indian women were common and could very easily have been the reason behind the bachelor Isaac Barksdale's freeing "Nancey and her two mulatto children, named Johney and Salley" in his will.[133]

George Galphin especially seems to have allowed his slaves more freedoms than were typical in the colonial Southeast, particularly in matters of religion. David George, who had mended deerskins in Indian towns while bonded to one of Galphin's traders, went to live at Silver Bluff, where Galphin used him as a house servant "to wait upon him." While in Galphin's employ, George attended Baptist sermons at Galphin's mill and was eventually baptized in the mill's stream. Baptism gave George a calling, and he began preaching himself. He helped found Old Springfield Baptist Church, one of the earliest black churches in Georgia. Not everyone was as comfortable with George's preaching as Galphin seemingly was, particularly as the Revolution neared. George remembered that as a period "when the Ministers were not allowed to come amongst us [slaves] lest they should furnish us with too much knowledge."[134] During the war, George escaped to Canada, where he turned missionary, and eventually led a body of over 1,000 souls to settle in Sierra Leone.[135] Although George's story perhaps indicated that Galphin was, as one historian wrote, "one of the least racially conscious persons in the vicinity," the Silver Bluff store, like other trading stores helped institutionalize slavery in Augusta more than it did to break down racial barriers in the Southeast.[136]

Despite the seeming opportunity that David George experienced through the Indian trade, and possibilities for kindness exhibited in the intimate relations between merchants, traders, and their slaves, Galphin's account books indicate that the system of slavery was already deeply ingrained in Augusta and limiting opportunities for African Americans. If Galphin was willing to allow his slaves more freedom than many of his colonial peers, his store account book revealed the extent to which racial distinctions had worked their way into everyday life. The ledger listed numerous categories of fabric, and these were divided between their prospective wearers. Entries listed the sale of "Whitemans Shirts" or "fine White Mans Check Shirts" alongside such items as "Negro Cloth" and "Negro Shoes." Even at the level of dress, Galphin was willing to delineate between the proper attire for a free man and that for a slave.[137] Galphin extended this distinction to his own children as well, dividing up his estate among his numerous children from various liaisons with Indian, African American, and mulatto women. He granted freedom to his "mulatto girls, daughters of a mulatto woman named Sappha" as well as his "mulatto girl named Barbara (Daughter of Rose, deceased)."[138]

Like other European southeasterners in the eighteenth and nineteenth centuries, Augustans dreamed of wealth based on slaveholding. A crucial component of the development and entrenchment of slaveholding in North America was the system's ingraining in its participants, be they actual slaveholders or merely would-be masters, the belief that holding their fellow humans in bondage granted them the possibility of future wealth and comfort.[139] The Malcontents of Georgia used Augusta's prosperity to demonstrate the necessity of slaveholding to whites' future prospects, and articulated the earliest slaveholding fantasies in Georgia. By the 1770s, it had become common wisdom that Trustee Georgia's inability to develop was a "Backwardness," stemming from "the Prohibition of introducing African Servants."[140] When the broken and bankrupt William Mylne came to the Augusta area, his future prosperity came only in a vision of himself as a planter, "to buy three negroes, to bring Willie and a white maid servant over, with these I could live easily and contented, [and] lay by some money yearly."[141]

Slaves allowed for dreams of individual achievement, but white Augustans also used them to cement social ties with their fellow slave owners. James Fraser helped his son-in-law Edward Barnard get started in life by selling him nine slaves, in addition to all Fraser's household furniture.[142] In December 1757, Thomas Bassett expressed his affection for his "beloved Son" Thomas and his daughter Louissa through the gift of fifteen and eleven slaves respectively. The gift was formalized "by the delivery of the lad named Dick" for Thomas and "by the delivery of Charles in the name of all the slaves mentioned" for Louissa.[143] In 1758 John Spencer became the benefactor of Thomas Millen when he gave the young man a stock of cattle and horses, as well as ten slaves.[144] The trader Daniel Douglass followed suit in 1760 with his own gift of a slave named June to Sarah Clark's son John.[145] In addition to their patronage of their neighbors' and friends' children, Augusta slaveholders used their slaves to cement bonds with lowcountry gentlemen. Hence, Lachlan McGillivray gave the Savannah planter Matthew Roche's daughter Bellamy a "Negro woman named Cassandra" in 1761.[146]

While Augustans used slaves to build wealth and community, their slaves obviously did not share in these bonds of affection. Galphin's slaves, who may have enjoyed some liberties from their owner, nonetheless took the first opportunity to leave. During the Revolution, when many slaves attempted to find their way to freedom by crossing over to British lines, the enslaved residents of Silver Bluff joined this short but important migration. As Archibald Campbell's British regiment marched toward Augusta in January 1779, his force met "90 of Golphin's Negroes" which had "deserted his Plantation, and joined the Troops under my Command."[147] Hoping for their freedom, these refugees found no friendship behind British lines. Campbell used the slaves as a bargaining chip with Galphin to dissuade him from influencing the Creeks to remain neutral in the war. The threat of his slaves' emancipation convinced Galphin, and three days later Campbell received "a penitential Letter from Golphin." Campbell sent the slaves downriver "to be preserved for Mr. Golphin, in Case he continued to act in the same friendly part toward us, during the rest of the Campaign."[148] It was almost certainly for this reason that Galphin amended his will to read, "None of the negroes may have any mourning or anything else (on account of their ingratitude)."[149] Even David George preferred freedom to bondage to his "kind" master, since he fled to Canada during the American Revolution.

As it did at Silver Bluff, the American Revolution revealed that the bonds tying Augusta together were temporary. The coming of the Revolution and the rapid disappearance of Indian traders from the Augusta landscape demonstrated the limitations of the trading company's power.

By 1780, the men who had dominated town life for forty years had largely disappeared. Death claimed many: Macartan died in 1768, John Rae in 1772, Edward Barnard and Robert Mackay in 1775, and George Galphin in 1780. Others left Augusta, such as Lachlan McGillivray, who moved to a plantation near Savannah in the 1760s and retired to his native Scotland in 1782. However, unlike the powerful families of Virginia or Massachusetts, the leaders of Augusta did not manage to transfer their legacies or social positions to their own descendants. By 1783, a new generation of men had taken over the government of Augusta and begun to remake the town into a market center for tobacco and later cotton. The lack of continuity resulted from the dislocations of war but also from Augustans' seeming inability to transfer their influence to a younger generation.[150]

The traders at Augusta, while amassing sizable estates, often did not keep that wealth within the community. Many traders kept close ties with relatives in Scotland and Ireland and transferred their property to those living across the Atlantic. William Sludders left two-thirds of his property to his siblings living in Scotland. Daniel Clark divided 2,500 pounds sterling, the bulk of his estate, between his brother and brother-in-law living in Inverness, Scotland. John Francis Williams remembered the family he left in Barbados much more generously than he did his own wife, Catherine. He left over 2000 pounds sterling to Barbadians, and only 50 pounds sterling to his widow, much to the chagrin of his former partner Mackay.[151] Lachlan McGillivray and George Galphin likewise remembered their overseas relatives.[152] These latter two men, though, also provided generously for their children by Indian wives, some of whom chose to remain in their respective towns for the duration of their lives. That each of these wills was divided among many in part might explain why the traders' wealth did not remain concentrated in Augusta from one generation to the next.

Another key factor in the disappearance of the Augusta traders was their heavy burden of debt. The Revolution's origins in Georgia began in part with a series of Indian attacks in response to the "New Purchase" of 1773. George Galphin and other Augusta traders had convinced the Cherokees to grant the British a large territory north and west of Augusta as a means of repayment of long-standing debts accrued through the deerskin trade. The traders would then use the land sales to pay off their lowcountry and British creditors. Governor James Wright of Georgia approved the measure, but the Creek Indians did not. They also claimed the lands so generously given by the Cherokees, and unhappy Creek warriors took out their frustrations on whites moving into the territory.

These events joined with Georgia Whigs' complaints against the British and formed the Revolutionary impulse in Georgia. However, the traders' debts were in part a direct result of the demands of keeping company in Georgia.

The cost of sociability composed part of the traders' debts. The shifts in the trade—fewer deer and increased competition—certainly contributed most to the traders' hardship. But the threat to their way of living was perhaps the most immediately felt. Robert Mackay's dozens of plates and expensive furniture were part of the huge debt owed to the Savannah merchant Thomas Netherclift, and they tied Mackay directly to the politics of the New Purchase. The cost of keeping company in Augusta was certainly astronomical, as evidenced by Netherclift informing Mackay of a bill for "£1538.14.1 Stlg. a very heavy sum to add to the old Ballance."[153] Only the credit afforded by the Indian trade could have allowed these Augustans to maintain their lifestyle, though even that was in danger. At that time, Netherclift hoped that the sales of lands from the proposed New Purchase would help settle the accounts, and that the free trade following the Proclamation of 1763 would be ended, allowing the large stores at Augusta to claim a proper share of the trade and make up their old debts. As Netherclift fumed, anyone who thought the trade should remain open "shoud go to the Devil." Netherclift feared, though, that "the people of England have such a notion of Monopoly . . . that I am affraid Mr Wright's sollicitations will be in vain."[154] In the end, Mackay and Netherclift got what they wanted, and the New Purchase was approved. It also eventually cost Augusta the heaviest price by severing the town from its old connections with both southeastern Indians and the British Empire.

After the Revolution, the estates of Indian traders became valuable property as Augusta became the new state capital of Georgia. The case of Robert Mackay's "White House" tract exemplified the ways in which the Augusta companies quickly collapsed in the face of the American Revolution. Mackay's son Robert went on to a successful career as a Savannah merchant and never again lived in Augusta. The house in and land on which young Robert had grown up became the property of Mackay's old friend, Andrew McLean, during the war. After his death in 1784, the White House tract was sold to pay McLean's outstanding debts to Mackay's old creditor, Thomas Netherclift. William Greenwood of Charles Town purchased the property. Greenwood quickly divided the 500 acres and sold them at a profit to Peter Carnes, Dr. John Hartford Montgomery, and Ezekial Harris. Harris further divided his share of the property to establish the town of Harrisburg around 1800, with himself as the hamlet's largest proprietor, building a large two-story house and tobacco warehouse to take advantage of the changing economy of the Augusta neighborhood. The little village's grid pattern eventually allowed its easy incorporation into the town of Augusta in the 1770s, but by 1800 the stone house owned by Mackay and whatever traces of his former residence that survived the war had been erased from the Augusta landscape.[155]

The rapidity with which the great traders vanished from Augusta was remarkable considering the central role they had played in shaping the colonial town. Once the vital connection between whites and Indians had been severed, their authority vanished along with their properties. They survived only in a few place-names such as Rae's Creek (now running through Augusta's most famous landmark, the Augusta National golf course). The severing of ties also spelled disaster for the Indians of the Southeast. The "Virginia men" who came to dominate the town devised land speculation schemes such as the Yazoo Fraud as a means of forming new wealth in Augusta. The greatest continuity lay in these new men's attitudes toward African Americans. They expanded upon the slaveholding of eighteenth-century Augusta and entrenched enslaved labor as the basis for the new town, which would be a center for the cotton boom of the early nineteenth century in the Southeast.

Augustans depended on the trading path. It was the key to their fortunes and their place atop Georgia's upcountry society. It took a revolution to undo the connection, but once the trade moved south to Pensacola and Mobile, the great trading companies vanished from the Augusta landscape. Dependent as they were on the path, Augustans did their best to maintain control over it. But the companies' dominion did not extend much beyond Augusta itself. On the path, the outcome of any individual journey remained in doubt, as traders had very little control over who might join them on their travels. The companies tried to limit access to the paths as best they could, but they had no real power to do so. Instead, Indian preferences, natural forces, and horses ruled the paths. Traders left Augusta knowing that they could only react to the challenges of the trails. They could in no way predict them.

4 / To Make the Path White and Clear: Possibilities and Problems in Southeastern Travel

It was an uncommon sight, the hatchet in the path. It was July 1752, and Thomas Bosomworth and his wife, Mary, had recently been commissioned to travel to the Creeks and resolve a dispute with the Cherokees that threatened the fresh peace between those Indian nations. The traders feared that the Bosomworths' unprecedented goal of extracting Creek concessions for a recently murdered Cherokee warrior would upset the Anglo-Creek peace. Such a development threatened the traders' profits, if not their very lives. The day after setting out from Augusta for the Creek town of Cowetas, the Bosomworths came across a "bloody Hatchett sticking right in the Path with some light coloured white Person's Hair about the Head of it." The hatchet's handle, "finely adorned with fresh Peacock's Feathers and Wood painted all over fresh with Vermilion," presented an exotic and singular appearance in southeastern history, since fresh peacock feathers were "seldom found in the Woods." Thomas Bosomworth recognized the ploy immediately as "Mean Artifice indeed," planted by the Augusta traders who "set to work all the Engines of their policy to bugbear and frighten us from executing the Commands of the Government."[1]

It was a feeble attempt. The Augusta merchants (if it was indeed they who planted the hatchet) hoped to assert their authority over the paths in the same way they asserted their authority in Augusta. In the end, however, they only revealed how little power they wielded over these crucial spaces. While the hatchet "a little intimidated Mrs. Bosomworth," the party, "still determined to proceed," simply sidestepped the object and continued on its way.² The traders' ploy revealed their powerlessness to prevent anyone from traveling the Georgia-Creek corridor or any of the other trading routes that crossed southeastern North America. Throughout the eighteenth century, travelers needed the paths as they were the only means of navigating the Southeast. Paths therefore became spaces where strangers found each other, leading to an ongoing dissolution and reformation of identity. The Bosomworths' journey, an effort to improve their standing in colonial society and lend credibility to their ambitious land claims, was but one of many such new beginnings that the paths afforded—status was not fixed along the trails. The Bosomworths, Indians, slaves, and the traders themselves all took advantage of the openness of paths to remake themselves in southeastern society.

Needed by all inland southeasterners and governed by none of them, paths were spaces where power was decentralized and therefore available in some measure to everyone. First and foremost, paths were the only reliable means of navigating the region; to get anywhere required the use of these well-worn paths. Because of this reality, paths were the crucial connection between Indian and European towns and made possible all the myriad physical, political, economic, and cultural interactions that defined southeastern history. They were thus a temporary home to peoples from all parts of eastern North America between Lakes Ontario and Pontchartrain. These were not simple roads: paths were areas of constant contest where identity and status were in constant flux, and the future was anything but certain.

Negotiating such spaces required adaptation on the part of the Southeast's most recent inhabitants. While Indians had been living with the realities of the paths for millennia, British sojourners and African Americans found new opportunities and new perils along the routes. British traders first and foremost had to adapt to a system of frequent, long-range travel unlike the roads of Britain or the American coast and had to accommodate themselves to the needs of weather and horses. More important, they had to adapt to spaces where English notions of property and status did not apply. By necessity, Europeans had to live by a system of personal property that was often closer to Indian ideas than English ones, and found numerous opportunities and rewards for doing so. Africans in many cases especially benefited from the mutable nature of property along the paths: if they could learn to travel these winding routes, they could change their status from property to person.

As important as adapting to the physical path, however, was adapting to the metaphorical path. The path was the central metaphor in southeastern relations and one that had to be grasped by traders and governors alike. A "white, clear, and straight" path in the context of Anglo-Indian talks signified peace and amity, an ideal route free of dangers and open equally to all sides. Materially, southeastern Indians represented friendly paths as strings of white beads. In 1758, Cherokee headmen reminded Governor William Henry Lyttleton of South Carolina that "the String of white Beads is your own Talk formerly when the Path was white and clear." Recently, however, relations had soured and the Indians gave Lyttleton a "String [of] black Beads" to "shew that the Path is foul and bloody."[3] Violence "bloodied" the path, making friendly communication more difficult and increasing hostility and mistrust on both sides. The goal of much Indian diplomacy, particularly for Augusta's leading trade partners, the Creeks, was to maintain a "white" path—friendship without compulsion extended to all Europeans, be they French, British, or Spanish. For the Creeks, the use of the trading path, a passive metaphor, reflected this desire to maintain their neutrality in the face of European conflicts. To ally themselves too closely would risk transforming the neutral path to a binding "covenant chain."

When the British hoped to replace the ambiguous path with the more clearly defined "chain," they quickly realized the breach of protocol. British governors new to the Southeast brought their familiarity with Iroquois diplomacy, referencing the "chain of friendship" when negotiating with southern Indians.[4] Very seldom did Indians echo the phrase, for they had long heard from the French that the English planned to make slaves of them all, preparing literal chains for their women and children. British governors who spoke too much of the "chain of friendship" risked calling these rumors to mind and further entrenching the association between British friendship and Indian enslavement. And the Creeks, who had long been involved in the Indian slave trade with the English, needed no French reminders of Britain's willingness to enslave Indians.[5] An effective communicator such as Georgia's Governor Henry Ellis quickly learned to adapt his speech to suit southern tastes. When Ellis arrived in Georgia in 1757, he greeted numerous Indian emissaries, and his talks frequently included references to the "chain of friendship." Only one Indian that year—out of dozens who talked with Ellis—employed the phrase. Ellis probably recognized his error, and even used French tactics to his advantage when he warned the Creeks that "[the French] had already begun to make Chains" for Creek hands.[6] By the end of his Georgia tenure in 1760, Ellis had completely abandoned the chain metaphor and referred to Anglo-Indian friendship solely in terms of the path.[7]

Ellis had little choice; Indians and especially Creeks preferred the path metaphor because it matched their political agenda of neutrality. From the 1710s onward, the Creeks had adopted a policy of commerce without commitment toward all Europeans.[8] As the Gun Merchant of Okchai reminded an English agent in 1757, "the Path was open both to French and English."[9] The Spanish may as easily have been added. In addition, the Creeks' openness toward outsiders extended to Indian refugees, as well, and Creek country became home to Yuchis, Yamasees, Shawnees, Chickasaws, and numerous others at various times during the eighteenth and nineteenth centuries.[10] The path metaphor accurately described Creek ambition: to have access to the world without being coerced by any part of it.

This policy benefited those Creeks who thus could access major pathways. Anglo-Indian trade relations in particular helped some Creek headmen attain considerable influence in the decentralized and town-oriented political world of Creek towns. The rise of Coweta as an early Creek town of influence, its later eclipse by Okfuskee and Okchai, and the still later rise of Little Tallassee after 1763 all depended partly on these towns' roles as British gateways to Creek country. The headmen of these towns recognized the political influence that access to British trade goods afforded them and contested among themselves the paths' courses as a means of defending that influence. Such was the power of paths that a man such as Emistisiguo of Little Tallassee could turn disputed trade routes to his personal advantage and increase his influence within the Creek confederacy.[11] Such "new men" in Indian politics had their closest analogues in the Augusta deerskin trade-merchants, whose trade connections gave them a great deal of political influence in Anglo-Indian affairs.[12]

Creek policy also meant that its paths were open to enemies as well as friends. As the Chickasaws' 1737 map demonstrated, paths were routes by which Indians conducted trade and war. The Creeks' frequent wars and the politics of their recent immigrants meant that trading paths were also frequented by enemies from as far away as the Great Lakes and Ohio Valley. The path between the Upper Creek town of Coosa and the Chickasaws served as a constant example of how easily paths turned from peaceful white to violent red. The Chickasaw-Choctaw wars, ongoing throughout most of the eighteenth century, made the Coosa-Chickasaw route dangerous as early as Thomas Nairne's 1708 journey to the Mississippi River. Nairne, in company with twenty-six Chickasaw warriors, opted to go "the straightest road," even though "it lay along close by the Chacta Country." Nairne opted to hazard the route rather than go "any of the other roundabout wayes which being safer are therefor more frequented."[13] In addition to Choctaw hostility, the Chickasaws faced constant threats from the Choctaw-allied French and French-allied northern Indians, especially in times of Anglo-French war. Further endangering the route were the sometimes anti-British and anti-Chickasaw sentiments of Upper Creek warriors, who in 1756 threatened to destroy the path entirely by making war on the Chickasaws. So bloody was the path that the trader Jerome Courtonne promised his Chickasaw clients that "in Case some Creeks should make War with us and stop the Path, I would go to the C[h]erokees and open a Path for them there."[14] The Chickasaws, for their part, resented such Creek meddling with their trade and bluntly informed the Upper Creeks that "we shall never be obliged to take no round about Path to go and see our Friends, the English."[15]

The Chickasaw path, connected to political events hundreds or even thousands of miles away, provided a small arena for continental conflict. The Wolf of Muccolasses, a headman of the Alabama Upper Creeks, explained the reasons for the path's dangers in 1757. When the French offered scalp bounties for the Chickasaws and their British allies, Choctaw warriors "for a trifling Consideration" took "both red and white scalps... without Distinction which the Chickesaw Path can well confirm by Bones remaining to this Day."[16] Even members of a supposedly friendly nation could bloody a path, given the decentralized nature of authority among southeastern Indians. Thus in 1755 two Chickasaw traders bore the brunt of an unsuccessful Cherokee war party. According to a Creek informant, the Cherokee warriors had gone against the Choctaws, "which proving fruitless they inclined a little towards our [Upper Creek] Nation with a View to kill some of us (the Creeks) but Meeting with the said two White Men, at the great Hill in the Chekesaw Path killed them."[17] The result of political circumstances, none of these acts was completely random. Taken together, they amounted to a general pattern where enemies were frequently fellow travelers.

For Europeans, the reward was worth the risk. Paths were opportunities for Europeans, a means of advancing oneself in the supposedly "lawless" Indian interior. Those who ventured to Indian towns frequently sought a better station for themselves than was offered in British settlements.[18] These plans included the grand schemes of Christian Gottlieb Priber's "Kingdom of Paradise" and Alexander Cuming's ambition to become viceroy of the Cherokees.[19] Even William De Brahm, who had earned a comfortable living as surveyor general of Georgia, could hope to "make himself a great Man" among the Cherokees.[20] The opportunities to be found along the paths formed the core of the nineteenth-century rags-to-riches legend of Lachlan McGillivray. McGillivray, it was said, had built his entire fortune on a single trading knife.[21] All of these people owed their fortunes or failures to Indian goodwill, but what they saw and hoped to exploit was the path's ability to transform one's status. European notions of property (and their attendant degrees of social standing) weakened on the trails. That uncertainty shaped much of southeastern history and acted as an agent in these men's search for new lives among Indians.

But just like Henry Ellis had to adapt to southeastern paths, so did other Europeans. Despite the seeming openness of the paths, numerous forces circumscribed travel in the Southeast. At the most basic level, simply knowing where to go was a precondition of setting off. Numerous routes crossed the region, and a wrong turn could cost a traveler days or even a life. Even when headed in the right direction, a person faced the elements, difficult terrain, and the sometimes terrifying prospect of fording a river at high flood. Added to that were the limitations of horse travel—one could move neither farther nor faster than one's mount. Travelers were also bound to human history through the series of Indian and European wars that frequently occasioned hostile encounters. For traders, the debt-based nature of the trade was its own limitation. They were bound by their creditors and their licenses to make the annual journey from Augusta to their Indian store, and the goods they carried were rarely their own.

The first and most important skill Europeans had to develop was learning where to go in the first place. Paths made it possible to move across long distances with some assurance of getting where one was going, but only if you already had some idea of how to get there. "The path" may have been a central metaphor in Anglo-Indian diplomacy, but no single path led directly from Indian towns to British ones. Even though paths were often marked, the web of trade routes and hunting paths proved daunting to inexperienced travelers. A few main roads did persist through the eighteenth century: the "Lower Creek Path" from Augusta to Coweta, the "Upper Creek Path" from Augusta to Okfuskee, and the "Dividing Paths" from Charles Town to the Cherokees. However, these intersected numerous small hunting paths which could lead a traveler far away from the known world of the main roads.

Maps—those increasingly popular European tools— were of no help. Southeastern travel proved frightening for map-bearing newcomers such as William Mylne. Even in the relatively long-settled district north of Augusta, Mylne was fearful that "I would loose myself for it is very difficult to travel in the woods, there are so many paths that intersect one another that ... one may go God knows where."[22] When Mylne consulted his map on a journey from Charles Town to Georgetown, South Carolina, the rustling of the paper startled Mylne's horse, and he spent an hour retrieving the items lost during the horse's mad gallop through the woods.[23] Mylne, new to the Southeast, understandably feared the unknown of a vast interior, but even those who spent their lives on the paths knew only small sections of them.

Even experienced traders did not always feel comfortable straying from the paths they knew. The most detailed maps of the southeastern interior only demonstrated the limits of traders' knowledge. The Stuart-Purcell Map of 1775, for example, offered no information other than what lay immediately along trade routes. All else remained something of a mystery. Owing to the uncertainty, John Pettygrew, a veteran Creek trader, refused a 1759 request to travel from Augusta to the Cherokees, admitting that "he did not know the way."[24] Pettygrew's reluctance was understandable, given the recent experience of Thomas Ross, one of Pettygrew's fellow Creek traders at Augusta. In 1756 Ross had stepped off the Coweta-Augusta path and onto a "Hunting Path," where he remained lost "seven Days and seven Nights." Ross's week-long wandering left him "sickly" and "very much swelled" in his "Body and Legs." He was spared starvation only by the chance discovery of "an Ear of Corn in the Path upon which I lived the seven Days."[25]

But knowing one's course was but the first part of travel. Path travel required a great deal of skill and endurance. A party could travel only twenty to twenty-five miles a day on average, making use of the numerous campsites that dotted the trails and all the while exposed to the vagaries of wind and weather. When Daniel Pepper described the route between the Lower and Upper Creeks in 1756, he noted that he was "very much fatigued" by the "very bad stoney and hilly Path which makes it tedious."[26] The Cherokee trader Anthony Dean likewise painted a bleak picture of southeastern travel to justify his colleagues' reliance on rum. He maintained that "there are no People ... that a little Spirit is more necessary for than the poor Traders" whose "Journies lie over Hills, and Dales, Rivers and Creeks, subject to Want, Danger, and all the Inclemencies of Weather."[27] Dean's story indicates that traders were inclined to emphasize the difficulty of travel, as it served as a defense against greater regulation of their trade.

While traveling, traders were constantly aware of how little control they had over their own lives, their personal comfort and safety dependent on chance meetings with friends or enemies and their economic future dependent on preserving goods from damage in transit. The weeks-long journeys, "the great Fatigue of carrying up Goods," defined the traders' role on the paths.[28] They were little more than vessels for carrying trade items and skins back and forth. Goods had to survive each leg of the journey to ensure the traders' continuation in both Indian esteem and economic standing. These men were often "great Sufferers as their Goods are often damaged; in carrying up, the Guns are often broken, and the Leather they receive in Exchange for Goods sometimes gets wet, and is spoiled in coming down."[29] Their goods were the most valuable property, even more so than the traders' bodies, a fact made evident during a thunderstorm, when "all our skins and bedding were cast over the packs of merchandize to prevent them from being injured by the deluge of rain."[30]

Traders also suffered from distant weather patterns; flooded rivers were a constant nuisance, if not a peril, for southeastern travelers. Unlike the Savannah River boatmen or the merchants of Augusta, for whom rivers were important connectors, traders on the path regarded rivers primarily as obstacles. The numerous river systems of the Southeast, with their regular flooding, offered the traveler a harrowing and unpredictable experience with each crossing. Adair described the path from Augusta to Fort Toulouse as "a great deal of hilly ground, and bad rivers, very full and rapid in the winter: Insomuch that, in our trading way, we have great hardships in crossing them."[31] Bosomworth at one point had to delay his mission because "the Creeks or rivulets were swelled so high with the late Rains, we could proceed no farther."[32] Moreover, the length of river courses and their origins in the Appalachian Mountains meant that floods could arise in areas where not a raindrop fell. As Adair recounted on one of his trips, three times he was delayed "on account of a very uncommon and sudden flow of the rivers, without any rain."[33]

The difficulty of travel, however, would have largely been familiar to the majority of Indian traders, even if they were setting out on their first journey. Many of them came from Ireland and Scotland, where travel was equally difficult. Eighteenth-century England had developed a system of regular roads and stagecoach routes, but many eighteenth-century roads on the "Celtic fringe" remained muddy, rocky, and difficult footpaths. As one commissioner of roads described the early highways of Scotland, they were "merely the tracks of black cattle and horses, intersected by numerous rapid streams, which being frequently swollen into torrents by heavy rains, rendered them dangerous or impassable."[34] Eighteenth-century Ireland experienced a similar development, with regular stagecoach routes in place only by the end of the eighteenth century.[35]

What would have been new were the Indian solutions to these problems. Facing raging southeastern rivers, traders turned to Indian material culture. The navigation of such capricious rivers relied on small, temporary watercraft built to Indian specifications. Traders rigged a leather skin with a frame of saplings and loaded their cargoes into these "leathorn canoes."[36] The traders would then swim the river, pushing the skin boats ahead of them—a practice learned from southeastern Indians, who had been crossing the same rivers for centuries.[37] Thomas Nairne had first observed the Chickasaws doing this in 1708, reporting that "to see every man make a Boat of his bed, and therein carry over Cloaths Arms and Ammunition very dry, was a thing I had not seen before."[38] The crossings were not always smooth, as trader Jeremiah Knott discovered in 1735. "In crossing Coosaw with his Goods, his Canoe was overset, and he lost in Goods to the Value of Two Hundred Weight of Deer Skins."[39]

What would have been even newer was the company one kept on southeastern paths. Even friendly travel would have required adaptation and conflict. Sojourners commonly traveled the paths with Indian companions. Headmen and warriors frequently traveled with Europeans in the eighteenth century. As the century wore on, Indians found ready employment as guards and scouts for packhorse trains.[40] While no packhorseman or other sojourner recorded his opinion of his Indian companions, one can reasonably suppose that the trek was not always smooth. The long history of European and Indian travel was marked by each culture asserting the superiority of its own way of moving from place to place. Travel tested European and Indian attachment to their respective cultures, and frequently served to harden cultural attitudes rather than lead to any sense of sharing.[41]

But sojourners also traveled with an even more constant Indian presence—having to adapt to Indian ideas of property. Since paths were meeting places for all the peoples of eastern North America, travelers could potentially encounter just about anyone. This fact was a key influence on life along the trails, forcing Europeans to adapt to an Indian world of goods and act according to Indian notions of property. But traders were also tasked with upholding the system of private property emanating from Augusta and points east. Every item they carried was, after all, carefully noted in Augusta store ledger books. Caught between these two systems, European and African sojourners had to adapt in numerous ways, but also found numerous opportunities in spaces where property was defined mostly by who was carrying it.

Indian concepts of property played a major role on southeastern paths. Indians recognized personal property—their guns, ammunition, and the products of their hunts, which included goods purchased with deerskins. However, Indian notions of property were more fluid and less certain than Britons'. Indians recognized each other's property but paid little regard to the amassing of personal property and wealth. Southeastern Indians, like other native North Americans, frequently "borrowed" from each other on the promise that the favor would be returned. Reciprocity and the welfare of the town took precedence over an individual's material comfort. By the end of the eighteenth century, Creeks (typically métis children of Indian traders) began amassing private estates and altering their view of "borrowing" to mirror the European concept of "stealing." But this process simply underscored that southeasterners were individually capable of selecting which system worked best for them.[42]

But sojourners also labored under the burdens of European notions of property. In addition to the physical challenges of traveling, there was the primary, though invisible, limitation of the deerskin trade's organization. The nature of the Indian trade imposed its own limits on those who carried deerskins from Indian towns to Augusta and returned with British manufactures. First was the economics of the trade itself. Traders maintained a store in a particular town and were forbidden from trading with Indians from any other town, under penalty of forfeiture of their goods and licenses. Even the licenses did not belong to them. The storekeepers and trading companies of Augusta held the official licenses, which meant that most traders were employees of Augusta firms rather than independent. The trade itself, conducted largely on debt and credit between Indians, traders, and merchants, ensured that one year's deerskins would go toward the purchase of next year's goods.[43]

The imperative to move flowed from the debt-based nature of the deerskin trade, since most Indian traders were not independent, but merely factors employed by the large Augusta firms. A list of licensees to Creek towns in 1761 revealed few independent traders among that nation. In that year, the governor and council of Georgia decided that "the Towns in the Indian Nations should be divided among the several Traders" and disproportionately favored the large Augusta houses. Out of thirty-eight Creek towns named, only William Fraser and James Cussings held individual licenses for their towns. The rest belonged to former members of the "Augusta Company," Macartan and Campbell, Cook and Company, and the various associates of William Trewin and Company (whose membership included former Augusta Company member William Sludders).[44] Most of those who held licenses lived in Augusta; thus reformers such as Edmond Atkin lamented "that Licences on the present footing may as well be given to Men living in Cheapside."[45] A person's continuation in the trade depended on his ability to satisfy the debts he owed to merchant-traders, as well as his ability to get along with his Indian customers.

Even the handful of independent traders felt the influence of Augusta companies. When the large firms chose to ignore an official ordinance or regulation of the trade, "the less Traders must of necessity follow the Way of the greater or they have no Business here."[46] If one trader sold rum, for example, another must do likewise for fear of losing his town's skins to another trader. John Elliott, a newcomer to the Cherokee trade in the 1750s, discovered the pressures of competition when he found that "he must either follow the Multitude, endanger his own Safety, or find some other Way of living, which at that Time he could not safely do, in respect of his Credit from his Merchants, without hurting both himself and them."[47] A trader had little say in what he traded or for how much.

Sojourners were expected, however, to defend "their" property against the uncertainties of southeastern travel. Traders earned the highest praise from their fellows when they suffered violence in the protection of their goods. When Samuel Benn's caravan came under attack near the Cherokee town of Natalee, Benn told his assailants that "the Goods that I have . . . are for the Upper [Cherokee] Towns" and refused the Indians any part of his packs.[48] Benn acted in a manner would have pleased James Adair in particular. In his *History*, Adair praised another trader who, "being intrusted by his employer with a cargo of goods," violently resisted a Creek Indian who threatened his cargo and "opposed lawless force by force."[49] More than bravery, defense of goods was likely economic self-interest, as well, since the sojourner owed someone in Augusta a lot of deerskins for those goods.

Sojourners' boasts recognized an important reality—the system of property that governed traders' lives was real only in Augusta and in English courts. On the paths, sojourners had to grapple with the fact that English property was no certain thing. Prideful traders usually gave no voice to their uncertainties; other southeastern travelers were not so stoic. John Ross, who left Augusta not knowing whether he would return, was a rare case and was derided for his lack of bravery (see below). However, William Bartram, a complete outsider to the Southeast's peoples and places, best expressed the fear of meeting a stranger on the paths. In the early 1770s, Bartram made a trip southward from Savannah. On the path to East Florida, past "the utmost frontier of white settlement," Bartram met a Seminole Indian traveling in the opposite direction. "I never before this was afraid of an Indian," Bartram claimed, "but at this time I must own that my spirits were quite agitated: I saw at once, that being unarmed I was in his power, and having now but a few moments to prepare, I resigned myself entirely to the will of the Almighty, trusting to his mercies for my preservation."[50] In Anglo-American settlements, roads were part of an ordered, hierarchical landscape, where all travelers knew both each other and their respective roles.[51] The loss of that comfort nettled travelers along the paths.

Paths were thus not like the typical colonial road. European colonists moved through known landscapes where an ongoing series of face-to-face encounters made everyone known to each other. While settlers marked their status with the usual combination of dress and demeanor, the context of social relations was stable enough that rank could easily be reformed at every moment of encounter. Even the roads themselves reinforced property-holders' status by respectfully circumventing fields.[52] Along southeastern paths, every traveler was far from home and the usual markers of status. The only marks were those things that travelers and traders carried with them.

As a matter of survival, southeastern travelers had to quickly recognize the attitude of an approaching party. Such recognition required some knowledge of the variety of Indian customs and costumes that prevailed east of the Mississippi. At first sight, it was frequently difficult to know whether an approaching party was friendly or hostile. A Creek hunting party "discover'd some strange Indians upon the Path [and] th[e]y could not tele wither they ware Savannas or Cherekees," but they did notice that the strangers "ware in a war Dress."[53] Adair told the story of a 1749 ride between the Flint and Ocmulgee rivers, which demonstrated the uncertainty of travel. He met a party of Shawnee Indians, whose hostility Adair could not determine until they were close enough for him to notice that "instead of carrying their bow and quiver over their shoulder, as is the traveling custom, they held the former in their left hand, bent." After convincing the party that he was an "English Chikkasah" at the head of a large war party, Adair managed to escape only to encounter another Indian party on the same path. Ready to flee into a nearby swamp, Adair recognized the approaching Indians as friendly Creek headmen returning from Charles Town. Relieved, he greeted his friends and warned them of the Shawnees, advising them to leave the path and "go home through the woods, to prevent a larger body of the lurking enemy from spoiling them."[54]

To identify others' intentions, southeasterners frequently relied on trade goods and personal property as markers of hostility. Personal property assisted the navigation of southeastern paths, in some cases quite literally, as when two British deserters carried with them "a large tin Pot on the Side of which was laid down the Path [a map]" to Fort Toulouse.[55] Indians recognized their own goods and those of their fellows, and finding one's personal possessions in the hands of another party identified former attackers and targets of revenge. In 1737, several Upper Creeks killed three men from Spanish Florida, when the Creeks "found a Gun belonging to one of their People, who had been killed with his Family some time ago, for which reason they killed them all that Night."[56] When three Savannah Indians robbed the house of white settlers, James Glen hoped that "an iron Pot, a frying Pan, some Shirts, some Sheets, and a blue Cloth Pettycoat.... may perhaps help to discover them."[57] A Cherokee warrior in 1752 explained his killing of a white man by the victim's association with stolen property. "He saw a horse that the Creeks took away when they killed one of his Relations, and thought then he should have Satisfaction, not knowing there was any white Man in the House."[58] Recognizing enemies at a distance, however, was of only so much advantage. Traders had to also adopt measures that protected them from all potential threats.

As with the trade boat, traders relied on a specialized form of transport to carry their business overland, the horse caravan. The hardships of travel, combined with political uncertainty, made large horse caravans the choice of southeastern traders. Supplying an entire village with a year's worth of goods required anywhere from sixty to a hundred horses, guided by a party of four or more men, each one armed to the teeth to ward off attacks. As Nairne described his company, "Our camp was not much unlike a crew of Gipsies, only that we were all armed men."[59] On a journey through the Lower Creek towns in 1773, with the Creeks and Choctaws at war, Bartram chose "for the better convenience and security" to join "company with a caravan of traders."[60] Bartram's companions, in "humanity and friendship," refused to let him travel alone, "saying I must not be left alone to perish in the wilderness."[61] The company of traders, maintained by a common bond of uncertainty, provided a sense of community, and the presence of arms gave the caravan a paramilitary aspect that was reflected in traders' choice of dress.

Traders' dress indicated that they considered paths to be separate and distinct spaces that required a certain costume. Traders marked themselves as adventurers with their choice in apparel. Though in some sense a practical matter, martial dress came to mark those who traveled the paths. On his death in 1757, Daniel Clark distributed horses, money, and property to a multitude of relatives, friends, and charitable societies. For traders John McGillivray and William Sludders, he reserved his "wearing apparel, riding saddle, bridle, furniture, swords, belts, guns, and pistols."[62] Sludders, for his part, distributed his property to his old partners John Rae, Lachlan McGillivray, and George Galphin, but he singled out one Nicholas Swarts to take his "best riding horse, saddle... my pistols and gun."[63] The Augusta merchant Isaac Barksdale remembered his partner John Rae's children according to their professions. Rae's daughter and eldest son, who remained in Augusta, each received money and property. Rae's son William, a trader to the Okfuskees, earned Barksdale's "gun and pistols."[64] Each of these heirs undoubtedly had their own weaponry, but there was likely a symbolic importance in passing one's own arms to another generation of Indian traders.

That packhorsemen wore a certain costume was perhaps evident from the unfortunate experience of William Bonar. Bonar, a surveyor and cartographer, had accompanied Daniel Pepper during his 1756–57 agency among the Creeks. Pepper hoped to use Bonar's skills to scout and map the French Fort Toulouse, and "privately sent him in Disguise as a Packhorseman to take a View of the Alabama Fort."[65] Pepper's idea of a disguise, though, consisted of "the very worst Cloaths he [Bonar] had" and mounted on "his worst Horse, leaving his favourite one in the Yard at the Oakchoy's."[66] While Bonar may have been captured for any number of reasons, his dress may have been a factor. Based on other descriptions, a packhorseman would not have presented so shabby an appearance. They had too much pride in themselves and in their horses to let themselves appear foolish before either French competitors or Indian clients.

Despite the impressive shows of arms that traders displayed for oncoming parties, there was no ignoring the fact that the traders' horses were the real authority in southeastern travel. For as much as the pressure of debt urged on the traders, they could move only as fast as their horses. The packhorse trains themselves lurched forward at an uneven pace, alternating between relentless progress and long periods of rest. William Bartram found their rhythms odd enough to remark on them.

The trains "seldom decamp until after the sun is high and hot" and come to camp "frequently in the middle of the afternoon, which is the pleasantest time of day for travelling." In the few hours they moved, "the chief drives with the crack of his whip, and a whoop or a shriek, which rings through the forests and plains, speaks in Indian, commanding them to proceed... keeping up a brisk and constant trot, which is incessantly urged and continued as long as the miserable creatures are able to move forward."[67] The pace was too much for Bartram's horse, which he had to sell for a fresh one in order to keep up.

No contest was more important or more common than the ongoing battle of wills between traders and their packhorses. These men took great pride in their ability to control and manage their animals. Bartram no doubt flattered one Cherokee trader when he noted with awe the trader's command over his horses. On seeing the trader, the horses "assembled together from all quarters... [and] saluted him with the shrill neighings of gratitude... as soon as their lord and master strewed crystalline salty bait on the hard beaten ground."[68] Horses who refused to show such deference were punished with "threats, the discipline of the whip and other common abuse." If such tactics failed, a packhorseman would resort to biting an animal on its ear, "when instantly the furious strong creature, trembling, stands perfectly still until he is loaded."[69]

In their attachment to animal cruelty, southern sojourners allied themselves with their more northern counterparts, the voyageurs. The voyageurs' torture of sled dogs, however, represented an early modern attachment to all things bodily and a more modern attachment to offending the bourgeois sensibilities of their employers who sometimes traveled with them.[70] Packhorse trains in the Southeast rarely included Augusta merchants, so the southeastern sojourners' treatment of horses was likely intended for a different audience. It was to demonstrate their mastery over their mounts and thus was directed at Indian companions, interested outsiders like Bartram, and the horses themselves. In this way, the sojourners shared other Anglo-Americans' conception of the ideal traveler as one who remained in firm control of his horses at all times.[71]

A constant march through the heat of a Gulf Coast summer quickly wore out packhorses. Bartram, himself tormented by the heat and biting flies, found a great deal of sympathy for the animals. Only a few days into the journey, the horses, "through fatigue of constant traveling, heat of the climate and season, were tired and dispirited." They thus "came to camp sooner than usual and started later the next day." Even so, the following day they traveled "but a few miles; the heat and the burning flies tormenting our horses to such a degree, as to excite compassion even in the hearts of pack-horsemen ... the head, neck and shoulders of the leading horses were continually in a gore of blood" from the fly bites. The day after that, they "halted at noon, being unable longer to support ourselves under such grievances."[72]

As Bartram discovered, the needs of horses dictated the pace of southeastern history. Daniel Pepper, hurriedly dispatched from South Carolina to calm Anglo-Creek relations in response to the Ogeechee incident in 1756, was delayed by his horses: "a very tedious journey occasioned by the great Drought which was so excessive upon the Path that the Pack Horses ... straggled away for want of Water, and obliged me to lye too for two Days till they were hunted up."[73] In some cases, delays could be extraordinary, both in duration and in importance. In 1746, James Glen of Carolina charged John Vann with carrying a large load of presents to win Choctaw affection during their revolt against the French. Glen hoped for a diplomatic coup, winning over France's strongest Indian allies, but the presents never arrived (and whether they would have done much good is debatable). In the investigation into the matter, Vann tried to exonerate himself by blaming his horses. Traveling in February proved too difficult, for "the horses grew lean and tir'd and could not proceed." Vann was therefore "under the necessity of lying by with them until the Spring, when by fresh food they might recover flesh, and strength."[74]

The deerskin trade involved more than the Indian consumption of British goods and British consumption of Indian leather. It also consumed a great many horses. Estimates of how many horses varied: in 1735, the leading deerskin merchants in Charles Town claimed that "Eight hundred Horses are yearly Employed," while in 1740 William Stephens of Georgia asserted that "above two thousand Horses" made their way to Augusta each spring.[75] Given forty-five Creek towns, forty-two Cherokee towns, and eleven Chickasaw towns, with even a modest figure of fifty horses for each and allowing that trains may have served more than one village, one may well assume that two or three thousand horses walked the Southeast each year.[76]

These yearly numbers needed continual replenishment, for packhorses did not last very long. Traders kept no records of how many horses they used, or for how long, but a packhorse probably lasted no more than three to six years. Stagecoach horses in Britain, similarly used to traveling long distances at a constant speed, could work only three years in the heavier traffic near London, or six years in outlying areas.[77] This was consistent with Bartram's experience in the Southeast; his horse, he said, "which had served me faithfully almost three years, having carried me on his back at least six thousand miles, was . . . almost worn out."[78] In short, traders as a group needed hundreds of new horses every year to transport their goods. Many traders supplied their trains from their own private stocks. Bartram recorded one visit to a trader's "horse-stamp" near the Cherokee town of Keowee. In a remote glen, the trader kept "a large squadron of those useful creatures."[79] Adair claimed that the Creek and Chickasaw traders likewise kept horses near their towns, where the riverbanks "abounded with great brakes of winter-canes.—The foliage of which is always green, and hearty food for horses and cattle. The traders used to raise there flocks of an hundred, and a hundred and fifty excellent horses."[80] Indeed, Augusta traders used horses as a secondary source of income. In 1763 John Rae advertised the sale of a "parcel of likely mares and horses of the Chickesaw breed."[81] The next year, Lachlan McGillivray offered "a Number of Mares, Stallions, and Geldings, of the Chickesaw blood" and was willing to furnish "any gentleman that may chuse to put a stock of that kind upon a plantation or island, and captains of vessels trading to the West-Indies."[82] Adair cautioned, however, that "a person runs too great a risk to buy any to take them out of the country, because, every spring-season most of them make for their native range."

Given the value of horses in the trade, it is small wonder that traders would supplement their incomes in this way. Macartan and Campbell's store ledger provided some glimpse of the horse trade along the paths and its value to its participants. In 1762–63, the going rate for a packhorse was about thirty-five pounds currency. John Buckles and Company paid this price for two horses "put into commssn. in the Chickesaws" in August 1762 and for ten other horses in that same month.[83] A year later, the price was the same, as trader James McQueen paid this price for sixteen horses in July 1763. At that time, one packhorse was worth the same amount as fifty pounds of dressed deerskins.[84] As few as five or six horses could go a long way, then, to helping a trader make ends meet. Although cheaper than riding horses, packhorses were a solid business so long as the trade continued.[85]

Looking at the activities of Samuel Paine reveals that certain traders could make a lot of money just by focusing on the horse trade. Paine was an employee of John Buckles and Company, traders to the Chickasaws and a firm heavily involved in the transport of horses in the Southeast.[86] In June 1764, Paine make a tidy sum by selling six horses to his employers, netting himself two hundred ten pounds credit at Macartan and

Campbell's store.[87] More than a horse seller, Paine also earned his wages "for horse hunting from 20th July to 22d Sept." in 1762.[88] Despite the tidy sums he made in the horse trade, Paine was not always the best judge of horses. He was one of the two men who had Macartan and Campbell cover their gambling debts "Lost at a Race."[89]

While mastery of horses and protection of property served their creditors' interests, many sojourners learned to use their knowledge of paths' uncertain definitions of property to their own advantage. Traders and packhorsemen did not always accept the prescribed limits of their world. They clearly felt aggrieved on occasion that, while they faced the uncertainties of southeastern travel, wealth tended to concentrate in the hands of Augusta and Charles Town merchants. Horse theft, along with other clandestine enterprises, gave traders some power over their employers. Provided with mobile and uncertain forms of property, enterprising and often unscrupulous traders managed to create alternate paths to wealth than those set by headmen and great merchants. Horses provided a crucial link in this largely hidden side of the deerskin trade.

Whatever English maps may have claimed, sojourners recognized that they were leaving the jurisdiction of English law when they moved past Augusta and into the world of trails and Indian towns. The lack of defined political and property borders fostered an attitude of personal autonomy among traders. One of the traders' most common traits was a stubborn independence in the face of British authority. Upon the urging of the commander at Fort Loudon, John Elliott refused to move away from Overhill Cherokees, even when his life was threatened by souring Anglo-Cherokee relations. Elliot would "have his own Way," lamented Captain Raymond Demere, "and does not want to be controlled by no body."[90] John Williams, who illegally traded rum with the Cherokees, reportedly told those Indians that "he values not the Governors either of So. Carolina and Georgia that it is what and how he pleases to trade."[91] Richard Street, a packhorseman among the Creeks, did Williams one better, and boasted that "he was not subject to any King and had nothing to do with any King." When informed that his words were "treason and more than your Life is worth," Street replied that "he never paid Tribute to any King, and had not any King at all."[92]

In the case of horses, traders frequently turned this sense of independence into personal advantage. Lowcountry residents early recognized the connection between packhorse trains and horse thieves when they noted that more horses seemed to leave Charles Town than returned there. The *South Carolina Gazette* in 1739 voiced the "many and daily

Complaints of Horse-stealing, occasioned either by Pack-horse-men and others picking up Horses in the Settlements and selling them in the Indian Countries."[93] Indians also suffered losses at the hands of traders. Thomas Bosomworth had to address a number of Creek complaints regarding stolen horses. Malatchi and Chiggili, two headmen of the Cowetas, pressed Bosomworth on the matter "of the white People stealing of the Indians' Horses, which made the Indians steal the white People's in Return." The Lower Creeks had heard of a number of their horses spotted in Augusta yards and forced Bosomworth to promise "he would take care to see them restored."[94]

From the 1740s on, Indians, Carolinians, and Georgians continually stole each others' horses, taking advantage of mobility and distance. Free-ranging horses made easy targets, and the lack of brands, the difficulty of identifying stolen horses, and often the desire for revenge created an ongoing black market for horses during most of the eighteenth century.[95] Traders, who needed horses more than almost anybody else, necessarily formed a part of this network. As the trader Anthony Dean wrote in 1751, "It is no Wonder, when every Horse Stealer can screen himself here from Justice ... which could not be if the Trade was regulated, and proper Officers kept here to see Justice done."[96] Horse thefts inspired the South Carolina Regulators to riot because they were unhappy with the loosely defined notions of property existing in the backcountry.[97] Indeed, Regulator Patrick Calhoun's early introduction to the southeastern economy came in the form of a Cherokee attack on his neighbors, and he went to the Cherokees where he suspected "thire Head Men by words endivering to clear themselves, of thire young fellows misconduct, both of killing some white People, & stealing of Hoarses."[98]

The case of John Branham illustrated the difficulty in distinguishing between horse thieves, horse traders, and Indian traders. Branham, though not a trader, had nonetheless taken up residence among the Cherokees and had earned native scorn for theft and other misbehavior. In 1755 the Cherokee trader James May carried a Carolina warrant for Branham's arrest, but could not seize Branham because of the interposition of the same Indians who had made the complaint. These men explained that they "talked to Branham and he has promised to be good and there should be no more bad Talks of him."[99] Tossitee, a Cherokee headman, promised May that "any Whiteman or Indian that misses or has missed their Horses he'l take care to see, if in Branham's Range" and, if so, "they shall be delivered."[100] The same town had also housed John Burn, a British deserter who had robbed the trader (and Branham's friend) Aaron Price of his deerskins. In the end, May threw up his hands, despairing that any order could be imposed when the law was "daily circumvented by a Parcel of idle People here."[101]

May's frustration, and the Cherokees' tolerance of a known thief, resulted from the Europeans' uncertainty over Indians' concepts of property. Raymond Demere made explicit the connection between traders' seeming lawlessness and their loose definition of legal property. "They are a Sett of bad People . . . a Kind of Bandite, the very refuse of all Provinces, who harbour themselves here from the Laws of the Land. They have no Principles of Liberty or Property."[102] It was not lawlessness, however, for traders had to conform to the laws of their Indian hosts. Indians had a well-developed notion of personal property, to the point of identifying relatives' goods months or years after their loss. But horses did not fit easily into Indian notions of personal property, and this ambiguity gave traders and other horse-swappers room to create a black market along the trails.

Recognizing the flexibility of laws and jurisdictions, sojourners learned to use southeastern connections to their advantage. By 1751 it had become customary for traders "to allow their Packhorsemen or Substitutes the Priviledge of carrying a Horse load or two of Goods into the Nation for their private Benefit."[103] But the hired factors learned to expand their "private benefit" to include the skins they purchased with Augusta goods, as well as the very horses they used to carry those goods into Indian towns. While Samuel Paine seemed to conduct his business with his employers' approval, not every trader did. After 1763, when the port of Pensacola offered Indian traders a supply of goods outside Augusta, it became common to "Carry off the Skins which they have purchased with goods and barter them at Pensacola for Rum, with which they purchase more Skins or the Horses which are stolen from Indian Traders, and from the different provinces."[104] David Taitt accused two of Robert Mackay's hired hands of this practice. If guilty, they were only two of many who sought ways to increase their share of the trade.

Packhorsemen also resorted to absenteeism, abandoning the trade to live somewhere else in the Southeast. Such behavior inspired the legend of "Herbert's Spring," according to Adair. The spring, near the headwaters of the Savannah River, was a natural place "for strangers to drink." Some Chickasaw packhorsemen took a longer rest than others, and "by some allurement or other, exceeded the time appointed" spending years in the mountains. On their return, they claimed that "the spring had such a natural bewitching quality that whosoever drank of it, could not possibly quit the nation, during the tedious space of seven years." Adair dismissed such supernatural overtones as a mere "excuse for their bad method of living," but the legend spread among other packhorsemen to the point that none would ever drink from Herbert's Spring. To have a drink there, they believed, would be to "basely renew, or confirm the loss of their liberty, which that execrable fountain occasions."[105] Runaway packhorsemen also took more direct measures against their Augusta employers, stealing goods and horses from them. In 1765, for example, the *Georgia Gazette* advertised two runaway packhorsemen, Benjamin Parrot and Jeremiah Holland, who "did feloniously steal and carry away from their said masters [Thomas Grierson and Frederick Myerson of Augusta] four head of horses, one riding saddle, two guns, three blankets, and other articles."[106]

Horses, the lifeline of southeastern commerce, provided a key example of the flexibility provided by competing systems of property. While colonial commentators such as David Taitt invariably attributed horse thieving to the criminal nature of most traders, horses were an uncertain property in the eighteenth-century Southeast. The large ranges and constant trading devalued horses moving along the paths. In Britain, a horse "was one of the most expensive pieces of capital equipment," and its theft a tremendous loss to the owner.[107] The value that new settlers in Carolina attached to their horses prompted the Regulator riots in the 1760s. By the time one traveled as far into the colonies as Augusta, though, the worth of a horse had lessened a great deal. William Mylne complained in 1775 that the large number of horses in and around Augusta lessened the value of his. Mylne feared that if he sold his horse in the Augusta market, he would "not get nigh what he is worth, the market being overstocked at present."[108]

Traders also took advantage of Indians' uncertainty over the value of horses or even the animals' status as property. The Choctaws referred to horses as *isuba*, or "deer-resembler."[109] The Creeks similarly referred to horses as "Echolucco" or "big deer."[110] While Creeks recognized any part of a deer they themselves had killed as their own personal property, no individual could claim ownership of an animal found wild in the woods.[111] The uncertain value of horses also stemmed from the fact that the animals seemingly lived to serve Indians, as Emistisiguo claimed in 1764: "The Young people its certain daily have Pilfered and stole horses from the Traders; which horses we regard as our property as they are wholly employed in the service of Trade to this Nation."[112] While horse stealing was a common complaint and a constant source of irritation,

Indians' major concerns remained the abuse of the rum trade, encroachment of white settlements, and the intrusion of that other proliferating livestock, cattle. Malatchi resolved in 1752 that "as the bad Talk was now made good, a few Horses should never make it crooked again," implying that horses were too trivial a matter to disturb the general peace between whites and Indians.[113]

The case of John Pigg illustrated the difficulty in determining when "borrowing" horses became "stealing." In 1772 David Taitt heard the Wolf of Muccolasses's complaint against Pigg for stealing two of his horses. Pigg defended himself from the charge by providing a lengthy account of what had happened to one of the Wolf's two horses. Another trader, James Gray, had the Wolf's permission to take the horse to Pensacola to carry back presents for Muccolasses. In Pensacola, Gray sold the horse to a British officer for seven guineas, but told the Wolf that the horse had "cut one of his feet almost off by some broken bottles in the Streets" of Pensacola and was unable to return. Gray gave the Wolf six gallons of rum as compensation. The same horse later returned to Muccolasses as part of another gang, much to the Wolf's surprise. Only at that point did Pigg seize the horse and send it down to Augusta, apparently believing that the original borrowing and rum payment by Gray had extinguished the Wolf's claims. At some undetermined point in the story, the "borrowed" horse became stolen property, but, according to Pigg's logic, it was not when he laid hands on the creature.[114]

While the Wolf's horse doubtless paid little heed to its change in ownership, there was a group of southeasterners for whom such a journey had the most profound implications—African Americans. Traders owned and employed slaves in the deerskin trade. Their role as traveling companions brought African Americans face-to-face with the same dangers as white traders, and their ability to pass the same tests as whites earned at least some enslaved packhorsemen a measure of respect from whites, though they were by no means equal. However, for a number of lowcountry slaves, the opportunities of the deerskin trade afforded an escape from lowcountry servitude. Runaway slaves in particular took advantage of the trade's uncertain definition of property, in particular Indians' lukewarm reception to the concept of human property, to "steal" themselves.

The hardships of travel and the idea of community in some ways enhanced African Americans' status along the trails. The deerskin trade certainly offered a more equal relationship between blacks and whites than that available on lowcountry plantations. For that reason, a number of slaves took advantage of the geography of the paths much as Indian traders did. As humans, they risked capture and punishment for the opportunity of leaving their slave status behind and remaking themselves as free men on the trails, an opportunity enhanced by the fact that, much like horses, it was harder for them to be identified as one man's property so far away from the place they had been purchased. In a society where "property" existed only as far as one's eyes could reach, African Americans could change their status as long as they moved fast enough.

Despite the worries and declarations of colonial officials, African Americans remained a common presence in trader caravans and Indian towns. Traders' slaves interacted with Creeks on a daily basis and some even married into Creek clans. A number of runaways likewise took advantage of Creeks' differing attitudes toward race and slavery and married into Creek society in a way that was forbidden on colonial plantations.[115] Despite colonial authorities' constant fears of such intimate connections between Indians and Africans, runaways continued to find a home in Indian towns throughout the eighteenth century.[116] After 1763, some Indians sold captured slaves back to the British for a bounty, but others did not participate in the activity, and Indian villages continued to attract black refugees.

Even after the Treaty of Augusta in 1763 formally required Indians' assistance in pursuing and returning escaped slaves, runaways still cast their lots in Indian towns, perhaps even with Indian connivance. As Joseph Gibbons of Georgia suspected in 1763, a slave named Primus "might have gone away with a gang of Creek Indians."[117] Others found less sympathetic treatment among the Indians. In 1769 two black men were brought to the Savannah workhouse "from the Creek nation." The previous year, an unfortunate runaway lost his scalp during a Creek manhunt for nine escaped slaves.[118] As John Stuart commented on the latter incident, "This cannot fail of having a very good Effect, by breaking that Intercourse between the Negroes & Savages which might have been attended with very troublesome Consequences had it continued."[119] Stuart was overly optimistic, for escaped African Americans continued to seek new employments in Indian towns. If one man died and eight escaped, the risk must have still seemed worth it.

Death was a risk run by all those employed in the Indian trade, white as well as black. Traders and Indians alike owed their lives to African Americans. Adair told of one Chickasaw trader and his slave who were attacked on the path by a party of "Canada Indians." Noticing that the northern war party was about to set upon two Chickasaw boys, the trader and his slave shouted out and drew the attack on themselves. The northern Indians shot the slave's horse, which carried him off a quarter of a mile before collapsing. While the black man lived, the white man had received two mortal wounds and died the following day. However, the two men did save the lives of two Chickasaw boys targeted by the northern war party.[120]

A similar story came from the Cherokees in 1751, when the trader Hugh Murphy and his African American companion "met with a Gang of 7 or 8 Indians one of whom pointed his Gun at Murphey and the Negro seeing it, said to Murphy, take care of yourself, the Indians is going to sute at you." Murphy wheeled his horse around, but was shot through the arm and disabled. The account made no mention of what happened to the other man.[121] Samuel Benn's slave had likewise "told him to go away as fast as he could ... saying, The Indians hearing that you have killed one of them will be here soon with their Arms, and will kill you. Perhaps finding you are gone, they won't kill us."[122] Benn, badly beaten, entrusted the man with care of his goods, and the Natale Indians allowed him to pass unmolested. The African American apparently returned Benn's goods to him, for no further mention of him was made.

That some African Americans earned a certain measure of respect from white traders perhaps explains a remarkable incident in May 1767. Two men, James McCormick and John Bowie, were carrying a "Mulatto or Negro fellow named Jacob Williams" prisoner to Pensacola. On their trip down, they stopped at the camp of a number of traders, including James Gray and Cornelius Doharty. Doharty and company tried to persuade the two men "to leave the Negro to lie with them at their Camp all night, which Mr Bowie & the Dep[onen]t refused." The traders then followed McCormick and Bowie on foot, seizing McCormick's horse and tearing his coat. Gray "promised to pay the Mulatto's Debt" and another of the traders "swore that if he had been a White man he should not have passed their camp as prisoner."[123] Williams, at least, had earned some loyalty from these men, even if he did not share a complete equality with "a White man."

More than respect, however, African American sojourners could use movement along the paths to earn something much more valuable—freedom. In the same way that a Virginia man's horse could easily become a Georgian's, slaves used movement along the paths as a way to change ownership. Unlike a horse, slaves used the paths to take ownership of themselves. The story of David George's flight from Virginia to the Creek nation followed the pattern of other backwoods property exchanges. Born in Essex County, Virginia, George worked as a field slave for a man named Chapel. George's brother had run away, "but they caught him, and brought him home ... and they hung him up to a cherry tree in the yard" and gave him 500 lashes. But David managed to escape beyond his owner's immediate grasp. He fled southward to the Pee Dee River in South Carolina and then later to a white settlement along the Savannah. In both places, George worked for a new white master and both times had to flee when his Virginia owners came calling. George then fled to the Ocmulgee River, where he was captured in the woods and made a slave of King Blue Salt, a Creek headman. George lived with Blue Salt in his hunting camp and then returned with him to his town. "I was his prize and lived with him ... but the people were kind to me," George recalled. Chapel's son eventually found George even among the Creeks and paid Blue Salt for George's return. But George again escaped and made his way to the remnant Natchez village in the Creek nation, where he made the acquaintance of John Miller, an employee of Galphin's. The Natchez headman gave George to Miller, and Miller put him to work as a packhorseman for a few years before Galphin honored George's own request to live and work as a slave at Silver Bluff. Prior to his final escape during the Revolution, George never fully changed his status—he remained a slave to one man or another, but enjoyed a remarkable ability to change owners, and he himself contrasted his early harsh usage in Virginia with his kinder reception in Indian towns and on Galphin's plantation. Like the Wolf's horse, George's status depended on another man's ability to claim him face-to-face, an ability that diminished the farther that George moved.[124]

George was not the only one who underwent such transformations in the Southeast, and not all runaways relied on white assistance to the degree that George did. Two runaway slaves, captured in 1768 and brought to Savannah, said "they both belong to one man, but can not tell his name. They also say the Indians gave them the names of Harry and Bear."[125] Like George, Harry and Bear escaped English dominion for Indian and took new names as a result. How long they maintained their new lives was uncertain, but such sojourns could prove lengthy. A few weeks later, a slave named Sampson joined Harry and Bear in the workhouse, saying "he went to the Indian nation about seven years ago, but cannot tell his master's name."[126]

Sampson's lengthy tenure marked him as a man of experience, and such men provided leadership for their new fellows, offering them guides and interpreters not necessarily associated with the Indian traders. For example, three slaves ran away from a Pensacola plantation along with "One Stout Seasoned Fellow, called Limerick, speaks good English.... It is imagined he has taken the conduct of the rest, and that they may have found their way through the Creek nation."[127] Robert Rae and George Whitefield of Augusta advertised in 1770 that they held a slave who could "speak no English, but can talk Indian, and says he came from Pensacola near twelve months ago."[128] The runaway, who had worked on his owner's schooner, had learned, probably from Creek Indians frequenting Pensacola, enough language to allow him to strike out on his own.

With Pensacola in British hands after 1763, slaves began taking advantage of the overland routes between Georgia and Florida to redefine their place in society. In 1769, Andrew Johnston of Augusta lost two of his slaves when Harry and his wife, Cassandra, struck off into the interior, aided by Harry's being "very artful and plausible ... it is supposed they may endeavour to get to the Indian nation, or to Mobille," where Cassandra's "parents and other relations live."[129] Rather than finding the distance between Pensacola and Augusta insurmountable, Cassandra and her husband saw the paths as a way of linking family. The following year, a man named Peter escaped from Thomas Netherclift's plantations near Savannah. Peter, like Harry, was "extremely artful, and will doubtless attempt to pass as a free man. He formerly belonged to a person at Pensacola, came from thence by land, and 'tis supposed may be gone toward the Creek nation."[130]

As it was on the Savannah River, so it was on the trading paths. Mobility, not proximity, was the key to slaves' maintenance of family ties. Riverboats, however, moved among centers of white power. Boats linked Africans with each other, and water culture linked Africans with their home culture. But boats also maintained white status and ensured the continuation of the slave-owning Augusta merchants. Although slave boatmen might enjoy the invisibility of their work and use it to their advantage, crews, boats, and cargos were all legal property. Slave watermen carved out small spaces of community and resistance but had little power to remake their status. The uncertainty of relationships along the path, however, had a powerful potential to transform slaves into freemen. But freedom from enslavement meant placing oneself under the same rules that governed all travelers on southeastern trails.

In the end the Bosomworths reached their destination, but not their goals. The Augusta Company's feeble hatchet job had done nothing to deter the ambitious couple; it only underscored how little power the companies had to restrict access to the paths. Leaving the domain of the Augusta merchants behind, the Bosomworths enjoyed a relatively uneventful trip among the Creeks before arriving at the trading house at the Creek villages of Coweta. Trying to circumvent the authority of the Augusta Company, the Bosomworths spent a great deal of time in the households of the village traders. The path may have been open, but the traders made sure that their houses stood as symbols of their authority in the Southeast. The path was uncertain and unpredictable, but traders believed that their houses could contain and control the potential chaos of the Southeast. Fortunately for the traders' lives and livelihoods, Indians shared this belief in the power of houses. Of course, the Indians believed it was *they* who could use the trading house to control the potential chaos of the deerskin trade.

5 / Breaking Houses: Trading Posts and Power in the Colonial Southeast

On August 26, 1765, a weary John Stuart reported to Whitehall that the southern Indian trade was in chaos. The superintendent for Indian affairs in the southern district of North America, Stuart had spent two years trying to bring order and regulation to the southern deerskin trade, achieving only mixed results. The spring and summer of 1765 had witnessed a series of trade conferences with Indian headmen from the Creeks at Pensacola and with the Choctaws and Chickasaws at Mobile. The Indians' "complaints of the disorderly Behaviour of Traders and Packhorse Men were incessant," Stuart reported, because "although every Town had White People who resided and traded in it, yet there were no more than three regularly licenced Traders in the whole Chactaw Nations." The confused state of the deerskin trade and the malicious influence of deerskin traders had thrown the Chickasaws into "a State of Civil War," argued Stuart. The traders, each seeking personal advantage, "availed themselves of the Avidity of the Indians for Rum, and when drunk, set them to rob and insult their competitors, and tear down their Houses."[1] Struggling to regulate an unregulated trade, Stuart painted a portrait of Indians besieged by legions of unruly traders, with the peace of southeastern North America similarly under siege.

Stuart's letter expressed a common consensus that the Southeast was on the verge of chaos, confusion, and war, brought on by the deterioration of the Augusta trade system. The Treaty of Paris in 1763 had left Britain in possession of Pensacola and Mobile on the Gulf Coast. British merchants and some Augustans, finding easier trade routes from the southern ports, relocated their capital and their warehouses to the Gulf. The deerskin trade, for decades tied to imperial contests in North America, had to accommodate a new British hegemony in the region. Most important, the old system of resident traders and semipermanent licenses for Indian towns had been rendered null by the Proclamation of 1763. The proclamation had created a new system of licensing traders, essentially allowing any British citizen who could post bond the freedom to trade with any Indians, anywhere, anytime. In issuing the proclamation, the British king had unmoored the Indian trade from the hidebound customs of Augusta and cleared a path for a new generation of adventurers and swindlers. When Stuart wrote of falling houses, he summarized the situation better than perhaps he recognized. Literally and figuratively, the houses that served as the defining feature of the southern Anglo-Indian trade were under attack. British officials, Augusta traders, and Indian headmen shared fears of an unhoused trade, for the houses had allowed each to feel in control of the deerskin trade. Without that foundation, each group felt powerless to control the future of the Southeast.

Stuart's complaint also revealed a common fixation on trading houses as the key spaces of the deerskin trade. Like rivers and paths, traders' houses in Indian towns were both metaphorical and physical spaces. As metaphor, the houses symbolized an orderly and regular trade. As buildings, they became the most scrutinized and contested spaces within the whole trade network as traders, Indians, and British officials sought to control these powerful points of exchange. English and Indian attitudes competed to shape the humble storehouses to their liking, giving all parties a sense that the trade could be controlled so long as the houses could. This focus on houses gave every participant influence over the trade but perhaps masked the larger forces shaping economic conditions in the Southeast. Nonetheless, as Europeans and Indians (and, to a lesser extent, Africans) negotiated these spaces, they made the trading house the central space of the deerskin trade.

The house was perhaps the most important of the meaningful, superficial links between Creek and European culture. Each possessed its own respective attachment to houses, and that made the trading house the most crucial space of the deerskin trade. But it also made it the most contested since Europeans and Indians obviously had different ideas of what a "house" was. For British traders, the trading "house" was an English cultural ideal of male-dominated symmetry and order that invested the traders with special power and influence in the Southeast. For Indians, the house-based nature of the trade gave women special influence due to

Indian beliefs about women's role in the household. Indian men, then, in asserting their authority over trading houses, had to assert that authority both as Indians and as men.

Europeans and Indians had a mutual interest in the house-based trade. For traders, the house was a marker of their individual and collective authority in the Southeast. As the daily representative between English and Indian worlds, they prided themselves on the possession of orderly and regular structures and resisted all attempts to regulate their households. By referencing their houses, the traders conferred legitimacy on themselves and their actions and defended their business from unwanted intruders such as unhoused traders and British imperial reformers. They also used the ideal symmetry of the house to amplify their ambitions into an idea to "civilize" and improve the course of eighteenth-century history. Pushing against the traders were Indian headmen who also elevated the importance of the trading stores, preferring that the system ran from these locations because the houses placed the trade firmly within Creek boundaries and provided headmen with a sense of control over the trade.

Traders preferred to think of the trade system as a proper English "house." The members of Brown, Rae, and Company outlined the full architecture of the trade in a 1751 letter. Writing to defend their business against charges of monopoly and to prevent any alteration in the trade licensing system, the leading Augusta trade-merchants argued that the architecture of their company provided the most harmonious method of conducting the trade. As they described their firm, the company drew a picture of a three-part edifice, running up the Savannah River, through Augusta, and reaching Indian villages by way of the paths. All contained under the roof of one "house," the trade-merchants envisioned their firm as a symmetrical whole formed of articulated parts that in combination provided for peace and harmony in the Southeast. The letter referred to the origins of the company as "formerly three Separate Houses" which had been combined into one. Referencing their connections along the most distant paths, they touted their ability "to supply the Chactaw Indians upon their revolt from the French to the British interest." The stores also entered the description, since the firm still had "a very Large Quantity of goods in their [the Choctaw] nation." The writers even felt the need to allude to the trading boat connections to Charles Town and Savannah as anchors of the trade when they added as an aside: "We doubt not in a short time to bring shipping to Savannah, & Import & Export our goods from thence."[2]

It was a very English way to describe a house. In the rest of British North America, colonists expected their houses to have a three-part symmetry. The Georgian (named after the Hanoverian kings, not the colony) housing style first appeared in the colonies in the late seventeenth century and spread outward from the large port cities in the eighteenth. Typically, Georgian houses emphasized a three-part façade, with a central vertical element (usually the entryway) separating two equal and symmetrical halves. Divided interior spaces separated tasks into specialized rooms. The owner's intention was to demonstrate his mastery over the surrounding landscape and the human relationships within the house's walls. The aim was to conflate harmony and hierarchy and emphasize the owner's social standing. The structures were also designed with a pedagogical purpose, instructing outsiders on the proper rank of the inhabitants and providing a literal schoolroom for the gentleman's children.[3]

Brown, Rae, and Company employed similar ideas in their description of their "house." Their first description of the structure emphasized their own vertical position as the top of a pyramid: seven traders from three separate companies now formed into one. As noted above, they emphasized their connections both to Indian villages and English ports. And, as they reminded their coastal audience, such symmetry produced harmony. From their house, the company "kept the Indians on good Terms... for some Years past." If the trade system was altered in any way, they argued, disorder and chaos would result. Should they be deprived of their centrality in the trade by letting new licensees compete with them, "an Inundation of Raw Unexperienced people among the Indians... would soon raise such a Combustion as would not easily be allayed."[4]

Even Creek headmen sometimes echoed this three-part division of the trade. In 1774, as the gathering tensions of the decade pushed the Southeast toward war and a complete dissolution of the Augusta-Creek trade, the Okfuskee headman Cujesse Mico arrived in Augusta to defend the old trade arrangement. Adapting a native symbol of peace and diplomacy, the white wing, Cujesse Mico used the item to identify a three-part relationship. Arriving at Robert Mackay's "White House" compound in Augusta, the headman referenced the path he had just walked and his desire for a white and straight path free of trees. He immediately then referred to the white wing in his hands: "We hold this Wing fast by the Root, and hope that Capt. Stuart at Charles Town will hold fast by the middle, and the Governor of Savannah the Point." Stuart had come to replace the Augusta traders in this articulation, but the speech delivered in front of Mackay's house certainly kept the Augusta traders prominent. But, even in the headman's description, an orderly trade was balanced between its parts.

Brown, Rae, and Company's letter was not the only articulation of the ideal trading "house." A trader who maintained peace considered his duties to his country fulfilled. He measured his service to the colonies primarily in terms of whether his Indian clients were friendly or hostile to Britain. When challenged by colonial leaders, provincial assemblies, or fellow traders, the leading Creek and Cherokee traders defended their honor as men who kept the peace. McGillivray, a member of Brown, Rae, and Company, repeated this defense in 1754 when he answered the South Carolina Assembly's censure with his claim that "he gave no Cause of Complaint to the Indians or his fellow Traders and kept the Indians of his Towns in good Order and well affected to this Government."[5] When Robert Goudy carried a South Carolina warrant against Cornelius Doharty, the fiery Cherokee trader replied that he would "be missed by the Government" and that he had been "a safe Guard to the Country and what I have lost and am in debt for, was to keep the Indians in Peace and Unity."[6]

Traders also echoed the sense that a proportional trade was a proper trade. From the traders' perspective, this meant that each trader had his own Indian town without competition. Within this town, he charged a fair rate that covered his debts to eastern merchants and provided enough profit to offset the hazards of living among and especially traveling between Indian nations. In its simplest terms, the ideal trade provided Indians "a quantity of goods proportioned to what the Indians were able to purchase."[7] Life in the Southeast was at its most peaceful when the trade stood "on such an equitable footing betwixt the Indian & the Trader that the former may have the just value of his Effects and the latter a moderate profit on his goods as a recompence for the labour he undergoes & the various hardships & difficulties as well as danger of a life led amongst Indians."[8] Traders perhaps expected too much symmetry and balance in a trade conducted by three separate British colonies and spread among five large Indian confederacies, each with its own divisions. Regardless of the impossibility of maintaining a perfect trade, the traders sensed the imminent demise of their occupation should the slightest shift occur in the flow of trade—particularly in the number of traders.

When anything threatened the trade system (i.e., any source of trade outside their own houses), traders believed that the Southeast would experience disaster—usually described in terms of a flood. Complaints of too many traders were frequent and enduring, especially when new competition threatened established traders' dominance of the deerskin traffic. In 1738, when Georgia and South Carolina competed for preeminence in the Indian trade, the Georgia Trustees attempted to sway royal favor by painting a portrait of a flooded trade. Having been asked to approve any and all South Carolina traders to the Creeks and Cherokees, the trustees protested that the trade would then "become entirely subject to the pleasure of S. Carolina, which Province may pour into ours such a number of Traders as may ruin the trade of both Provinces, and disgust the Indians."[9] The image of chaos and disorder reappeared fourteen years later when James Habersham wrote the trustees that Georgia and South Carolina traders were every day attempting "to rival each other in trade, trample on all the good Rules prescribed them" which had occasioned "almost all the Jealousies and Disturbances we have had with the Indians."[10] Even during the height of the "golden age" of the deerskin trade, it seemed that any alteration in the trade threatened to unleash chaos upon the Southeast.[11]

In this link between proper architecture and orderliness, traders demonstrated a common set of beliefs with other eighteenth-century English thinkers. The eighteenth-century concern with harmonious plans and proper social relations expressed itself in numerous concerns from palaces to prisons. The Georgia Trustees, who believed so strongly in governing society through city planning and had fought with Augustans over the proper layout of the town, might have smiled at the traders' statements regarding proportion and harmony in the trade's social relations. Coming from this Anglo-American worldview, traders understandably believed that a properly structured trade laid a course for future prosperity.[12]

Some traders did sense a greater purpose in their employment and appointed themselves as cultural missionaries to the Indians. One evening in 1772, David Taitt dined in the Creek town of Little Tallassee, the guest of one Vanden Velden, a factor for Robert Mackay. Under the influence of alcohol, Velden became "Troublesome in his discourse, which was chiefly about the Indians, afirming [sic] that he Could make them as Obedient and Submissive as any Civilized Nation in the world." Velden asserted he could complete his task without any governmental expense and "only in the space of Six Months."[13] Taitt, unimpressed, considered Velden's plan for civilization as nothing more than the ravings of a "Cracked brained dutchman."[14] However, Velden's belief in his ability to direct Indians to European arts and culture would have found sympathy from traders whose brains had not "cracked."

Such calls as Velden's grew louder and more public as the post-1763 reforms threatened the Augusta "house." In particular, people connected to the trade began arguing for a return to the old Augusta system and the preservation of trading houses. They believed that history had been set on a proper course before 1763 but that the interference of the proclamation had upset the "natural" course of history. Two of the Southeast's more famous authors, James Adair and William Bartram, specifically composed their works in order to convince readers that a reformed trade was the proper route to a happy and harmonious Southeast. Echoing the traders' views that commerce "civilized" Indians, Adair and Bartram (erroneously) believed that Indians were eager to become just like Europeans.

James Adair, the Chickasaw trader and passionate defender of the Augusta trade system, argued in his 1775 *History of the American Indians*, that village traders were then in the process of "civilizing" southeastern Indians. A longtime trader who had resided among the Cherokees and the Chickasaws, Adair believed mightily in the power of the Augusta system. More verbose than Velden, Adair took his readers through the numerous ways in which the balanced trading "house" had led Indians to adopt European customs through the process of emulation. Adair made this argument as a means of opposing the crown's decision to allow unlicensed (and unhoused) traders from upsetting the balance of the system.

Adair justified the traders' influence with the customary references to peacekeeping and public-mindedness. In advocating a restoration of the old Augusta system, Adair pointed to the advancements that his fellow traders had made in "civilizing" the Indians and believed that their management of the trade would produce more good results. He cited specifically his literary patrons Lachlan McGillivray and George Galphin. Readers of Adair's *History* were introduced to McGillivray and Galphin before Adair said word one about Indian customs. They were praised for their "public spirit ... zealous and faithful service of your country ... social and domestic virtues, etc., which have endeared you to your acquaintances, and to all who have heard your names."[15] Rather than leave things in the hands of Stuart, Adair openly advocated for the two men to be named superintendents over southeastern Indian affairs.

> There might be introduced among the Indian nations I have described, a spirit of industry, in cultivating such productions as would agree with their land and climates; especially, if the

super-intendency of our Indian affairs, westward, was conferred on the sensible, public-spirited, and judicious Mr. George Galphin, merchant, or Lachlan McGillivray, Esq; of equal merit. Every Indian trader knows from long experience, that both these gentlemen have a greater influence over the dangerous Muskohge, than any other besides.[16]

In one passage, Adair summed up the basic argument of his book—that the old Augusta system had proved the best path to harmony and civility in the Southeast, and that a failure to reinstate it would prove disastrous to whites and Indians alike. There was a "plan of civilization" in Adair's writing—the natural order of things that had been abruptly and rudely interrupted by the Seven Years' War and the even more diabolical Proclamation of 1763.

Adair's vision of the Southeast was based on the ideas of the Scottish enlightenment. Like many of his fellow Southeasterners, Adair had clearly read something of John Millar and Adam Smith. In particular, Adair followed Smith's belief in sympathy and emulation as the guiding forces of human history. Smith argued in his *Theory of Moral Sentiments* (1759) that humans understood their fellows and their selves through the mechanism of sympathy—of understanding other humans as actors and judging the appropriateness of their actions. Sympathy then turned on the spectator through the motor of emulation—correcting one's own actions so as to be viewed with sympathy by other human beings. Out of this constant back-and-forth arose morals and the desire for improvement of self and society.

Adair revealed his Smithian beliefs in his description of Indians adopting European mores from the traders, such as Chickasaw Indians raising domesticated livestock. "This is to be ascribed to their long intercourse with us," he explained, "and the familiar easy way in which our traders live with them, begetting imperceptibly an emulous spirit of imitation, according to the usual progress of human life."[17] Adair sincerely and condescendingly believed that "with proper cultivation" Indians "would shine in higher spheres of life," but that it was no easy matter "to seduce them from their supposed interests, to the incoherent projects, that our home-bred politicians confidently devise over their sparkling bowls and decanters." Adair advocated governmental involvement to restore the old trade system by revoking general licenses and removing the post-1763 traders. The restored system would then provide "an opportunity of civilizing and reforming the savages."[18]

Adair provided his readers with examples of ways in which the traders had taught Indians to renounce their "savage" ways. Adair believed that the Creeks had learned to avoid epidemics because "the traders with them have taught them to prevent the last contagion from spreading among their towns."[19] The Chickasaws, he asserted, had recently "grown fond of the ornaments of life, of raising live stock, and using a greater industry than formerly, to increase wealth."[20] The Cherokees, "by the reiterated persuasion of the traders," had "entirely left off the custom of burying effects with the dead body; the nearest of blood inherits them."[21] Adair believed that these good works had all commenced under the pre-1763 trade system and only a return to that system could allow those good works to continue. The general licenses were ruining what the Augusta system had built.[22] Adair's *History* had organized Indian-white relations into a program for civilization—a benign commerce between the two peoples that would "tame" the Indians and provide a harmonious future for all. But it could only occur if the household system of Augusta was restored and the Proclamation of 1763 revoked.

Though published much later than Adair, William Bartram's *Travels* was just as much a product of the old Augusta system. The deerskin trade most obviously shaped Bartram's *Travels* in that it determined where he traveled. Bartram's sojourn among the Cherokees and Creeks depended on the letters of introduction he carried with him. Arriving in Charles Town in 1773, he first applied to Dr. Lionel Chalmers "for counsel and assistance for carrying into effect my intended travels." From Charles Town, Bartram moved to Savannah, where Governor James Wright of Georgia provided him with "letters to the principal inhabitants of the state, which were of great service." Shortly after his Savannah arrival, Bartram made his first visit to Augusta, at the request of John Stuart. Bartram had met Stuart in Charles Town and the superintendent would use the Augusta Congress of 1773 to introduce Bartram "to the chiefs of the Cherokees, Creeks, and other nations, and recommend me to their friendship and protection." Before setting off for the Cherokees in 1776, Bartram made certain to visit George Galphin at Silver Bluff, an acquaintance made most likely through either Wright's or Stuart's introduction. Galphin provided Bartram with the necessary "letters of recommendation and credit to the principal traders residing in the Indian towns." These traders, whose friendship Galphin secured with his letters, would provide a crucial support for Bartram's lengthy travels and an influence in the Pennsylvanian's understanding of Indians.[23]

Bartram himself acknowledged his intellectual debts to deerskin traders. On numerous occasions Bartram faced inscrutable Indian ruins and turned to his trading friends for information. Bartram's lengthy description of the abandoned Creek town of Apalachicola proceeded from a trader leading him to the site. Once there, Bartram further "enquired of him what were his sentiments with respect to their [Creeks'] wandering, unsettled disposition." When surveying a field of Indian stone tables near the Cherokee town of Keowee, Bartram "enquired of the trader what they were, who could not tell me certainly." One of Bartram's most detailed contributions to Creek ethnohistory—his description of a Creek council house and its attendant rituals—was only possible because he was "in company with the traders." How many of Bartram's ideas were his own and how many the traders' would be difficult to determine, but clearly Bartram traveled in the same company as Adair. It is not surprising, then, that the Quaker's work harmonized with the trader's.[24]

Connected as he was with traders, it is unsurprising that Bartram prescribed much the same solution as Adair had. The "civilization question" loomed large in Bartram's mind and was possibly a major motive for his travels.[25] Though he was willing to criticize Indian traders, Bartram recognized the same merits of the old system as Adair. Remembering one Galahan, the trader at the Cherokee town of Cowe, Bartram criticized the "new traders" of the 1760s at the same time he lauded the abilities of his host. Galahan was "an ancient and respectable man who had been many years a trader in this country ... esteemed and beloved by the Indians for his humanity, probity, and equitable dealings with them." Bartram, referring to less noble traders, lamented that these noble qualities made Galahan "somewhat of a prodigy."[26] But Bartram recognized the need for men such as Galahan in his plan for the United States's dealings with the Creeks and Cherokees.

> It may, therefore, not be foreign to the subject, to point out the propriety of sending men of ability and virtue, under the authority of the government, as friendly visitors, into the towns; let these men be instructed to learn perfectly their languages, and by a liberal and friendly intimacy, become acquainted with their customs and usages, religious and civil; their system of legislation and police, as well as their most ancient and present traditions and history. These men thus enlightened and instructed, would be qualified to judge equitably, and when returned to us, to make true and just report, which might assist the legislature of the United States to form, and

offer them [the Indians] a judicious plan, for their civilization and union with us.[27]

Bartram did not explicitly advocate that traders should alone fill this diplomatic role, but he clearly believed that moral men educated in Indian ways could provide the proper example and lead Indians toward an improved state of civilization.

The heavy ideological significance with which traders and their apologists invested their houses meant that these structures easily became the scene of serious contestation. As they elevated the house to be the symbol of their standing in the Southeast, traders made them easy targets for European competitors, both economic and political. Economically, trading houses could be targeted by newcomers who sought to dislodge an established trader. Politically, the British government took a keen interest in these powerful little structures and attempted to make sure that they were closely scrutinized and regulated.

The frequent references to the trade's houselike qualities necessarily linked the larger ideology of the trade to traders' physical residences. While some few trade-merchants lived in the large Augusta compounds, the overwhelming majority of traders lived in Indian-built homes perched on the edge of their client villages. As buildings, traders' stores were perhaps less imposing than the great trading compounds that circled Augusta. Physically, they resembled southern Indian houses: simple wood-framed structures, covered with wooden clapboards and daubed with mud. One of these, opened on one side, provided the trader a summer residence. Two or three others would act as corncribs or chicken coops, and one or two more would serve as the trader's storehouses. A round winter hothouse would complete the complex. Here lived the resident trader, usually an employee of one of the large Augusta firms. He would share his home with his wife (usually an Indian woman) and several of his employees—a storekeeper, three or four packhorsemen, and other servants. The latter provided the household even more ethnic diversity since they could easily be white, African American, or mestizo. As the colonial period wore on, traders increasingly located their growing compounds a mile or two outside of Indian villages, to accommodate the trader's livestock and to assert the trader's independence from the village where he resided.[28]

Houses, the markers of authority in the deerskin trade, understandably became targets for competitors. In the 1730s, Carolina traders warned Georgia interlopers not to meddle in the trade by dispatching Thomas

Wright "a transported Convict...to animate the Indians...which occasioned the pulling down of an House within the Bounds of the Province of Georgia."[29] When the French at Fort Toulouse wished to reduce British influence in their neighborhood, they insisted that the Alabama Creeks "remove the Trader Jon. Spencer from the Muckalooses and that if he refused to go by fair means to take his Goods by force and level his House, with the Ground, for that some years agoe the Indians had served a house of theirs after the same manner."[30] When John Stuart wrote John Pownall about falling houses among the Chickasaws, he was merely reporting the latest instance of a pattern in the Southeast: intimidate or eliminate competitors' advantages by tearing down their houses.

Stuart's note, though, might be read differently given Anglo-Americans' fondness for tearing down eighteenth-century houses. During the 1700s, Britain transformed into an industrial power, and British society slowly and unevenly began adapting to newer capitalist and global economies. One of the main points of contest involved houses, and house-breaking was a common form of protest when Anglo-Americans believed that older, early modern notions of community and commonwealth were being sacrificed in favor of greed-driven exploitation of world markets. From Bristol to Boston, grain merchants, cheese makers, and butchers faced public wrath against their warehouses and stores whenever prices seemed to work against the community's favor. Coincidentally, as Stuart wrote his note in August 1765, Boston had been the scene of two dramatic house-breaking incidents, as protests over the Stamp Act called into question the British government's concern for local welfare.[31] While the attacks in Creek and Chickasaw country seem to have been motivated by less noble interests, the Boston actions serve as a reminder that house-breaking was rarely a simple statement in the English eighteenth century.

Traders' beliefs about their households were partly correct, because Indians regarded an occupied trading house as continuing proof of British allegiance and peace. The Cherokees, for example, were extremely cautious about the future and wary of the dangers inherent in sudden and unexpected changes.[32] Should a trader suddenly abandon his post for no apparent reason, concern quickly turned to fear, as was the case in 1751, when rumored Cherokee attacks sent Lower Towns traders fleeing. Whatever the source of this rumor, the traders' flight greatly concerned the Cherokees, the more mistrustful of whom saw in it the first step toward a British military invasion of their country. As the Overhill Cherokees informed James Glen, it was "a great Trouble...to see the white People's Houses empty in this Nation, that used to be full of goods."[33] The traders' abrupt departure quickly lent credibility to a number of other Cherokee suspicions about the British and helped created what one historian has termed "the Panic of 1751" among the Cherokees and South Carolinians.[34] What was true of the Cherokees was also true of the Creeks, as evidenced by the Creeks' response to Richard Henderson's fleeing Okfuskee in 1755. As with the Cherokee panic, Henderson's empty house required explanation, and the Indians quickly gave free rein to their worst suspicions about the British.[35]

British officials worried about the proximity of such households to Indian villages and the power they granted to their inhabitants. From their perspective, stores were powerful objects that were as dangerous as they were necessary. Waging a contest for empire on the cheap, the British governments in the South were unwilling to pay for forts, ambassadors, or Indian presents. Instead, they relied on the trade to convey official messages and to return intelligence of interior happenings, giving traders a quasi-official role as backcountry diplomats. The British also feared the power that such reliance gave to men of low breeding and questionable character. The trading house was the vehicle by which indigent men could spread their pernicious influence among Britain's Indian allies. The houses thus required regulation. Fortunately for the British sense of order, the household also allowed British governors and superintendents to maintain the belief that they were in control of the trade.

As a practical matter in imperial politics, the trading houses were Britain's most direct and concrete claim to jurisdiction over southern Indians. The "houses... Gardens and small plantations" that the traders had built in Indian villages served as the stakes for Britain's territorial claims in the Southeast.[36] James Glen considered trading houses to be little embassies and a part of British soil. In 1750 an army of lower Creeks attacked the Cherokees, destroying two towns as part of an ongoing war between the two confederacies. What worried Glen was that the Creeks showed "very little regard to this Country [Carolina], for they set fire to our Traders house."[37] The Indians most likely considered the house as part of the targeted village and thus open to attack. That Glen considered it part of the British realm revealed how much weight the houses had for British legitimacy in the Southeast.

From the standpoint of a British governor, the trading houses were his primary source of information on Indian affairs. The frequent (and often conflicting) reports from Indian towns allowed officials to believe that nothing could transpire in Indian villages without their knowledge.

In 1756, Daniel Pepper argued that surveillance was one of the traders' primary functions and that the trade should be structured so that each trader kept "a certain Number of Indians under their Care and Eye."[38] A year later, Pepper made clear his dependence on trader reports: "I must expect my Intelligence from them," he wrote, "as I cannot possibly be every where."[39] It was such trade-gathered intelligence that allowed James Glen to boast to the Board of Trade that he could "strictly watch the smallest motions" among the Indian nations.[40] Their dependence on the traders made men such as Glen and Pepper doubly uneasy with the characters of men who would willingly live among Indians.

Though not frequently spoken, Europeans felt that traders had taken advantage of a system where lowly whites could become men of influence simply by marrying an Indian woman and taking up residence at a store. William Stephens, tireless guardian of Georgia's moral virtue, expressed most clearly the unease that British officials felt toward traders' elevated status. Based more on social than racial lines, Stephens disapproved of Jacob Matthews's marriage to Mary Musgrove and his assumption of her trading post near Savannah. Matthews was "a hail, lusty young Fellow, an Englishman, and her Servant: Such a Promotion from Obeying to Commanding, had the usual Effect," clucked Stephens.[41] The newlywed Matthews soon grew "vain, dressing gaily (which ill became him)," and he began "to behave most insolently among all he kept Company with, looking on himself at least equal to the best Man in the Colony."[42] Matthews's presumption, though, came crashing down when he tried to assert his authority over Mary's Creek cousins, and he received "a good Thrashing from them, to convince him of his Error: For though they shew some Regard to Mary (as they call his Wife) they shew none to him."[43] What was true of Matthews was true of Indian traders in general—while their marriage to important Indian women secured their influence among their fellow Britons, their status in Indian towns was not necessarily so secure.

The same disapproval of Matthews echoed in a more general concern with "beaver catchers" in the 1750s. Informal members of the traders' households, "beaver catchers" were those whites seeking their fortunes among the Indians, living on the fringes of the deerskin trade as hunters and trappers. Irritated at the catchers' presence, Indians complained that they "not only kill Beaver which is an Infringement of their Property, but even kill Deer and so impoverish them in their hunts."[44] While a nuisance to Indians, the catchers particularly rankled older traders and British agents in Indian country. The catchers posed an even greater threat to

British notions of order, for they were men without status who openly sought influence among Indians. Poaching animals was one thing, but poaching rank was an altogether more serious matter where the British were concerned.

The beaver catchers elicited more concern for their naked ambition than their denuded quarry. James Beamer, an Indian trader among the Cherokees, referred to the "Beaver Catchers (of whom and such idle Fellows here there are more than ought to be allowed)."[45] These men were not so much prodigious hunters as useless layabouts who frequented traders' homes in the hopes of finding some station among the Indians. White hunters frequently elicited scorn from genteel Europeans for being indolent and uncivilized, but the focus on beaver catchers had more to do with their seeking a station among the Indians.[46] Daniel Pepper, British agent among the Creeks, defined the beaver catchers as nothing more than "A Sett of Idle Vagrants... who frequently raise bad Blood" with their "romancing Stories to ingratiate themselves among the Indians to procure a Livelyhood and gett an Indian Wife, which is all their Desire."[47] Pepper, proposing reforms for the deerskin trade, noted the Indians' complaints against the white hunters, but felt the greater danger they posed was "telling Storys to the Indians and Infusing bad Notions in their heads."[48] It was the catchers' undue influence that posed a threat to British-Indian friendship, and their search for unearned status in southeastern society that bothered colonial commissioners. The beaver catchers could be banned outright; not so the traders who housed and occasionally employed the catchers. At best, traders could only be regulated.

Houses that could elevate such disreputable men needed careful regulation. The trade's would-be reformers always expressed concern for the composition of the traders' households. In his 1751 effort to reform the Indian trade, James Glen paid special attention to the composition of the trading households. "No Trader," he proclaimed "shall carry with him in the Indian country any Negro, whether he be free or Slave, or any other Person whatever, unless it be the Servants or the Pack Horse Men whose names he shall give in before he sets off for the Nation."[49] Edmond Atkin paused in his lengthy assessment of Anglo-Indian relations to lament that traders' long absences during the year left the "worthless Fellows their Servants... at Liberty to deal wholly with the Indians one half the Year."[50] Being "left to themselves... without Control," Indian traders were allowed too free a hand to shape Indian affairs from their houses.[51]

A decade after Atkin's "Report," regulation of the trading household remained a key component of John Stuart's proposed reforms of the deerskin trade. During Stuart's tenure as superintendent, one of his greatest challenges was to assert his authority over a trading population he viewed as licentious, ill-behaved, and dangerously out of control. In 1765, Stuart submitted a lengthy list of regulations he deemed necessary for improving the Indian trade. Significantly, four of the first six involved the composition of Indian trader households. Stuart recommended that no trader be allowed to employ any person as a clerk or factor without that person's being expressly named in the trader's license. Stuart demanded that none be hired or dismissed from the house without the approval of one of Stuart's deputies, especially if that person had been in the employ of another trader. Multiracial stores were also prohibited, as Stuart hoped to bar traders from employing "any Negro or Indian or half breed, who from his Manner of Life shall in the Conscience of a Jury be considered as living under the Indian Government as a Factor or deputy."[52] All in all, Stuart hoped that by asserting his authority over traders' households, he could gain greater power in the regulation and management of the trade.

Traders responded to these attempts to regulate their households by asserting their ownership and independence of their houses. When Superintendent Edmond Atkin made his journey among the Creeks in 1759, he confronted trader John Spencer about the Muccolasses store being too far from town and threatened to revoke his trading license. Spencer, affronted that Atkin would dictate his store's location, replied that "he might take his Licence from him . . . and if he did that, he the said Spencer did not value it that, (snapping his fingers)."[53] Spencer then mounted his horse, threw his hat at Atkin's feet, and rode off, claiming that "if he never was to sell a bit of goods whilst he lived, he would not let his goods go into Mocolussah."[54] Spencer's goods were his, and he alone would determine where his house would be situated.[55] Asserting their independence was the means by which traders kept greater control over the sale of their goods. If they acted as dutiful servants of the crown, governors might be allowed to set the prices of trade goods. Therefore the traders took every opportunity to remind their clients that the stores' goods belonged to the traders and no one else. Glen noted in 1751 that traders frequently ignored trade regulations, telling the Indians "not to mind what was said by the government for their Goods were their own and they would then sell them how, and in what Manner they pleased."[56]

But asserting household independence in the face of British regulation was seemingly targeted at Indian audiences rather than European ones. As Atkin indicated, the real audience for traders' boasts of independence were Indians themselves. After leaving Atkin's presence, Spencer made "brags to some Indians, that he had talked strong to the Great Beloved Man [Atkin]."[57] In 1755, Creek traders echoed Spencer's sentiment, but this time directed them at Creek headmen, telling the Indians that "their Goods were their own" and that they "would dispose of them or give them away as they thought proper."[58] Spencer and the other Creek traders believed that their success depended on their separation from both British and Indian authorities, leading them to use the same language to defy both. Their primary assertion was that they were in complete control over the goods within their households.

The traders also used the slippery definition of "household" to suit their position. They could define themselves as both master of the household and humble servants of the larger trading "house" depending on which identity suited their needs at the time. In particular, traders' carefully guarded independence would vanish the instant that Indians tried to negotiate trade prices. At that moment, the trader became very concerned with proper channels and authority. Creeks recognized traders' slippery justifications for their prices and occasionally expressed their frustration in extreme ways, as indicated by the Gun Merchant's April 1755 seizure of Lachlan McGillivray and other leading Upper Creek traders. Recently returned from a hunting trip among the Cherokees, the Gun Merchant was startled at the good prices Cherokee hunters received for their skins and returned to his town of Okchai determined to get a Cherokee rate from the Creek traders. The traders refused to negotiate, telling the Gun Merchant "we were sorry that we could not gratify him in his Request, that Matters of such publick and great Consequence as that, ought to be decided before the Governor and Council." The headman "in a great Heat replyed that he expected such an Answer," but that he knew "it was of no Use to apply to the Governor on that Head, that they were told the Traders might do as they pleased." He then ordered the traders to be tied up. Despite the ropes around their wrists, the traders maintained that the Carolina council chamber "was the proper Place for desiring a Favour of that Kind" and that it was not within the traders' "Province" to comply with his demand.[59] The tactic worked: while the Gun Merchant refused to see the governor, the traders were allowed to go to Charles Town to negotiate a lower rate. In the end, obviously, nothing was altered. But Indians were not helpless in the trade. As the Okchai headmen learned, traders knew they were at Indian mercies and that a little violence could always bring them to heel.

But all the traders' boasts, dodges, and declarations were perhaps a case of protesting too much. For all the traders' vaunted independence from the authorities in their life, there was no escaping the fact that their actual houses were not completely their own. These structures were not Georgian mansions but were Indian-constructed buildings, designed to demonstrate the household's place in a Creek landscape and not an Englishman's mastery. On a daily basis, traders were reminded that they lived under Indian custom, and most seemingly embraced that fact. Creek customs governed trading houses. They did not, however, govern the larger Augusta system. And therein lay the seeds of constant contest within the trading house.

Creeks, particularly their headmen, were themselves very concerned that the house-based trade continue. The Proclamation of 1763 did not sit well with them, for it cost them influence over the deerskin trade. While the increased competition among traders did lower the price of European goods, it came with higher costs. Trader abuses became more common as rum increasingly made up trade deficits and even formerly honest traders did everything possible to balance the books and claim their share of ever-dwindling profits. As abuse increased, Indian methods of redress decreased. Southern Indians, particularly the Cherokees and Creeks, had pledged in numerous treaties following the Seven Years' War not to molest even the most abusive trader but instead to make formal complaints to the superintendent or to the governors.[60] More important, trading houses' diminished role also signified a reduction of Indian control over the traders, for the houses operated primarily according to Indian customs and laws.

Trading houses were part of the Indian landscape and had likely been built by Indians. By the mid-eighteenth century, trading houses had become a part of almost every southeastern Indian town, and descriptions indicated that the Indians themselves built the traders' houses, given the usual method of building in southern Indian towns.[61] Trading houses were most often described as resembling nothing more than larger versions of Indian habitations. At the Upper Creek town of Muccolasses, William Bartram saw a trader's house and stores that "formed a compleat square, after the mode of the habitations of the Muscogulges, that is, four oblong buildings of equal dimensions."[62] James Adair agreed that traders' and Indians' houses resembled each other. He described the "clean, neat, dwelling houses" of the Indians, "white-washed within and without," and noted that "the Indians, as well as their traders, usually decorate their summer-houses with this favourite white-wash."[63] Adair did note a subtle distinction between the Indians' compounds and the traders'—Indian squares contained "a corn-house, fowl-house, and a hot-house" whereas "the traders [have] likewise separate store-houses for their goods, as well as to contain the proper remittances received in exchange."[64] Traders adapted the Indian building form for the sake of commerce.

Trading houses were not just productions of the local vernacular, either. Descriptions indicated that their form depended somewhat on Creek geopolitics. Although based on Indian traditions, it seems that not all trading houses were equal. Commentators singled out Creek stores in particular—a focus that might indicate that those traders enjoyed larger houses, but one that also precludes any comparison among traders. The most detailed portrait of a trading house, for example, came from Bartram's visit to the Boatswain, a Creek Indian who began trading at Apalachicola in the years before the American Revolution. "His villa was beautifully situated and well constructed," Bartram enthused. The Boatswain's household, like other Creek and trader households, included four buildings forming a square: a "large and commodious" dwelling, a "cookhouse," a "skin or ware-house" and a "vast open *pavilion,* supporting a canopy of cedar roof by two rows of columns or pillars. . . . Between each range of pillars was a platform, or what the traders call cabins, a sort of sofa raised about two feet above the common ground."[65] Adair described the house of another "considerable trader" among the Upper Creeks as being at least one-and-a-half stories tall, for that trader had eluded an attacker by escaping "round a large ladder that joined the loft."[66] When Adair referred to a third Upper Creek trader's house as "a gentleman's dwelling house," he may have been remembering yet another substantial structure.[67] Certainly some traders were better off than others, which might explain variations in house size. But consideration might also be given to the political circumstances in which traders lived.

The Creeks were fond of political neutrality, and their traders may have reaped the benefit. The Southeast's Indian traders had realized the benefit of (European) neutrality for commerce. Rumors persisted throughout the colonial period that British traders dealt with the French at Fort Toulouse, even during times of war.[68] While British governors smelled treason in such commerce, the case of John Spencer proved the benefit of neutrality to traders. Spencer's store near Muccolasses was an international market among the Alabama Creeks. Spencer had specifically ordered his storekeeper "*to buy all the skins that came, (or were brought) let them come from where they might.*"[69] The storekeeper, Thomas

Perriman, witnessed French men and women bringing deerskins to Spencer's store to exchange for blankets, calico, and other sundries, and that "Spencer did sometimes go to the French Fort, and Frenchmen & Women belonging to that Fort came often to Mr Spencer's House to see him & his Indian woman."[70] In this manner, Spencer ensured that the deerskins traded to the French in small-scale local exchange ended up in his own warehouses—personal neutrality allowed Spencer to convert a competitor into a client and to reap the profits.

Perhaps coincidentally, the more elaborate trader dwellings described were those among the Creeks, and the Upper Creeks in particular. It is also worth noting that the majority of house descriptions came during the 1760s, when British hegemony made neutrality an untenable position. But even during times of war, the Upper Creek traders had fewer burdens and higher profits, and they faced fewer hostile parties than did the traders among the British-allied Chickasaws.[71] If true, the Upper Creeks' decades-long campaign for neutrality in the Southeast would have created benefits for the traders who resided near their towns. If the traders' clients were at war, the trading houses were "built in the middle of the town . . . on account of greater security." But if the Indians made peace, "both the Indians and traders chuse to settle at a very convenient distance, for the sake of their [traders'] live-stock."[72] The trader who enjoyed a loft in his storehouse also "stood in the secure affection of his savage brethren."[73] For this reason, it was quite likely that a trader's house grew to fit its environment—larger dwellings and stores in areas that were not at war, and smaller ones in areas beset by constant attack.[74]

That houses should be so influenced by Indian preferences is no surprise, given that the Creeks believed that the houses belonged to the village. Traders operated under Indian law and Indian custom, a fact that no trader could afford to ignore for long. From his first welcome into an Indian town, the trader's life was in the hands of Indian clan traditions. A headman would welcome the trader to town, offering him protection. The formal alliance between headman and trader would be reinforced and secured by the headman's female relations, acting as hostesses. One of them would usually marry the trader, further cementing the trader's status as an adoptive member of the headman's clan.[75] Every aspect of the trader's daily life and household would continue to function according to Indian tradition: Indians would build the house, protect it, and destroy it if the trader's actions warranted.

In Creek country, houses were largely women's domains. Households were overseen by the *huti*, a local network of related households whose membership was determined by matrilineal descent, so that husbands joined their wives' families but were not actually part of the kinship system, meaning they had little direct control over their household affairs (women's male relatives did have such influence, however). Since most traders married into Creek villages, traditional Creek ideas of household relations would not give traders much of a role. But within the house, Creek women oversaw household management and the distribution of goods. While men oversaw the management of town and national matters, women were charged with the daily operations within household walls. Women thus had a great deal of control over Creek life, since they saw to it that everyone was fed and everyone was clothed. It was women's work that made the trade possible, as well, since their dressed deerskins fetched higher prices and were the standard trade item for many decades.[76]

Moreover, the trade actually served to enhance women's power in Creek life. Women who married or lived with European traders had direct access to a powerful trove of desirable items and many used that access to conduct their own trade on the side. The need for deerskins also enhanced women's roles as dressers of deerskins, or at least until the rise of Augusta slavery and the new trade in raw skins after 1760 began diminishing the importance of this role. Creek women could even use their access to European livestock to take up ranching, transforming themselves into livestock producers and selling their animals for personal profits.[77]

Changes in Creek settlement patterns likely only enhanced women's house-linked power. As the eighteenth century progressed, Creek towns became less nucleated, as Creeks opted to string their households along the country's river valleys rather than cluster together in more traditional centralized town sites. As settlement moved farther away from male-dominated town centers, life likely became increasingly household-based. Traders certainly recognized the independence that living away from town allowed, and they joined this migration outward during the eighteenth century.[78] This increasingly dispersed settlement pattern was possibly another contributing factor to Creek men's sense that their women were gaining too much power over the trade, and perhaps life in general.[79]

The trading house was thus a key space where cultures overlapped but never quite meshed. European ideas of the household privileged masculine ownership and largely denied female agency, whereas Creek notions privileged female ownership and left husbands without much of a role.

And yet these structures, perhaps because they were so ill-defined, served as the main locus of trade and communication between the Creeks and the English. As Andrew Frank has shown, Creek and European notions of identity made these households places where people could easily slip between European and Indian cultures. But part of that power may also have stemmed from the household itself.[80]

Focusing on the household also helps explain why so many of the documented instances of cultural exchange of beliefs and practices seemed to follow along an axis between European men and Creek women. When the traders praised cultural transformation in Indian villages, they were in part praising the new adoptions of women. Adair singled out livestock husbandry as a key marker of growing Indian "civilization" (see above). In the later eighteenth century, Indian men and women were both adopting livestock as a source of trade. But, as Robbie Ethridge has shown, Creek women were aggressive in raising their own livestock, as it allowed them to participate in the trade more equally than traditional agriculture had.[81] Moreover, European adoption of Creek customs seems to have followed this same axis. When Europeans described traders as "going native," they most commonly indicated food and clothing as points of transformation, both provisions of Creek women's influence.

Food provided many with their first taste of Indian life, and it proved most enticing. Traders' homes were provided with the most fashionable repasts of both European and Indian palates. The traders' servants and employees apparently spent their winters hunting, and "every servant that each of them [the traders] fits out for the winter's hunt, brings home to his master a large heap of fat barbecued briskets, rumps, and tongues of buffalo and deer."[82] The game would be complemented with the finer tastes from eastern seaports that traders brought to their Indian homes. James Adair assured his readers that these items were "laid up and used not for necessity, but for the sake of variety." Adding to the variety were the "chocolate, coffee, and sugar" obtained in Charles Town or Augusta. These products of the West Indies allowed the traders to improve their own "numberless quantity of fowl-eggs, fruit, &c. to have puddings, pyes, fritters, and many other articles of the like kind."[83] Though not a purely English diet, Adair had no regrets, asserting that the traders enjoyed "as great plenty, as in the English settlements."[84]

Traveling in the 1770s, William Bartram enjoyed the traders' hospitality at their well-set tables. While visiting a trader in the Cherokee lower towns, he breakfasted on "excellent coffee, relished with bucanned venison, hot corn cakes, [and] excellent butter and cheese."[85] Later, at the

Boatswain's well-appointed table, Bartram again dined on "excellent coffee served up in china ware, by young negro slaves," along with "excellent sugar, honey, choice warm corn cakes, venison steaks, and barbecued meat."[86] Bartram's enthusiasm was typical of Europeans who ventured to try North American game—an enthusiasm that quickly extended to the native lifestyle that provided the delicious treats.

The shock of the exotic made Europeans hesitant to try such foods, but such prejudices were quickly overcome. Food provided many their first entry into an Indian life. Thomas Nairne's description of his 1708 journey to the Mississippi extolled the virtues of the hunter's diet of roast turkey, bear, deer, and buffalo. Nairne considered buffalo tongue to be "extraordinary fine atasting like marrow" and thought that "no Beef exceeds them."[87] Nairne extended his enthusiastic praise to the Indian hunters who made "happiness consist in a few things," and gave his readers a warm description of happy Indians sitting with "their mistresses, by some prety Brook under the shady trees . . . ther belleys were full."[88] Adair claimed to have known "gentlemen of the nicest taste, who on beginning their first trip into the Indian country" refused to eat bear meat, protesting they "would as soon eat part of a barbecued rib of a wolf, or any other beast of prey."[89] The long days of travel brought these gentlemen a healthy appetite, Adair continued, and after they "ventured to taste a little," these gentlemen proceeded to devour all the bear's meat they could get, "to make up the loss they had sustained by their former squeamishness and neglect."[90]

If visitors relished bear ribs as a treat, traders far outdid their countrymen in their zeal for Indian cultural ways. Traders spent the majority of their lives living among Indians. James Adair began trading in the 1730s and did not quit the trade until the 1770s. Cornelius Doharty, who appeared as a trader in the 1741 census of Augusta, was still trading well into the 1760s. James Germany and Thomas Perriman, both acting as storekeepers for John Spencer in the late 1750s, had already spent many (if not most) of their adult years living with Indians. Germany had been "26 years in the [Creek] Nation" as of 1759 and Perriman the same year reckoned he had been "employed in the Indian Trade in the Creek nation 21 Years."[91] If they entered the trade hoping for a quick profit, most of these men found that life among the Indians was either too pleasant or too debt-ridden to give up. In either case, traders tended to adopt a when-in-Rome approach to their lives in Indian towns.

Given their long tenures, most traders clearly felt that their stores were not houses but homes. Spending so much of their lives among Indians, it was small wonder that many traders came to resemble their hosts. Upon his annual return to his store, the seasoned trader immediately changed into something more comfortable than European woolens. Bartram was welcomed to Muccolasses by a trader "entirely naked except for a breechclout, and encircled by a company of red men in the like habit."[92] Adair told of another trader who was always "nearly in the same light dress, as that of his [Indian] visitants, according to the mode of their domestic living."[93] At another time, Adair crossed paths with "a fellow-traveller, an old Indian trader, inebriated and naked, except his Indian breeches and maccaseenes," whom Adair offended by killing a rattlesnake and thereby violating an Indian custom.[94]

Creek women, however, helped ensure that the transfer of knowledge between traders and their children remained under their supervision. In the case of educating children, one of the Georgian house's most important functions, the European ideal quickly lost out to Creek ideals. The *huti*, not the father, was responsible for a child's education, and European traders often found that their desire to have their children educated in European schools was outweighed by their wives' desires to have their children educated according to Creek preferences. Even when educated in European schools, Creek wives closely monitored their children's education.[95] Even Benjamin Hawkins seemed to acknowledge women's role in the transfer of culture by being particularly solicitous of women when enacting the U.S. "plan for civilization."[96]

Obviously, European-Indian exchanges were not entirely limited to this gender axis. European men and Indian men exchanged ideas as well, and plenty of Indian men adopted European ideas of property alongside their European goods. Traders also partook of Indian beliefs about hunting, as evidenced by Adair's encounter with traders who kept deer hooves sewn into their gunshot pouches, which enabled the men "according to Indian creed, to kill deer, bear, buffaloe, beaver and other wild beasts."[97]

But there was definitely a strong connection between European men and Indian women made possible by the two cultures' differing ideas of households. Europeans envisioned the house as a place where they held ultimate and unchallenged sway. Creek women saw the household as their domain. It is difficult to know how these overlapping and competing ideas of ownership played out between husbands and wives in Creek trading houses, given the scarcity of eighteenth-century sources, but it seems clear that each side felt comfortable adopting those ideas brought into the house by the other.

What also seems clear is that Creek men sometimes felt themselves on the outside looking in. Male Creeks had authority within their own clans' households and certainly had a role to play in household management. The opportunities that trading houses offered both European men and Creek women challenged male Creek authority over the trade, and the relationship between European traders and Creek women was a source of concern to Creek men. Indeed, Creek headmen worried about the damaging effects of the trade on relations between Creek men and women, a concern hinted at in Emistisiguo's 1764 complaint that most trade disturbances resulted from "white people, who are very guilty with women that have husbands, if a woman brings any thing to the house of a white Man, let him pay her & let her go again."[98] Clearly Emistisiguo associated the daily interactions of traders and women with the breakdown in Creek gender norms. Nor was he alone—Creek men linked high trade prices to the traders' showing favor to their Indian wives.[99]

The combination of Creek men's concerns over gender authority, trade prices, and their own control revealed themselves in the Gun Marchant's 1755 seizure of McGillivray and other Upper Creek traders. During his harangue of the traders, the Gun Merchant sniffed that "he was not a Child to say one Thing Today and unsay it Tomorrow."[100] The Gun Merchant, holding the traders hostage in his own home, asserted his authority over his house and his town with reference to his status as an adult man. In other words, the Gun Merchant mirrored the traders' own sense of household authority and used it to claim control over the way the trade should be conducted. As the Gun Merchant's example shows, Creek men preferred the household system, as it did afford them a sense of control over the trade. It was just that Creek men would have to constantly assert their authority both as men and as Indians, given the dual nature of trading households.

Creek men's assertions of authority, like traders' and women's, rested in large measure on the physical form of the house itself. The houses enhanced the Indian sense of control. Built by Indians according to Indian construction methods, they were quite obviously Indian buildings. European traders who married into Indian clans also placed themselves at least partly, if never quite definitively, under Indian law. Creek headmen and warriors alike used the buildings' Indian appearance as a basis for their own assertions of authority, as indicated by headmen's speeches and more common warriors' practice of store-breaking.

The physical structure of the houses benefited Indian men more than whites. Trading houses were more easily and more frequently invaded than were fortified Augusta homes. Aggrieved Indians employed the simple and effective tactic of store-breaking to remind their storekeepers that they were guests in town. While the Upper Creeks' 1760 attacks were a striking (and strikingly violent) example, they were part of a pattern of violence in the deerskin trade. Historians have tended to focus on the most dramatic examples of Indian correction in the deerskin trade, attributing Indian attacks against traders to political or personal motivations. The 1760 attacks themselves have been variously attributed to the political motives of an anti-British Creek faction and to a lovers' dispute over a Creek woman.[101] In both of these interpretations, however, Indian violence was expressly punitive, a response to trade abuses of one kind or another—a familiar pattern in historians' accounts of the trade, whereby abusive traders press their Indian hosts too far and spark either a beating, a murder, or a war.[102]

Store-breaking, however, was not always a catastrophic or even punitive event. Sometimes the act was nothing more than kicking open a trader's door and perhaps strewing his goods about the yard. In this action, Creek warriors echoed the actions of English housebreakers in the eighteenth century. Whether learned from the English or not, there was a clear parallel between Creek men breaking the lock off of a trader's door and English men breaking the locks off a local warehouse. In each case, the building's "owner" (an obviously contested term) had violated community ideas of fair prices. The punishment was to assert the community's control over the individual by breaking into the building and distributing the "owner's" goods to everyone.

As was true in English mob action, doors were the target of Indian housebreakers. Given that trading houses were otherwise built according to Indian custom, the presence of a large iron padlock on the door of a trading house would have stood out in sharp relief, especially given Indians' distaste for iron chains and shackles. Trading house doors were particular targets for store-breakers. Given storehouses' close resemblance to Indian houses, the locked door stood out as a clear symbol of competing Indian and European notions of property and propriety. Cherokee trader Matthew Toole complained of the Indians' getting drunk, so much so that "they drives us all out of our Houses, and breaking open our Doors."[103] Twenty years later, David Taitt recorded an incident in which the Creeks of Tallasseehatchee attacked the store of John Bell. The Indians "broke Bells doors and destroyed his household utensils such as pots, bowles etca and Spoiled all his Victuals."[104]

Though seemingly quite violent, these small-scale attacks were enabled by the unusual fragility of Indian doors. In his lengthy and detailed description of Indian construction methods, Adair noted that the Indians "always make their doors of poplar, because the timber is large, and very light when seasoned, as well as easy to be hewed." Doors were usually made of a single plank, but could also be made of two planks with cross bars tied with strips of leather. Adair praised the strength of the leather bindings, which were "almost as strong as if it were done with long nails," but there seemed little evidence that the doors were as sturdy as English oak.[105] Poplar was a favorite of Indian canoe-builders because of its softness.[106] It was probably also a favorite of Indian store-breakers, given the ease with which one "young fellow run against one of the Traders doors and broke it in pieces by a thrust with his foot."[107]

Store-breaking was frequently nothing more than a bargaining tactic between Indian men and their storekeepers, usually in pursuit of a lower rate of exchange. As the Cherokees told Upper Creek headmen in the 1750s, the Cherokees earned their lower trade prices "with all Manner of bad Usage" of the traders. "Tumble their Goods out of their Houses," they advised the Creeks, "take some of their Goods by Force . . . that was the Method the Cherrockee Warriours fell upon to get a Low Trade."[108] The Upper Creeks took the message to heart, and promptly tied up Lachlan McGillivray and some other Augusta traders. Almost twenty years later, the Creeks still practiced the Cherokees' advice. The headman of Tallasseehatchee, explaining the breaking of John Bell's store, told David Taitt it had happened because Bell "would not give them such a good Trade as the people of puckantallahassie [sic] did."[109]

Indian/trader violence was also a part of an ongoing social negotiation between the town and its fictive kinsman, the trader. It was a mark of a respected trader that he would return violence with violence in kind. William Rae died in the 1760 attacks in Okfuskee, but apparently earned the respect of his fellow traders and even of the Creeks who killed him. According to Adair, a trader such as Rae had earned the respect of the Okfuskee Creeks because "it was usual for him to correct as many of the swaggering [Indian] heroes, as could stand round him in his house, when they became impudent and mischievous."[110] Adair asserted that Indians respected "martial spirit, and contemn the pusillanimous."[111] Given Indians' preoccupation with concepts of manliness and its close association with diplomacy and trade, these small-scale battles between Indian clients and European traders were attempts to assert or maintain a dominant position in daily transactions.[112] Whereas John Ross, almost universally loathed by European and Indian alike, was "cut to Pieces" in the nearby village of Sugatspoges, William Rae was only killed, with no apparent disrespect paid to his body.[113] Even the other employees of Ross's trading store were spared Ross's fate, which Adair took as proof that "the worst people, in their worst actions, make a distinction between the morally virtuous, and vicious."[114]

Although Creek negotiation tactics seldom, if ever, produced any long-term alteration in trade prices, their assertions of control did challenge one established English notion of ownership—human bondage. While no Creeks broke open stores to liberate African American bondsmen, Indian preferences did shape the material lives of slaves living in Creek country.

Indian traders apparently had no way to physically restrain runaways and had to shield their intentions lest their "captives" simply flee at the first sign of danger. This lack of restraint may have been owing to traders' good natures, but it was more likely a result of Indian attitudes in the 1750s and 1760s. Amid numerous rumors that the British sought to enslave Indians and steal their land, traders were perhaps circumspect in their displays of human bondage. The sight of an escaped slave tied in a trader's house, or even more insidiously, the mere presence of iron shackles and chains, would have alarmed Indians fearful of their own enslavement. As an example, a group of nine slaves in 1768 were held in Creek country without physical restraint, and it was only on "finding that they were to be delivered" to their former owners that they realized their situation and fled.[115] A decade earlier, the Cherokee trader James Beamer in a similar manner hosted two runaways without informing them of their impending return to their former enslavement. He warned any who might apply for their return to "acquaint me privately that I may have the Negroes seized, for they are always on their Watch and the least mistrust they have, they will fly directly to the Woods."[116] Even in the case of escaped runaways, there does not seem to be much evidence that slaves were physically restrained in Indian country.

Traders did not carry iron chains because Indians had no use for them. Moreover, their presence in British traders' hands would have marked Europeans as slavers rather than friends. In 1756 the French governor of New Orleans encouraged the association between British traders and iron shackles. He informed a body of assembled Cherokee and Shawnee headmen that "already thirty Horses laden with Irons have been sent into your Nation." To make clear the significance of this, the governor added, "The Uses they are to be put to you may easily guess is to enslaving your Women and Children after having knocked all the Men on the Head."[117] Surveyors' chains were no better, since their use was associated with Indian land cessions and British encroachment; the experiences of Bernard Romans and David Taitt underscored the wisdom of keeping survey equipment hidden from Indian view.[118]

While the presence of iron chains would have alarmed Indians, the natives proved just as unwilling to countenance white acts of coercion in their towns. Indians were deeply suspicious of whites who came to forcibly remove slaves from Indian towns. In 1757, a Cherokee trader named Robert Goudy caused an alarm in Hiwassee when he arrested Doharty's slaves. Neighboring Indians "about the House, who seeing white Men carrying away the Negroes and taking the Goods, were frighted" and "alarmed the Women and those that were not gone a hunting . . . that the white People were coming to carry them away, and told them what they had seen."[119] For this reason, probably, runaways reaped the benefit of Anglo-Indian tensions, even if they themselves did not know the intricacies of southeastern diplomacy. Runaways also benefited from the uncertain definitions of property that traders themselves had helped create.

While Indians and English alike focused most of their attention on houses, the ground was shifting below their feet. However much the trade's participants believed that they could control the trade by controlling their houses, global and local forces were combining to dramatically reshape the trade for everyone. Creeks' material and intellectual life changed as a result of the trade, and their reliance on hunting set a price that the local deer population could not bear forever. As Indians' inability to meet payments burdened traders with their own debts, small-scale exchanges became large-scale land deals and set the stage for a revolution in the South. When the upheavals came in the 1770s, however, traders renewed their attachment to their houses by abandoning the other spaces of the Augusta-Creek path and embracing their trading houses as their refuge.

Although Indian social mores shaped everyday life at the store, the stores' presence had the long-term effect of dramatically altering those mores. Indians preferred European manufactures to their own stone tools. The increasing dependence on European goods weakened Indians' material independence. Greater reliance on commercial hunting to secure basic needs also strained southeastern deer populations and decreased the importance of agriculture. Indians' increasing dependence on European goods, and their decreasing ability to pay for those goods, increased tensions, sparked wars, and ultimately led to Indian land cessions as confederacies sought to absolve their debts to traders. This story gradually unfolded among the Catawbas, the Cherokees, and the Creeks alike throughout the eighteenth and nineteenth centuries.[120]

Internally, the trade undermined Indians' traditional village life. Extended contact with traders influenced Indians to adopt some form of private property. This was particularly true of mestizo sons fathered by white traders who remained a part of their mothers' villages. These men owned land and slaves and introduced European notions of status and ownership into Indian towns. In doing so, they provided a new generation of leadership among Indians, but their accommodationist sentiments clashed with nativists, dividing Indians and providing opportunities for further wars and loss of land in the first years of the United States government.[121] The trade also undermined traditional gender roles, placing a greater emphasis on hunting as an economic enterprise, and reducing the importance of agriculture.[122] In ways no individual could have witnessed, but obvious to historians, the trade was a precursor to dispossession: Indians eventually began trading land instead of leather, and the trade ran itself out of business. Beyond the level of daily interaction, however, more obvious forces were combining to alter Indian life in the Southeast.

The 1760s witnessed a series of land trades between the Creeks and the British. When the Cherokees traded a large swath of Creek-claimed territory in exchange for debt forgiveness, tempers boiled over. The 1774 New Purchase set off hostilities between Creeks and English and eventually merged into the unfolding hostilities of the American Revolution. That war, and its years of violence and instability, severed the Augusta-Creek connection and forced traders to find a new place in the Southeast.

The traders chose, unsurprisingly, to claim their trading houses as their most valuable space. They left the town of Augusta, which traded hands a couple of times during the Revolution, to the fortunes of war. The Savannah River and the Georgia-Creek path became little more than a highway for armies and raiding parties. Most Creeks and traders chose to stay home. During the war, traders moved into Creek country, taking advantage of the Creeks' willingness to house and shelter refugees from all over. English traders became "Indian countrymen" and carried out their old business supplied from the British-occupied ports of Mobile and Pensacola. Their houses again served as valuable gateways, as these men and their families would continue to move between Euro-American and Native American identities into the nineteenth century.[123] The spaces that the traders abandoned did not vanish when the

Augusta-Creek connection was severed. But they did change meaning as a new generation of southeasterners reoccupied the river, the town, and even the paths. What they brought with them was a new concept of spatial and human arrangements that would dramatically reshape the course of southeastern history.

The American Revolution and the new occupation of the Georgia-Creek corridor did not mean an end to the contest over space that marked the colonial era. The ideas that emanated from the trading houses reached a new generation of empire-builders: George Washington's administration. Building on the idea of house-directed civilization developed in part by Creek, Cherokee, and Chickasaw traders, the new administration's "plan for civilization" ensured that some echo of the former trade geography would remain under debate even in those areas where the actual trade geography had vanished.

Conclusion. To Remove All Obstructions: Southeastern Geography after the American Revolution

The fence was in the way. In September 1783 the Richmond Academy Board of Trustees met for the first time in one of the few houses remaining in postwar Augusta. The Georgia legislature had given the trustees the task of remaking the old trader town into something more orderly, and they convened their first meeting hoping to begin that work. They had set their sights on the old common lands, which the legislature had "lately ordered to be laid out into lots, and to form part of the town of Augusta" (fig. 14). Standing in their way, however, was one of the last vestiges of Augusta's old trader elite—Andrew McLean's fence.[1]

McLean was one of the last traders left in Augusta after the American Revolution. Most of his old friends and partners had either died or fled. Loyalist in their sentiments, most traders moved their operations to West Florida to reestablish their business and avoid hostile Augusta Whigs. Others, like McLean, had simply returned to their village stores and households and stayed put. Whatever the reasons for his decision to stay, he suffered accordingly. His property had apparently been subject to seizure and insult from the Revolutionary government. As Mary Mackay wrote in the summer of 1783, "While his Estate was in the hands of the public, devastation [and] destruction prevail'd, I never saw such ruin."[2] Amid the slow process of sorting out his affairs, McLean now had to go defend his fence.

It was a small contest, but it pitted Augusta's old leadership against its new. After the trade and the traders left Augusta during the Revolution, the Georgia legislature and Richmond Academy trustees decided to create a more regular and orderly street plan for their new home. The physical layout of Augusta, for decades based more on the contours of the trading path than any natural feature of formal survey, was ordered changed into a more orderly grid pattern by an act of the Revolutionary legislature in 1780. The trustees took control of Augusta's former common lands along the river; they noted that "there are few buildings and none of them very valuable" and believed that "a street or a common upon the bay, bounded by a straight and regular line, will be of considerable and general utility."[3] McLean's fence had delayed this project but could not sway the trustees from their goal.

At their second meeting, the Academy Trustees demanded that McLean attend them and prove his claims. McLean demurred, claiming that he did not have his personal papers handy. But he responded to the trustees' order with reference to his former associations and powers within the town. The "Parish of St. Paul having been indebted to the house of James Jackson, & Co.," McLean claimed, "application was made to the Governor & Council, during the late government, and the same now granted accordingly, and is now his property."[4] The fence thus stood as a final reminder of the enormous influence the traders had once wielded over the town. McLean's refusal to attend the board meeting was perhaps intended as one final denial of the authority of outsiders.

The world around Augusta had changed dramatically, however, and history was not on McLean's side. McLean did attend the trustees meeting in November of 1783 and laid his claims before them. They referred the matter to the legislature.[5] McLean lost his claim, and the survey of the new town began in the spring of 1784. The trustees, whose numbers included such prominent men as Georgia Governor George Walton and Speaker of the Assembly William Glascock, clearly had the upper hand. The trustees were not men who took kindly to obstructions. In 1785, they ordered the entire town of Augusta to work "to remove all obstructions out of the Streets of the town." They commanded "all white male Inhabitants . . . with their Negroes . . . to proceed to the removal of all such obstructions."[6]

The dispute between McLean and the trustees also symbolized a new concern in the Southeast. As Georgia's new planners began laying out their schemes, they had to contend with all of their other neighbors as well. The term "neighborhood" began appearing with greater frequency in their letters and speeches when referring to the region and in particular Georgia's relationship with Spanish Florida and the Creek Indians. The term was significant, as Georgians increasingly saw themselves less as parts of a connected whole and more as one of a number of discrete polities, each vying for exclusive control over the region. In their schoolhouses and newspapers, Georgians began reimagining this contentious geography of the Southeast and slowly erasing the old trader geography from the landscape.

Despite the radical change in leadership, the Revolution in Augusta was not a coup against an entrenched elite. The traders themselves had largely created the conditions for their own removal. By 1773, the Cherokees had lost much of their leather resources as deer herds decreased and white settlements increased. As hunts grew less productive, Cherokee debts increased. Augusta's traders hit upon a classic solution for this problem—the Cherokees would be forgiven their debts in exchange for a cession of hunting grounds to the north and west of Augusta. Since the Creeks claimed the same grounds, the Augusta traders extended the same exchange of land for absolution. In June 1773, Augusta hosted a second major Indian congress that resulted in the 2.5 million-acre New Purchase of 1773. It was an attempt to preserve peace and maintain the old trading system, but it had the unintended consequence of hastening its demise.[7]

The treaty did not sit well with younger Creek warriors. Angry at their leadership and angrier at white settlers, Creeks attacked white settlements throughout the winter of 1773-74. Governor James Wright's response to these attacks dissatisfied backcountry whites. They believed him too beholden to the Indian traders' pacifistic policies and not sufficiently ardent in pressing white claims to Indian lands. Their local protests eventually joined them to the larger independence movement and touched off the Revolutionary War in the Georgia upcountry. For the remainder of the war, Augusta would serve as a center for Whig sentiment and even as a capital for the Whig government when the British seized Savannah in 1778.[8]

Due to its centrality to the Whig movement, Augusta and its environs also saw a lot of Indian-white violence during the war. While the majority of Indians remained neutral during the war, bands of disaffected warriors used the war as an opportunity to press their grievances against white settlements. Creek warriors in particular were active around Augusta, continuing the war begun in 1774 and encouraged in their operations by British supplies and soldiers from loyalist Florida. Creeks and British made raids against Whig settlers throughout the war and Creek warriors continued to attack Georgia for years after the war, as well.[9]

The Revolution signaled the end of Augusta's influence in the deerskin trade. Some traders, such as Lachlan McGillivray, had already moved to the Georgia lowcountry and had lost their influence in the Indian country, while others fled the colony to Florida. Those who stayed in Augusta lost their homes and property due to the events of the war; and some, such as George Galphin, worked with the rebels to preserve Indian neutrality and to secure some future for the trade. Others, such as John Rae and Robert Mackay, simply died. But, as rebels and British forces alternately besieged and occupied Augusta, the traders found themselves bereft of their former economic and political influence. In fact, the new legislature targeted a law to exclude Scotsmen from entering the state at the largely Scottish former Indian traders.[10] By the end of the war, the British had evacuated the upcountry, and the anti-Indian backcountry leadership had formally taken control of the new state capital at Augusta and made themselves sovereign over all the lands from the Savannah to the Mississippi rivers.

Within Creek country, the Revolution did not radically alter the deerskin trade at its most basic levels. The basic business of exchanging skins for European goods remained the same in the 1780s as it had been in the 1760s. Indian hunters still brought in their annual harvest of skins, and European traders still eagerly purchased them with the usual assortment of tools, cloth, alcohol, and other sundries. The war certainly did lead to frequent disruptions in the supply of goods from Europe, but the everyday exchanges of the trade likely did not seem so different, either during the war or after it. Even the spaces remained largely the same: rivers, paths, houses, and even trading compounds remained the key places of the trade.

But those places had been physically relocated during the war, a move that signaled a generational shift on all sides of the trade that would set Anglo-American-Creek relations on new paths after the war. The trade's spaces, once strung along hundreds of miles of southeastern geography, now existed almost entirely within Creek country. The old Augusta traders, whether dead or fled, abandoned the old town and left the trade in the hands of younger partners who either reestablished themselves on the Gulf Coast of Florida or built large warehouses and trading stores near their client villages. The increasing presence of the traders (and their Indian children) also coincided with the loss of an older generation of Creek leadership. The new politics combined with the old economy shaped Creek country in ways that would have seemed both familiar and odd to the average Creek resident.

Adding to the newness of the post-Revolutionary Southeast were other new generations on all sides of Creek country. To the south, Creeks could find a new Spanish government that had reoccupied Spain's former colony of Florida after 1783. To the distant northeast, a new United States government was finding its feet and increasingly asserting itself in southern Indian affairs. And, strangest of all, a new generation of Georgian leaders began occupying Augusta, turning the familiar into the unfamiliar, since these new leaders had little firsthand knowledge of Indians. While the deerskin trade remained the same, there is little doubt that most Creeks were aware that this was indeed a revolutionary age.

The Creeks had to adjust to the rearrangement of both physical space and political authority after the war. Pursuing their decades-old policy of strengthening themselves through the absorption of refugee groups, the Creeks allowed many of their loyalist-leaning traders to take up permanent residence in Creek villages. Other European refugees followed and soon these English "Indian countrymen" were planting themselves in Creek towns, bringing familiar livestock and enslaved African Americans in increasing numbers.[11]

The refugees alone would not have been more than an increased headache had not their presence also begun to blur the lines of authority in Creek villages. European traders were managed with relative ease, but their children posed a real problem. Born to Indian mothers of European fathers, this new generation of traders and property owners began to claim leadership during and after the Revolution. With a foot in both European and Creek culture, they used their fathers' property and their mothers' kinship to position themselves as spokesmen for the Creeks, taking advantage of the fact that older headmen such as Emistisiguo and the Handsome Fellow had died during the Revolution.[12]

These new men among the Creeks blurred the lines of authority that had existed before the war. Attached to powerful Creek clans, they separated themselves from Creek villages, living on plantations some distance removed from their kinsmen. Raised partly by their European fathers, they typically spoke and read European languages but used those languages on behalf of their fellow Creeks. Backed by (and sometimes partners in) powerful trading firms, these men did have economic influence among the Creeks. But unlike their fathers, these men's status as Creeks gave them more prestige in the eyes of European leaders who curried Creek favor and craved Creek lands. They thus used their dual position to enrich themselves, sometimes at the expense of their Indian kinsmen.[13]

And thus did they find a great deal of opposition within Creek councils. Other headmen claimed authority after the war, those who did not have trader fathers. And despite the military honors and trading arrangements lavished on the new Creeks, other Creeks claimed as much authority based on older Creek notions of clan membership and political lineages. And these Creeks competed for European and American favors as well, resulting in decades' worth of conflicting agreements and political factionalism.[14]

Although life remained relatively peaceful within Creek villages, the situation between the Creeks and the state of Georgia grew more chaotic. The divided authority within Creek country met the federated authority within Anglo-America, which also sought to sort out its own lines of authority as the new state of Georgia competed with the United States government for primacy in Indian affairs. The 1780s and 1790s thus witnessed a continuation of the uptick in Anglo-Creek violence that had started the Revolution in Georgia. As with the beginning of the war, Anglo settlers rushed onto lands ceded by some Creeks in treaties that other Creeks did not recognize as legitimate.

While Georgia's new leaders did occasionally envision a return to the deerskin trade, there was in actuality very little interest in returning the Southeast to its prewar geography. Georgians, suffering from a postwar economic slump in the years before cotton, sometimes reminisced about the Indian trade and contemplated reviving it. In 1788, one Georgian remembered that "the supply of this nation [the Creeks] with goods and the monopoly of the furs and peltry formed a very profitable branch of the commerce of this state before the revolution" and then asserted, without any real basis in reality, that the trade "since has been almost exclusively in the hands of the citizens of this state."[15] Governors and leading merchants in the state believed that the trade could provide the financial support that it once had. As Joseph Clay wrote to Governor Edward Telfair, "I see no opening or prospect we have of accelerating the payment of our debts by any other means so eligible as from that quarter.... Skins is the only commodity we can make a whole remittance with shipping."[16] Even in 1795, after two decades of conflict, Governor George Mathews could posit that "if the friendship of the Indians can be secured by any means, the opening a trade with them is the most probable one."[17] The trade never recovered, as Georgians lacked the resources of British traders in Florida as well as the necessary access to British markets for deerskins.[18]

Despite the occasional memory of the trade, however, Georgia's new leadership was quickly moving toward a new understanding of geography, one that had no space for Indians. Partly this was the result of warfare—the raids of the Revolution certainly hardened whites' attitudes toward Indians and the Creeks in particular. Borders and their meaning thus increasingly occupied the minds of early republican Georgians. This preoccupation was no surprise given Georgians' desire for Indian lands. But Georgians divided their ideas of borders between two audiences. When speaking to Creek Indians, borders were held up as a means of establishing peaceful relations. But in an act of either unthinking contradiction or cold-blooded duplicity, Anglo-Georgians told themselves that borders were a cause of ongoing warfare and conflict. As Creeks signed more and more treaties to ensure the peace, little did they realize that Georgians were increasingly viewing such boundaries as dangerous obstacles that should be eliminated.

When Georgia and United States agents discussed boundaries with the Creeks after the Revolution, they were held up as guarantors of the peace between Indians and Euro-Americans. As Georgia governor Samuel Elbert told the Creeks in the 1780s, marking a boundary between Georgia and the Creeks was a step to preventing "bad people from going over it." U.S. Indian agent James Seagrove assured the Creeks that the Spanish-U.S. boundary being established in Florida was nothing to worry about. "Lines of a similar kind," he claimed, "are established between all white nations, whereby wars and much injury is prevented."[19] And although the U.S. agents may have believed in these pacific images, Georgians were reconceptualizing the geography of the Southeast through new media: geographic education and especially the proliferation of newspapers in the Georgia upcountry. And these new media claimed that borders were the ongoing cause of conflict and bloodshed in human history.

Georgians believed that a proper understanding of geography was crucial for the next generation. To help them, the Trustees of the Richmond County Academy in Augusta made sure that their students were provided with maps, globes, and atlases, as well as surveyor's instruments.[20] Moreover, when one of their students "so far excelled as to be entitled to particular attention," he was given his own copy of Jedediah Morse's popular geography textbook.[21] When the anonymous author "Neocomi" used the pages of the *Georgia State Gazette* to lay out his elaborate plan to improve the education and citizenship of Georgia students, he emphasized geographic education, so that students would know "by theory the whole world, and give a well founded preference to their native soil, which they will be thoroughly acquainted with. There will be no river, no road, no creek, but they will have seen or crossed."[22] And, as they pressed for better instruction of children, Georgia's political leaders made sure that they, too, were fully educated in geography. James Jackson, for example, made sure that he had a copy of William Guthrie's geography textbook even while he was leading the repeal of the Yazoo sales in 1796.[23]

In its drive for geographic education, Georgia followed a national pattern. Geographic study was a key component of early republican education. As a means of creating a sense of nationalism, American educators promoted students' instruction in geography as a means of providing students with a virtual "grand tour" of the young nation with the goal of diminishing the localism that typically defined the politics of the age. To ensure standardization and uniformity of lessons, geography textbooks also privileged textual representations of boundaries and geographic features over the supposedly more ambiguous visual representations of maps. Students thus learned to recite by heart the boundaries of nations, states, and counties.[24]

In addition to the schoolhouse, Georgians relied heavily on a fully literary medium—the newspaper—to arrange their notions of landscape. Perhaps because maps were not yet a readily available means of landscape representation, Georgians relied heavily on newspapers to shape their ideas of spatial and human relationships. The newspaper was an innovation in upcountry Georgia. Although the *Georgia Gazette* had been printed in Savannah since 1763, the upcountry did not have any established newspapers until after the American Revolution. First was the *Georgia State Gazette*, which began publication in Augusta in 1787, changing its name to the *Augusta Chronicle* in 1789. It was joined by the *Augusta Southern Centinel*, which began publishing in the mid-1790s. It was in these pages that Georgians debated major political issues of their day: the Treaty of New York, the Yazoo controversy, and the best method of securing their borders from Spanish and Creek invasion.

Newspapers presented a new medium of geographic representation in the Southeast, one that had not been prominent in the debates over the trade geography. Historians of geography have paid a great deal of attention to the various forms of geographic representation but have not paid much attention to newspapers.[25] This oversight is unfortunate, as the case of Georgia after the Revolution indicates that newspapers had a remarkable ability to help Euro-Americans organize their world into discrete spaces. With their columns of text devoted to news of foreign countries and Indian affairs, newspapers presented a neat grid on which human history could be arranged even as it unfolded. When Georgians began defining the Southeast anew after the Revolution, it is clear that they used the medium of newsprint to help map and organize their region.

Like most Americans in the eighteenth century, Georgians invested print with a special authority to reveal the truth about the world around them. When the poet "Tantarobus" wished to prove a political opponent wrong, he merely had to include the line "Look at the papers, they will shew it."[26] When the federal government defended the wisdom of the Treaty of New York based on the necessity of peace with the powerful Creeks, the anonymous author "Investigatio" derided their attempt to fool the citizens of Georgia. In earlier years, he argued, governments might have gotten away with such tactics, but "the literary genius of the present age, aided by the freedom of the press" could easily prove the Creeks to be "a mere handful of savages, living amongst woods and wild beasts."[27] Even the Creeks themselves (or at least their self-appointed white spokesman, William Augustus Bowles) relied on the ability of print to reveal truth.[28]

The association of textual and geographic authority is revealed most clearly in a trope common to the land speculation disputes that marked Georgia politics in the 1780s and 1790s. Numerous land companies competed for legitimate claims along the Mississippi and Tennessee Rivers. When each of these companies had to defend or define their claims, they almost always included a recitation of their boundaries.[29] Although one source suggested that such recitations were the means of hiding territory's true extent from public scrutiny, they nonetheless took on a similarity of form and became a source of authority.[30] The *Augusta Chronicle* employed this trope when it described a Yazoo purchase in 1789. "To bring into view the value of the territory disposed of," the newspaper asserted, "it is only necessary to mention its limits generally, which begin at the mouth of Coe's Creek on the Mississippi, about twenty miles above the Natches, continuing from thence to the source thereof, thence a due east course one hundred and twenty miles, thence north fifty miles to the northern boundary, thence due west to the Mississippi."[31] To give the reader an understanding of the value of disputed territory, it was "only necessary to mention its limits generally," indicating that the author expected his readers to both understand his geographic recitation and recognize its authority.

Perhaps more prevalent and more immediate than the spread of geographic literacy through formal education was the spread of geographic literacy through the medium of newsprint. The pages of the *Augusta Chronicle* and the *Southern Centinel* provided their readers with an ongoing and seemingly endless narrative of border warfare and frontier conflict. Combining news from European warfare, U.S.-Indian conflicts, and reports on the progress of the town of Augusta, the papers created a series of juxtapositions that allowed Georgians to create a sense of their place between the degradation of Europe and the wildness of American warfare.

Newspapers had begun amplifying border-related, anti-Indian sentiment in Georgia in the years just prior to the Revolution, if the words of "Ekanichski" are any indication. In 1768, only five years after the *Georgia Gazette* began publication, the author, an anonymous poet (although quite possibly Bernard Romans), claimed to be a surveyor recently returned from marking the Georgia-Creek boundary established by the 1763 Treaty of Augusta. Angry over what he labeled Creek duplicity, the author conflated boundaries, violence, and Georgia's expansion in the brief space of six rhymed couplets. In perhaps the most vehement statement on colonial Georgia-Creek relations, this anonymous author penned a small poem in which he portrayed the Creeks as an "infernal, treach'rous race" that would "cut your throat, while smiling in your face." He then went on to celebrate the unknown future date "that they were at once exterminate."[32] Given the ways in which later Georgians used their newsprint to define the geography of the Southeast, Ekanichski's poem appears something of a harbinger.

Reading the newspaper, Georgians could easily learn the lessons of neighborhood that Europe had to teach. Georgia's newspapers, like most American newspapers, featured European warfare prominently, usually on the front page. Especially in the 1790s, as the wars of the French Revolution engulfed the continent, American newspapers had plenty of stories of troop movements, border skirmishes, and territorial conquest to fill their pages. Indeed, Americans seemed to have a decided taste for it, as the printer of the *Southern Centinel* made clear in 1795. The paper recognized that "Domestic concerns and legislative proceedings . . . are not sufficiently interesting to engage the attention of those who delight in carnage and blood." To assuage its readers, the *Centinal* promised "battles obstinately fought—fortresses taken by storm—thousands of our fellow creatures left weltering in blood or made prisoners of war by a successful army" and that these topics would "entertain the sanguine and animated politicians of the day."[33] Lest his readers grow too concerned that the newspaper might forever slip into local news, the printer reminded them that "business is going on rapidly in Europe . . . and thousands will probably be buried in its ruins."[34]

Certainly the papers printed enough battle accounts to satisfy readers' curiosity and also provide them with an ongoing lesson in the history of borders. Consider the example of the December 13, 1788, issue of the *Georgia State Gazette*, which contained dispatches from "near the Frontiers of Turkey." That issue contained a report of Turkish soldiers who charged into southeastern Europe "and set fire to the watchhouse there, in which there were 150 men." The same issues also carried news that the Turks had made attempts to invade Transylvania, "overthrowing the first corps of Imperial troops opposed to them ... and making a considerable slaughter."[35] Once the French Revolution began the next year, the papers had no shortage of battles with which to entertain their readers. To read the newspapers, then, was to see constant proof that countries living in neighborhood experienced near-constant violence and the near-constant presence of soldiers.

The lesson almost certainly struck close to home for Georgians in the 1780s and 1790s. Printers certainly did their best to make this point clear. In 1788, when the above account of the Turks was published, Georgians had witnessed several attacks by Creek warriors. The *Southern Centinel* printer from 1795 published a letter directly below his description of constant European warfare which reminded readers "that a number of the frontier citizens of the state of Georgia, have for several years, past remained captives to a cruel and barbarous enemy."[36] Almost as constant as the accounts of European warfare were the accounts of clashes between Indians and whites in the Southeast.

Newspapers encouraged readers to draw contrasts between their peaceful homes and the violence taking place on seemingly distant frontiers. Alongside the accounts of European battles, readers in Augusta read of attacks on Georgia's borders and probably sighed with relief when they read the advertisements and announcements that reminded them that they no longer lived on such a violent border. For example, in November 1790, Augusta readers learned that Creeks had murdered two white men in separate attacks in outlying counties. Immediately below those accounts, though, came the reassuring message that members of the Augusta Dramatic Society "are earnestly requested to meet at the Theatre this evening at 7 o'clock, upon particular business."[37] In 1792, the pages of the *Chronicle* carried news that "savage outrage still continues" on the Oconee River (less than one hundred miles from Augusta) and that the settlers there were in a "state of alarm." But the advertisements in the back of the paper informed Augusta readers that they could stroll into town for linens, silk stockings, satin, "French scented Hair Powder," and "Fresh Sallad Oil."[38]

Authors also used newspapers to publish more explicit celebrations of the progress of certain regions. Civic boosters penned paeans to their home towns, celebrating their rise from rough frontier to polished civility. In newsprint, upcountry readers could celebrate the creation of schools and the education of pupils, even in places like Wilkes County. In 1788, a newspaper essayist named "Auditor" boasted of the progress of Wilkes, which had been the farthest edge of settlement less than ten years earlier. The county's youth "two years ago were lying almost in the field of nature" but were now "capable of treating even political subjects with perspecuity and precision."[39] In 1790, George Walton praised the town of Augusta, which was still a ruin in 1780, claiming, "Perhaps no place from natural causes ever made a more rapid progress," including such European cities as Constantinople and St. Petersburg.[40]

Thus did upcountry Georgians see the world's daily operations. Neighbors inevitably came to blows; conflict and proximity went hand in hand. The only hope for civility was to keep one's invaders at bay, restricting violence to some distant line. In America, this meant fighting off the countless "invasions" of Indians and pushing them farther and farther from population centers. Once this was achieved, then the real business of history could commence with the maturation of schools and villages in the wake of conquered Indian opponents. Thus did newspapers help prepare Georgia's political leadership for their response to the political situation of the 1780s and 1790s.

Minds shaped in part by newspaper accounts quickly adopted a theory of human relations common in the early republic. Gone were the old references to paths or channels; instead, southeasterners and others began using the term "neighborhood" to describe the region. Governor Edward Telfair of Georgia, when addressing Creek headman Alexander McGillivray, referred to Georgia and the Creeks as "neighbours."[41] McGillivray himself used the term, referring to Georgia as "our neighbours toward the sun rising."[42] George Washington referred to Spanish Florida as "the neighboring colonies."[43] Even anonymous poets in the *Augusta Chronicle* referred to their home region as "the neighbourhood."[44] The word was not new to the region, but it had suddenly become the most common means of describing the situation of the Southeast.[45]

The term "neighborhood" was more than a benign metaphor for a complex region; its appearance in early national discourse revealed a changing set of beliefs about relationships in the Southeast. The term, unlike the older metaphors of paths and channels, implied no real connection between the various peoples that lived in the Southeast. It instead implied semisovereign groups whose only relationship was that they happened to live near to each other. Their relationship, in many ways, was defined by placement on the map—who lived in proximity to whom. But "neighborhood" was not a valueless term in the 1780s and 1790s: it was in fact a term laden with fears and anxieties, as it implied aggression and antagonism between those who dwelled side by side.

The early Republic was marked by a general fear of neighbors. The historian James Lewis Jr. has identified a broad consensus over what he termed "the problem of neighborhood." In the 1780s and 1790s, Americans feared the establishment of sovereign nations on their borders, and later expanded this into a general fear of any non-American neighbors. Whether created out of new settlements or by the dissolution of the United States, America's policymakers believed that a potential neighborhood of sovereign states threatened to undermine republicanism and the goals of the Revolution. The logic of neighborhood was driven by fears of America's replicating the European situation, in which numerous bordering nations competed with each other in an ongoing balance of power. Such struggles had led to constant warfare, the buildup of armies and absolutist monarchies, and had thus threatened to extinguish the liberty that the American Revolution had sought to preserve.[46]

Georgia's residents were well prepared to believe in the problem of neighborhood, given the fact that they had so many neighbors. With the Spanish returned to their south and the Creeks to their west, Georgians believed themselves beset on all sides and, thus, continually exposed to conflict. John Milledge, speaking in the U.S. Congress, articulated this belief in 1793. Arguing in favor of military appropriations for the defense of the southern state, Milledge provided his hearers a lesson in geography and history. Georgia was constantly threatened by its neighbors, he argued, because "if the customs of the savage tribes did not direct them toward us, "they were incessantly excited by the British and Spaniards."[47] He reminded his fellow Congressmen that this had been true since at least the Yamasee War. Ignoring the actual history of the conflict, Milledge blamed the war on the "Spaniards, at the same spot where they are now." Milledge claimed that, because of Spanish intrigue, "the Yamasees, Creeks, and Cherokees . . . massacred one hundred and thirty of their [the English] inhabitants."[48]

Milledge's reading of history should not be surprising, as Georgians were beginning to fear the combination of the Creeks' "savage" warfare and Europeans' constant territorial ambitions. Increasingly, the Creeks and the Spanish seemed to be the same problem. The Creeks were dangerous because they were Indians, but they were especially dangerous because they were Indians with connections to Spanish Florida. When

Georgia's Indian agent Timothy Barnard believed the Creeks ready to attack, he cited as proof only that "Some of the Lower Towns have lately been at Pensacola, and returned with a large supply of ammunition."[49] As the *Georgia State Gazette* described the situation in 1788, "New settlements cannot with safety be made under the present dissatisfied state of the Indians,—whose minds have been kept uneasy and inflamed by the emissaries of a certain neighbouring power."[50]

Georgians' concerns over Spanish influence among the Creeks focused in particular on the figure of Alexander McGillivray. In the 1780s and early 1790s, he adopted the Creeks' decades-old strategy of using European powers against each other, which meant frequent negotiations with the Spanish governors in Florida and the British traders who also resided there; he even took a military commission as a Spanish general.[51] Because of these negotiations, McGillivray was considered as much a European threat as an Indian one. In the pages of the *Georgia State Gazette*, one writer described McGillivray as "a British subject— a Spanish officer—an Indian chief."[52] The same writer also described McGillivray as a "mongrel chief, who, joined to all the vices industriously acquired by a long residence among cultivated libertines, possesses all the cunning, ferocity, and vindictive rage of Indian assassins."[53] In another formulation, McGillivray was referred to as "a *half-breed Spanish Colonel*."[54] James Jackson, speaking in Congress, conflated the two sides of McGillivray's character when he informed his fellow representatives that McGillivray was a "half-breed chief" who "has his emissaries in Georgia and the Carolinas; he may have them, for aught I know, in this very city [New York]."[55] In Jackson's rhetoric, McGillivray became a sort of barbarian king, capable of sending his emissaries abroad, and who plotted "the total ruin of the State."[56]

It is perhaps because of this conflation of Creeks and Europeans that Georgians began a slow expulsion of the Indians from their jurisdiction and into a realm of semi-autonomy. The Creeks lived in territory that Georgia claimed, and the state believed that it alone had the authority to conduct diplomacy and treaties with the Creeks. When the federal government began signing treaties that violated Georgia's claims, the state was quick to defend its jurisdiction over the Creeks. Nonetheless, Georgians in the 1780s began thinking of the Creeks as outsiders and foreigners. This shift in thinking was symbolized by a 1787 act of legislature that mandated that "the Creek Indians shall be considered as without the protection of this state and it shall be lawful for the Government and people of the same, to put to death or capture the said Indians wheresoever they may be found within the limits of the same." The legislature complicated the simple division between Georgia and the Creeks by excepting "such tribes of the said Indians which have not or shall not hereafter commit hostilities against the people of this state."[57] Trying to have their cake and eat it, Georgia's assemblymen wanted Creeks to be both within and without the state—whichever status served their interests at the time.

But some Georgia leaders were increasingly convinced that the Creeks were not a part of Georgia at all. James Jackson, in particular, was apt to describe Creeks as a sort of quasi nation, whose attacks demonstrated the inevitability of conflict along borders. When Creeks attacked settlements in Georgia in the late 1780s, Jackson stood before Congress to "demand that protection and support which the Union is compelled to give to a sister State, who is unjustly attacked by a neighboring foe."[58] Jackson believed that the Creeks were like any other foreign power: "Georgia has been invaded; the fact is absolute and notorious. She has attempted to treat with her invaders."[59] Georgians had thus reached a conclusion—as long as the Creeks existed on their borders, Georgia was under threat of attack. Small wonder that Georgia's policymakers increasingly used the word "annihilated" in reference to the Creek Indians.[60]

Georgia's belief in the inevitability of conflict with Indians brought it into another conflict with the federal government. Despite the seeming consensus over neighborhood in the 1780s and 1790s, the issues of neighborhood actually drove Georgia and federal leaders into an oppositional relationship. Each agreed that sovereign neighbors were inherent trouble, but the two sides differed over who constituted a "neighbor." For the federal government, Indians did not merit such classification and could be considered candidates for assimilation into the Union. Following the unionist logic of Federalism, Washington's administration did all it could to win southeastern Indians away from the United States's actual "neighbors" in Spanish Florida, going so far as to grant Indians some unspecified rights to their own lands.[61] Georgians balked at the idea of Indians being granted a status of equality and even began to view the federal government's actions as a means of granting Indians sovereignty and further escalating violence and hostility in the Southeast.

Though none seemed to realize it, even this policy debate with the federal government was part of Georgians' efforts to remove the vestiges of the old trade system. When Washington's administration drew up its "plan for civilization," it relied on the words of Indian traders, both directly and indirectly. Thomas Jefferson considered James Adair an authority on southern Indians.⁶² William Bartram in particular had the ear of the Washington administration. Jefferson was a neighbor and frequent visitor to Bartram's house. Washington subscribed to Bartram's book and visited him twice. James Madison, Alexander Hamilton, and George Mason visited Bartram on occasion. And it is even possible that Henry Knox consulted Bartram's ideas when putting together the "plan for civilization."⁶³

The plan was essentially a means of pursuing a peaceful reconciliation with southern Indians while attempting to win land cessions from them.⁶⁴ Part of the plan required recognizing, at least to some degree, the Indians' rights to their land. Secretary of War Henry Knox articulated the basic principle when he allowed that Indians had an inherent "right of the soil"—an ambiguous phrase that suggested Indians had some claim to their hunting lands that the federal government was bound to recognize. Knox did not really mean that Indians had full and legal possession of their territory in any European sense. He meant mostly that no whites could settle Indian lands unless the United States government had properly acquired those lands through purchase.⁶⁵

When Washington's administration negotiated the Treaty of New York of August 1790, their ideas about the plan for civilization guided their talks. The Creeks gave the United Stated a stretch of territory on the south side of the Oconee River. In exchange, the United States recognized the Creeks' rights to the rest of their territory and negated numerous Georgia claims in the region. The Washington administration also named McGillivray a brigadier general in the United States Army with a pension of $1,200 a year, following an old tradition of giving Indians European commissions but also demonstrating the Federalist fondness for using patronage to cement alliances to the new government.⁶⁶ The federal government then promised to trade livestock and agricultural equipment to the Creeks and to establish a southern superintendent to manage U.S.-Creek relations as well as demonstrate the proper methods of husbandry. The Washington administration hoped that they had set the path for peace in the South and created a new model for American Indian relations.⁶⁷

The Treaty of New York created a boundary in the Southeast that crystallized Georgians' fears and prompted a furious backlash from the state's residents and literary defenders. For them, the treaty was a violation of trust between the state and federal governments. Georgians opposed every article and believed themselves endangered by its principles. From their perspective, the treaty created a new sovereignty among the Creeks and threatened the southern states with the incessant warfare found along formal boundaries. Worse, the treaty granted sovereignty to what they considered an inferior race of humans, elevating their "savagery" to nationhood and threatening the autonomy of Georgia.

Although Georgians had economic motivations to resist the Treaty of New York, it is the language of opposition that is most instructive.[68] Georgians' immediate objection to the treaty was that it legitimized the Creeks as a kind of sovereign power in the Southeast. They believed that the federal government had debased itself when it elevated McGillivray and the Creeks to a position of power that they did not deserve. The United States, "a power who would not think herself too much honored by the alliance of the greatest monarch on earth," had leagued with "Indians, who have hitherto despised civilization" and placed them "in the same dignified point of view with the plenipotentiaries of powerful nations."[69] Georgians believed that the Washington administration had "strained constructions" of the Constitution to believe that it could place "negotiations with tribes of Indians, within the boundaries of a state" on the same legal plane as treaties with actual sovereign nations.[70] Over a year after the treaty was signed, Governor Edward Telfair still believed that "the United States had in contemplation to place the Creek Indians in the same point of view with nations in civilization."[71]

Feeling like the federal government preferred the Creeks over them, Georgians developed their identity around local circumstances rather than national ones. As others have noted, Georgia's response to the Treaty of New York foreshadowed its later alienation and secession from the federal union.[72] It is also important to remember that political identity was still primarily based on local conditions after the American Revolution.[73] However, in turning to their neighborhood as the means of defining themselves, Georgians developed a local identity that would have long-lasting and even national implications. By responding to the problems of their "neighborhood," Georgians helped turned federal policy away from the "empire of land" model favored by Washington and toward the "empire of liberty" model favored by Thomas Jefferson.[74]

During the debates over Georgia's relationship to its various rivals, the state began defining itself increasingly in relation to its boundaries. Boundaries were at the center of Georgians' ideas of neighborhood, fears of Indian "savagery," and frustration at U.S. policy. Thus, in the 1780s and 1790s, Georgians' discourse on boundaries took older intellectual and political threads and tied them to new definitions of citizenship in a young republic. What emerged was a language of boundaries new to the Southeast that bundled militarism, citizenship, and racial superiority into Georgians' sense of self.

Georgia had early believed that militarization was necessary for the preservation of peace. One of the state's main objectives in ratifying the Constitution was the hope that federal arms would be sent to defend Georgia against Creek attacks.[75] Jackson initially believed that the power of federal armies "may keep them [the Creeks] in awe; but Congress must show a disposition to exert it."[76] But the Washington administration quickly proved itself more willing to spend federal monies on the Ohio Valley, and Jackson and his fellow Georgians increasingly grew frustrated with the administration's seeming neglect. They thus joined a growing community of aggrieved settlers south of the Ohio River.[77] Receiving an ambitious plan of civilization instead of armies, Georgians began translating their beliefs about militarism and peace into a local sense of citizenship.

Faced with the "foreign" invaders of the Creek confederacy, Georgians increasingly adopted a policy that a militarized border was the only means of preserving peace. Georgians rejected the Federalist notion that peace was maintained by clear boundaries enforced by a central authority. As Jackson noted in Congress, "Paper negotiations they [the Creeks] are taught to despise; nothing but an armed force can restrain them."[78] And if that armed force was not federal, then it would have to be Georgian.

Georgians began to depict local militarism as more than expediency. They quickly began to identify it as a core virtue. As "Neocomi" wrote in the *Georgia State Gazette,* "We wait the instructions of a confederated power, which we durst not, perhaps, anticipate.... Let us see whether we are able to insure the safety of our frontiers."[79] Neocomi quickly elevated his rhetoric, calling on his *"Brother citizens and Soldiers"* and "friends to their country" to serve in militias and "do duty on the line which Congress has determined between us and the Creeks."[80] In this discourse, borders not only made enemies, but they also made citizens. For lack of proper citizens, Neocomi argued, the Creeks "are grown bold, and soon a great part of the country will become desolate."[81] Appropriating the old metaphor of the Southeast, Neocomi believed that a militarized citizenry was "the only means of keeping the *paths between us and the Creeks always open, bright and clear.*"[82]

In Georgians' thinking, frontiers were where men became citizens by fighting Indians and keeping them at bay. It was the only means of preserving peace in the face of a constant threat. It became an assumption in Georgia that a militarized citizenry would preserve peace with the Indians. One proponent of the 1789 Yazoo land sales believed that settlements should be spread quickly so that "the Indians, who have been the terror of this state for many years, will find themselves so enclosed, they will gladly be at peace with us."[83] Another Georgia speculative group believed that their "uniting in general combination the frontier inhabitants of this state" was the best means "to secure their peace and safety from the hostilities of the Indians."[84] More than a means of winning an immediate peace with Creeks, neighborhood required that Georgians always remain on a war footing; Neocomi reminded his readers: "Let every citizen keep himself always at the ready, as if he was to start the next morning on another expedition; this continual state of preparation is the only guarantee to an everlasting peace."[85]

These ideas were not unique to Georgia in the 1780s and 1790s, but they were new to the state and becoming increasingly entrenched in the minds of its inhabitants. Georgia had been formed as a buffer colony, after all, but the rhetoric of early republican Georgia indicated a new idea of frontier settlement than existed previously. Georgia's early settlers were to be settlers first and take up arms only if slaves, Indians, or, most likely, Europeans threatened the peace of the whole. Peace was the assumed condition. In the language of Georgia, an active military was the only means of ensuring peace. War was considered the natural condition of the region, an idea in keeping with the rhetoric of neighborhood.

Moreover, violent defense of one's home had become the true mark of manhood, rather than older attachments to "reason." James Jackson made the argument in 1789 that rational debates in Congress were not the mark of citizenship in Georgia—fighting Indians was. Thomas Sumter of South Carolina charged Jackson that he had "suffered himself to be too much affected by the situation of his country to apply arguments to the reason of his hearers."[86] Jackson paid little attention, believing that reason had no place in Indian policy. "It is easy for men who, with their families, are secure from being plundered and butchered, whose wives and daughters are not exposed to the brutal ravisher, to reason upon and contemplate distant evils," he answered. But, Jackson made it known that he was not one of these men: "Were they, like me, acquainted with the desolation of my country, the wretchedness of my fellow-citizens ... they would feel, and their arms would hurl vengeance like vivid lightning upon the cause of such misfortunes."[87]

Thus did U.S.-Georgia conflicts over the future of the Southeast come down to a contrasting view of neighborhood. On the one hand, the

Washington administration believed that conflict arose from the "desires of too many frontier white people, to seize by force or fraud upon neighboring Indian lands."[88] On the other hand, Georgians believed that they had "little prospect of peace with such a faithless, restless neighbour," and that the only solution was to be even more aggressive toward the Creeks.[89] Increasing the tensions between state and nation, Georgians' newspapers warned them that the federal government was, through treaties such as New York, actually encouraging "a dangerous, formidable, perfidious foe, to hang forever on your borders, and prevent your growth."[90] Small wonder, then, that Georgians attached their sense of self not to the federal union but to the violent defense of their borders with the Creeks.

Georgians were not unique in this definition of self and other. They reached much the same attitude toward Indians that those in other parts of the Republic, particularly the Ohio Valley, also exhibited. Federalist policy, however, quickly accommodated Ohio settlers by treating Ohio Indians as enemies and targets of U.S. arms. Georgia, like Tennessee, faced a federal policy at odds with those beliefs and even flirted with Spanish or British help to pursue their policy of Indian warfare.[91] The Republicans, recognizing the real danger of such threats, quickly adopted a policy of catering to western settlers rather than allow them to establish separate and rival sovereignties in North America.[92] Thus did Georgia's political leadership finally begin to help push federal policy toward its ultimate end of removal.

This part of the story is familiar: western settlers, eager for Indian lands, helped drive an accommodating federal government toward a more aggressive anti-Indian policy in the early 1800s. But what is significant here is understanding the source of that aggression. Certainly, Anglo-Americans had a deep tradition of hating Indians, one that drew from both the lived experiences and literary accounts of warfare. But, at least in this one instance in Georgia, the particular beliefs about Indians—the fears of a semisovereign Indian nation that would forever bring chaos and warfare—owed much to the particulars of time and place. In this case, the American Revolution was absolutely crucial in creating the power dynamics that drove Georgians toward both their idea of the frontier and their specific policies toward that frontier. As important was the new language of geographic relations made possible by public schooling and in particular the newspapers that daily formed and enforced Georgians' beliefs about how the world worked. Indeed, more than literary productions or captivity narratives, Georgians seemingly shaped their attitudes in accordance with the weekly juxtapositions of European warfare, Indian warfare, and domestic comfort that the newspapers provided.

By the 1810s, these policies were becoming fully implemented. Georgia gave up its claims to its western lands in 1802, but Georgians' belief in the aggressive removal of Indian competitors did not go away. Indeed, their discomfort with their neighbors was matched by the growing movement among younger Creek warriors. Increased American aggression pushed these younger warriors into a stronger adversarial stance against the United States. These "Red Stick" Creeks sparked civil war within the Creek confederacy and attacks on white settlements without. Merging with the conflicts of the War of 1812, the Red Sticks' attacks allowed Southern statesmen to realize their vision for the Southeast. Armies from Tennessee, South Carolina, and Georgia marched into Creek territory, launching the national career of Andrew Jackson in the process. By the end of the war, the Creeks had lost millions of acres of hunting ground, and even villages had to be abandoned. Whites rushed into the region and began the countdown to the final removal of the Creeks in the 1830s.[93]

It was also in these decades when Georgians' sense of place began appearing in maps. Daniel Sturges, the state of Georgia's first surveyor general, produced a large-scale map of the state in 1818. The states' counties, outlined in color, were the dominant feature on a largely featureless map. A geological assessment of the state's topography appeared at the map's right, and a statistical table appeared in the lower right corner to chart the progress of settlements, listing populations from the 1810 census and including a blank column to be filled in with data from the 1820 census. Indians belonged to administrative territories, outlined in color the same as any of Georgia's counties.[94]

The process of removal was well under way by the time of Sturges's map. A number of legends recounted important events from the recent War of 1812, including the march of the American army against British forts during the conflict. Large, empty stretches of territory in the south and west of the state bore the label "Indian claim extinguished by the Treaty of Fort Jackson." One Creek town bore the legend "Destroyed by the Georgians Sep. 27th 1793." More subtly, Sturges removed Indians as people inhabiting the landscape and blended them into the "natural" landscape. In a legend next to "Chatta-hochee Old Town" on the Chattahoochee River, Sturges helpfully identified the source of the river's name: "This Town gives name to the River from Chatto a Stone and Hachee flowered. There being Stones of that description in the River." In one stroke, the provenance of the name, "Chattahoochee River," the Indian town that stood on its banks, was transformed into a benign natural feature, removed from human history.[95] As with Chattahoochee Old Town, the old Indian trade geography persisted in certain elements of Sturges's map, but its meaning had changed dramatically. The old path that stretched from Augusta to the Cowetas appeared on Sturges's map, but rather than bearing any indication of the old mutuality of the trade, Sturges labeled the path simply, "Route which the Army took."[96]

Once removal had become a fact and Anglo-American settlements had covered almost all of the former Creek lands, cartographers once again began emphasizing connections between points. The path, for example, continued as a major transportation route, though nineteenth-century travelers experienced it in a very different manner. No longer the required route through the Southeast, the old path from Augusta to the Chattahoochee was but one of many roads crisscrossing the region. In 1835, Samuel Augustus Mitchell published a "Map of the States of North Carolina, South Carolina, and Georgia," which showed each state as a series of colored counties, stretching from border to border. The map's main feature was an intricate series of "Stage Roads," "Common Roads," "Canals," and "Rail Roads," which connected the county seats to each other. By the time of the Mitchell map, Augusta was still a common point for travelers, serving as a transfer point for Georgia's main stage routes: Savannah-to-Augusta, Augusta–Milledgville, Augusta–Chattahoochee, Augusta–Columbia, South Carolina. For those entering Georgia from the north on their way west to Alabama and Mississippi, Augusta was the gateway to the former Indian territories, as one copy of the 1835 Mitchell map attests. In a copy held in the Newberry Library, an unknown traveler inked a heavy black line from Raleigh, North Carolina, to Columbia, Georgia, presumably tracing his intended southern route. The line passed through Augusta and closely followed the old Indian trading path. In the era of Indian removal, travelers through Georgia still followed the old geography, even if they were unaware of it.[97]

More than a century after Augusta's founding and more than fifty years after the Revolution had severed the town from the Indian trade, travel through the Southeast had finally shaken most of the legacies of the deerskin trade. White settlements had pushed across the Chattahoochee River, and the "Black Belt" of the cotton south was quickly subsuming the older trading path. Relations between places no longer included the human relationships of the Indian trade. Instead, geography had become a neutral servant of the traveler, masking the human history that had created the antebellum landscape. The lands that such famous travelers as Frederick Law Olmsted experienced were the result of this conscious creation of southeasterners, a product of the decisions that men such as the Richmond Academy trustees made in the decade after the American Revolution.

Movement had changed in this new Southeast and was shifting increasingly in one direction. In their treaties with the Creeks, Anglo-Americans insisted on free travel through Creek territory with no fear of the attacks and uncertainty that marked travel along eighteenth-century trade routes.[98] White travelers poured into the new states of Alabama and Mississippi to claim lands and raise cotton. Their movement also signaled one-way travel for many Indians and African Americans. Many Creeks, like the Cherokees, found themselves on the road to removal and a reservation in Oklahoma. For slaves, movement westward meant a new life in the Mississippi cotton fields or the deadly sugar plantations of Louisiana as the slave system quickly spread beyond the Southeast.

In the eighteenth century, southeasterners had been drawn to the possibilities of the deerskin trade. As a system and as a business, the trade had created a unique and flexible procession of spaces and institutions. The flexibility of traffic between Indian towns and European ones had allowed both groups some power to shape the trade to suit their own ends. So long as the Southeast remained within the boundaries of the trade's personal connections, opportunity existed for Europeans, Indians, and Africans to seek each other out and carve out autonomous spaces in the greater Southeast. By the middle of the nineteenth century, it was clear that movement along the Southeast's roads increasingly favored only one particular subset of southeasterners.

Flexible as they were, these spaces and institutions of the deerskin trade were nevertheless concrete and enduring. The winding and scattered town of Augusta stubbornly resisted attempts to "order" and straighten its streets. Its assemblage of large trading houses and outlying settlements was a testament to the entrenched authority of the deerskin traders. The well-worn trading paths were an important neutral space that allowed easy entry into the Southeast but that required the constant reassertion of identities. The village storehouses were the small arenas in which Indians and Europeans waged mighty cultural contests. And in each of these spaces Africans and African Americans took advantage of the uncertainties of an improvised system to remake themselves as people rather than property. As the eighteenth-century maps show, this supposed transitional space in American history remained a stubborn imprint that powerfully affected the history that surrounded it.

The stubbornness of the geography was evident in how quickly Europeans and Indian reestablished it during the American Revolution. Although the war brought upheaval and disorder to the Carolinas and Georgia, Creek headmen and British traders continued their contact. Resident storekeepers became more permanently attached to their houses in Indian villages. Packhorse trains wended their way through the Southeast. All that changed was the direction of these spaces. Moving to the Gulf Coast, the trade's movements became oriented southward.

But along the Georgia-Creek corridor, the old spaces of the trade became fundamentally different. Men like the Richmond Academy Trustees sensed no opportunity in the trade. Surveying the Indian interior, these men instead saw competitors for the valued resource of land. The history that turned toward dispossession hinged on this shift in attitudes and spelled doom for the old Indian trade geography. Lacking a competing system of property or opportunity, African Americans found themselves increasingly bound to white definitions of slavery and society. For them, the post-Revolutionary landscape must have looked sadly familiar.

Amid all the upheaval and grand transformations, one aspect of the southeastern trade geography remained. The slave boatmen of the Savannah River continued to drift downstream and row upstream for many years after the American Revolution. The war drastically remade the Southeast, but it did not fundamentally alter the boatmen's roles. Augustans raised tobacco and no longer traded for leather, but their goods still required water passage to the port of Savannah. Plank-sided pole boats replaced dugout trading canoes, but the similarly shaped craft still required skilled hands to navigate the snags in the river. Cotton flats joined the pole boats, but a fundamental change in river life would not come until the 1830s with the rise of steam power on the Savannah. Given the influence black watermen had in other parts of antebellum America, it would seem natural that the long-practiced Savannah boatmen would continue to fulfill their role as links in the Southeast's network of slave communication and resistance.[99]

The story of Augusta began atop Yamacraw Bluff when James Oglethorpe first noticed the slave-rowed Indian trade boats on the river below. It is fitting and also telling that the story should end here as well. The deerskin trade provided opportunity and freedom of movement for Indians, Europeans, and African Americans in the Southeast. It bound people together in complicated ways that challenged the notions of order and hierarchy that prevailed in eighteenth-century Anglo-America. But slave boatmen were the only trade participants whose livelihood continued after the deerskin trade moved to Florida. That is almost certainly because the boatmen occupied the same place in both the pre-Revolutionary and post-Revolutionary Southeast. In both regimes, they acted as nearly invisible agents allowed to practice their skills so long as they did not overtly challenge whites' presumed mastery of the landscape. If there was commonality between traders like Andrew McLean and trustees like George Walton, it was their mutual commitment to unfree labor. Along this common bond would lay the eventual future and ultimate tragedy of the American South.

NOTES

Introduction

1. James Oglethorpe to the Georgia Trustees, March 8, 1739, Allen D. Candler, Kenneth Coleman, and Milton Ready, eds., *The Colonial Records of the State of Georgia*, 30 vols. (Atlanta: C. P. Byrd, 1904–16; Athens: University of Georgia Press, 1974–76), 22, pt. 2, p. 109.

2. Edward J. Cashin, "The Gentlemen of Augusta," in *Colonial Augusta: "Key of the Indian Countrey,"* ed. Cashin (Macon, Ga.: Mercer University Press, 1986), 31–33; Cashin, "Oglethorpe's Contest for the Backcountry, 1733–1749," in *Oglethorpe in Perspective: Georgia's Founder after Two Hundred Years*, ed. Phinizy Spalding and Harvey H. Jackson (Tuscaloosa: University of Alabama Press, 1989), 101–2.

3. Eric Hinderaker, *Elusive Empires: Constructing Colonialism in the Ohio Valley, 1673–1800* (New York: Cambridge University Press, 1997), xii.

4. Verner Crane, *The Southern Frontier, 1670–1732* (Durham, N.C.: Duke University Press, 1928); Frederick Jackson Turner, "The Significance of the Frontier in American History," in Frederick Jackson Turner, *The Frontier in America* (New York: Holt, 1947, 1967).

5. John R. Alden, *John Stuart and the Southern Colonial Frontier: A Study of Indian Relations, War, Trade, and Land Problems in the Southern Wilderness, 1754–1775* (Ann Arbor: University of Michigan Press, 1944); Alan Gallay, *The Formation of a Planter Elite: Jonathan Bryan and the Southern Colonial Frontier* (Athens: University of Georgia Press, 1989); Edward J. Cashin, *Lachlan McGillivray, Indian Trader: The Shaping of the Southern Frontier* (Athens: University of Georgia Press, 1992); J. Russell Snapp, *John Stuart and the Struggle for Empire on the Southern Frontier* (Baton Rouge: Louisiana State University Press, 1996).

6. Robert Mitchell, *Commercialism and Frontier: Perspectives in the Shenandoah Valley* (Charlottesville: University Press of Virginia, 1977). Historical archaeologist Kenneth Lewis has updated Mitchell's ideas and applied them to the South Carolina backcountry in his *The American Frontier: An Archaeological Study of Settlement Pattern and Process*

(Orlando: Academic Press, 1984) and his "The Metropolis and the Backcountry: The Making of a Colonial Landscape on the South Carolina Frontier," *Historical Archaeology* 33, no. 3 (1999): 3–13. For the political expressions of these settlers' goals, see Rachel Klein, *Unification of a Slave State: The Rise of the Planter Class in the South Carolina Backcountry, 1760–1808* (Chapel Hill: University of North Carolina Press, 1990); Albert Tillson, *Gentry and Common Folk: Political Culture on a Virginia Frontier, 1740–1789* (Lexington: University Press of Kentucky, 1991); Richard Beeman, *Evolution of the Southern Backcountry: A Case Study of Lunenburg Country, Virginia, 1746–1823* (Philadelphia: University of Pennsylvania Press, 1984); for a fuller review of all of this literature, see Robert D. Mitchell, "The Southern Backcountry: A Geographical House Divided," in *The Southern Colonial Backcountry: Interdisciplinary Perspectives on Frontier Communities.* ed. David Colin Crass et al. (Knoxville: University of Tennessee Press, 1998).

7. James Merrell located this development in native sensibilities in his study of the formation of the Catawba Nation in South Carolina, *The Indian's New World: Catawbas and Their Neighbors from European Contact through the Era of Removal* (Chapel Hill: University of North Carolina Press, 1989; New York: W. W. Norton, 1991). Hahn has done something similar for the Creeks, locating the genesis of their national sensibility in their adapting to the presence of Spanish and English colonies in his *The Invention of the Creek Nation, 1670–1763* (Lincoln: University of Nebraska Press, 2004). Robbie Ethridge has built a thorough portrait of the Creeks' idea of nation from her exhaustive comparative study of Creek communities in her *Creek Country: The Creek Indians and Their World* (Chapel Hill: University of North Carolina Press, 2003). David Corkran also deserves credit for first attempting to define Indians' motivations in southeastern history in his *The Cherokee Frontier: Conflict and Survival, 1740–1762* (Norman: University of Oklahoma Press, 1962) and *The Creek Frontier, 1540–1783* (Norman: University of Oklahoma Press, 1967).

8. Kathryn Holland Braund first traced the effects of the deerskin trade on Creek ideas of community and property in her *Deerskins and Duffels: The Creek Trade with Anglo-America, 1685–1815* (Lincoln: University of Nebraska Press, 1993). Recent studies have complicated and deepened this basic story of the trade. Claudio Saunt's *A New Order of Things: Property, Power, and the Transformation of the Creeks, 1733–1816* (New York: Cambridge University Press, 1999) focused in particular on the alterations in Creek systems of property ownership created by the trade (particularly among the mestizo children of traders) and how this transformation created factions within Creek politics that ultimately weakened their response to colonialism; Joshua Piker has provided a close examination of the trade's effects on the definition of community within a single village in his *Okfuskee: A Creek Indian Town in Colonial America* (Cambridge, Mass.: Harvard University Press, 2004)

9. D. W. Meinig, *The Shaping of America: A Geographical Perspective on 500 Years of History*, Vol. 1: *Atlantic America, 1492–1800* (New Haven, Conn.: Yale University Press, 1986), 258–59.

10. Ibid., 260–61, fig. 46.

11. Meinig included this uncertainty as a mark of Anglo-Indian encounters (ibid., 211). Stephen Aron has also suggested an emphasis on uncertainty as a means of correcting the triumphalism of Turner's thesis in his *How the West Was Lost: The Transformation of Kentucky from Daniel Boone to Henry Clay* (Baltimore: Johns Hopkins University Press, 1996), 1–4.

12. Nancy Shoemaker has argued that the similarities between English and Indian opened the door to both cultural exchange and cultural conflict and required the English to distance themselves from Indians through the invention of a red/white racial divide. See Shoemaker, *A Strange Likeness: Becoming Red and White in Eighteenth-Century North America* (New York: Oxford University Press, 2004). For the Southeast, this school of similarity has emphasized comparison between Indian and European culture. Piker positions his *Okfuskee* as a comparative study between a Creek village and the colonial processes in other American settlements made possible by English and Indians' mutual attachments to town-based cultures. See Piker, *Okfuskee*, 5–9; Julie Ann Sweet has argued that diplomacy was possible between Creeks and English because of the two sides' willingness to accept the other's superficial nods to diplomacy without requiring any meaningful adaptation to the other. See Sweet, *Negotiating for Georgia: British-Creek Relations in the Trustee Era* (Athens: University of Georgia Press, 2005), 3–6.

1 / Strung Together

1. J. B. Harley, "Power and Legitimation in the English Geographical Atlases of the Eighteenth Century," in *Images of the World: The Atlas through History*, ed. John A. Wolter and Ronald E. Grim (New York: McGraw-Hill, 1997); also Gregory F. Nobles, "Straight Lines and Stability: Mapping the Political Order of the Anglo-American Frontier," *Journal of American History* 80, no. 1 (1993): 9–35.

2. This idea of imperial contest within empires comes from Eric Hinderaker's work on the Ohio Valley. Hinderaker identifies three models of empire within British policy: an "empire of commerce" that was based on the local creations of traders that seemed too anarchic and dangerous to British officials who preferred an "empire of land" where British royal authority was absolute. The "empire of land" was predictable due to the predictability of unquestioned British hegemony; it also only existed as a fantasy and was replaced by an "empire of liberty" after the American Revolution, when settlers themselves created, from the ground up, an idea of a disciplined landscape that required the dispossession of Indians. See Hinderaker, *Elusive Empires: Constructing Colonialism in the Ohio Valley, 1673–1800* (New York: Cambridge University Press, 1997), xi–xiii.

3. For biographical details of Nairne's life, see Alexander Moore's introduction to Thomas Nairne, *Nairne's Muskhogean Journals: The 1708 Expedition to the Mississippi River*, ed. and intro. Alexander Moore (Jackson: University Press of Mississippi, 1988), 3–32; on Barnwell, see Verner Crane, *The Southern Frontier, 1670–1732* (Durham, N.C.: Duke University Press, 1928), 163. On the importance of their two maps, see William P. Cumming, *The Southeast in Early Maps*, 3rd ed. revised and enlarged by Louis De Vorsey Jr. (Chapel Hill: University of North Carolina Press, 1998), 22, 24–25.

4. Memorial of Thomas Nairne, July 8, 1708, in Great Britain, Public Record Office, *Records in the British Public Record Office Relating to South Carolina, 1701–1710*, indexed by A. S. Salley, printed for the Historical Commission of South Carolina, 5 vols. (Columbia, S.C.: Crowson-Stone Printing, 1947), 5:193, 196.

5. Moll's outrage was not limited to the Southeast. Legends on the map expressed frustration over Britain's failure to conquer Quebec. Herman Moll, "A New and Exact Map of the Dominions of the King of Great Britain on ye Continent of North America" [1715]. The above information comes from a circa 1731 copy of the map held at the Newberry Library, Chicago, Illinois. Cumming, *Southeast in Early Maps*, 207.

6. Delisle was a student of Jean Dominique Cassini, whose astronomically based map of France was a major innovation in the science of cartography. Norman J. W. Thrower, *Maps and Civilization: Cartography and Culture in Society* (Chicago: University of Chicago Press, 1996), 95, 110; Cumming, *Southeast in Early Maps*, 20–21.

7. See Patricia Galloway, "Debriefing Explorers Amerindian Information in the Delisles' Mapping of the Southeast," in *Cartographic Encounters: Perspectives on Native American Mapmaking and Map Use*, ed. Malcolm G. Lewis (Chicago: University of Chicago Press, 1998), 223–40.

8. Guillame Delisle, "Map of Louisiana and the Course of the Mississippi" [1730], copy held in Newberry Library; Cumming, *Southeast in Early Maps*, 20–21.

9. Cumming calls the Beresford map the best backcountry map until the 1721 Barnwell-Hammerton map. Cumming, *Southeast in Early Maps*, 23–24.

10. Herman Moll, "A New Map of the North Parts of North America claimed by France" [London, 1720], Newberry Library.

11. Azilia was the ambitious plan of Robert Montgomery, but Montgomery's charter expired before he could settle the colony. The territory was later granted to the Trustees for the Colony of Georgia.

12. Crane, *Southern Frontier*, 213–14, 228–31.

13. Ibid., 234.

14. On the development of Carolina's Indian trade after the Yamasee War, see James Merrell, *The Indian's New World: Catawbas and Their Neighbors from European Contact through the Era of Removal* (Chapel Hill: University of North Carolina Press, 1989; New York: W. W. Norton, 1991), 80–91.

15. Allen D. Candler, Kenneth Coleman, and Milton Ready, eds., *The Colonial Records of the State of Georgia*, 30 vols. (Atlanta: C. P. Byrd, 1904–16; Athens: University of Georgia Press, 1974–76), 3:20. Hereafter cited as *CRG*.

16. Louis De Vorsey Jr., "Oglethorpe and the Earliest Maps of Georgia," in *Oglethorpe in Perspective: Georgia's Founder after Two Hundred Years*, ed. Phinizy Spalding and Harvey H. Jackson (Tuscaloosa: University of Alabama Press, 1989), 36–40.

17. Edward J. Cashin, "Oglethorpe's Contest for the Backcountry, 1733–1749," in Spalding and Jackson, *Oglethorpe in Perspective*, 103–5.

18. Ibid., 105–6. For a fuller history of the Augusta-based Indian trade, see Kathryn Holland Braund, *Deerskins and Duffels: Creek Indian Trade with Anglo-America, 1685–1815* (Lincoln: University of Nebraska Press, 1993).

19. This is work that began with the revisionist interpretations of the late J. B. Harley in the 1980s. His most influential essays have been collected and reprinted in J. B. Harley, *The New Nature of Maps: Essays in the History of Cartography*, ed. Paul Laxton, intro. J. H. Andrews (Baltimore: Johns Hopkins University Press, 2001). Harley, following the work of Michel Foucault, interpreted maps as a form of power/knowledge that privileged a "scientific" understanding of geography that ultimately served the interests of rising nation-states while delegitimizing native systems of geographic understanding. An example of this approach applied to the Southeast can be found in Gregory Nobles, "Straight Lines and Stability: Mapping the Political Order of the Anglo-American Frontier," *Journal of American History* 80 (June 1993): 9–35. Other works in this school of thought that have influenced this book are Denis Wood with John Fels, *The Power of Maps* (New York: Guilford Press, 1992), and Walter Mignolo,

The Darker Side of the Renaissance: Literacy, Teritoriality, and Colonization (Ann Arbor: University of Michigan Press, 1997).

20. Here I am following the lead of recent cartographic historiography. Matthew Edney has argued for a multivalent approach to maps, recognizing that cartography is not a monolithic endeavor. It is one means of engagement between humans and their environment and not always the most significant one. Further, separate elements within the map are as much connected to these other discourses as to each other. As an example, Edney cites the ways in which topographical maps and landscape art both entail the "appropriation, reconfiguration, and modification of the landscape." Matthew Edney, "The Irony of Imperial Mapping," in *The Imperial Map: Cartography and the Mastery of Empire*, ed. James R. Akerman (Chicago: University of Chicago Press, 2009), 19. Edney's approach thus focuses on maps as artifacts and requires a study of how maps were made, circulated, and used in the wider culture (18). For an excellent overview of this historiographic trend, see D. Graham Burnett, "Hydrographic Discipline among the Navigators," in Akerman, *Imperial Map*, 185–259, 216–17.

21. Harley, "Power and Legitimation," 162, 173–76.

22. Journal of the Georgia Commons House of Assembly, Dec. 10, 1763, *CRG*, 14:78.

23. James Glen to the Board of Trade, Dec. 1751, in Great Britain, Public Record Office, *Documents of the British Public Record Office Relating to South Carolina, 1663–1782* (Columbia: South Carolina Department of Archives and History, 1973), 12 reels, microfilm, 24:406. Hereafter cited as *SCPRO*.

24. Proceedings of the Georgia President and Assistants, Nov. 16, 1744. *CRG*, 6:119.

25. Barbara Belyea, "Inland Journeys, Native Maps," in Lewis, *Cartographic Encounters*, 140.

26. Louis De Vorsey Jr. "American Indians and the Early Mapping of the Southeast," in Cumming, *Southeast in Early Maps*, 71.

27. On indigenous mapping in colonial contexts, see the essays in Lewis's *Cartographic Encounters*, in particular the following: Elizabeth Hill Boone, "Maps of Territory, History, and Community in Aztec Mexico," 111–34, which identifies and analyzes a "path map" produced by sixteenth-century Central American Indians in Tochpan; Patricia Galloway, "Debriefing Explorers: Amerindian Information in the Delisles' Mapping of the Southeast," 223–40, which identifies indigenous mapping traditions in eighteenth-century French maps of the Southeast; and Gregory A. Waselkov, "Indian Maps of the Colonial Southeast: Archaeological Implications and Prospects," 205–22, which provides an overview of southeastern mapping. See also Gregory Waselkov, "Indian Maps of the Colonial Southeast," in *Powhatan's Mantle: Indians in the Colonial Southeast*, ed. Waselkov, Peter H. Wood, and Tom Hatley, rev. and exp. ed. (Lincoln: University of Nebraska Press, 2006), 435–453, which provides the most encyclopedic description of colonial Indian maps of the Southeast.

28. For a full description and interpretation of the Chickasaw map, see Waselkov, "Indian Maps," 481–84; also Peter Wood, "Circles in the Sand: Perspectives on the Southern Frontier at the Arrival of James Oglethorpe," in Spalding and Jackson, *Oglethorpe in Perspective*, 19–21.

29. See Waselkov, "Archaeological Implications," 225–26, for other examples.

30. Joshua Piker, "'White and Clean' and Contested," *Ethnohistory* 50, no. 2 (2003): 322–23.

31. Emistisiguo quoted ibid., 327.
32. Ibid.
33. Ibid.
34. For a description of the basic trade route, see Crane, *Southern Frontier*, 132–36; also see maps in Braund, *Deerskins and Duffels*, 90, and Piker, "Contested," 316.
35. John Pettycrow to Governor James Glen, Dec. 4, 1752, in *Documents Relating to Indian Affairs*, ed. William L. McDowell, Colonial Records of South Carolina, series 2: Indian Books, published for the South Carolina Department of Archives and History, 2 vols. (Columbia: University of South Carolina Press, 1958, 1970), 1:351–52. Hereafter cited as *DRIA*.
36. Joshua Piker has recently made the first argument for a stable pattern of relations in the eighteenth-century Southeast: "Colonists and Creeks: Rethinking the Pre-Revolutionary Southern Backcountry," *Journal of Southern History* 70 (August, 2004): 506–7.
37. Magali Carrera, "Entangled Spaces: Mapping Practices of Eighteenth-Century New Spain" (paper presented at the seventeenth Kenneth Nebenzahl Jr. Lectures in the History of Cartography, Chicago, November 2010), 3–9.
38. "Appendix to the Journal of Thomas Bosomworth," *DRIA*, 1:329.
39. "Brown, Rae, & Company to the Georgia Trustees," Feb. 13, 1751, *CRG*, 26:153.
40. Crane, *Southern Frontier*, 93–94, Cumming, *Southeast in Early Maps*, 22
41. The trustees' promotional literature for Georgia included maps of the Southeast that were essentially Nairne's 1708 map with the bounds of Georgia marked upon them. See De Vorsey, "Oglethorpe and the Earliest Maps," 30–33.
42. Nairne, *Muskhogean Journals*, 51.
43. For a reproduction of the Crisp inset, see Cumming, *Southeast in Early Maps*, plate 45. For a comparison with a modern reconstruction of the path's actual course through the Southeast, compare the Nairne map with the one found in Braund, *Deerskins and Duffels*, 90. Also see Steven C. Hahn's updated version of Braund's map in his *The Invention of the Creek Nation, 1670–1783* (Lincoln: University of Nebraska Press, 2004), iix.
44. Crane, *Southern Frontier*, 228–34.
45. The Barnwell-Hammerton map is reprinted in Cumming, *Southeast in Early Maps*, plates 48, 48A–D. See also 218–19.
46. Braund, *Deerskins and Duffels*, 26–29; John Philip Reid, *A Better Kind of Hatchet: Law, Trade, and Diplomacy in the Cherokee Nation during the Early Years of European Contact* (University Park: Pennsylvania State Unversity Press, 1976), 72–73.
47. Crane has said that Popple used the Barnwell map, but "not very intelligently." Crane, *Southern Frontier*, 351; Cumming described the Popple map as "impressive in conception and elaborate in detail, if at times faulty in execution." Cumming, *Southeast in Early Maps*, 233.
48. Cumming, *Southeast in Early Maps*, 233.
49. Henry Popple, "A Map of the British Empire in North America" [London, 1733]. Copy held in the Graff Collection, Newberry Library.
50. The emphasis on individual autonomy in Indian social order has been emphasized in most recent accounts of Anglo-Indian relations. On Creek notions of autonomy, see Braund, *Deerskins and Duffels*, 20–22, and Piker, "Contested," 318–20; for the Cherokees, see Reid, *Hatchet*, 2–5.
51. "James Glen to Board of Trade," Dec. 1751, *SCPRO*, 24:403–4.

52. Popple, "Map of the British Empire in North America."
53. Cumming, *Southeast in Early Maps*, 233.
54. John Mitchell, "A Map of the British and French Dominions in North America" [London, 1755]. Copy held in the Ayer Collection, Newberry Library.
55. Cumming, *Southeast in Early Maps*, 274.
56. Ibid., 323. On De Brahm's career and his role as Surveyor General, see Louis De Vorsey Jr.'s introduction to John Gerar William De Brahm, *De Brahm's Report of the General Survey in the Southern District of North America*, ed. and intro. Louis De Vorsey Jr. (Columbia: University of South Carolina Press, 1971), 3–5, 33–36.
57. Thrower, *Maps and Civilization*, 105–113.
58. De Brahm, "Map of South Carolina and Part of Georgia" [1757]. Copy held in the Ayer Collection, Newberry Library.
59. De Vorsey's introduction to De Brahm, *Reports*, 45; De Brahm quoted in De Vorsey, *Report*, 45.
60. Harley, "Power and Legitimation," 191.
61. Robert Paulett, "The Bewildering World of William De Brahm: An Eighteenth-Century Map Maker Surveys the End of Time," *Eighteenth-Century Studies* 42 (July 2009): 492–94.
62. Thomas Boone to the Board of Trade, Jan. 20, 1764, *SCPRO*, 29:397.
63. William Bull to the Board of Trade, Sept. 3, 1764, *SCPRO*, 30:195.
64. James Wright to the Board of Trade, Aug. 27, 1764, *CRG*, 28, pt. 2:51–52.
65. John Stuart on General Indian relations in the Southern Department, 1765 in Great Britain, Public Record Office, *Records of the British Colonial Office, Class 5, Part 1: Westward Expansion, 1700–1783* (Frederick, Md.: University Publications of America, 1981–1984), 12 reels, microfilm. 66:386. Hereafter cited as *CO-WE*.
66. On Stuart's plan for regulating the deerskin trade, see J. Russell Snapp, *John Stuart and the Struggle for Empire on the Southern Frontier* (Baton Rouge: Louisiana State University Press, 1996), 55–61.
67. Ibid., 61.
68. Letter from John Stuart, Aug. 8, 1766, *CO-WE*, 67: 590.
69. Ibid., 591.
70. Piker, "Contested," 325–26.
71. Stuart quoted in Louis De Vorsey Jr., *The Indian Boundary in the Southern Colonies, 1763–1775* (Chapel Hill: University of North Carolina Press, 1961), 229.
72. William Bartram, *The Travels of William Bartram: Naturalist's Edition*, ed. Francis Harper (New Haven, Conn.: Yale University Press, 1958), 23.
73. Philip Yonge, "A Map of the Lands Ceded to His Majesty by the Creek and Cherokee Indians at a Congress held in Augusta the 1st June 1773," photocopy in the Newberry Library.
74. On Stuart's opposition to the New Purchase, see Snapp, *John Stuart*, 121–27.
75. Stuart quoted in Newton D. Mereness, ed. *Travels in the American Colonies* (New York: Macmillan, 1916), 493.
76. Instructions to David Taitt, ibid., 493.
77. Journal of David Taitt, ibid., 497–98.
78. De Brahm listed Purcell as "Draughtsman, Mathematician, Navigator," in his "A List of the Inhabitants of East Florida, their Employs, Business and Qualifications in Science from 1763 to 1771," included in De Brahm, *Report*, 185.

79. Hachuring involved the use of straight lines whose thickness indicated the steepness of a slope. See Thrower, *Maps and Civilization*, 113.

80. On the contests Stuart faced from British governors and traders, see Snapp, *John Stuart*, 63–77, 93–107.

81. The quote actually serves as a heading in Cashin, "Gentlemen of Augusta," 48; Braund, *Deerskins and Duffels*, 100–102, also employs 1763 as the date which brought the Indian trade into decline due to increased competition among traders following the Proclamation of 1763.

82. Both tables reproduced in De Vorsey, "Colonial Georgia Backcountry," 11.

83. On the specifics of the American Revolution's origins in Georgia, see Snapp, *John Stuart*, 147–88; Edward J. Cashin, "'But Brothers, It Is Our Land We are Talking About': Winners and Losers in the Georgia Backcountry," in *An Uncivil War: The Southern Backcountry during the American Revolution*, ed. Ronald Hoffman, Thad Tate, and Peter Albert (Charlottesville: University of Virginia Press, 1985), 240–75; on the emergence of the backcountry political leadership, see Harvey H. Jackson, "The Rise of the Western Members: Revolutionary Politics and the Georgia Backcountry," in Hoffman, Tate, and Albert, *Uncivil War*, 276–320.

84. As Cashin has noted, the debate over the Indian trade served more to define Whig and Tory allegiance in Georgia than any debate over taxation or representation. Cashin, "Brothers," 245–53.

2 / The Life of the Region

1. Rae's comings and goings were recorded most meticulously by William Stephens, the Georgia Trustees' Secretary in Savannah. See Journal of William Sephens in *The Colonial Records of the State of Georgia*, ed. Allen D. Candler, Kenneth Coleman, and Milton Ready, 30 vols. (Atlanta: C. P. Byrd, 1904–16; Athens: University of Georgia Press, 1974–76), vol. 4 and supplement. Hereafter cited as *CRG*.

2. "Patroon" was the most common term for the boats' masters. For a biography of Rae, see George Fenwick Jones, "Portrait of an Irish Entrepreneur in Colonial Augusta: John Rae, 1708–1772," *Georgia Historical Quarterly* 83 (Fall 1999): 427–47.

3. Examples of this relationship between Augusta and its river can be found in Edward J. Cashin, *The Story of Augusta* (Augusta: Richmond County Board of Education, 1980), 3. Cashin repeats the basic story in his introduction, "The Setting," to his edited volume, *Colonial Augusta: "Key of the Indian Countrey"* (Macon, Ga.: Mercer University Press, 1986), 1–2, and historical geographer Louis De Vorsey Jr. elaborates on the theme in his essay, "The Colonial Georgia Backcountry," in the same volume, 4–10. Kathryn Holland Braund's landmark study, *Deerskins and Duffels: Creek Indian Trade with Anglo-America, 1685–1815* (Lincoln: University of Nebraska Press, 1993), also repeats the town-river association, 41. Historical archaeologist Kenneth E. Lewis included Augusta in his study of settlement patterns in the South Carolina backcountry. For an overview of this theory, and the centrality of riverine networks in frontier settlements, see Lewis, "The Metropolis and the Backcountry: The Making of a Colonial Landscape on the South Carolina Frontier," *Historical Archaeology* 33, no. 3 (1999): 3–13, 6. For a more general overview of the importance of river systems in backcountry history, see Robert D. Mitchell, "The Southern Backcountry: A Geographical House Divided," in *The Southern Colonial Backcountry: Interdisciplinary Perpsectives*

on *Frontier Communities*, ed. David Colin Crass et al. (Knoxville: University of Tennessee Press, 1998), 1–35.

4. Robbie Ethridge provides the most detailed description of Creek town environments in her *Creek Country: The Creek Indians and Their World* (Chapel Hill: University of North Carolina Press, 2003), 32–91.

5. Theda Perdue, *Cherokee Women: Gender and Culture Change, 1700–1835*, (Lincoln: University of Nebraska Press, 1998), 34; Charles Hudson, *The Southeastern Indians* (Knoxville: University of Tennessee Press, 1976), 125–44, 172, 324, 355.

6. Paul Kelton, "The Great Southeastern Smallpox Epidemic, 1696–1700: The Region's First Major Epidemic?," in *Light on the Path: The Anthropology and History of the Southeastern Indians*, ed. Thomas J. Pluckhahn and Robbie Ethridge (Tuscaloosa: University of Alabama Press, 2006), 21–37, 27–28. The Savannah River Valley was abandoned in this way because it served as a "buffer zone" between the Mississippian chiefdoms of Ocute and Cofitachequi. On the concept of buffer zones between chiefdoms, see David J. Hally, "The Nature of Mississippian Regional Systems," in *The Transformation of the Southeastern Indians, 1540–1760*, ed. Robbie Ethridge and Charles Hudson (Jackson: University Press of Mississippi, 2002), 26–42.

7. On the history of the Westos, the Savannahs, and the Yuchis, see Alan Gallay, *The Indian Slave Trade: The Rise of the English Empire in the American South, 1670–1717* (New Haven, Conn.: Yale University Press, 2002), 40–41, 55–61, 319. On the history of the eastern Chickasaws, see Edward J. Cashin, *Guardians of the Valley: Chickasaws in Colonial South Carolina and Georgia* (Columbia: University of South Carolina Press, 2009).

8. Angela Pulley Hudson, *Creek Paths and Federal Roads: Indians, Settlers, and Slaves and the Making of the American South* (Chapel Hill: University of North Carolina Press, 2010), 19–20; for other examples of watery boundaries in Indian cultures, see William Cronon, *Changes in the Land: Indians, Colonists, and the Ecology of New England* (New York: Hill and Wang, 1983), 63–64.

9. John Juricek, *Colonial Georgia and the Creeks: Anglo-Indian Diplomacy on the Southern Frontier, 1733–1763* (Gainesville: University Press of Florida, 2010), 37.

10. Hudson, *Creek Paths*, 50–51.

11. Louis De Vorsey Jr., "American Indians and the Early Mapping of the Southeast," in William P. Cumming, *The Southeast in Early Maps*, 3rd ed., rev. and enl. by Louis De Vorsey Jr. (Chapel Hill: University of North Carolina Press, 1998), 71.

12. T. S. Willan, *River Navigation in England, 1600–1750* (London: Oxford University Press, 1964), 21–22; L. T. C. Rolt, *The Inland Waterways of England* (London: George Allen and Unwin, 1966), 17.

13. Willan, *Navigation*, 30.

14. Speaker of House of Commons to House of Lords, quoted ibid., 29.

15. For a survey of some of these contests, see ibid., 24–51.

16. "A Description of the Golden Islands, with an Account of the Undertaking now on Foot for making a Settlement there [London, 1720]," in *The Most Delightful Country of the Universe: Promotional Litrature of the Colony of Georgia, 1717–1734*, ed. Trevor R. Reese (Savannah: Beehive Press, 1972), 42.

17. Jean Pierre Purry, "Memorial of Jean Pierre Purry," in Reese, *Most Delightful Country*, 59.

18. Sir Robert Montgomery, "The Most Delightful Country of the Universe," in Reese, *Most Delightful Country*, 17.

19. Benjamin Martyn, "Reasons for Establishing the Colony of Georgia," in Reese, *Most Delightful Country*, 177–81.

20. Barnwell's letter printed in "Description of the Golden Islands," in Reese, *Most Delightful Country*, 43.

21. John Gerar William De Brahm, *De Brahm's Report of the General Survey in the Southern District of North America*, ed. and intro. Louis De Vorsey Jr. (Columbia: University of South Carolina Press, 1971), 150.

22. Ibid., 105.

23. James Adair, *History of the American Indians*, ed. Samuel Cole Williams (Johnson City, Tenn.: Watauga Press, 1930), 484.

24. James Oglethorpe to the Georgia Trustees, March 8, 1739, *CRG* 22 (2): 109. Edward Cashin, "The Gentlemen of Augusta," in Cashin, *"Key of the Indian Countrey,"* 31–33.

25. James Oglethorpe to the Georgia Trustees, March 12, 1733, *CRG* 20:13–14.

26. An Act to Prevent the Importation and Use of Rum and Brandies in the Province of Georgia, January 9, 1745, *CRG* 1:44.

27. An Act for Rendering the Colony of Georgia more Defencible by Prohibiting the Importation and Use of Black Slaves or Negroes into the Same, January 9, 1734, *CRG* 1:50.

28. Benjamin Martyn, "An Account Showing the Progress of the Colony of Georgia in America from its First Establishment," 1741, *CRG* 3:377.

29. Ibid., 3:377.

30. James Oglethorpe to the Georgia Trustees, Oct. 20, 1739, *CRG* 22 (1): 253.

31. Thomas Jones to Harman Verelst, July 15, 1740, *CRG* 22 (1): 391–92.

32. Journal of the Earl of Egmont, March 6, 1741, *CRG* 5:464.

33. See Chapter 3.

34. Georgia Charter, 1732, quoted in Louis De Vorsey Jr., *The Georgia-South Carolina Boundary: A Problem in Historical Geography* (Athens: University of Georgia Press, 1982), 23.

35. Ibid., 23–31.

36. *South Carolina Gazette*, May 1, 1736. See also Cashin, *Story of Augusta*, 10. Cashin notes that the boats belonged to Kennedy O'Brien, a New Windsor trader who would soon become one of Augusta's first residents.

37. *South Carolina Gazette*, May 1, 1736.

38. Petition and Representation of the Council and Assembly of South Carolina, 1736, Great Britain, Public Record Office, *Documents of the British Public Record Office Relating to South Carolina, 1663–1782* (Columbia: South Carolina Department of Archives and History, 1973), 12 reels, microfilm. 18:90, 97. Hereafter cited as *SCPRO*.

39. Ibid., 18:97.

40. Ibid., 18:98.

41. Ibid., 18:95–96.

42. Thomas Broughton to the Board of Trade, Aug. 6, 1736, *SCPRO*, 18:60.

43. Petition and Representation of the Council and Assembly of South Carolina, *SCPRO*, 18:95.

44. Broughton to Board of Trade, Aug. 6, 1736, *SCPRO*, 18:63.

45. Ibid., 18:63.

46. Robert Mackay to Mary Chilcott Mackay, Jan. 4, 1775, Mackay-Stiles Family Papers, Southern Historical Collection, University of North Carolina at Chapel Hill.

47. William Bartram, *The Travels of William Bartram, Naturalist's Edition*, ed. Francis Harper (New Haven, Conn.: Yale University Press, 1958), 25.

48. Ibid., 199.

49. Ibid., 200.

50. Hammond quoted in Charles C. Jones and Salem Dutcher, *Memorial History of Augusta, Georgia* (Syracuse: D. Mason, 1890; Spartanburg, S.C.: Reprint Company, 1966), 441.

51. Kristian Hvidt, ed., *Von Reck's Voyage: Drawings and Journal of Philip Georg Friedrich von Reck* (Savannah: Beehive Press, 1980), 36.

52. De Brahm, *Report*, 159.

53. Hvidt, *Von Reck's Voyage*, 37.

54. The weirs on English rivers were designed to elevate the water level for the use of mills and the seasonal flooding of farmlands. Discussion of river navigation thus centered on human actions rather than natural ones. Willan, *Navigation*, 17–19, 86. See also P. A. L. Vine, *London's Lost Route to the Sea: An Historical Account of the Inland Navigations which Linked the Thames and the English Channel* (Newton Abbot, Eng.: David and Charles, 1965), 5.

55. Hvidt, *Von Reck's Voyage*, 50.

56. Proceedings of the President and Assistants, April 3, 1742, *CRG*, 6:28.

57. Robert G. McPherson, ed., *Journal of the Earl of Egmont : Abstract of the Trustees Proceedings for Establishing the Colony of Georgia, 1732–1738* (Athens: University of Georgia Press, 1962), 132.

58. Hvidt, *Von Reck's Voyage*, 36.

59. Bartram, *Travels*, 31.

60. Ibid., 33.

61. Willan, *Navigation*, 96–100.

62. Quoted in Hvidt, *Von Reck's Voyage*, 84.

63. Rusty Fleetwood provides the best overview of southeastern craft types in his *Tidecraft: An Introductory Look at the Boats of Lower South Carolina, Georgia, and Northeastern Florida: 1650–1950*, principal research by Antionette Goodrich (Savannah: Coastal Heritage Society, 1982), 4–6, 33–35. On the use of European oars, see Hvidt, *Von Reck's Voyage*, 37.

64. Timothy Silver, *A New Face on the Countryside: Indians, Colonists, and Slaves in South Atlantic Forests, 1500–1800* (New York: Cambridge University Press, 1990), 57.

65. W. Jeffrey Bolster, *Black Jacks: African American Seamen in the Age of Sail* (Cambridge, Mass.: Harvard University Press, 1997), 60–61; John Thornton, *Africa and Africans in the Making of the Atlantic World, 1400–1800*, 2nd ed. (New York: Cambridge University Press, 1998), 36–40.

66. Proceedings of the President and Assistants, June 7, 1745, *CRG*, 6:135; Hugh Ross, a freeholder of Savannah was found guilty of pilfering the trustees' timber, which prompted the further complaint of the "frequent Spoil . . . made in the Woods by sundry People in cutting the choicest of Timber," Proceedings of the President and Assistants, June 15, 1745, *CRG*, 6:136–37.

67. McPherson, *Egmont*, 195.

210 / NOTES TO CHAPTER 2

68. Journal of William Stephens, July 14, 1740, *CRG*, 4:619.
69. Ibid., 4:620.
70. McPherson, *Egmont*, 133.
71. Journal of William Stephens, March 21, 1739, *CRG*, 4:303.
72. Eugene D. Genovese, *Roll, Jordan, Roll: The World the Slaves Made* (New York: Vintage Books, 1976), 25–37.
73. "Journal of William Stephens [supplement]," March 10, 1741, *CRG*, 4(sup): 102.
74. William Stephens, *The Journal of William Stephens*, ed. E. Meron Coulter, 2 vols. (Athens: University of Georgia Press, 1958–1959), 2:120.
75. Journal of William Stephens, Sept. 16, 1738, *CRG*, 4:201.
76. Journal of William Stephens, March 26, 1741, *CRG*, 4(sup): 114.
77. Patrick Tailfer et al., "A True and Historical Narrative of the Colony of Georgia in America," in *The Clamorous Malcontents: Criticisms and Defenses of the Colony of Georgia, 1741–1743*, ed. Trevor R. Reese (Savannah: Beehive Press, 1973), 104.
78. In England, boatmen did not receive much in the way of respect. Opponents of river improvements often pointed to the bad things that boatmen would bring to their towns and farms: theft, drunkenness, and overall bad behavior. These characterizations must be taken with a grain of salt, given the contests over who could and should use a river in England, but the public reputation of a boatman was not in general a positive one. Willan, *Navigation*, 45, 107–11.
79. McPherson, *Egmont*, 193.
80. John Gerar William De Brahm, "A Map of Carolina and Part of Georgia" [1757]. Copy held in the Ayer Collection, Newberry Library.
81. Hvidt, *Von Reck's Voyage*, 34.
82. "A New Voyage to Georgia by a Young Gentleman" [1737], *Collections of the Georgia Historical Society* 2 (1842): 37–60, 46.
83. Bartram, *Travels*, lvii.
84. Stephens, *Journal of William Stephens*, 2:53, 67–68.
85. White Outerbridge to William Henry Lyttelton, July 10, 1759, William Henry Lyttelton Papers, William L. Clements Library, University of Michigan.
86. Edmond Atkin to William Henry Lyttelton, Jan. 31, 1760, Lyttelton Papers.
87. Robert Mackay to Mary Chilcott Mackay, undated, in the Mackay and Stiles Family Papers #470, Southern Historical Collection, Wilson Library, University of North Carolina at Chapel Hill; Robert Mackay to Mary Chilcott Mackay, Jan. 10, 1775, Mackay and Stiles Family Papers.
88. Export figures from Joshua Piker, *Okfuskee: A Creek Indian Town in Colonial America* (Cambridge, Mass.: Harvard University Press, 2004), 148. The number of boat trips is an estimate based on the fact that the largest trading boats could carry about one thousand skins, each weighing between one and two pounds. For boat capacity, see Fleetwood, *Tidecraft*, 34–35. On the weight of the average deerskin, see Braund, *Deerskins and Duffels*, 88–89. Piker has noted the increasingly year-round nature of the trade in Creek towns in his *Okfuskee*, 149.
89. *South Carolina Gazette*, Sept. 15, 1749.
90. *Georgia Gazette*, March 22, 1764.
91. *South Carolina Gazette*, Dec. 19, 1748.
92. Philip D. Morgan, *Slave Counterpoint: Black Culture in the Eighteenth-Century*

Chesapeake and Lowcountry (Chapel Hill: University of North Carolina Press, 1998), 243–44.

93. *Georgia Gazette*, March 22, 1769.

94. Henry Laurens, *The Papers of Henry Laurens*, ed. Philip M. Hamer (Columbia, S.C.: University of South Carolina Press for the South Carolina Historical Society, 1968), 16 vols., 5:475.

95. On slaves adopting Indian water culture, see Peter Wood, *Black Majority: Negroes in Colonial South Carolina from 1670 through the Stono Rebellion* (New York: W. W. Norton, 1974), 114–17; David Cecelski, *The Waterman's Song: Slavery and Freedom in Maritime North Carolina* (Chapel Hill: University of North Carolina Press, 2001), 5–12. On African antecdents of Carolina's enslaved watermen, see Bolster, *Black Jacks*, 48–50, and Morgan, *Slave Counterpoint*, 242–44.

96. Bolster, *Black Jacks*, 62–65; Leland Ferguson, *Uncommon Ground: Archaeology and Early African America, 1650–1800* (Washington: Smithsonian Institution Press, 1992), 109–16.

97. Martyn, "Account," in *CRG*, 3:377.

98. Ibid., 3:377.

99. *South Carolina Gazette*, April 12, 1739.

100. Bolster, *Black Jacks*, 52.

101. Ibid., 52–53. Wood, in his *Black Majority*, 202–5, first recognized the importance of black boatmen in South Carolina, noting that they "literally provided the backbone of the lowland transportation system during most of the colonial era." Morgan has further elaborated and explored the lives of Carolina's slave watermen in his *Slave Counterpoint*, 236–44, 337–42.

102. On slave boatmen as agents of refuge, see Morgan, *Slave Counterpoint*, 339–41. A quantitative breakdown of slave boatmen as a percentage of runaways can be found in Philip D. Morgan, "Colonial South Carolina Runaways: Their Significance for Slave Culture," *Slavery and Abolition* 6 (December 1985): 57–78, 63–65; their role in an intraslave economy has been documented in Wood, *Black Majority*, 217. On watermen's roles in spreading abolitionism and rebellion against slave owners, Bolster offers a broad study of the subject in *Black Jacks*, 190–214; Cecelski offers a much more in-depth study of watermen's lives within a region in his *The Waterman's Song*.

103. Cecelski, *Waterman's Song*, xv–xvii.

104. *South Carolina Gazette*, July 25, 1748.

105. *South Carolina Gazette*, Nov. 5, 1737.

106. Morgan, "Colonial South Carolina Runaways," 69–74.

107. James Oakes has argued that the erasure of Africans' legal ability to maintain kinship ties, or slaves' "kinlessness," underpinned the brutality and idea of slavery. Oakes, *Slavery and Freedom: An Intepretation of the Old South* (New York: W. W. Norton, 1990), 4.

108. Journal of the Earl of Egmont, Jan. 6, 1742, *CRG*, 5:583.

109. Journal of William Stephens [supplement], March 10, 1741, *CRG*, 4(sup): 102.

110. Ibid.

111. Kenneth Coleman, *Colonial Georgia: A History* (New York: Scribner, 1976), 230.

112. *South Carolina Gazette*, April 6, 1738.

113. *South Carolina Gazette*, Oct. 19, 1738.

114. *Georgia Gazette*, Feb. 24, 1768.
115. *Georgia Gazette*, May 25, 1768.
116. *Georgia Gazette*, May 3, 1769.
117. *Georgia Gazette*, June 2, 1769.

3 / Keeping Company, Keeping Store

1. James Adair, *History of the American Indians*, ed. Samuel Cole Williams (Johnson City, Tenn.: Watauga Press, 1930), 278.
2. National Society Colonial Dames of America, *Abstracts of Colonial Wills of the State of Georgia* (Atlanta: Georgia Department of Archives and History, 1962), 120.
3. On Ross's death in the context of Okfuskee politics, see Joshua Piker, *Okfuskee: A Creek Town in Colonial America* (Cambridge, Mass.: Harvard University Press, 2004), 52–63.
4. Kenneth Coleman, *Colonial Georgia: A History* (New York: Charles Scribner's Sons, 1976), 51. Coleman's work tended to criticize the trustees' "interference" in the natural course of southeastern development, and he saw Augusta's early success as proof that the carefully managed settlements near Savannah could not thrive until slavery was introduced after 1750.
5. Helen Callahan, "Colonial Life in Augusta," in *Colonial Augusta: "Key of the Indian Countrey,"* ed. Edward J. Cashin (Macon, Ga.: Mercer University Press, 1986), 96–97, 119. Callahan, the only historian to study Augusta's daily life, emphasized its development through formal institutions such as schooling, church-building, and the development of a court system. Edward Cashin's textbook of Augusta history, *The Story of Augusta*, likewise emphasized Augusta's formal development and its transition from "an Indian town" to a market town through "civilizing influences at work among the rough frontier folk." Edward J. Cashin, *The Story of Augusta* (Augusta: Richmond County Board of Education, 1980), 17.
6. See Heard Robertson and Thomas H. Robertson, "The Town and Fort of Augusta," in Cashin, *Key of the Indian Countrey*, 60–63, map on 64.
7. Phinizy Spalding, "James Edward Oglethorpe's Quest for an American Zion," in *Forty Years of Diversity: Essays on Colonial Georgia*, ed. Harvey H. Jackson and Phinizy Spalding (Athens: University of Georgia Press, 1984), 68–71.
8. John W. Reps, "C2 + L2 = S2? Another Look at the Origins of Savannah's Town Plan," in Jackson and Spalding, *Diversity*, 117–20.
9. Robertson and Robertson, "The Town and Fort of Augusta," 60; see also Cashin, "Gentlemen," in Cashin, *Key of the Indian Countrey*, 30–31.
10. See maps in Martha F. Norwood, *A History of the White House Tract, Richmond County, Georgia, 1756–1975* (Atlanta: Georgia Department of Natural Resources, Historical Preservation Section, 1975), 5, 16, 51. On the formation of Harrisburg, see ibid., 46–51.
11. William Stephens's Journal, Sept. 19, 1738, in *The Colonial Records of the State of Georgia*, ed. Allen D. Candler, Kenneth Coleman, and Milton Ready, 30 vols. (Atlanta: C. P. Byrd, 1904–16; Athens: University of Georgia Press, 1974–76), 4:203. Hereafter cited as *CRG*.
12. Mackay quoted in Callahan, "Colonial Life in Augusta," 97.
13. Thomas Boone, Arthur Dobbs, and Francis Fauquier to James Wright, Oct. 4, 1763, in Great Britain, Public Records Office, *Records of the British Public Records*

Office Relating to South Carolina, 1663-1782 (Columbia: South Carolina Department of Archives and History, 1973), 12 reels, microfilm, 30:18. Hereafter cited as *SCPRO*.

14. Wright to Boone, Dobbs, and Fauquier, Oct. 8, 1763, *SCPRO*, 30:37.

15. Archibald Campbell, "Sketch of the Northern Frontiers of Georgia" [London, 1780], William L. Clements Library, University of Michigan, Ann Arbor.

16. Archibald Campbell, *Journal of an Expedition against the Rebels of Georgia in North America Under the Orders of Archibald Campbell Esquire, Lieut. Colol. of His Majesty's 71st Regimt. 1778*, ed. Colin Campbell (Darien, Ga.: Ashantilly Press, 1981), 54.

17. William Stephens, "A State of the Province of Georgia. Attested upon Oath in the Court of Savannah, Nov. 10, 1740," in *The Clamorous Malcontents: Criticisms and Defeses of the Colony of Georgia, 1741-1743*, ed. Trevor Reese (Savannah: Beehive Press, 1973), 6.

18. Patrick Tailfer, Hugh Anderson, and David Douglass, "A True and Historical Narrative of the Colony of Georgia in America," in Reese, *Malcontents*, 116-17.

19. Tailfer et al., "Narrative," 117. The trustees in London clearly preferred to promote Stephens's vision, as Benjamin Martyn repeated it nearly verbatim in his "Impartial Enquiry into the State and Utility of the Province of Georgia, 1741," in Reese, *Malcontents*, 153-54.

20. Thomas Stephens, "A Brief Account of the Causes that have Retarded the Progress of the Colony of Georgia, 1743," in Reese, *Malcontents*, 282.

21. Deposition of Kennedy O'Brien, July 9, 1741, in Reese, *Malcontents*, 311.

22. Deposition of Sir Richard Everard, in Reese, *Malcontents*, 312.

23. Stephens's Journal, September 19, 1738, *CRG*, 4:203.

24. Ibid.

25. Ibid.

26. William Stephens's Journal [supplement], Oct. 28, 1740, *CRG*, 4 (sup): 19.

27. Ibid., June 25, 1741, *CRG*, 4 (sup): 175.

28. Ibid., June 29, 1741, *CRG*, 4 (sup): 179.

29. Ibid., July 9, 1741, *CRG*, 4 (sup): 187.

30. Ibid., Oct. 24, 1741, *CRG*, 4 (sup): 271.

31. Ibid., 272.

32. Deposition of W. Williams, July 4, 1735, incl. with Memorial of Benjamin Gooden, Richard Hill, James Crockat et al., July 4, 1735, *SCPRO*, 17:424.

33. Deposition of Thomas Johns, July 4, 1735, *SCPRO*, 17:436.

34. Deposition of Jeremiah Knott, July 4, 1735, *SCPRO*, 17:433.

35. Deposition of W. Williams, July 4, 1735, *SCPRO*, 17:425.

36. Ibid.

37. Memorial of Benjamin Hill et al., July 4, 1735, *SCPRO*, 17:412-41.

38. Edward J. Cashin, *Lachlan McGillivray, Indian Trader: The Shaping of the Southern Colonial Frontier* (Athens: University of Georgia Press, 1992), 34-35.

39. Appendix no. 10 to Stephens, "A Brief Account" in Reese, *Malcontents*, 309-10.

40. Stephens's Journal, March 24, 1738, *CRG*, 4:111.

41. Ibid., June 30, 1740, *CRG*, 4:608.

42. Ibid.

43. Stephens's Journal, June 3, 1740, *CRG*, 4:585.

44. *CRG*, 6:129.

45. *Abstract of Colonial Book C-1*, 126–27.

46. On the formation of Brown, Rae, and Company, see Kathryn Holland Braund, *Deerskins and Duffels: Creek Indian Trade with Anglo-America, 1685–1815* (Lincoln: University of Nebraska Press, 1993), 44–49; also Cashin, *Lachlan McGillivray*, 34–36.

47. Edmund Atkin to William Henry Lyttelton, January 31, 1760, Lyttelton Papers.

48. Gavin Cochrane to Thomas Gage, November 27, 1764, Thomas Gage Papers, William L. Clements Library, University of Michigan.

49. Histories of Augusta's founding have emphasized these factors to greater and lesser degrees. Edward Cashin and Louis De Vorsey Jr. emphasized the connection between Augusta, the Savannah, and the indigenous pathways of the Southeast. See Cashin, "Contest," 102–5, and "The Gentlemen of Augusta," in *Colonial Augusta: "Key of the Indian Countrey,"* ed. Cashin (Macon, Ga.: Mercer University Press, 1986), 29–32, and De Vorsey, "The Colonial Georgia Backcountry," in Cashin, *Key*, 5–10. Braund emphasizes both the location and the human networks in her *Deerskins and Duffels*, 41–43.

50. Robert Mitchell first created this developmental model for frontier history in his study of the Shenandoah Valley, *Commercialism and Frontier: Perspectives in the Shenandoah Valley* (Charlottesville: University Press of Virginia, 1977). Kenneth Lewis, a historical archaeologist, adapted Mitchell's model to the South Carolina backcountry in his *The American Frontier: An Archaeological Study of Settlement Pattern and Process*, Studies in Historical Archaeology (Orlando: Academic Press, 1984). In both cases, the authors occupy themselves with what Lewis terms "agricultural colonization," or the development of commercial agriculture along the southern Piedmont. Lewis, *American Frontier*, 19–26. Both authors have revisited and restated their theses in more recent essays. See Mitchell, "The Southern Backcountry: A Geographical House Divided," in *The Southern Colonial Backcountry: Interdisciplinary Perspectives on Frontier Communities*, ed. David Colin Crass et al. (Knoxville: The University of Tennessee Press, 1998), 1–35, and Lewis, "Economic Development in the Southern Backcountry: A View from Camden," in the same volume. The best summary of the model comes from Lewis in his "The Metropolis and the Backcountry: The Making of a Colonial Landscape on the South Carolina Frontier," *Historical Archaeology* 33, no 3 (1999): 3–13.

51. Howard J. Nelson, "Walled Cities of the United States," *Annals of the American Association of Geographers* 51 (March 1961): 1–22.

52. Lewis, *American Frontier*, 80–81.

53. The Chickasaws' involvement in Augusta's defense was ongoing and has been chronicled in Edward Cashin, *Guardians of the Valley: Chickasaws in Colonial South Carolina and Georgia* (Columbia: University of South Carolina Press, 2009).

54. Piker, *Okfuskee*, 112–15; Robbie Ethridge, *Creek Country: The Creek Indians and Their World* (Chapel Hill: University of North Carolina Press, 2003), 95–96.

55. *Georgia Gazette*, March 22, 1769. Although no name appeared on the advertisement, the presence of the store as well the directive to contact either John Gordon of Charles Town or Thomas Netherclift of Savannah indicated that this was the home of someone connected with the Indian trade. Gordon and Netherclift were both low-country merchants closely tied to the Augusta storekeepers.

56. William Bartram, *The Travels of William Bartram, Naturalist's Edition*, ed. Francis Harper (New Haven, Conn.: Yale University Press, 1958), 199.

57. *Abstracts of Colonial Book C-1*, 203.

58. As evidenced by Mary Mackay's reference to her daughter's sitting "up-stairs" in their house. Mary Mackay to Robert Mackay, Jan. 19. 1775, in the Mackay and Stiles Family Papers, #470, in the Southern Historical Collection, Wilson Library, University of North Carolina at Chapel Hill.

59. Mylne to Robert Mylne, June 26, 1774, in Ted Ruddock, ed. *Travels in the Colonies in 1773-1775: Described in the Letters of William Mylne* (Athens: University of Georgia Press, 1993), 30, 33.

60. *South Carolina Gazette*, September 26, 1741.

61. *Georgia Gazette*, April 20, 1768.

62. *Georgia Gazette*, February 28, 1770.

63. Robert Mackay to Mary Chilcott Mackay, January 8, 1775, Mackay and Stiles Family Papers.

64. Robert Mackay to Mary Chilcott Mackay, January 24, 1775, Mackay and Stiles Family Papers.

65. *Georgia Will Abstracts*, 10, 28, 110, 125–26.

66. *Georgia Gazette*, April 6, 1768.

67. *Georgia Gazette*, June 24, 1767.

68. Brown, Rae, & Company to the Georgia Trustees, Feb. 13, 1751, *CRG*, 26:152–53.

69. Augusta Store Journal, 163, 194, 309, 324. Clemson.

70. President and Assistants to Benjamin Martyn, Feb. 25, 1751, *CRG*, 26:161.

71. President and Assistants to Benjamin Martyn, Feb. 28, 1751, *CRG*, 26:169–71.

72. Edmund Atkin to William Henry Lyttelton, Nov. 24, 1758, William Henry Lyttelton Papers, William L. Clements Library, University of Michigan, Ann Arbor.

73. Edmund Atkin to William Henry Lyttelton, January 25, 1760, Lyttelton Papers.

74. Atkin to Lyttelton, Jan. 25, 1760, Lyttelton Papers.

75. Robert Mackay to Mary Mackay, Jan. 24, 1775, Mackay and Stiles Family Papers.

76. Mary Malbone Chilcott to John Malbone, May 14, 1770, Mackay and Stiles Family Papers.

77. Chilcott to Malbone, May 14, 1770, Mackay and Stiles Family Papers.

78. William Mylne to Anne Mylne, May 29, 1774, in Ruddock, *Travels*, 26.

79. William Mylne to Robert Mylne, June 26, 1774, ibid., 31.

80. Ibid.

81. Mary Malbone Chilcott to John Malbone, Oct. 24, 1770, Mackay and Stiles Family Papers.

82. Chilcott to Malbone, Oct. 24, 1770, Mackay and Stiles Family Papers.

83. William Mylne to Anne Mylne, Oct. 13, 1774, in Ruddock, *Travels*, 48.

84. Ibid., 50.

85. Kathleen Brown, *Good Wives, Nasty Wenches, and Anxious Patriarchs: Gender, Race, and Power in Colonial Virginia* (Chapel Hill: University of North Carolina Press,1996), 260–67.

86. Mary Chilcott to John Malbone, May 14, 1770, Mackay and Stiles Family Papers.

87. William Mylne to Anne Mylne, Oct. 13, 1774, in Ruddock, *Travels*, 50.

88. Mary Mackay to Robert Mackay, Jan. 19, 1775, Mackay and Stiles Family Papers.

89. Ibid.
90. Ibid.
91. Ibid.
92. William Mylne to Robert Mylne, June 26, 1774, in Ruddock, *Travels*, 30.
93. Mylne to Anne Mylne, May 29, 1774, ibid.
94. Mylne to Anne Mylne, Oct. 13, 1774, ibid., 47–48.
95. Mylne to Robert Mylne, June 26, 1774, ibid., 32.
96. Mylne to Anne Mylne, Oct. 13, 1774, ibid., 48.
97. The term "frontier exchange economy" was originally coined by Daniel Usner in his *Indians Settlers and Slaves in a Frontier Exchange Economy: The Lower Mississippi Valley before 1783* (Chapel Hill: University of North Carolina Press, 1992). Joshua Piker has adapted Usner's thesis for the British Southeast in his *Okfuskee: A Creek Town in Colonial America* (Cambridge, Mass.: Harvard University Press, 2004), 88–89, 92–101.
98. Henry Ellis to William Henry Lyttelton, April 13, 1758, Lyttelton Papers.
99. Ibid.
100. Henry Ellis to William Henry Lyttelton, May 3, 1758, Lyttelton Papers.
101. James Germany to Rae and Barksdale, undated, incl. in White Outerbridge to William Henry Lyttelton, July 17, 1756, Lyttelton Papers.
102. In September 1756, word reached Augusta of an altercation between Creek warriors and the Ogeechee settlers. Seven of the settlers, led by Andrew and James Lambert, believed that an Indian hunting party had stolen some of their horses. They set out after the alleged thieves the next day and caught up with the hunting party. An exchange of fire left two Indians dead and wounded some of the whites. The sudden threat of an Indian war chased the Ogeechee settlers to Augusta and threatened a full-scale Indian war, one that the "Virginia Men" would have been all too familiar with, having just left a colony in the early, brutal stages of the Seven Years' War. But the conflict came to a surprisingly quick resolution, because neither the Creeks nor the British had any interest in going to war with the other. For more on the Ogeechee incident, see Cashin, *Lachlan McGillivray*, 148–49.
103. John Reynolds to William Henry Lyttelton, Sept. 14, 1756, Lyttelton Papers.
104. Talk of Lower Creek Headmen to John Reynolds, incl. in James Reynolds to William Henry Lyttelton, Oct. 6, 1756, Lyttelton Papers.
105. Henry Ellis to William Henry Lyttelton, March 17, 1758, Lyttelton Papers.
106. Ellis to Lyttelton, March 17, 1758, Lyttelton Papers.
107. Petition of the Inhabitants of Augusta to John Reynolds, Aug. 30, 1756, in Minutes of the Governor and Council, Sept. 15, 1756, *CRG*, 7:399.
108. Petition of Inhabitants of Augusta, Aug. 30, 1756, *CRG*, 7:398
109. David Douglass, John Rae, and Martin Campbell to John Reynolds, Sept. 12, 1756, Minutes of Governor and Council, Sept. 15, 1756, *CRG*, 7:393.
110. Memorial in behalf of the Inhabitants of the Town and Township of Augusta, April 12, 1750, in Berry Fleming, *The Autobiography of a Colony: The First Half-Century of Augusta, Georgia* (Athens: University of Georgia Press, 1957), 35.
111. Petition of the Inhabitants of Augusta, Aug. 30, 1756, *CRG*, 7:398 Signatories to the letter included David Douglass, Martin Campbell, Lachlan McGillivray, John Williams, John Spencer, Daniel Clark, Edward Barnard, John Pettycrow, George Galphin, Moses Nunes, Patrick Clark, John Rae, and Isaac Barksdale, all of them involved in the Indian trade.

112. Cambric was a very fine (and expensive) linen; osnaburg was a cheaper and much coarser linen, used primarily for work clothes.

113. Compiled from Silver Bluff Trading Post Account Book, December 3, 1767–January 18, 1768 [old style, 1769 by modern reckoning], George Galphin Papers, MS no. 269, Georgia Historical Society, Savannah, Georgia.

114. Silver Bluff Account Book, Galphin Papers.

115. Ibid.

116. Augusta Store Journal of Accounts, Mss 197, 248–50, Special Collections, Clemson University Libraries.

117. Ibid.

118. Mylne to Anne Mylne, May 29, 1774, in Ruddock, *Travels*, 26.

119. Mylne to Robert Mylne, June 26, 1774, ibid., 32.

120. George F. Walker, comp., *Abstracts of Georgia Colonial Book J, 1755–1762* (Atlanta: R. J. Taylor Jr. Foundation, 1978), 117.

121. *Abstracts of Colonial Book J*, 115, 109.

122. My reasoning for including such a large range of territory was based on a quote from William Mylne: "Their [sic] are few stores in this part, people comes twenty mile." Mylne to Anne Mylne, May 29, 1774, in Ruddock, *Travels*, 26. I also took into account the fact that, while few of the Augusta traders owned land upriver from Augusta, many owned land in Halifax, and their slaves might be expected to live and work in both districts.

123. Compiled from petitions recorded in the Minutes of the Governor and Council, *Colonial Records of Georgia*, from 1754–69, vols. 7–10. For persons making multiple petitions, I counted only the last in each of two time frames: 1754–59, and 1760–69. I included in the Augusta count the settlements nearest Savannah River (Augusta, Kioka Creek, Little River) but not those for Briar Creek, as there was no easy way to determine where along Briar Creek the claims were made, and many or most of those could have been too far south to count as part of the Augusta neighborood. I included the district of Halifax because it was closely tied to Augusta, and it bordered George Galphin's trading store across the river at Silver Bluff, and many of Augusta's inhabitants held land in Halifax. For those with grants in both districts, I counted only the largest number of slaves on the latest petition in each of my two time windows. The count also includes petitions for the Town and Township of Augusta, where petitioners were not required to give account of their household, which I counted as zero slaves. Thus, these numbers almost certainly underestimate the actual numbers of slaves in and around Augusta. The parish numbers come from the Rev. Samuel Frink and are quoted in Cashin, *Guardians*, 125.

124. Augusta Store Journal, 137, 242, 265.

125. Ibid., 101.

126. Ibid., 255.

127. Edmond Atkin to William Henry Lyttelton, February 16, 1760, Lyttelton Papers.

128. Peter Wood, *Black Majority: Negroes in Colonial South Carolina from 1670 through the Stono Rebellion* (New York: W. W. Norton, 1974), 95–130.

129. On the shift to raw skins, see Piker, *Okfuskee*, 148–50; Braund, *Deerskins*, 68–69.

130. David George, "An Account of the Life of Mr. David George, from Sierra

Leone in Africa; given by himself in a Conversation with Brother Rippon of London, and Brother Pearce of Birmingham," in John D. Rippon, *The Baptist Annual Register for 1790, 1791, 1792, and part of 1793: including sketches of the state of religion among the different denominations of god men at home and abroad* ([1793?]): 473–84, 474.

131. Augusta Store Journal, 333.

132. *Abstracts of Colonial Book J*, 17, 109, 98–99, 137, 176.

133. Kathryn Holland Braund, "The Creek Indians, Blacks, and Slavery," *Journal of Southern History*, 57 (November 1991): 615–16, 619–20; *Abstracts of Colonial Wills*, 10.

134. George, "Life," 474, 476.

135. Edward J. Cashin, *Old Springfield: Race and Religion in Augusta, Georgia* (Augusta: Springfield Village Park Foundation, 1995), 1–7; Mechal Sobel, *Trabelin' On: The Slave Journey to an Afro-Baptist Faith* (Princeton: Princeton University Press, 1979), 105–6.

136. Cashin, *Old Springfield*, 7.

137. Silver Bluff Trading Post Account Book, George Galphin Papers. Macartan and Campbell used the same terminology in their ledger; Augusta Store Journal, 97, 109, 240.

138. Galphin's will quoted in John Shaw Billings, "Analysis of the Will of George Galphin," *Richmond County History* 13, no. 1–2 (1981): 31.

139. Joyce Chaplin has identified this myth's appeals in lowcountry South Carolina during the eighteenth century in her *An Anxious Pursuit: Agricultural Innovation and Modernity in the Lower South, 1730–1815* (Chapel Hill: University of North Carolina Press, 1993). Walter Johnson has perhaps most ably demonstrated the power slavery held over whites' imaginations at the height of the slave regime in the nineteenth century in his *Soul by Soul: Life Inside the Antebellum Slave Market* (Cambridge, Mass.: Harvard University Press, 1999), chap. 3, 78–116.

140. John Gerar William De Brahm, *De Brahm's Report of the General Survey in the Southern District of North America*, ed. and intro. Louis De Vorsey Jr. (Columbia: University of South Carolina Press, 1971), 163. De Brahm enumerated the costs necessary to create a profitable rice plantation and listed forty slaves as a necessary expenditure for such an operation, 162.

141. William Mylne to Anne Mylne, May 29, 1774, in Ruddock, *Travels*, 26.

142. *Colonial Book J*, 17.

143. *Colonial Book J*, 98–99. Thomas Bassett Jr. received eight more of his father's slaves the following April. *Colonial Book J*, 107.

144. Ibid., 176.

145. Ibid., 189–90; Clark was the son of the Indian trader Patrick Clark.

146. Ibid., 214–15.

147. Campbell, *Journal*, 53.

148. Ibid., 56.

149. Quoted in Billings, "Analysis," 33.

150. Edward J. Cashin, "But Brothers, It Is Our Land We Are Talking About," in Ronald Hoffman, Thad Tate, and Peter Albert, eds. *An Uncivil War: The Southern Backcountry during the American Revolution*, ed. Ronald Hoffman, Thad Tate, and Peter Albert (Charlottesville: University of Virginia Press, 1985), 274–75.

151. *Abstracts of Colonial Wills*, 28, 125–26, 145–46. Mackay was outraged that

Williams "has left upwards of a dozen legacies to people in Barbadoes—A thousand Pounds to his daughter and only fifty Pounds to Mrs W when she chooses to cal for it." Robert Mackay to Mary Mackay, Jan. 10, 1775, Mackay and Stiles Family Papers.

152. Cashin, *Lachlan McGillivray*, 256–57, Billings, "Analysis," 32.

153. Thomas Netherclift to Robert Mackay, May 29, 1772, House Family Papers, MS 1196, Georgia Historical Society, Savannah, Georgia.

154. Ibid.

155. Norwood, *White House*, 42–50.

4 / To Make the Path White and Clear

1. Journal of Thomas Bosomworth, July 13–14, 1752, in *Documents Relating to Indian Affairs*, ed. William L. McDowell, 2 vols. (Columbia: University of South Carolina Press, 1958, 1970), 1:269–70. Hereafter cited as *DRIA*. On the specifics of the Bosomworths' agency, David H. Corkran provides the best narrative in his *The Creek Frontier, 1540–1783* (Norman: University of Oklahoma Press, 1967), 131–44, 153–59.

2. Appendix to the Journal of Thomas Bosomworth, *DRIA*, 1:330.

3. Headmen of the Cherokee Lower Towns to William Henry Lyttleton, March 4, 1758, in Lachlan McIntosh to Lyttleton, March 4, 1758, *DRIA*, 2:444.

4. On the idea of the "covenant chain," its basis in Iroquois customs, and its formation in Anglo-Iroquois diplomacy, see the essays in *Beyond the Covenant Chain: The Iroquois and their Neighbors in Indian North America, 1600–1800*, ed. Daniel K. Richter and James Merrell (Syracuse, N.Y.: Syracuse University Press, 1987), especially Mary A. Druke, "Linking Arms: The Structure of Iroquois Intertribal Diplomacy," and Richard L. Haan, "Covenant and Consensus: Iroquois and English, 1676–1760."

5. For the full history of English slaving in the Southeast, see Alan Gallay, *The Indian Slave Trade: The Rise of the English Empire in the American South, 1670–1717* (New Haven, Conn.: Yale University Press, 2002).

6. Minutes of Governor and Council, May 18, 1757, in *The Colonial Records of the State of Georgia*, ed. Allen D. Candler, Kenneth Coleman, and Milton Ready, 30 vols. (Atlanta: C. P. Byrd, 1904–16; Athens: University of Georgia Press, 1974–76), 7:568. Hereafter cited as *CRG*.

7. Ellis's first talks with Indians typically included a reference to the "chain of friendship." Minutes of Governor and Council, May 18, 1757, September 13, 1757, and November 3, 1757. *CRG*, 7:567, 630, 663. By the end of his governorship in 1760, Ellis had abandoned the chain metaphor altogether and employed the path metaphor. Minutes and Proceedings of Governor and Council, April 28, 1760, May 20, 1760, June 5, 1760, *CRG*, 8:293, 313, 320. For his part, Ellis's successor James Wright used the path metaphor rather than the chain in his first talk with Indians. Minutes and Proceedings of Governor and Council, Nov. 7, 1760, *CRG*, 8:415.

8. Creek diplomacy centered on acquiring trade with as many Europeans as possible while avoiding any long-term entanglements in European wars or politics. Steven C. Hahn has traced the origins of this policy to Coweta negotiations in the wake of the Yamasee War. See Hahn, *The Invention of the Creek Nation, 1670–1713* (Lincoln: University of Nebraska Press, 2004), 110–19.

9. Daniel Pepper to Lyttleton, May 25, 1757, *DRIA*, 2:378.

10. On the acceptance and incorporation of other Indian groups into Creek life, see Andrew K. Frank, *Creeks and Southerners: Biculturalism on the Early American*

Frontier (Lincoln: University of Nebraska Press, 2005), 26–45; Robbie Ethridge, *Creek Country: The Creek Indians and Their World* (Chapel Hill: University of North Carolina Press, 2003), 92–93

11. Coweta's rise to prominence in the Apalachicola Indian province began with their close contact to English-supplied Westo Indians in the late seventeenth century. Hahn, *Invention of the Creek Nation*, 29–39. Okfuskee and Okchai enjoyed the prestige and diplomatic influence that geography provided them as the gateway to the Upper Creek towns for British traders and agents, and struggled to maintain that superiority when the British occupied Pensacola post-1763 and trade began entering the Upper Creeks from the south. The possibility of a southern trade route, combined with British desires to undermine the influential Okchai headmen, allowed Emistisiguo's rise to prominence. Joshua A. Piker, "'White, Clean, and Contested': Creek Towns and Trading Paths in the Aftermath of the Seven Years' War," *Ethnohistory* 50 (Spring 2003): 315–47, 321–24. See also Piker, *Okfuskee: A Creek Indian Town in Colonial America* (Cambridge, Mass.: Harvard University Press, 2004).

12. Historians studying the southeastern deerskin trade have all recognized the large role that traders played in Anglo-Indian diplomacy. See Kathryn Holland Braund, *Deerskins and Duffels: The Creek Trade with Anglo-America, 1685–1815* (Lincoln: University of Nebraska Press, 1993), 40; Edward J. Cashin, "The Gentlemen of Augusta," in *Colonial Augusta: "Key of the Indian Country,"* ed. Edward J. Cashin (Macon, Ga.: Mercer University Press, 1986); John Philip Reid, *A Better Kind of Hatchet: Law, Trade, and Diplomacy in the Cherokee Nation during the Early Years of European Contact* (University Park: Pennsylvania State University Press, 1976), 145–50. For the particular role played by an individual trader, see Edward J. Cashin, *Lachlan McGillivray, Indian Trader: The Shaping of the Southern Colonial Frontier* (Athens: University of Georgia Press, 1992).

13. Thomas Nairne to Robert Fenwick, April 13, 1708, in *Nairne's Muskhogean Journals: The 1708 Expedition to the Mississippi River*, ed. and intro. Alexander Moore (Jackson: University of Mississippi Press, 1988), 51.

14. Jerome Courtonne to John Brown, Oct. 23, 1756, *DRIA*, 2:292.

15. Chickasaw Headmen to the Gun Merchant of Okchai, Nov. 26, 1756, in Courtonne to Brown, Nov. 26, 1756, *DRIA*, 2:294.

16. Daniel Pepper to William Henry Lyttleton, April 7, 1757, *DRIA*, 2:364.

17. Journal of an Indian Trader, May 24, 1755, *DRIA*, 2:69.

18. Frank, *Creeks and Southerners*, 31–32.

19. On Priber, see Knox Mellon Jr., "Christian Priber's Cherokee 'Kingdom of Paradise,'" *Georgia Historical Quarterly* 57 (Spring 1973): 319–31.

20. Raymond Demere to Lyttleton, Feb. 5, 1757, *DRIA*, 2:334.

21. According to an early historian of Alabama, McGillivray was a sixteen-year-old who ran away from his wealthy Scottish parents to seek adventure in America. He arrived with "no property, except a shilling in his pocket." He joined a packhorse train from Charles Town to the Chattahoochie River, earning a knife for his troubles. He traded the knife for some deerskins, "and the proceeds of his adventure laid the foundation of a large fortune." Albert James Pickett, *History of Alabama, and Incidentally of Georgia and Mississippi, from the Earliest Period*, 2nd ed. 2 vols. (Charleston: Walker and James, 1851), 31. McGillivray, in reality, owed his entry into the trade and the foundation of his fortune to his well-connected family members in colonial Charles Town. Cashin, *Lachlan McGillivray*, 34–37.

22. William Mylne to Anne Mylne, Sept. 1, 1774, in *Travels in the Colonies, 1773–1775: Described in the Letters of William Mylne*, ed. Ted Ruddock (Athens: University of Georgia Press, 1993), 44.

23. William Mylne to Anne Mylne, March 1, 1775, ibid., 61.

24. Lt. White Outerbridge to Lyttleton, Dec. 19, 1759, William Henry Lyttleton Papers, William L. Clements Library, University of Michigan.

25. Thomas Ross to David Douglass, Oct. 15, 1756, in Outerbridge to Lyttleton, Oct. 22, 1756, *DRIA*, 2:212. Ross's ordeal resulted from his fleeing his own execution, discussed below.

26. Daniel Pepper to Lyttleton, Nov. 18, 1756, *DRIA*, 2:55–56

27. Anthony Dean to James Glen, April 13, 1752, in *DRIA*, 1:259–60.

28. Proceedings of the Council Concerning Indian Affairs, May 31, 1753, *DRIA*, 1:398

29. Ibid., 398–99.

30. William Bartram, *The Travels of William Bartram: Naturalist's Edition*, ed. Francis Harper (New Haven, Conn.: Yale University Press, 1958), 244.

31. "Lauglin McGilvery" to William Henry Lyttleton, July 14, 1758, Lyttleton Papers. Although signed with McGillivray's name, the author of this letter was almost certainly Adair. See Cashin, *Lachlan McGillivray*, 170–71.

32. Journal of Thomas Bosomworth, Nov. 6, 1752, *DRIA*, 1:319.

33. James Adair, *History of the American Indians*, ed. Samuel Cole Williams (Johnson City, Tenn.: Watauga Press, 1930), 291.

34. Thomas Telford quoted in Anne Gordon, *To Move with the Times: The Story of Transport and Travel in Scotland* (Aberdeen: Aberdeen University Press, 1988), 5.

35. Philip Bagwell and Peter Lyth, *Transport in Britain: From Canal Lock to Gridlock* (London: Hambledon and London, 2002), 37–49; Gordon, *To Move with the Times*, 1–15; J. L. McCracken, "The Age of the Stage Coach," in *Travel and Transport in Ireland*, ed. Kevin B. Nowlan (New York: Barnes and Noble Books, 1973), 47; see also John G. Barry, "Transport and Communication in Medieval and Tudor Ireland," in Nowlan, *Transport and Travel*, 32–46.

36. McGilvery to Lyttleton, July 14, 1758, Lyttleton Papers.

37. Rusty Fleetwood, *Tidecraft: The Boats of South Carolina, Georgia, and Northeastern Florida—1500–1950* (Tybee Island, Ga.: WBG Marine Press, 1995), 9.

38. Nairne to Fenwick, April 13, 1708, in Nairne, *Journals*, 55.

39. Deposition of Jeremiah Knott, in Memorial Benjamin Goodin et al., July 4, 1735, in Great Britain, Public Record Office, *Documents of the British Public Record Office Relating to South Carolina, 1663–1782* (Columbia: South Carolina Department of Archives and History, 1973), 12 reels, microfilm, 17:431. Hereafter cited as SCPRO.

40. Piker, *Okfuskee*, 95

41. Philip Levy, *Fellow Travelers: Indians and Europeans Contesting the Early American Trail* (Gainesville: University Press of Florida, 2007), 67–69.

42. Creek notions of property have been well studied. See Braund, *Deerskins and Duffels*, 129–30; Claudio Saunt, *A New Order of Things: Property, Power, and the Transformation of the Creeks, 1733–1816* (New York: Cambridge University Press, 1999), 38–45; Ethridge, *Creek Country*, 180–81.

43. Braund, *Deerskins and Duffels*, 53–54.

44. Minutes of Governor and Council, July 3, 1761, *CRG*, 8:522–24.

45. Edmond Atkin to Lyttleton, Dec. 10, 1758, Lyttleton Papers.
46. Ludovic Grant to James Glen, July 22, 1754, *DRIA*, 2:20.
47. Ludovic Grant to James Glen, March 27, 1755, *DRIA*, 2:41.
48. Paul Demere to Lyttleton, Dec. 30, 1757, *DRIA*, 2:427.
49. Adair, *History*, 156.
50. Bartram, *Travels*, 14–15.
51. Rhys Isaac, *The Transformation of Virginia, 1740–1790* (New York: W. W. Norton, 1988), 53–57.
52. Ibid., 53–56; Carter Hudgins, "Robert 'King' Carter and the Landscape of Tidewater Virginia," in *Earth Patterns: Essays in Landscape Archaeology*, ed. William M. Kelso and Rachel Most (Charlottesville: University of Virginia Press, 1990), 59–70, 64–65.
53. George Galphin to William Henry Lyttleton, June 11, 1759, Lyttleton Papers.
54. Adair, *History*, 295–96, 297.
55. Daniel Pepper to Lyttleton, May 25, 1757, *DRIA*, 2:377–78.
56. *South Carolina Gazette*, March 5, 1737.
57. James Glen to Heads of the Creek Nation, Dec. 14, 1753, in *DRIA*, 1:465.
58. Talk of Skiagunsta of Keowe and the Good Warrior of Estatoe, [1752], in *DRIA*, 1:249.
59. Nairne to Fenwick, April 13, 1708, in Nairne, *Journals*, 51–52.
60. Bartram, *Travels*, 277.
61. Ibid., 279.
62. National Society Colonial Dames of America, *Abstracts of Colonial Wills of the State of Georgia, 1733–1777* (Atlanta: Georgia Department of Archives and History, 1962), 28.
63. Ibid., 125–26.
64. Ibid., 10.
65. Pepper to Lyttleton, May 7, 1757, *DRIA*, 2:373.
66. Pepper to Lyttleton, May 25, 1757, *DRIA*, 2:378.
67. Bartram, *Travels*, 278.
68. Ibid., 225.
69. Ibid., 238–39.
70. Carolyn Podruchny, *Making the Voyageur World: Travelers and Traders in the North American Fur Trade* (Lincoln: University of Nebraska Press, 2006), 187–92.
71. Levy, *Travelers*, 105–20.
72. Bartram, *Travels*, 242–43.
73. Daniel Pepper to William Henry Lyttleton, Oct. 10, 1756, Lyttleton Papers.
74. Examination of John Vann, included in James Glen to Board of Trade, Dec. 1751, *SCPRO*, 24:425.
75. Memorial of Goodin et al., July 4, 1735, *SCPRO*, 17:413; William Stephens, "A State of the Province of Georgia, Nov. 10, 1740," in *The Clamorous Malcontents: Criticisms and Defenses of the Colony of Georgia, 1741–1743*, ed. Trevor R. Reese (Savannah: Beehive Press, 1973), 6.
76. Town numbers based on the Stuart-Purcell MS Map in the Newberry Library, Chicago. Braund estimated the typical horse caravan to be between sixty and one hundred horses. Braund, *Deerskins and Duffels*, 92.

77. Bagwell and Lyth, *Transport in Britain*, 44–45.
78. Bartram, *Travels*, 278.
79. Ibid., 225.
80. Adair, *History*, 241.
81. *Georgia Gazette*, Sept. 29, 1763.
82. *Georgia Gazette*, Oct. 11, 1764
83. Augusta Store Journal of Accounts, Mss 197, 90–91, Special Collections, Clemson University Libraries.
84. Deerskins traded at 14 shillings/lb. at Macartan and Campbell's during this time period. Augusta Store Journal, 169, 175.
85. As an example, John Buckles paid over fifty-three pounds for "a Black pacing horse."
86. Between 1753 and 1754, Buckles and Company moved 233 horses, either on their way to or from the Chickasaws. Piker, *Okfuskee*, 122.
87. Augusta Store Journal, 211.
88. Ibid., 102.
89. Ibid., 249.
90. Raymond Demere to Lyttleton, Aug. 26, 1757, *DRIA*, 2:406.
91. James Beamer to Glen, Feb. 21, 1756, *DRIA*, 2:106.
92. Affidavit of Lachlan McIntosh, Nov. 14, 1752, *DRIA*, 1:343
93. *South Carolina Gazette*, July 14, 1739.
94. Journal of Thomas Bosomworth, *DRIA*, 1:304–6.
95. Historians of Anglo-Creek relations have universally noted horse thefts as important both to Indian-white relations and the development of a Creek notion of personal property differing from their traditional one. See Braund, *Deerskins and Duffels*, 76–77; Piker, *Okfuskee*, 119–123; and Ethridge, *Creek Country*, 180–85.
96. Anthony Dean to Cornelius Doharty, May 1, 1751, in *DRIA*, 1:73.
97. Rachel M. Klein, *Unification of a Slave State: The Rise of the Planter Class in the South Carolina Backcountry, 1760–1808* (Chapel Hill: University of North Carolina Press, 1990), 67–77.
98. Patrick Calhoun to William Henry Lyttleton, Sept. 21, 1759, Lyttleton Papers.
99. James May to James Glen, Sept. 27, 1755, *DRIA*, 2:81.
100. Ibid.
101. Ibid.
102. Demere to Lyttleton, Jan. 1, 1757, *DRIA*, 2:328.
103. President and Assistants of Georgia to Benjamin Martyn, Feb. 28, 1751, *CRG*, 26:169.
104. Journal of David Taitt, in *Travels in the American Colonies*, ed. Newton D. Mereness (New York: Macmillan, 1916), 512
105. Adair, *History*, 243–44.
106. *Georgia Gazette*, Aug. 8, 1765.
107. Bagwell and Lyth, *Transport in Britain*, 44–45.
108. Mylne to Anne Mylne, Jan. 4, 1775, in Ruddock, *Travels*, 55–56.
109. James Taylor Carson, "Horses and the Economy and Culture of the Choctaw Indians, 1690–1840," *Ethnohistory* 42 (Summer 1995): 497.
110. Braund, *Deerskins and Duffels*, 76.

111. Ibid., 129–30; Saunt, *New Order*, 38–44; Ethridge, *Creek Country*, 180–85.

112. Talk of Emistisiguo to John Stuart, in John Stuart to Thomas Gage, May 20, 1764, Thomas Gage Papers, William L. Clements Library, University of Michigan.

113. Journal of Thomas Bosomworth, Oct. 4, 1752, *DRIA*, 1:304.

114. Journal of David Taitt, in Mereness, *Travels*, 510.

115. Kathryn Holland Braund, "The Creek Indians, Blacks, and Slavery," *Journal of Southern History*, 57 (November 1991): 601–36.

116. Southern whites feared the revolutionary implications of a joint African-Indian uprising, knowing that they were outnumbered should such an event take place. For a good overview of whites' attempts to maintain Indian-African hostility, see Philip Morgan, *Slave Counterpoint: Black Culture in the Eighteenth-Century Chesapeake and Lowcountry* (Chapel Hill: University of North Carolina Press, 1998), 477–85.

117. *Georgia Gazette*, June 9, 1763.

118. *Georgia Gazette*, Dec. 13, 1769; John Stuart to Thomas Gage, July 2, 1768, Gage Papers.

119. Stuart to Gage, July 2, 1768, Gage Papers.

120. Adair, *History*, 441–42.

121. Affidavit of Robert Gandy, June 5, 1751, *DRIA*, 1:71.

122. Paul Demere to William Henry Lyttelton, Dec. 30, 1757, *DRIA*, 2:428.

123. Deposition of James McCormick, May 21, 1767, in John Stuart to Thomas Gage, July 21, 1767, Gage Papers.

124. David George, "An Account of the Life of Mr. David George, from Sierra Leone in Africa; given by himself in a Conversation with Brother Rippon of London, and Brother Pearce of Birmingham," in *The Baptist Annual Register for 1790, 1791, 1792, and part of 1793: including sketches of the state of religion among the different denominations of god men at home and abroad*, ed. John D. Rippon ([1793?]), 473–84, 473–74.

125. *Georgia Gazette*, June 22, 1768.

126. *Georgia Gazette*, July 13, 1768.

127. *Georgia Gazette*, Aug. 24, 1768.

128. *Georgia Gazette*, Jan. 31, 1770.

129. *Georgia Gazette*, Nov. 1, 1769.

130. *Georgia Gazette*, March 7, 1770.

5 / Breaking Houses

1. John Stuart to John Pownall, August 26, 1765, in Great Britain, Public Record Office, *Records of the British Colonial Office, Class 5, Part 1: Westward Expansion, 1700–1783* (Frederick, Md.: University Publications of America, 1981–84), 12 reels, microfilm, 389–90. Hereafter cited as *CO-WE*.

2. Brown, Rae, and Company to the Georgia Trustees, Feb. 13, 1751, *The Colonial Records of the State of Georgia*, ed. Allen D. Candler, Kenneth Coleman, and Milton Ready, 30 vols. (Atlanta: C. P. Byrd, 1904–16; Athens: University of Georgia Press, 1974–76), 26:152–54. Hereafter cited as *CRG*.

3. James Deetz, *In Small Things Forgotten: An Archaeology of Early American Life*, exp. and rev. ed., illustrated by Amy Elizabeth Grey (New York: Doubleday, 1996), 156–64. The Georgian house was meant to demonstrate to its observers proper social

hierarchy, with more educated gentlemen sitting atop a social pyramid and directing local life with the community's interest in mind. Rhys Isaac, *The Transformation of Virginia, 1740-1790* (New York: W. W. Norton, 1988), 34-39. Dell Upton has demonstrated how Georgian architecture was also designed to coordinate the physical movements of its inhabitants and visitors alike. Dell Upton, *Holy Things and Profane: Anglican Parish Churches in Colonial Virginia* (Cambridge, Mass.: MIT Press, 1986), 206-14.

4. Brown, Rae, and Company to the Georgia Trustees, Feb. 13, 1751, *CRG* 26:152-54.

5. Petition of Lachlan McGillivray [1754], *Documents Relating to Indian Affairs*, ed. William L. McDowell (Columbia: University of South Carolina Press, 1958, 1970), 1:518. Hereafter cited as *DRIA*.

6. Cornelius Doharty to Paul Demere, Dec. 4, 1757, *DRIA*, 2:432. For the circumstances surrounding Goudy's actions, see David H. Corkran, *The Cherokee Frontier: Conflict and Survival, 1740-1762* (Norman: University of Oklahoma Press, 1962), 139-40.

7. Memorial of the Merchants and Traders of the Province of Georgia, in John Stuart to Thomas Gage, July 21, 1767, Thomas Gage Papers, William L. Clements Library, University of Michigan,

8. Ibid.

9. Georgia Trustees' Petition to King George II, in the Journal of the Earl of Egmont, July 17, 1738, *CRG*, 5:51.

10. James Habersham to Benjamin Martyn, June 26, 1752, *CRG*, 26:402.

11. Edward Cashin defined the "golden age" of the deerskin trade as the period between 1750, when military officers lost their civic authority in Augusta, and 1763, when the Proclamation of 1763 ushered in an era of decline and conflict in the trade. See Cashin, "The Gentlemen of Augusta," in *Colonial Augusta: "Key of the Indian Countrey,"* ed. Cashin (Macon, Ga.: Mercer University Press, 1986), 35-48.

12. For a few examples of this idea in the eighteenth century, see Isaac, *Transformation of Virginia*, 36-38; Gary Nash, *The Urban Crucible: The Northern Seaports and the Origins of the American Revolution*, abridged ed. (Cambridge, Mass.: Harvard University Press, 1986), 116-17; Gregory Nobles, "Straight Lines and Stability: Mapping the Political Order of the Anglo-American Frontier," *Journal of American History* 80 (June 1993): 9-35, 29-34. For an early nineteenth-century example, see James A. Delle, *An Archaeology of Social Space: Analyzing Coffee Plantations in Jamaica's Blue Mountains* (New York: Plenum Press, 1998), 36-40. The classic statement of physical architecture and social control comes from Michel Foucault's analysis of Mettray prison in his *Discipline and Punish: The Birth of the Prison*, trans. Alan Sheridan (New York: Vintage Books, 1977), 293-308.

13. Journal of David Taitt, March 2, 1772, in *Travels in the American Colonies*, ed. Newton D. Mereness (New York: Macmillan, 1916), 507.

14. David Taitt to John Stuart, March 16, 1772, in Mereness, *Travels*, 522. Taitt also described Velden as "a man that loves to hear himself speak and would wish to be thought of Consequence among the Indians." Journal of David Taitt, Feb. 19, 1772, in Mereness, *Travels*, 506.

15. Ibid., xxxiv.

16. Ibid., 393.

17. Ibid., 390. On the Scottish Enlightenment's influence on the southern colonies, see Joyce Chaplin, *An Anxious Pursuit: Agricultural Innovation and Modernity*

in the Lower South, 1730–1815 (Chapel Hill: University of North Carolina Press, 1993), 28–37.

18. Ibid., 459, 393.

19. James Adair, *History of the American Indians*, ed. Samuel Cole Williams (Johnson City, Tenn.: Watauga Press, 1930), 276; Adair also singled out the Creeks' unparalleled gift for politics and their ability to incorporate remnant nations into their own confederacy as the other major reasons why the Creek population had increased.

20. Ibid., 390.

21. Ibid., 187.

22. Ibid., 393.

23. William Bartram, *The Travels of William Bartram: Naturalist's Edition*, ed. Francis Harper (New Haven, Conn.: Yale University Press, 1958), 2–3, 6, 199.

24. Ibid., 247, 235, 231.

25. His "investigation of the manners of the Indian nations" was so that "I might judge for myself whether they were deserving of the severe censure, which prevailed against them among the white people, that they were incapable of civilization" (ibid., lx). Bartram's "investigation" was perhaps even a part of the instructions given him by Dr. John Fothergill when Bartram began his trip. Kathryn Braund and Gregory Waselkov, "William Bartram and the Southeastern Indians: An Introduction," in *William Bartram on the Southeastern Indians*, ed. Kathryn Braund and Gregory Waselkov (Lincoln: University of Nebraska Press, 1995), 11–12.

26. Bartram, *Travels*, 223.

27. Ibid., lxi.

28. For a full description of Indian construction methods, see Adair, *History*, 448–52. On traders' stores, see Kathryn Holland Braund, *Deerskins and Duffels: The Creek Trade with Anglo-America, 1685–1815* (Lincoln: University of Nebraska Press, 1993), 85–86. Joshua Piker has attributed the change in trading house location to traders' desire to be less dependent on village food supplies, and thus less dependent on village politics. See Joshua A. Piker, *Okfuskee: A Creek Indian Town in Colonial America* (Cambridge, Mass.: Harvard University Press, 2004), 145–47.

29. Petition of Georgia Trustees, Jan. 19, 1737, Great Britain, Public Record Office, *Documents of the British Public Record Office Relating to South Carolina, 1663–1782* (Columbia: South Carolina Department of Archives and History, 1973), 12 reels, microfilm, 18:190–91. Hereafter cited as *SCPRO*. The house's unidentified owner was almost certainly an early Augusta trader, as William Stephens noted in his journal that Wright had been arrested at Augusta and accused of "demolishing, by his own Hands, one of the first Huts we had built there." Journal of William Stephens, July 4, 1738, *CRG*, 4:166.

30. Alexander Wylly to Captain [?] Croft, May 10, 1740, *SCPRO*, 20:258.

31. E. P. Thompson, *The Making of the English Working Class* (New York: Pantheon Books, 1963), 62–68. Nash, *Urban Crucible*, 46–48, 184–89.

32. Theda Perdue, *Cherokee Women: Gender and Culture Change, 1700–1835* (Lincoln: University of Nebraska Press, 1998), 28, 34–35.

33. Talk of Tacite of Euphassee and others, July 30, 1751, *DRIA*, 1:107–8, quoted in Gregory Evans Dowd, "The Panic of 1751: The Significance of Rumors on the South Carolina-Cherokee Frontier," *William and Mary Quarterly*, 3rd ser., 53 (July 1996): 536.

34. Dowd, "Panic of 1751," 531–36.
35. See above, Chapter 4.
36. James Glen, "An Account of the Boundaries of South Carolina, and of the Encroachments upon the said Privince by Foreign Princes," Feb. 1751, *SCPRO*, 24:282. See Chapter 1 above.
37. James Glen to the President and Assistants of Georgia, Oct. 1750, *CRG*, 26:65.
38. Daniel Pepper, "Some Remarks in the Creek Nation," 1756, William Henry Lyttelton Papers, William L. Clements Library, University of Michigan.
39. Daniel Pepper to William Henry Lyttelton, March 30, 1757, Lyttelton Papers.
40. James Glen to Board of Trade, April 14, 1748, *SCPRO*, 23:108.
41. Journal of William Stephens, Feb. 22, 1740, *CRG*, 4:518.
42. Ibid.
43. Ibid., 519.
44. Daniel Pepper to William Henry Lyttelton, March 30, 1757, *DRIA*, 2:355.
45. James Beamer to James Glen, Feb. 21, 1756, in *DRIA* 2: 105.
46. On European views toward white hunters, see Rachel Klein, *Unification of a Slave State: The Rise of the Planter Class in the South Carolina Backcountry, 1760–1808* (Chapel Hill: University of North Carolina Press, 1990), 51–56; Stephen Aron, *How the West Was Lost: The Transformation of Kentucky from Daniel Boone to Henry Clay* (Baltimore: Johns Hopkins University Press, 1996), 13–15.
47. Pepper to Lyttelton, March 30, 1757, *DRIA*, 2:355.
48. Daniel Pepper, "Some Remarks in the Creek Nation," 1756, Lyttelton Papers.
49. Glen, "Scheme for Regulating the Indian Trade" [August 1751], *DRIA*, 1:88.
50. Edmond Atkin, *Indians of the Southern Colonial Frontier: The Edmond Atkin Report and Plan of 1755*, ed. Wilbur R. Jacobs (Columbia: University of South Carolina Press, 1954), 25.
51. Ibid., 27.
52. John Stuart, "Regulations Settled as Necessary for the better carrying on the Trade with the Indian Nations," in John Stuart to Lord Halifax, April 16, 1765, *CO-WE*, 66:162.
53. Memorial of James Germany, Aug. 18, 1759, in Edmond Atkin to William Henry Lyttelton, Jan. 9, 1760, Lyttelton Papers.
54. Ibid.
55. Ibid.
56. Glen, "Scheme for Regulating the Indian Trade" [1751], *DRIA*, 2:87–88.
57. Memorial of James Germany, Aug. 18, 1759, Lyttelton Papers.
58. Journal of an Indian Trader, April 22, 1755, *DRIA*, 2:65.
59. Ibid., 2:64.
60. Braund, *Deerskins and Duffels*, 101, 105–17. In his attempts to regulate trade prices, Stuart held numerous conferences specifically devoted to issues regarding the trade, so as to redress Indian complaints and prevent the Indians from taking matters in their own hands. Stuart held three such conferences: with the Creeks at Pensacola in 1765, with the Choctaws and Chickasaws the same year at Mobile, and with the Creeks again at Augusta in 1767. Braund, *Deerskins and Duffels*, 112–14.
61. Adair described the building of a house as a town-wide concern, with all the men assisting in the building. See Adair, *History*, 448–49.
62. Bartram, *Travels*, 282.

63. Adair, *History*, 443.
64. Ibid.
65. Bartram, *Travels*, 549.
66. Adair, *History*, 281. Adair did not specify the location of this trading house, but did identify it as one of those attacked by the Upper Creeks in 1760 (279–81).
67. Ibid., 279.
68. See, for example, Edmond Atkin, *Indians of the Southern Colonial Frontier: The Edmond Atkin Report and Plan of 1755*, ed. and intro. Wilbur R. Jacobs (Columbia: University of South Carolina Press, 1954), 23.
69. Deposition of Thomas Perriman, Nov. 23, 1759 in Edmond Atkin to William Henry Lyttelton, Jan. 9, 1760, Lyttelton Papers.
70. Deposition of Perriman, Nov. 23, 1759.
71. Kathryn E. Holland Braund, "James Adair: His Life and History," in Adair, *History*, 30–33.
72. Adair, *History*, 442–43.
73. Ibid., 281.
74. Traders, it should be noted, preferred neutrality only between European nations. Indians they hoped would continue to war with each other for as long as they could. Indian wars meant increased demand for arms, ammunition, and provisions and consequently higher prices for the traders' goods. Indians warring with each other also reduced the threat of a pan-Indian alliance that could wipe out the British colonies. William Stephens summarized the basic policy of the traders as early as 1739 when he described a possible Creek-Choctaw war "which our Traders would rather chuse than not; for whilst these Nations are most at Variance with one another, it prevents any dangerous uniting, to the Detriment of us." Journal of William Stephens, April 29, 1739, *CRG*, 4:326. Stephens later restated this policy as "a never-failing Maxim, that the Indians falling out with one another, never forbodes any Ill to us." Journal of William Stephens, Dec. 18, 1740, *CRG*, 4(sup.): 55.
75. Piker, *Okfuskee*, 136–40, 165–67, 59–61; Braund, *Deerskins and Duffels*, 84–86; Perdue, *Cherokee Women*, 46, 81. For a fuller elaboration on Indians' matrilineal kinship systems, see Charles Hudson, *The Southeastern Indians* (Knoxville: University of Tennessee Press, 1976), 185–202.
76. Robbie Ethridge, *Creek Country: The Creek Indians and Their World* (Chapel Hill: University of North Carolina Press, 2003), 74–75.
77. On the roles of women in the trade and their increasing power, see Piker, *Okfuskee*, 165–70. On women as ranchers, see Ethridge, *Creek Country*, 161–162.
78. Piker, *Okfuskee*, 145–147.
79. On shifting settlement, see Ethridge, *Creek Country*, 71–72. On Creek men's gender crisis, see Piker, *Okfuskee*, 170–75.
80. Andrew K. Frank, *Creeks and Southerners: Biculturalism on the Early American Frontier* (Lincoln: University of Nebraska Press, 2005), 4–6.
81. Adair, *History*, 390. Ethridge, *Creek Country*, 161–62.
82. Adair, *History*, 447.
83. Ibid.
84. Ibid.
85. Bartram, *Travels*, 221.
86. Ibid., 549.

87. Thomas Nairne, *Nairne's Muskhogean Journals: The 1708 Expedition to the Mississippi River*, ed. and intro. Alexander Moore (Jackson: University Press of Mississippi, 1988), 52.

88. Ibid., 53.

89. Adair, *History*, 446.

90. Ibid.

91. Edmond Atkin to John Cleland, Dec. 23, 1759; Deposition of Thomas Perriman, Nov. 23, 1759; both included in Edmond Atkin to William Henry Lyttelton, Jan. 9, 1760, Lyttelton Papers.

92. Bartram, *Travels*, 282.

93. Adair, *History*, 281-82.

94. Ibid., 251.

95. Frank, *Creeks and Southerners*, 66-67.

96. Ethridge, *Country*, 148-149.

97. Adair, *History*, 251.

98. "Talk of Emistisiguo," in John Stuart to Thomas Gage, May 20, 1764, Gage Papers. Piker, *Okfuskee*, 190-91.

99. Piker, *Okfuskee*, 170-71.

100. "Journal of an Indian Trader," April 22, 1755, in *DRIA*, 1:64.

101. David H. Corkran, *The Creek Frontier, 1540-1783* (Norman: University of Oklahoma Press, 1967), 216-19; Braund, *Deerskins and Duffels*, 108. Piker provides an excellent overview of the historiographic disputes over the 1760 attacks in his *Okfuskee*, 54-56. Piker argues that the attacks took place within a specifically Creek notion of clan justice, whereby Okfuskee Indians killed their British "kinsmen" as a means of correcting traders' lapses in Indian protocol. Piker, *Okfuskee*, 56-61.

102. Corkran tended to view attacks on traders as simply local manifestations of larger political issues, whether Creek or Cherokee. In addition to *Creek Frontier*, see also his account of the Cherokees' breaking of Bernard Hughs's store in Corkran, *Cherokee Frontier*, 26. More recent historians of the southeastern Indian trade have tended to associate Indian violence with a litany of trader abuses. See for example Braund, *Deerskins and Duffels*, 106-8; James Merrell, *The Indian's New World: Catawbas and Their Neighbors from European Contact through the Era of Removal* (Chapel Hill: University of North Carolina Press, 1989; New York: W. W. Norton, 1991), 63-68. Tom Hatley, for his part, has given both motivations equal weight and also tried to understand trader attacks in a specifically Indian context, as attacks were sometimes messages of strength sent to rival Indian groups. Hatley, *The Dividing Paths: Cherokees and South Carolinians through the Era of Revolution* (New York: Oxford University Press, 1993), 44-47. Piker's study, the most recent, still understands violence against traders in a primarily punitive sense. See n. 15 above.

103. Matthew Toole to James Glen, Oct. 2, 1752, *DRIA*, 1:359.

104. Journal of David Taitt, March 28, 1772, in Mereness, *Travels*, 533.

105. Adair, *History*, 450.

106. Rusty Fleetwood, *Tidecraft: The Boats of South Carolina, Georgia, and Northeastern Florida—1500-1950* (Tybee Island, Ga.: WBG Marine Press, 1995), 4-5.

107. Journal of David Taitt, May 13, 1772, in Mereness, *Travels*, 555.

108. Journal of an Indian Trader, April 1755, *DRIA*, 2:66.

109. Journal of David Taitt, March 28, 1772, in Mereness, *Travels*, 533.
110. Adair, *History*, 280.
111. Ibid.
112. On the importance of gender metaphors in Indian diplomacy and trade, see Nancy Shoemaker, "An Alliance between Men: Gender Metaphors in Eighteenth-Century American Indian Diplomacy East of the Mississippi," *Ethnohistory* 46 (Spring 1999): 240–48.
113. Narration of Robert French Pack-Horseman in Minutes of Georgia Council and Governor, May 26, 1760, *CRG*, 8:315; Piker, *Okfuskee*, 58–59.
114. Adair, *History*, 278.
115. Stuart to Gage, July 2, 1768, Gage Papers.
116. James Beamer to William Henry Lyttleton, May 20, 1758, Lyttleton Papers.
117. Abstract of a Talk between the Governor of New Orleans and the Cherokee and Shawanese Indians, Dec. 4, 1756, in Daniel Pepper to William Henry Lyttelton, April 25, 1757, *DRIA*, 2:368.
118. Romans, appointed by John Stuart to survey the Chickasaw and Choctaw nations, reported Chickasaw thefts of his surveying equipment. Taitt, appointed as Romans's counterpart for the Creek nation, kept his surveying activities carefully hidden and reported no such thefts. Braund, "Romans's History as a Source for Understanding the Eighteenth-Century South," in Bernard Romans, *A Concise Natural History of East and West Florida*, ed. Kathryn Holland Braund (Tuscaloosa: University of Alabama Press, 1999), 65–66.
119. Paul Demere to William Henry Lyttelton, Dec. 30, 1757, *DRIA*, 2:426.
120. The deerskin trade has played a prominent role in most major works of southeastern Indian history. For the Catawbas, see Merrell, *The Indians' New World*; for the Cherokees, see Hatley, *Dividing Paths*, and Perdue, *Cherokee Women*; for the Creeks, see Braund, *Deerskins and Duffels*; Piker, *Okfuskee*; and J. Leitch Wright Jr., *Creeks and Seminoles: The Destruction and Regeneration of the Muscogulge People*, Indians of the Southeast (Lincoln: University of Nebraska Press, 1986); also James Axtell, *The Indians' New South: Cultural Change in the Colonial Southeast*, Walter Lynwood Fleming Lectures in Southern History (Baton Rouge: Louisiana State University Press, 1997), chap. 3.
121. Claudio Saunt in particular emphasized the role of these mestizo leaders in his *A New Order of Things: Property, Power, and the Transformation of the Creeks, 1733–1816* (New York: Cambridge University Press, 1999); see also Ethridge, *Creek Country*.
122. Perdue, *Cherokee Women*, 75–77.
123. Frank, *Southerners*, 26–45. Frank's work focuses on the lives of resident traders in the eighteenth and nineteenth centuries, but the bulk of his evidence comes from after the American Revolution.

Conclusion

1. Minutes of the Richmond Academy Trustees, September 18, 1783, Bound Volume, Papers of the Trustees of the Richmond County Academy, Robinson Trust Fund, and Tubman Home, Augusta State University, Augusta, Georgia.
2. Mary Chilcott Mackay to [John Malbone?], July 26, 17[8]3, Colonial Dames of

America, Georgia Historical Society Collections, MS #965, Georgia Historical Society, Savannah Georgia.

3. Minutes of the Richmond County Academy Trustees, Sept. 18, 1783, Papers of the Trustees.

4. Minutes of the Richmond Academy Trustees, September 19, 1783, Papers of the Trustees.

5. Minutes of the Richmond Academy Trustees, November 20, 1783, Papers of the Trustees.

6. Minutes of the Richmond County Academy, August 27, 1785, Papers of the Trustees.

7. Kathryn Holland Braund, *Deerskins and Duffels: Creek Indian Trade with Anglo-America, 1685–1815* (Lincoln: University of Nebraska Press, 1993), 150–51.

8. Edward J. Cashin, "But Brothers, It Is Our Land We Are Talking About," in *An Uncivil War: the Southern Backcountry during the American Revolution*, ed. Ronald Hoffman, Thad W. Tate, and Peter J. Albert (Charlottesville: University Press of Virginia, 1985), 245–47.

9. For a good account of the Revolution in Georgia's upcountry, see Cashin, "Brothers."

10. Ibid., 274.

11. Braund, *Deerskins and Duffels*, 180–88; Kathryn Holland Braund, "The Creek Indians, Blacks, and Slavery," *Journal of Southern History* 57 (November 1991): 618–21; J. Leitch Wright, *Creeks and Seminoles: The Destruction and Regeneration of the Muscogulge People* (Lincoln: University of Nebraska Press, 1986), 83–85; Robbie Ethridge, *Creek Country: The Creek Indians and Their World* (Chapel Hill: University of North Carolina Press, 2003), 77–78; Andrew Frank provides perhaps the most detailed study of the "Indian countrymen" in his *Creeks and Southerners: Biculturalism on the Early American Frontier* (Lincoln: University of Nebraska Press, 2005), 26–45.

12. Braund, *Deerskins and Duffels*, 164–170. Frank, *Creeks and Southerners*, 96–113; Claudio Saunt, *A New Order of Things: Property, Power, and the Transformation of the Creeks, 1733–1816* (New York: Cambridge University Press, 1999), 111–35.

13. Wright, *Creeks and Seminoles*, 60–62; Saunt, *New Order*, 67–79; Frank, *Creeks and Southerners*, 77–95.

14. Saunt, *New Order*, 79–83.

15. *Georgia State Gazette*, Sept. 20, 1788.

16. Joseph Clay to Edward Telfair, Dec. 30, 1790, Edward Telfair Papers, MS 791, Georgia Historical Society, Savannah Georgia.

17. *Augusta Chronicle*, May 9, 1795.

18. Kathryn Braund provides a summary of the obstacles to postwar trade in her *Deerskins and Duffels*, 169–70.

19. Samuel Elbert and Jams Seagrove quoted in Angela Pulley Hudson, *Creek Paths and Federal Roads: Indians, Settlers, and Slaves and the Making of the American South* (Chapel Hill: University of North Carolina Press, 2010), 38 and 41, respectively. On the pacific language of American speeches to Creeks, see Hudson, *Creek Paths*, 41–42, 49–51.

20. Minutes of Richmond County Academy Trustees, April 4, 1785, Papers of the Trustees.

21. *Augusta Chronicle*, Nov. 7, 1789.

22. *Georgia State Gazette*, Nov. 8, 1788. Neocomi's plan required students to attend school in every county in Georgia for one year before moving on to the next.

23. James Jackson to John Milledge, April 11, 1796, in *Correspondence of John Milledge, Governor of Georgia, 1802–1806*, ed. Harriet Milledge Salley and intro. Victor Davidson (Columbia, S.C.: State Commercial Printing Company, 1949), 43.

24. Martin Brückner, *The Geographic Revolution in Early America: Maps, Literacy, and National Identity* (Chapel Hill: University of North Carolina Press, 2006), 142–58.

25. Brückner in his recent volume spends a great deal of time discussing plat maps, textbooks, novels, and other literary productions in the eighteenth century but mentions newspapers hardly at all.

26. *Augusta Chronicle*, Oct. 2, 1790.

27. *Augusta Chronicle*, Nov. 27, 1790.

28. In 1791, Bowles sent a message to a U.S. delegation saying that, despite talk of peace, "we also see that numbers of men have solemnly engaged themselves and are now forming plans to get possession of our lands, this we see in a publication of this year." *Augusta Chronicle*, Nov. 19, 1791.

29. See, for example, Application of John Twigg, William Few, John Wereat, and William Gibbons Jr., Dec. 11, 1794, Telfair Family Papers, MS 793, Georgia Historical Society, Savannah, Georgia; Richard Call to Jacob Weed [undated], Thomas Carr Family Papers, MS 21, Hargrett Rare Book and Manuscript Library, University of Georgia Libraries; Anonymous to Capt. Saunders, "Thoughts on a Western Purchase," Yazoo Papers, 1798–1809, MS 888, Georgia Historical Society.

30. One speculator suggested that "I would recommend a purchase of all this tract, which probably might as easily be obtained as a part. Should it be apprehended that the quantity will create an alarm, it would be best to omit it, and purchase intirely by the boundaries or if some quantity must be mentioned, let it be much smaller than the true one 7, 8, or 10,000,000 for instance with a [tweaking?] clause of 'more or less . . . ' and a very exact description of the boundaries." Anonymous to Capt. Saunders, Yazoo Papers.

31. *Augusta Chronicle*, Dec. 19, 1789.

32. *Georgia Gazette*, December 14, 1768. Romans seems a likely candidate given the few clues Ekanichski provided for his identity. Romans was a member of the Georgia-Creek survey party, an author, and occasional poet. The frequent postings coincided with the brief period when Romans would have likely been in Savannah between the end of the Georgia-Creek survey and his removal to Florida to begin work for De Brahm. See Kathryn Holland Braund, "Romans's History as a Source for Understanding the Eighteenth-Century South," in Bernard Romans, *A Concise Natural History of East and West Florida*, ed. Kathryn Holland Braund (Tuscaloosa: University of Alabama Press, 1999), 4, 19. Braund gives January 1768 as the date of Romans's leaving Georgia, but likely means January 1769, given the dates for the Georgia-Creek survey she provides and Romans's appointment following that survey. The in-text evidence for Romans's authorship is also compelling, since the harsh tone and insulting sarcasm of the January 4 response, and the general loathing of Indians throughout, is highly reminiscent of Romans's style in his *Concise Natural History of East and West Florida*, ed. and intro. Kathryn E. Holland Braund (Tuscaloosa: University of Alabama Press, 1999).

33. *Augusta Southern Centinel*, April 30, 1795.
34. Ibid.
35. *Georgia State Gazette*, Dec. 13, 1788.
36. *Augusta Southern Centinel*, April 30, 1795.
37. *Augusta Chronicle*, Nov. 20, 1790.
38. *Augusta Chronicle*, June 9, 1792.
39. *Georgia State Gazette*, July 26, 1788.
40. *Augusta Chronicle*, August 21, 1790.
41. Letter from Edward Telfair to Alexander McGillivray, *Augusta Chronicle*, May 29, 1790.
42. Alexander McGillivray to the Governor of Nassau, *Georgia State Gazette*, Dec. 1, 1787.
43. Address of George Washington, August 21, 1789, in United States, *The Debates and Proceedings in the Congress of the United States, with an Appendix containing Important State Papers and Public Documents, and all the Laws of a Public Nature; with a Copious Index; Compiled from Authentic Materials*, comp. Joseph Gales, 42 vols., microform (Washington, D.C.: Gales and Seaton, 1834–56), 1:58. Hereafter cited as *DPC*.
44. *Augusta Chronicle*, Oct. 2, 1790.
45. The terms "neighbour," "neighbouring," or "neightbourly" were sometimes used in the colonial Southeast, although never by Indian headmen (at least in no reference that the author has seen). Usually, it was in reference to either the Indians nearby or to adjacent colonies. For the first sense, see Herman Moll, "A New Map of the North Parts of North America claimed by France" [London, 1720], as well as Romans's *Concise Natural History*, 218. For the second sense, see *South Carolina Gazette*, May 1, 1736, as well as James Glen to the President and Council of Georgia, June 15, 1751, in *Documents Relating to Indian Affairs, Colonial Records of South Carolina*, ed. William L. McDowell (Columbia: University of South Carolina Press, 1958, 1970), 1:171. Otherwise, the term almost always referred to its common sense of people living within a town or community.
46. James E. Lewis Jr., *The American Union and the Problem of Neighborhood: The United States and the Collapse of the Spanish Empire, 1783–1829* (Chapel Hill: University of North Carolina Press, 1998), 1–11.
47. Journal of the House of Representatives, Jan. 3, 1793, *DPC*, 2:786.
48. Ibid. Milledge's interpretation of history demonstrated that old ideas were being given new shape and new emphasis in the early republic. At the time of the Yamasee War, English colonists did indeed blame the war on Spanish intrigue, but were more likely to fault the Indian traders who had abused Indians. Europeans had also long believed that Indians could easily be swayed by the nearest and friendliest European power. This had been the underlying thinking of much of British policy in the Southeast since at least the early 1700s, when Thomas Nairne made his proposals. And it remained a powerful sentiment in the early republic, as the U.S. Congress believed that the presence of British forts in the Ohio Valley kept the Indians outside the reach of U.S. influence. James Merrell, *The Indian's New World: Catawbas and Their Neighbors from European Contact through the Era of Removal* (Chapel Hill: University of North Carolina Press, 1989; New York: W. W. Norton, 1991), 68; Journal of the House of Representatives, Jan. 26, 1792, *DPC*, 2:338.

49. *Georgia State Gazette*, Sept. 1, 1787.
50. *Georgia State Gazette*, May 10, 1788.
51. McGillivray has been the subject of much analysis among historians. Portraits of the headman have been mostly critical, ranging from the hostile to the more nuanced critiques of his role and legacies. For the former, see Florette Henri, *The Southern Indians and Benjamin Hawkins, 1796–1816* (Norman: University of Oklahoma Press, 1986), 72–82. Ethnohistorians have provided much needed context and better analysis of McGillivray's position among the Creeks, emphasizing his role as part of a larger development of mestizo leadership among the Creeks. Wright, *Creeks and Seminoles*; also Saunt, *New Order*.
52. *Georgia State Gazette*, Oct. 30, 1790.
53. Ibid.
54. *Augusta Chronicle*, Sept. 25, 1790.
55. Journal of the House of Representatives, Aug. 11, 1789, *DPC*, 1:695–96.
56. Ibid., 696.
57. *Georgia State Gazette*, Nov. 10, 1787.
58. Journal of the House of Representatives, Aug. 11, 1789, *DPC*, 1:695.
59. Ibid.
60. Ibid., 700; *Augusta Chronicle*, Sept. 18, 1790; *Augusta Chronicle*, Nov. 27, 1790.
61. Federalists generally believed that the best way to secure the Union was to place competing polities (such as state governments) under the control of a strong central authority (such as the federal government). The unquestioned sovereignty of the central government would thus prevent state governments from competing with each other and re-creating the divided balance-of-power politics in Europe. Lewis, *Neighborhood*, 17–18.
62. Thomas Jefferson to John Adams, June 11, 1812, in *Thomas Jefferson: Writings*, ed. Merrill D. Peterson (New York: Viking Press, 1984), 1261–62.
63. Edward J. Cashin, *William Bartram and the American Revolution on the Southern Frontier* (Columbia: University of South Carolina Press, 2000), 247–50; Kathryn Holland Braund and Gregory Waselkov, eds., *William Bartram on the Southeastern Indians* (Lincoln: University of Nebraska Press, 1995), 187–90.
64. The literature on the Plan for Civilization is quite extensive, but Ethridge's *Creek Country*, 7–21, serves as an excellent introduction to the topic and its historiographical debates.
65. For an excellent parsing of Knox's phrase, see Henri, *Benjamin Hawkins*, 83–87.
66. As an example of colonial military commissions given to Indians, see Merrell, *Indians' New World*, 150–51. On Federalist beliefs in military patronage and national attachment, see Andrew R. L. Cayton, "'Separate Interests' and the Nation-State: The Washington Administration and the Origins of Regionalism in the Trans-Appalachian West," *Journal of American History* 79 (June 1992): 51–52.
67. It should be noted that part of Washington and Knox's plan was to pacify southern Indians so that a cash-strapped federal army could devote its full attention to war with the Indians of the Ohio Valley. Cayton, "Separate Interests," 47–49.
68. Georgia in 1790 claimed territory all the way to the Mississippi and was hoping to profit from sales of this vast territory to speculators. When the Treaty of New York upheld Creek rights to much of this land, the schemes were in jeopardy.
69. *Augusta Chronicle*, Sept. 25, 1790.

70. Ibid.
71. *Augusta Chronicle*, Nov. 12, 1791.
72. Edward Cashin, *Lachlan McGillivray, Indian Trader: The Shaping of the Southern Colonial Frontier* (Athens: University of Georgia Press, 1992), 304.
73. George R. Lamplugh, *Politics on the Periphery: Factions and Parties in Georgia, 1783–1806* (Newark: University of Delaware Press, 1986), 28; Andrew McMichael, *Atlantic Loyalties: Americans in Spanish West Florida, 1785–1810* (Athens: University of Georgia Press, 2008), 1–4.
74. Eric Hinderaker, *Elusive Empires: Constructing Colonialism in the Ohio Valley* (New York: Cambridge University Press, 1997), xii–xiii.
75. As Milledge noted quite succinctly, "My constituents . . . adopted the Federal system, from a hope that we should be protected." Journal of the House of Representatives, Jan. 3, 1793, *DPC*, 2:785.
76. Journal of the House of Representatives, August 11, 1789, *DPC*, 1:696.
77. Georgians were thus part of a larger community of aggrieved settlers south of the Ohio who were displeased at the Federalists' preferment of northern engagements. Cayton, "Separate Interests," 60–62.
78. Journal of the House of Representatives, Aug. 11, 1789, *DPC*, 1:696.
79. *Georgia State Gazette*, Oct. 25, 1788.
80. Ibid.
81. Ibid.
82. Ibid.
83. *Augusta Chronicle*, March 20, 1790.
84. *Augusta Chronicle*, Sept. 18, 1790.
85. *Georgia State Gazette*, Oct. 25, 1788. It should be noted that these ideas were not unique to Georgia in these years. Members of the U.S. Congress asserted that "frontier militia, are not only equal, but infinitely superior to any regular troops whatever, for the defence of borders. . . . [Regular troops] being collected in the heart of populous cities, where the face of an Indian is seldom seen, hardly know whether the Indian and his horse are not the same animal." Journal of the House of Representatives, Jan. 26, 1792, *DPC*, 2:341.
86. Journal of the House of Representatives, August 12, 1789. *DPC*, 1:699–700.
87. Ibid., 699.
88. Henry Knox, Plan to Preserve Peace with the Indians, Dec. 29, 1794, *DPC*, 3:1400.
89. *Augusta Chronicle*, Oct. 30, 1790.
90. Ibid.
91. Hinderaker, *Empires*, 253–54; Cayton, "Interests," 62–65. James Jackson in 1789 threatened that, if the United States would not send soldiers to Georgia, Georgia would seek Spanish or British help in its war with the Creeks. Journal of the House of Representatives, August 12, 1789, *DPC*, 1:701.
92. Lewis, *Neighborhood*, 22.
93. For an account of the Creek War of the 1810s, see Wright, *Creeks and Seminoles*, 155–84.
94. Daniel Sturges, "Map of the State and Province of Georgia Prepared from actual Surveys and other Documents for Eleazar Early," [1818], copy held at Newberry Library.

95. Ibid.

96. Ibid.

97. Samuel Augustus Mitchell, "Map of the States of North Carolina, South Carolina, and Georgia" [Philadelphia: Published by S. Augustus Mitchell, 1835], copy held at the Newberry Library.

98. Angela Pulley Hudson, *Creek Paths and Federal Roads: Indians, Settlers, and Slaves and the Making of the American South* (Chapel Hill: University of North Carolina Press, 2010), 56.

99. Rusty Fleetwood, *Tidecraft: The Boats of South Carolina, Georgia, and Northeastern Florida—1500–1950* (Tybee Island, Ga.: WBG Marine Press, 1995), 75–90. See also W. Jeffrey Bolster, *Black Jacks: African American Seamen in the Age of Sail* (Cambridge, Mass.: Harvard University Press, 1997) and David Cecelski, *The Waterman's Song: Slavery and Freedom in Maritime North Carolina* (Chapel Hill: University of North Carolina Press, 2001) for more detailed histories of nineteenth-century black watermen and resistance to slavery.

Bibliography

Manuscript Collections

Georgia Historical Society, Savannah Georgia

George Galphin Papers, MS #269
House Family Papers, MS #1196
Edward Telfair Papers MS #793
Georgia Historical Society Collections, MS #965
Yazoo Papers, MS #888

Hargrett Library, University of Georgia

Thomas Carr Family Papers

Reese Library, Augusta State University Special Collections

Papers of the Trustees of the Academy of Richmond County, Robinson Trust Fund, and Tubman House

William L. Clements Library, University of Michigan, Ann Arbor

Thomas Gage Papers, American Series
William Henry Lyttelton Papers

Southern Historical Collection, University of North Carolina, Chapel Hill

Mackay and Stiles Family Papers

Special Collections, Clemson University Libraries, Clemson University

Augusta Store Journal of Accounts

Newspapers

Augusta Chronicle, 1790–95
Augusta Southern Centinel, 1795–
Georgia Gazette, 1763–75
Georgia State Gazette, 1787–90
South Carolina Gazette, 1736–75

Maps

Campbell, Archibald. "Sketch of the Northern Frontiers of Georgia" [London, 1780]. William L. Clements Library, University of Michigan, Ann Arbor.

De Brahm, John Gerar William. "Map of South Carolina and Part of Georgia" [1757]. Newberry Library, Chicago, Illinois.

Delisle, Guillaume. "Map of Louisiana and the Course of the Mississippi" [1730]. Newberry Library, Chicago, Illinois.

Mitchell, John. "A Map of the British and French Dominions in North America" [London, 1755]. Ayer Collection, Newberry Library, Chicago, Illinois.

Mitchell, Samuel Augustus. "Map of the States of North Carolina, South Carolina, and Georgia" [Philadelphia, 1835]. Ayer Collection, Newberry Library, Chicago, Illinois.

Moll, Herman. "A New and Exact Map of the Dominions of the King of Great Britain on ye Continent of North America" [ca. 1731, copy of 1715 original]. Newberry Library, Chicago, Illinois.

———. "A New Map of the North Parts of North America claimed by France" [London, 1720]. Newberry Library, Chicago, Illinois.

Popple, Henry. "A Map of the British Empire in North America" [London, 1733]. Newberry Library, Chicago, Illinois.

Sturges, Daniel. "Map of the State and Province of Georgia Prepared from actual Surveys and other Documents for Eleazar Early" [Philadelphia, 1818]. Ayer Collection, Newberry Library, Chicago, Illinois.

Yonge, Philip. "A Map of the Lands Ceded to His Majesty by the Creek and Cherokee Indians at a Congress held in Augusta the 1st June 1773" [photocopy of original]. Newberry Library, Chicago, Illinois.

Published Primary Sources

Adair, James. *History of the American Indians*. Edited by Samuel Cole Williams. Johnson City, Tenn.: Watauga Press, 1930.

———. *The History of the American Indians*. Edited and annotated by Kathryn E. Holland Braund. Tuscaloosa: University of Alabama Press, 2005.

Atkin, Edmond. *Indians of the Southern Colonial Frontier: The Edmond Atkin Report and Plan of 1755*. Edited by Wilbur R. Jacobs. Columbia: University of South Carolina Press, 1954.

Bartram, William. *The Travels of William Bartram: Naturalist's Edition*. Edited by Francis Harper. New Haven, Conn.: Yale University Press, 1958.

Bartram, William. *Travels and Other Writings*. Edited by Thomas P. Slaughter. Library of America, no. 84. New York: Library of America, 1996.

Campbell, Archibald. *Journal of an Expedition against the Rebels of Georgia in North America Under the Orders of Archibald Campbell Esquire, Lieut. Colol. of His Majesty's 71st Regimt. 1778*. Edited by Colin Campbell. Printed for the Richmond County Historical Society, Augusta, Georgia. Darien, Ga.: Ashantilly Press, 1981.

Candler, Allen D., Kenneth Coleman, and Milton Ready, eds. *The Colonial Records of the State of Georgia*. 30 vols. Atlanta: C. P. Byrd, 1904–16; Athens: University of Georgia Press, 1974–76.

De Brahm, John Gerar William. *De Brahm's Report of the General Survey in the Southern District of North America*. Edited by Louis De Vorsey Jr. Columbia: University of South Carolina Press, 1971.

Fleming, Berry. *The Autobiography of a Colony: The First Half-Century of Augusta, Georgia*. Athens: University of Georgia Press, 1957.

George, David. "An Account of the Life of Mr. David George, from Sierra Leone in Africa; given by himself in a Conversation with Brother Rippon of London, and Brother Pearce of Birmingham." In *The Baptist Annual Register for 1790, 1791, 1792, and part of 1793: including sketches of the state of religion among the different denominations of god men at home and abroad*, ed. John D. Rippon, 473–84. [1793?].

Great Britain, Public Record Office. *Documents of the British Public Record Office Relating to South Carolina, 1663–1782*. Microfilm, 12 reels. Columbia: South Carolina Department of Archives and History, 1973.

———. *Records of the British Colonial Office, Class 5, Part 1: Westward Expansion, 1700–1783*. Microfilm, 12 reels. Frederick, Md.: University Publications of America, 1981–84.

———. *Records in the British Public Record Office Relating to South Carolina, 1701–1710*. Edited by A. S. Salley. Printed for the Historical Commission of South Carolina, 5 vols. Columbia, S.C.: Crowson-Stone Printing Company, 1947.

Hvidt, Kristian, ed. *Von Reck's Voyage: Drawings and Journal of Philip Georg Friedrich von Reck*. Editing assisted by Joseph Ewan, George F. Jones, and William C. Sturtevant. Savannah: Beehive Press, 1980.

Laurens, Henry. *The Papers of Henry Laurens*. Ed. Philip M. Hamer. 16 vols. Columbia: University of South Carolina Press for the South Carolina Historical Society, 1968.

McDowell, William L., ed. *Documents Relating to Indian Affairs*. Colonial Records of South Carolina, series 2: Indian Books, published for the South Carolina Department of Archives and History, 2 vols. Columbia: University of South Carolina Press, 1958, 1970.

McPherson, Robert G., ed. *Journal of the Earl of Egmont: Abstract of the Trustees Proceedings for Establishing the Colony of Georgia, 1732–1738*. Athens : University of Georgia Press, 1962.

Mereness, Newton D., ed. *Travels in the American Colonies*. Edited under the Auspices of the National Society of the Colonial Dames of America. New York: Macmillan, 1916.

Nairne, Thomas. *Nairne's Muskhogean Journals: The 1708 Expedition to the Mississippi River*. Edited by Alexander Moore. Jackson: University Press of Mississippi, 1988.

National Society Colonial Dames of America. *Abstracts of Colonial Wills of the State of Georgia*. Atlanta: Georgia Department of Archives and History, 1962.

"A New Voyage to Georgia by a Young Gentleman" [1737]. *Collections of the Georgia Historical Society* 2 (1842): 37–60.

Peterson, Merrill D., ed. *Thomas Jefferson: Writings*. Library of America. New York: Viking Press, 1984.

Reese, Trevor R., ed. *The Clamorous Malcontents: Criticisms and Defenses of the Colony of Georgia, 1741–1743*. Savannah: Beehive Press, 1973.

———. *The Most Delightful Country of the Universe: Promotional Litrature of the Colony of Georgia, 1717–1734*. Savannah: Beehive Press, 1972.

Romans, Bernard. *A Concise Natural History of East and West Florida*. Edited by Kathryn Holland Braund. Tuscaloosa: University of Alabama Press, 1999.

Rudock, Ted, ed. *Travels in the Colonies in 1773–1775: Described in the Letters of William Mylne*. Athens: University of Georgia Press, 1993.

Salley, Harriet Milledge, ed. *Correspondence of John Milledge, Governor of Georgia, 1802–1806*. Intro. Victor Davidson. Columbia, S.C.: State Commercial Printing Company, 1949.

Stephens, William. *The Journal of William Stephens*. Edited by E. Meron Coulter. Athens: University of Georgia Press, 1958–59.

United States. *The Debates and Proceedings in the Congress of the United States, with an Appendix containing Important State Papers and Public Documents, and all the Laws of a Public Nature; with a Copious Index; Compiled from Authentic Materials*. Comp. Joseph Gales. 42 vols. [Microform]. Washington, D.C.: Gales and Seaton, 1834–56.

Walker, George F., ed. *Abstracts of Georgia Colonial Book J, 1755–1762*. Atlanta: R. J. Taylor Jr. Foundation, 1978.

Secondary Sources

Akerman, James R., ed. *The Imperial Map: Cartography and the Mastery of Empire*. Chicago: University of Chicago Press, 2009

Alden, John R. *John Stuart and the Southern Colonial Frontier: A Study of Indian Relations, War, Trade, and Land Problems in the Southern Wilderness, 1754–1775*. Ann Arbor: University of Michigan Press, 1944.

Aron, Stephen. *How the West Was Lost: The Transformation of Kentucky from Daniel Boone to Henry Clay*. Baltimore: Johns Hopkins University Press, 1996.

Axtell, James L. "The First Consumer Revolution: The Seventeenth Century." In *Natives and Newcomers: The Cultural Origins of North America*, 104–20. New York: Oxford University Press, 2001.

———. *The Indians' New South: Cultural Change in the Colonial Southeast*. Walter Lynwood Fleming Lectures in Southern History. Baton Rouge: Louisiana State University Press, 1997.

Bagwell, Philip, and Peter Lyth. *Transport in Britain: From Canal Lock to Gridlock*. London: Hambledon and London, 2002.

Barry, John G. "Transport and Communication in Medieval and Tudor Ireland." In *Travel and Transport in Ireland*, ed. Kevin B. Nowlan, 32–46. New York: Barnes and Noble Books, 1973.

Beeman, Richard. *Evolution of the Southern Backcountry: A Case Study of Lunenburg Country, Virginia, 1746–1823*. Philadelphia: University of Pennsylvania Press, 1984.

Belyea, Barbara. "Inland Journeys, Native Maps." In *Cartographic Encounters: Perspectives on Native American Mapmaking and Map Use*, ed. Malcolm G. Lewis, 135–56.

Billings, John Shaw. "Analysis of the Will of George Galphin." *Richmond County History* 13 (1981): 29–38.

Bolster, W. Jeffrey. *Black Jacks: African American Seamen in the Age of Sail*. Cambridge, Mass.: Harvard University Press, 1997.

Boone, Elizabeth Hill. "Maps of Territory, History, and Community in Aztec Mexico." In *Cartographic Encounters: Perspectives on Native American Mapmaking and Map Use*, ed. Malcolm G. Lewis, 111–34.

Braund, Kathryn Holland. "The Creek Indians, Blacks, and Slavery." *Journal of Southern History* 57 (November 1991): 601–36.

———. *Deerskins and Duffels: Creek Indian Trade with Anglo-America, 1685–1815*. Lincoln: University of Nebraska Press, 1993.

Braund, Kathryn, and Gregory Waselkov. "William Bartram and the Southeastern Indians: An Introduction." In *William Bartram on the Southeastern Indians*, ed. Kathryn Braund and Gregory Waselkov, 1–24. Lincoln: University of Nebraska Press, 1995.

Brown, Kathleen. *Good Wives, Nasty Wenches, and Anxious Patriarchs: Gender, Race, and Power in Colonial Virginia*. Chapel Hill: University of North Carolina Press for the Omohundron Institute of Early American History and Culture, 1996.

Brückner, Martin. *The Geographic Revolution in Early America: Maps, Literacy, and National Identity*. Chapel Hill: University of North Carolina Press for the Omohundro Institute of Early American History and Culture, 2006.

Burnett, D. Graham. "Hydrographic Discipline among the Navigators." In *The Imperial Map: Cartography and the Mastery of Empire*, ed. James R. Akerman, 185–259.

Callahan, Helen. "Colonial Life in Augusta." In *Colonial Augusta: "Key of the*

Indian Countrey," ed. Edward J. Cashin. Macon, Ga.: Mercer University Press, 1986.

Carrera, Magali. "Entangled Spaces: Mapping Practices of Eighteenth-Century New Spain." Paper presented at the Seventeenth Kenneth Nebenzahl Jr. Lectures in the History of Cartography, Chicago, November 2010.

Carson, James Taylor. "Horses and the Economy and Culture of the Choctaw Indians, 1690–1840." *Ethnohistory* 42 (Summer 1995): 495–513.

Cashin, Edward J. "'But Brothers, It is Our Land We Are Talking About': Winners and Losers in the Georgia Backcountry." In *An Uncivil War: The Southern Backcountry during the American Revolution*, ed. Ronald Hoffman et al., 240–75.

———. "The Gentlemen of Augusta." In *Colonial Augusta: "Key of the Indian Countrey,"* ed. Edward J. Cashin. Macon, Ga.: Mercer University Press, 1986.

———. *Guardians of the Valley: Chickasaws in Colonial South Carolina and Georgia*. Columbia: University of South Carolina Press, 2009.

———. *Lachlan McGillivray, Indian Trader: The Shaping of the Southern Colonial Frontier*. Athens: University of Georgia Press, 1992.

———. "Oglethorpe's Contest for the Backcountry, 1733–1749." In *Oglethorpe in Perspective: Georgia's Founder after Two Hundred Years*, ed. Phinizy Spalding and Harvey H. Jackson, 99–111. Tuscaloosa: University of Alabama Press, 1989.

———. *Old Springfield: Race and Religion in Augusta, Georgia*. Augusta: Springfield Village Park Foundation, 1995.

———. *The Story of Augusta*. Augusta: Richmond County Board of Education, 1980.

———. *William Bartram and the American Revolution on the Southern Frontier*. Columbia: University of South Carolina Press, 2000.

Cayton, Andrew R. L. "'Separate Interests' and the Nation-State: The Washington Administration and the Origins of Regionalism in the Trans-Appalachian West." *Journal of American History* 79 (June 1992): 39–67.

Cecelski, David. *The Waterman's Song: Slavery and Freedom in Maritime North Carolina*. Chapel Hill: University of North Carolina Press, 2001.

Chaplin, Joyce. *An Anxious Pursuit: Agricultural Innovation and Modernity in the Lower South, 1730–1815*. Published for the Omohundro Institute of Early American History and Culture. Chapel Hill: University of North Carolina Press, 1993.

Coleman, Kenneth. *Colonial Georgia: A History*. A History of the American Colonies in Thirteen Volumes, ed. Milton M. Klein and Jacob E. Cooke. New York: Scribner, 1976.

Corkran, David H. *The Cherokee Frontier: Conflict and Survival, 1740–1762*. Norman: University of Oklahoma Press, 1962.

———. *The Creek Frontier, 1540–1783*. Norman: University of Oklahoma Press, 1967.

Crane, Verner. *The Southern Frontier, 1670–1732*. Durham, N.C.: Duke University Press, 1928.
Cronon, William. *Changes in the Land: Indians, Colonists, and the Ecology of New England*. New York: Hill and Wang, 1983.
Cumming, William P. *The Southeast in Early Maps*. 3rd ed. Revised and enlarged by Louis De Vorsey Jr. Chapel Hill: University of North Carolina Press, 1998.
Deetz, James. *In Small Things Forgotten: An Archaeology of Early American Life*. Expanded and revised edition, illustrated by Amy Elizabeth Grey. New York: Doubleday, 1996.
Delle, James A. *An Archaeology of Social Space: Analyzing Coffee Plantations in Jamaica's Blue Mountains*. Contributions to Global Historical Archaeology. Series edited by Charles E. Orser Jr. New York: Plenum Press, 1998.
De Vorsey, Louis, Jr. "American Indians and the Early Mapping of the Southeast." In William P. Cumming, *The Southeast in Early Maps*, ed. Louis De Vorsey Jr. Chapel Hill: University of North Carolina Press, 1998.
―――. "The Colonial Georgia Backcountry." In *Colonial Augusta: "Key of the Indian Countrey,"* ed. Edward J. Cashin, 5–10. Macon, Ga.: Mercer University Press, 1986.
―――. *The Georgia-South Carolina Boundary: A Problem in Historical Geography*. Athens: University of Georgia Press, 1982.
―――. *The Indian Boundary in the Southern Colonies, 1763–1775*. Chapel Hill: University of North Carolina Press, 1961.
―――. "Oglethorpe and the Earliest Maps of Georgia." In *Oglethorpe in Perspective: Georgia's Founder after Two Hundred Years*, ed. Phinizy Spalding and Harvey H. Jackson. Tuscaloosa: University of Alabama Press, 1989.
Dowd, Gregory Evans. "The Panic of 1751: The Significance of Rumors on the South Carolina-Cherokee Frontier." *William and Mary Quarterly*, 3rd series, 53 (July 1996): 527–60.
Druke, Mary A. "Linking Arms: The Structure of Iroquois Intertribal Diplomacy." In *Beyond the Covenant Chain*, ed. Daniel K. Richter and James Merrell, 29–40.
Earle, Carville, and Ronald Hoffman. "Staple Crops and Urban Development in the Eighteenth-Century South." *Perspectives in American History* 10 (1976): 7–80.
Edney, Matthew. "The Irony of Imperial Mapping." In *The Imperial Map*, ed. James R. Akerman, 11–46.
Ethridge, Robbie. *Creek Country: The Creek Indians and Their World*. Chapel Hill: University of North Carolina Press, 2003.
Ferguson, Leland. *Uncommon Ground: Archaeology and Early African America, 1650–1800*. Washington, D.C.: Smithsonian Institution Press, 1992.
Fleetwood, Rusty. *Tidecraft: The Boats of South Carolina, Georgia, and Northeastern Florida—1500–1950*. Tybee Island, Ga.: WBG Marine Press, 1995.
―――. *Tidecraft: An Introductory Look at the Boats of Lower South Carolina,*

Georgia, and Northeastern Florida: 1650–1950. Principal research by Antoinette Goodrich. Savannah: Coastal Heritage Society, 1982.

Foucault, Michel. *Discipline and Punish: The Birth of the Prison*. Translated by Alan Sheridan. New York: Vintage Books, 1977.

Frank, Andrew K. *Creeks and Southerners: Biculturalism on the Early American Frontier*. Indians of the Southeast. Series edited by Michael D. Green and Theda Perdue. Lincoln: University of Nebraska Press, 2005.

Gallay, Alan. *The Formation of a Southern Planter Elite: Jonathan Bryan and the Southern Colonial Frontier*. Athens: University of Georgia Press, 1989.

———. *The Indian Slave Trade: The Rise of the English Empire in the American South, 1670–1717*. New Haven, Conn.: Yale University Press, 2002.

Galloway, Patricia. "Debriefing Explorers Amerindian Information in the Delisles' Mapping of the Southeast." In *Cartographic Encounters*, ed. Malcolm G. Lewis, 223–40.

Genovese, Eugene D. *Roll, Jordan, Roll: The World the Slaves Made*. New York: Vintage Books, 1976.

Gordon, Anne. *To Move with the Times: The Story of Transport and Travel in Scotland*. Aberdeen: Aberdeen University Press, 1988.

Haan, Richard L. "Covenant and Consensus: Iroquois and English, 1676–1760." In *Beyond the Covenant Chain*, ed. Daniel K. Richter and James Merrell, 41–60.

Hahn, Steven C. *The Invention of the Creek Nation, 1670–1763*. Lincoln: University of Nebraska Press, 2004.

Hally, David J. "The Nature of Mississippian Regional Systems." In *The Transformation of the Southeastern Indians, 1540–1760*, ed. Robbie Ethridge and Charles Hudson. Jackson: University Press of Mississippi, 2002: 26–42.

Harley, J. B. *The New Nature of Maps: Essays in the History of Cartography*. Edited by Paul Laxton. Introduction by J. H. Andrews. Baltimore: Johns Hopkins University Press, 2001.

———. "Power and Legitimation in the English Geographical Atlases of the Eighteenth Century." In *Images of the World: The Atlas through History*, ed. John A. Wolter and Ronald E. Grim, 161–204. New York: McGraw-Hill, 1997.

Hatley, Tom. *The Dividing Paths: Cherokees and South Carolinians through the Era of Revolution*. New York: Oxford University Press, 1993.

Henri, Florette. *The Southern Indians and Benjamin Hawkins, 1796–1816*. Norman: University of Oklahoma Press, 1986.

Hinderaker, Eric. *Elusive Empires: Constructing Colonialism in the Ohio Valley, 1673–1800*. New York: Cambridge University Press, 1997.

Hoffman, Ronald, Thad Tate, and Peter Albert, eds. *An Uncivil War: The Southern Backcountry during the American Revolution*. Charlottesville: University of Virginia Press, 1985.

Hudgins, Carter. "Robert 'King' Carter and the Landscape of Tidewater Virginia." In *Earth Patterns: Essays in Landscape Archaeology*, ed. William M.

Kelso and Rachel Most, 59–70. Charlottesville: University of Virginia Press, 1990.

Hudson, Angela Pulley. *Creek Paths and Federal Roads: Indians, Settlers, and Slaves and the Making of the American South.* Chapel Hill: University of North Carolina Press, 2010.

Hudson, Charles. *The Southeastern Indians.* Knoxville: University of Tennessee Press, 1976.

Isaac, Rhys. *The Transformation of Virginia, 1740–1790.* New York: W. W. Norton, 1988.

Johnson, Walter. *Soul by Soul: Life inside the Antebellum Slave Market.* Cambridge, Mass.: Harvard University Press, 1999.

Jones, Charles C., and Salem Dutcher. *Memorial History of Augusta, Georgia.* Syracuse: D. Mason, 1890; Spartanburg, S.C.: Reprint Company, 1966.

Jones, George Fenwick. "Portrait of an Irish Entrepreneur in Colonial Augusta: John Rae, 1708–1772." *Georgia Historical Quarterly* 83 (Fall 1999): 427–47.

Juricek, John. *Colonial Georgia and the Creeks: Anglo-Indian Diplomacy on the Southern Frontier, 1733–1763.* Gainesville: University Press of Florida, 2010.

Kelton, Paul. "The Great Southeastern Smallpox Epidemic, 1696–1700: The Region's First Major Epidemic?" In *Light on the Path: The Anthropology and History of the Southeastern Indians*, ed. Thomas J. Pluckhahn and Robbie Ethridge, 21–37. Tuscaloosa: University of Alabama Press, 2006.

Kerber, Linda K. *Women of the Republic: Intellect and Identity in Revolutionary America* With a preface by the author. Originally published for the Omohundro Institute of Early American History and Culture. Chapel Hill: University of North Carolina Press, 1980; New York: W. W. Norton, 1986.

Klein, Rachel M. *Unification of a Slave State: The Rise of the Planter Class in the South Carolina Backcountry, 1760–1808.* Chapel Hill: University of North Carolina Press, 1990.

Lamplugh, George R. *Politics on the Periphery: Factions and Parties in Georgia, 1783–1806.* Newark: University of Delaware Press, 1986.

Levy, Philip. *Fellow Travelers: Indians and Europeans Contesting the Early American Trail.* Gainesville: University Press of Florida, 2007.

Lewis, James E., Jr. *The American Union and the Problem of Neighborhood: The United States and the Collapse of the Spanish Empire, 1783–1829.* Chapel Hill: University of North Carolina Press, 1998.

Lewis, Kenneth E. *The American Frontier: An Archaeological Study of Settlement Pattern and Process.* Orlando: Academic Press, 1984.

———. "Economic Development in the Southern Backcountry: A View from Camden." In *The Southern Colonial Backcountry: Interdisciplinary Perspectives on Frontier Communities*, ed. David Colin Crass et al., 87–107. Knoxville: University of Tennessee Press, 1998.

———. "The Metropolis and the Backcountry: The Making of a Colonial Landscape on the South Carolina Frontier." *Historical Archaeology* 33, no. 3 (1999): 3–13.

Lewis, Malcolm G., ed. *Cartographic Encounters: Perspectives on Native American Mapmaking and Map Use.* Chicago: University of Chicago Press, 1998.

McCracken, J. L. "The Age of the Stage Coach." In *Travel and Transport in Ireland*, ed. Kevin B. Nowlan. New York: Barnes and Noble Books, 1973.

McMichael, Andrew. *Atlantic Loyalties: Americans in Spanish West Florida, 1785–1810.* Athens: University of Georgia Press, 2008.

Meinig, D.W. *The Shaping of America: A Geographical Perspective on 500 Years of History, vol. 1: Atlantic America, 1492–1800.* New Haven, Conn.: Yale University Press, 1986.

Mellon, Knox, Jr. "Christian Priber's Cherokee 'Kingdom of Paradise.'" *Georgia Historical Quarterly* 57 (Spring 1973): 319–31.

Merrell, James. *The Indian's New World: Catawbas and Their Neighbors from European Contact through the Era of Removal.* Chapel Hill: University of North Carolina Press, 1989; New York: W. W. Norton, 1991.

Mignolo, Walter. *The Darker Side of the Renaissance: Literacy, Teritoriality, and Colonization.* Ann Arbor: University of Michigan Press, 1997.

Mitchell, Robert D. *Commercialism and Frontier: Perspectives in the Shenandoah Valley.* Charlottesville: University Press of Virginia, 1977.

———. "The Southern Backcountry: A Geographical House Divided." In *The Southern Colonial Backcountry: Interdisciplinary Perspectives on Frontier Communities*, ed. David Colin Crass et al., 1–35. Knoxville: University of Tennessee Press, 1998.

Morgan, Philip D. "Colonial South Carolina Runaways: Their Significance for Slave Culture." *Slavery and Abolition* 6 (December 1985): 57–78.

———. *Slave Counterpoint: Black Culture in the Eighteenth-Century Chesapeake and Lowcountry.* Published for the Omohundro Institute of Early American History and Culture. Chapel Hill: University of North Carolina Press, 1998.

Nash, Gary. *The Urban Crucible: The Northern Seaports and the Origins of the American Revolution.* Abridged ed. Cambridge, Mass.: Harvard University Press, 1986.

Nelson, Howard J. "Walled Cities of the United States" *Annals of the American Association of Geographers* 51 (March 1961): 1–22.

Nobles, Gregory F. "Straight Lines and Stability: Mapping the Political Order of the Anglo-American Frontier." *Journal of American History* 80, no. 1 (1993): 9–35.

Norwood, Martha F. *A History of the White House Tract, Richmond County, Georgia, 1756–1975.* Produced for the Department of Natural Resources, Office of Planning and Research, Historical Preservation Section. Atlanta: Georgia Department of Natural Resources, Historical Preservation Section, 1975.

Oakes, James. *Slavery and Freedom: An Interpretation of the Old South.* New York: W. W. Norton, 1990.

Paulett, Robert. "The Bewildering World of William De Brahm: An Eighteenth-Century Map Maker Surveys the End of Time." *Eighteenth-Century Studies* 42 (July 2009): 481–99.
Perdue, Theda. *Cherokee Women: Gender and Culture Change, 1700–1835*. Lincoln: University of Nebraska Press, 1998.
Pickett, Albert James. *History of Alabama, and Incidentally of Georgia and Mississippi, from the Earliest Period*. 2nd ed. Charleston, S.C.: Walker and James, 1851.
Piker, Joshua. "Colonists and Creeks: Rethinking the Pre-Revolutionary Southern Backcountry." *Journal of Southern History* 70 (August 2004): 503–40.
———. *Okfuskee: A Creek Town in Colonial America*. Cambridge, Mass.: Harvard University Press, 2004.
———. "'White, and Clean' and Contested: Creek Towns and Trading Paths in the Aftermath of the Seven Years' War." *Ethnohistory* 50 (Spring 2003): 315–47.
Podruchny, Carolyn. *Making the Voyageur World: Travelers and Traders in the North American Fur Trade*. Studies in Empire and Decolonization. Series edited by Philip Boucher, A. J. B. Johnston, James D. Le Sueur, and Tyler Stovall. Lincoln: University of Nebraska Press, 2006.
Reid, John Philip. *A Better Kind of Hatchet: Law, Trade, and Diplomacy in the Cherokee Nation during the Early Years of European Contact*. University Park: Pennsylvania State University Press, 1976.
Reps, John W. "C2 + L2 = S2? Another Look at the Origins of Savannah's Town Plan." In *Forty Years of Diversity: Essays on Colonial Georgia*, ed. Harvey H. Jackson and Phinizy Spalding, 101–51. Athens: University of Georgia Press, 1984.
Richter, Daniel K., and James Merrell, eds. *Beyond the Covenant Chain: The Iroquois and Their Neighbors in Indian North America, 1600–1800*. Syracuse, N.Y.: Syracuse University Press, 1987
Robertson, Heard, and Thomas H. Robertson. "The Town and Fort of Augusta." In *Colonial Augusta: "Key of the Indian Countrey*," ed. Edward J. Cashin, 59–74. Macon, Ga.: Mercer University Press, 1986.
Rolt, L. T. C. *The Inland Waterways of England*. London: George Allen and Unwin, 1966.
Saunt, Claudio. *A New Order of Things: Property, Power, and the Transformation of the Creeks, 1733–1816*. New York: Cambridge University Press, 1999.
Shoemaker, Nancy. "An Alliance between Men: Gender Metaphors in Eighteenth-Century American Indian Diplomacy East of the Mississippi." *Ethnohistory* 46 (Spring 1999): 239–63.
———. *A Strange Likeness: Becoming Red and White in Eighteenth-Century North America*. New York: Oxford University Press, 2004.
Silver, Timothy. *A New Face on the Countryside: Indians, Colonists, and Slaves in South Atlantic Forests, 1500–1800*. New York: Cambridge University Press, 1990.

Snapp, J. Russell. *John Stuart and the Struggle for Empire on the Southern Frontier.* Baton Rouge: Louisiana State University Press, 1996.

Sobel, Mechal. *Trabelin' On: The Slave Journey to an Afro-Baptist Faith.* Princeton: Princeton University Press, 1979.

Spalding, Phinizy. "James Edward Oglethorpe's Quest for an American Zion." In *Forty Years of Diversity: Essays on Colonial Georgia,* ed. Harvey H. Jackson and Phinizy Spalding, 60–79. Athens: University of Georgia Press, 1984.

Sweet, Julie Ann. *Negotiating for Georgia: British-Creek Relations in the Trustee Era.* Athens: University of Georgia Press, 2005.

Thompson, E. P. *The Making of the English Working Class.* New York: Pantheon Books, 1963.

Thornton, John. *Africa and Africans in the Making of the Atlantic World, 1400–1800.* 2nd ed. New York: Cambridge University Press, 1998.

Thrower, Norman J. W. *Maps and Civilization: Cartography and Culture in Society.* Chicago: University of Chicago Press, 1996.

Tillson, Albert. *Gentry and Common Folk: Political Culture on a Virginia Frontier, 1740–1789.* Lexington: University Press of Kentucky, 1991.

Turner, Frederick Jackson. "The Significance of the Frontier in American History." In Frederick Jackson Turner, *The Frontier in America.* New York: Holt, 1947, 1967.

Upton, Dell. *Holy Things and Profane: Anglican Parish Churches in Colonial Virginia.* Architectural History Foundation Books. Cambridge, Mass.: MIT Press, 1986.

Usner, Daniel. *Indians Settlers and Slaves in a Frontier Exchange Economy: The Lower Mississippi Valley before 1783.* Published for the Omohundro Institute of Early American History and Culture. Chapel Hill: University of North Carolina Press, 1992.

Vine, P. A. L. *London's Lost Route to the Sea: An Historical Account of the Inland Navigations which Linked the Thames and the English Channel.* Newton Abbot: David and Charles, 1965.

Waselkov, Gregory A. "Indian Maps of the Colonial Southeast: Archaeological Implications and Prospects." In *Cartographic Encounters,* ed. Malcolm G. Lewis, 205–22.

———. "Indian Maps of the Colonial Southeast." In *Powhatan's Mantle: Indians in the Colonial Southeast,* rev. and exp. ed., ed. Gregory A. Waselkov, Peter H. Wood, and Tom Hatley, 435–53. Lincoln: University of Nebraska Press, 2006.

Willan, T. S. *River Navigation in England, 1600–1750.* London: Oxford University Press, 1964.

Wood, Denis, and John Fels. *The Power of Maps.* New York: Guilford Press, 1992.

Wood, Peter. *Black Majority: Negroes in Colonial South Carolina from 1670 through the Stono Rebellion.* New York: W. W. Norton, 1974.

———. "Circles in the Sand: Perspectives on the Southern Frontier at the Arrival of James Oglethorpe." In *Oglethorpe in Perspective: Georgia's Founder after Two Hundred Years*, edited by Phinizy Spalding and Harvey H. Jackson. Tuscaloosa: University of Alabama Press, 1989.

Wright, J. Leitch, Jr. *Creeks and Seminoles: The Destruction and Regeneration of the Muscogulge People*. Indians of the Southeast. Lincoln: University of Nebraska Press, 1986.

Index

References to illustrations are italicized.

Adair, James (Chickasaw Trader), 125–27, 131, 134–35, 164, 165, 168–69; and idea of "civilization," 148–50, 163; and Scottish Enlightenment, 149

African Americans, enslaved, 195; as boatmen, 8, 9, 49, 66–71; networks among, 72–76, 140; in Augusta, 79, 82–83, 85–86, 94, 107–8, 110–11; dress deerskins, 79, 108–9; and paths, 116, 136–39; in Creek towns, 137, 152, 170; runaways, 72, 75–76, 138–40; in nineteenth century, 195–96

Albany, New York, 50, 91

American Revolution, 7, 19, 28, 39, 111–12, 189; influence on Indian trade, 10–11, 48, 171–72, 196; influence on Southeast, 45, 47–48, 52, 192–93, 195–96; effects on Augusta, 79, 173–174, 177; local origins in Georgia, 112–13, 170, 175; and Creeks, 175–76

Archibald McGillivray and Company, 87–89, 95

Atkin, Edmund, 70, 90, 98, 108, 125, 156–58

Augusta, 31, 48, 99–100, 195; founding of, 1, 7, 9, 14, 20, 28, 79–80, 85–88; place in Indian trade, 3, 9, 20, 27, 49, 56, 78–79, 91–92, 105–6, 115–20, 134, 144; relationship with Savannah River, 50, 55–56, 61, 76, 90; relationship with New Windsor, 57, 58, 61, 83, 84–86, 88; descriptions of, 81–84, 90–93; settlement pattern in, 50, 78–81, *82*, 84, 89–93, 103–4; slavery in, 75, 79, 82–83, 85–86, 94, 107–8, 110–11; effects of American Revolution on, 79, 113, 173–75, 176, 177; population of, 81–84, 107–8; civil government of, 83, 88–89, 93–94, 97–98; defenses of, 89–90, 92; Indian presence in, 92, 102; as portrayed in newspapers, 182, *183*–184; in nineteenth century, 196. *See also* Augustans, Non-trader; Towns, British; Traders, Merchant; Trading Companies; Trustees for Establishing the Colony of Georgia

"Augusta Company." *See* Brown, Rae, and Company

Augusta Congress of 1773, 150, 175

Augustans, non-trader, 78–79, 94, 98; relations to trading companies, 93, 94–95, 97, 99–100, 105–8

Barksdale, Isaac (Merchant-Trader), 96, 104, 128; as slaveowner, 109. *See also* Rae, John

Barnard, Edward (Merchant-Trader), 98, 112; as slaveowner, 75–76, 108, 111; fortified compound of, 90, 94. *See also* Fraser, James

Barnard, Timothy (Cherokee Trader), 105

Barnwell, John, 19, 34, 35; plans for Southeast, 16–18, 32; manuscript map, 17–18, *18*, 23, 30, 31–34

Bartram, William, 43–44; on rivers, 62, 63–64; on paths, 126, 128–29; and "civilization," 148, 151–52
Beamer, James (Cherokee Trader), 156
"Beaver Catchers," 155–56
Beresford, Richard, 16–17; manuscript map, 17, *18*; plans for Southeast, 17–18
Boatmen, European, 66–68
Boatmen, Indian Trade, 48, 49, 65, 69, 122; roles in Indian trade, 1, 8; landscapes experienced, 1–2, 49, 61, 68–69; enslaved, 8, 9, 49, 66–74, 76, 109, 140; careers of, 49–50, 65; as "patroons," 49–50, 65–69; in nineteenth century, 196–97. *See also* Augusta; Caesar; Indian Trade; Pompey; Rae, John; Savannah River; Shepherd, Peter; Traders, Merchant
Boatmen, West African, 65, 72
Boatswain, The (Upper Creek Indian), 160, 164
Borders, 179; idea of, in Georgia, 179, 181, 189–90; in newspapers, 181–83; between Georgia and the Creeks, 188–89; and citizenship in Georgia, 189–93
Bosomworth, Mary Musgrove, 115–16, 140–41, 155
Bosomworth, Thomas, 28, 29, 115–16, 133, 140–41
Branham, John (Cherokee Trader), 133–34
Britain, Royal Government of, 17–18, 19, 32, 35–36, 59, 141, 155; imperial plans for Southeast, 3, 8, 12, 13, 21, 33–34, 36–38, 141–42, 154; desires to regulate Indian trade, 7, 9, 13, 20, 29–30, 35–36, 39–47, 142–44, 154–56. *See also* Atkin, Edmund; Proclamation of 1763; Stuart, John
Brown, Patrick (Merchant-Trader), 88, 89, 96, 106. *See also* Archibald McGillivray and Company; Brown, Rae, and Company; Sludders, William (Elder)
Brown, Rae, and Company ("Augusta Company"), 50, 104; formation of, 88–89; fortified compounds of, 94; as "house," 96, 144–45; control over trade, 124–25, 140–41
Brown, Samuel (Cherokee Trader), 88

Caesar (Boatman), 70
Campbell, Archibald, 81, 111; *Sketch of the Northern Frontiers of Georgia*, 81, *82*
Campbell, Martin (Merchant-Trader), 88, 96, 98, 112; complains of Ogeechee settlers, 104. *See also* Pettygrew, John
Camden, South Carolina, 50, 91–92
Canoes, Dugout: African, 65; American Indian, 65, 123, 168; Anglo-American, 65, 123
Catawbas, 24, 171
Charles Town, South Carolina, 1, 3, 7, 30, 48, 53, 91; role in Indian trade, 20, 49, 60, 61, 70, 76, 90, 120, 145; Georgia Trustees' views of, 56
Chattahoochee River, 12, 27, 31, 193–94
Cherokee War, 39, 41, 42, 78, 108
Cherokees, 2, 15, 16, 20, 24, 70, 92; relations with British, 39, 41, 49, 78, 92, 132, 141, 153–54; and "New Purchase," 44, 112–13; relations with Creeks, 115, 154, 168; and paths, 120; number of towns, 130; relations with traders, 119, 133–34, 153–54, 175; effects of trade on, 171; and "plan for civilization," 151–52
Chickasaws, Eastern, 52, 78, 92
Chickasaws, Western, 2, 7, 20, 28, 70; as mapmakers, 24; relations with French, 28, 119; relation to trade, 27; relations with English colonies, 30, 39, 49, 141; relations with other Indians, 118–19; number of towns, 130; and livestock, 149–50. *See also* Mingo Ouma
Choctaws, 2, 20, 24, 27; relations with French, 30, 119, 130; relations with Chickasaws, 118–19; and horses, 130, 155; relations with English, 130, 141
Clark, Daniel (Merchant-Trader), 88, 89, 96, 112, 128. *See also* Archibald McGillivray and Company; Brown, Rae, and Company; McGillivray, John; McGillivray, Lachlan; Sludders, William (Elder); Sludders, William (Younger)
Cook and Company, 125
"Covenant Chain," 117
Coweta (Lower Creek Town), 27, 115, 118, 120, 141
Creek Men: fear loss of authority, 162, 166; attempts to maintain control over trade, 166–168; ideas of masculinity, 168. *See also* Creeks (General References)

Creek Women: roles in trading houses, 10, 142–43, 152, 161–62; links to slave labor, 79, 108–9, 162; relations with English traders, 87–88, 163–64; as ranchers, 162–63; oversee children's education, 165; and "Plan for Civilization," 165. *See also* Creeks (General References)

Creeks (General References), 7, 29, 34, 70, 75, 78, 81, 98, 104, 156; relations with English colonies, 2, 20, 44, 49, 92, 117, 141; adopt European ideas of property, 5, 124, 165, 171, 177–78; and American Revolution, 10, 175, 176, 177; views of rivers, 51–53; seek lower trade prices, 102, 158–59, 166, 168–69; relations with other Europeans, 117–18; relations with other Indians, 118; suspicion of chains, 117, 169–70; and slavery, 117, 137, 169–71; complain of horse thefts, 133, 135–36; attempts to control trade, 143–44, 166–69; and "Plan for Civilization," 151–52; ideas of trading houses, 159–60, 161–62; family structure of, 161–62; households of, 161–62, 165; effects of trade on, 170–71; factionalism within, 171, 177–78, 193; relations with United States, 171, 176–77, 179, 180, 187–88, 193–95; relations with state of Georgia, 176–79, 180, 183, 185–87, 193; and post-Revolutionary leadership, 177–78; removal of, 193–95. *See also* Creek Men; Creek Women; Creeks, Lower; Creeks, Upper; Towns, Creek;

Creeks, Lower, 7, 24, 27, 31, 62; relations with English colonies, 44, 78, 103, 111–13, 115, 171, 182; use Savannah River as boundary, 50, 52; relations with settlers, 102–5, 113, 175; relations with Cherokees, 115, 154. *See also* Creeks (General Reference); "New Purchase" of 1773; Yamasee War

Creeks, Upper, 7, 17, 24, 27, 47; relations with French, 17, 117–18, 153; relations with English colonies, 78, 119; relations with traders, 78, 158–59, 167, 168 relations with other Indians, 115, 118–19, 168. *See also* Creeks (General References)

Crisp, Edward, 30, *14*

Cussings, George (Creek Trader), 87

Cussings, James (Creek Trader), 124

De Brahm, John Gerar William, 40, 119–20; *Map of South Carolina and Part of Georgia*, 40, *41*, 69

Deerskin Leather, 8, 49; Quantities shipped to England, 47, 70; "Raw" skin trade, 108, 162

Delisle, Guillame, 15–16

Doharty, Cornelius (Cherokee Trader), 138, 146, 164, 170

Douglass, David (Merchant-Trader), 98, 104; as slaveowner, 75, 111

Education: in post-Revolutionary Georgia, 175, 179–80, 192–93; of traders' children, 165

Ellis, Henry, 103, 117–18

Emistisiguo (Upper Creek Headman), 118, 166, 177

Emulation, 148–50

Enlightenment Cartography: definition of, 12, 15; relationship with empire, 21, 40, 45; in Southeast, 30, 40–41, 43; as attempt to regulate Indian trade, 39–40; and Indians, 40

Florida (Spanish), 17, 19, 34, 39, 72, 176–77; relations with Creeks, 118, 127, 185–86; relations with Georgia (state), 180, 185–86; relations with United States, 184, 187

Florida, East (British), 40, 176–77

Florida, West (British), 175, 176–77; becomes center of Indian trade, 47, 142–43, 173, 176

Fort Augusta, 20, 90, 92, 104–5; Fort Toulouse ("Alabama Fort"), 17, 127, 128, 153; exchanges with English traders, 28, 160–61

France: contest with Britain, 1, 13–15, 20, 30–31, 37, 78, 119, 142–43, 153; claims on Southeast, 15–16, 21; removal from eastern North America, 39, 47; stoke Creek fears of enslavement, 117, 169; relations with Chickasaws, 119

Fraser, James (Merchant-Trader), 94, 97, 111. *See also* Barnard, Edward.

Fraser, William (Creek Trader), 124

"Frontier:" idea of, 4–5, 6, 79, 190–93; in newspapers, 181–84

Galphin, George (Creek Trader, Merchant-Trader), 89, 94, 96, 112, 150, 176; as storekeeper, 105–7; other economic endeavors, 106; as slaveowner, 107–8, 109–10, 111; as literary patron, 148. *See also* Bartram, William; Brown, Rae, and Company; McGillivray, Lachlan; Silver Bluff

Gender: in Augusta, 100–1; in Creek villages, 162–68. *See also* Traders, Merchant, Claims to independence and authority; Traders, Village, Claims to authority

Geography: as subject in Georgia schools, 175, 179–80; and newspapers, 181–82

George, David, 109–11, 138–39; dresses deer skins, 109; runs away along paths, 138–39

Georgia (Colony): founding of, 3, 7, 12, 14–15, 19–20, 54, 72; boundaries of, 20, 45–46, 52, 57; conflicts with Carolina traders, 20–21, 56–59, 86–87, 147, 152–153; and American Revolution, 47–48; relations with Creek Indians, 52–53. *See also* Augusta; Oglethorpe, James; Trustees for Establishing the Colony of Georgia

Georgia (State): ideas of geography in, 10–11, 178–84, 193–94; and Indian trade, 10, 173, 176, 178; Augusta and, 173–74; relationship with Creeks, 174–75, 178–79, 185–87, 188–93; relationship with Spanish Florida, 174–75, 185–86, 192; relationship with United States, 178, 186–92, 193; effects of American Revolution on, 48,178–79; idea of borders within, 179–80, 181–83, 189–90; and "Neighborhood," 182–85

Germany, James (Creek Trader), 47, 103, 164

Glen, James, 22, 34–35, 130, 154–55, 156

Greenwood, William, 113–14

Gun Merchant of Okchai (Upper Creek Headman): and neutrality, 118; attempts to control trade, 158–59, 166

Hawkins, Benjamin, 165

Henderson, Richard (Creek Trader), 154

"Herbert's Spring," 134–135

Horses, 7, 10, 28, 87, 89; trade of, 106, 131–35; influence on paths, 114, 116, 120, 121, 128–29; as uncertain "property," 127, 134–36; used in trade, 129–31; in England, 130; theft of, 132–36; links to South Carolina Regulators, 133, 175. *See also* Indian Trade; Packhorse Trains; Packhorsemen

House-breaking: in Anglo-America, 153, 167; in Creek country, 167–68

Houses: British ideas of, 10, 143–45, 152; trader ideas of, 29, 143–50, 152, 157–58; Creek ideas of, 143–44, 159–60, 161–62; educational function of, 165. *See also* Trading Companies; Trading Compounds; Trading Stores

Indian Trade, 5, 9, 19, 124, 145–150, 152, 194; diplomatic roles of, 2, 7, 13–15, 19, 153–55; human geography of, 2–3, 6–11, 20–30, 32–39, 43–48, 175, 184, 194–96; as route to power for Europeans, 2, 23, 27, 47, 195, 196–97; as route to power for Indians, 2, 27, 47, 195, 196–97; British attempts to reform, 7, 9, 13, 20, 29–30, 32, 35–36, 39–47, 142–144, 154–56; reliance on slave labor, 8, 9, 66–67, 70, 76–77, 79, 108–9, 136; influence on British maps, 21–23, 29–30, 32–39, 46–47; changes in, post-1763, 108–9, 141–142, 149, 159. *See also* American Revolution; Augusta; Boatmen; Britain, Royal Government of; Creeks (General References); Gender; Horses; Paths; Savannah River; Traders, Merchants; Traders, Village; Trading Stores

Indian Trade Goods, 49, 60, 105; influence on Creek politics, 118, 122, 170–71; traders' "ownership" of goods, 122, 124–25, 127, 134, 157–58; Indian attempts to lower prices, 158–59, 167–68

Jackson, James, 98, 186–87, 190, 191

Jefferson, Thomas, 53, 187–88, 189

John Buckles and Company, 97; and horse trade, 131–32

Kent, Richard, 84, 88, 97

Knox, Henry, 188

Little Tallasee (Upper Creek Town), 118, 147

Livestock, 106, 149, 152, 177; influence on Anglo-Creek relations, 53, 136; and "Plan for Civilization," 149–50, 188. *See also* Chickasaws, Western

Macartan, Campbell, and Company, 88, 90, 94, 97, 106–7, 108; and slavery, 107–8, 109; and horse trade, 131–32. *See also* Deerskin Leather; Galphin, George; John Buckles and Company; Maclean, Andrew; Trading Licenses, Private; Trewin, Sludders, and McGillivray

Macartan Francis (Merchant-Trader), 88, 90, 94, 96, 98. *See also* Macartan, Campbell and Company; Pettygrew, John; Trading Compounds

Mackay, Mary Chilcott, 99, 100–1. *See also* Gender, in Augusta; Mackay, Robert

Mackay, Patrick: conflict with Carolina traders, 86–88; role in Augusta's founding, 87–88

Mackay, Robert, 60–61, 70, 81, 95, 98–99, 100, 101, 112, 176; house of, 94, 145, 173–74; debts of, 113–14; employees of, 134, 147–48. *See also* Caesar; Mackay, Mary Chilcott; MacLean, Andrew; Williams, John Francis

MacLean, Andrew, 60–61, 70, 97, 113, 197; conflict with Richmond County Trustees, 173–74. *See also* Macartan, Campbell, and Company; Mackay, Robert; Pompey

Malatchi (Lower Creek Headman), 133, 136

"Malcontents," 57, 82–83, 110

Mapmakers, Colonial, 22–23. *See also* Nairne, Thomas; Barnwell, John; Mitchell, John; De Brahm, John Gerar William; Stuart, John; Purcell, Joseph

Mapmakers, French, 15–16, 40

Mapmakers, Indian, 24–26, 53, 117

Mapmakers, United States, 193–94

Maps, British, 8; cartographic contest with France, 12–16; relationship to British Empire, 12–13, 21; relationship with trade geography, 13–14, 16, 21, 29–32; of the Southeast, 14–23; as private property, 22–23; methods of production, 22–23, 30; uselessness for travel, 120–21

Maps, French, 15–16

Maps, Indian, 23–26, 117–18; influences on traders, 22; influences on European maps, 22; combine water and land routes, 53; mapping of pathways, 53, 118

McGillivray, Alexander, 184, 186, 188, 189

McGillivray, John (Trader), 128

McGillivray, Lachlan (Creek Trader, Merchant-Trader), 78, 89, 96, 98, 104; leaves Augusta, 98, 112, 175–76; protects business partners, 98; as millowner, 106; as slaveowner, 107–8, 111; leaves property to Scottish relatives, 112; rags-to-riches legend of, 120; defends Indian trade, 146; as literary patron, 148; held captive by Gun Merchant, 158–59, 166, 168. *See also* Brown, Rae, and Company; Clark, Daniel; Galphin, George; Ross, John; Sludders, William (elder).

Merchant-Traders. *See* Traders, Merchant

Mingo Ouma (Chickasaw Headman): map of Southeast, 24, *25*, 53

Mitchell, John, 42, 45; *A Map of the British and French Dominions of North America*, 30, 32–34, 36–39, *37*, *38*, 43

Mitchell, Samuel Augustus, 195

Mobile, Alabama, 114, 142, 171

Moll, Herman, 15–16, 19, 30–31; *A New Map of the North Parts of America Claimed by France*, 16, 17

Montgomery, Robert, 55

Mortar of Okchai (Upper Creek Headman), 25–26

Muccolasses (Upper Creek Town), 136, 157, 160–61

Mylne, William: house of, 94; relation to trading companies, 99–100; and slavery, 110; gets lost traveling, 121. *See also* Augusta; Augustans, Non-trader; Traders, Merchant; Trading Companies

Nairne, Thomas, 118–19, 164; map by, 14–15, *14*, 23, 30, 32; plan for Southeast, 14–15, 30–31, 39

"Neighborhood," 10; as common term for Southeast, 174–75; and newspapers, 182–83; idea of, 182–88, 190–91; and Georgian identity, 189–91

Netherclift, Thomas, 61, 113, 140

Neutrality: Creek policy of, 117–18; influence on trading stores, 160–61; during American Revolution, 176

256 / INDEX

"New Purchase" of 1773, 44, 150; and American Revolution, 48, 112–13, 171, 175; effects on Indian trade, 113–14, 145. *See also* Augusta Congress of 1773

New Windsor, South Carolina ("Savannah Town"), 20; trading boats and, 56; relation with Augusta, 57, 58, 61, 83, 84–86, 88

Newspapers: as geographic documents, 10–11, 175, 179, 180–82; borders and frontiers in, 181–82, 192–93; and idea of "Neighborhood," 182–84

Ninety-Six, South Carolina, 91–92

O'Brien, Kennedy (Cherokee Trader), 83
Ogeechee Settlements: unlicensed trade at, 102–5; and horses, 130
Oglethorpe, James, 196; plan for Augusta, 1, 55–56, 80; plan for Georgia, 1, 15, 20; and Indian trade, 1, 19–20, 52, 56–58, 86–87; and Savannah River, 1, 56, 62; and cartography, 19–20. *See also* Georgia (Colony); Stephens, William; Trustees for Establishing the Colony of Georgia
Ohio Valley, 52, 118, 190, 192
Okchai (Upper Creek Town), 118, 158–59
Okfuskee (Upper Creek Town), 27, 28, 145, 154; 1760 attacks at, 78, 167, 168; and trade in settlements, 102; and paths, 118, 120

Packhorse Trains, 3, 43, 78, 196; in Augusta, 100; speed of travel, 121; employ Indians, 123; as adaptation to Southeastern travel, 127–28; description of, 127–29; and horse thefts, 132–33. *See also* Horses; Indian Trade; Packhorsemen
Packhorsemen: and paths, 122–23; dress of, 128; and horse thieving, 132–33; relation to employers, 134–35; enslaved, 136–38, 139; live in trading stores, 152. *See also* Horses, Indian Trade; Packhorse Trains
Paine, Samuel (Chickasaw Trader), 131–32
Paths, 27, 171, 195; African Americans and, 9, 116, 136–40; traders and, 7, 8, 9, 27, 78, 116, 119, 121–23; Indians and, 8, 9, 24, 27, 116–18, 123, 126–27; packhorsemen and, 9, 121–23; travel along, 9–10, 116, 120–23, 125–26, 129–30; as feature on European maps, 23, 31, 45–47, 127, 195; as feature on Indian maps, 25, 53; uncertainty of, 28, 114, 118–28; influence on Augusta settlement, 78–79, 89–90, 103–4, 114; power relations on, 115–16; and opportunity, 116, 118–19, 136–37; private property on, 116, 120, 123–25; personal property on, 116, 123–24; as metaphor, 116–18; influence on Indian politics, 118. *See also* Horses; Packhorse Trains; Packhorsemen; Traders, Village

Pensacola, 138, 139, 142, 186; becomes center of Indian trade, 114, 134, 140, 171; and horse trade, 134, 136
Pepper, Daniel, 128, 130, 156
Perriman, Thomas (Creek Trader), 164
Pettygrew, John (Creek Trader), 28; estate of, 96; and paths, 121
Pigg, John, 136
"Plan for Civilization," 10–11, 147–50, 151–52 187–88, 190; and Creek women, 165
Pompey (Boatman), 70
Popple, Henry: *A Map of the British Empire in America*, 19–20, 30, 33, 33–35, 36, 37–38; and trade geography, 32–35
Proclamation of 1763, 43, 45; establishes system of general licenses, 42, 47, 108, 113; effects on Indian trade, 108–9, 113, 143, 149; trader complaints about, 148–49; Creek complaints about, 159. *See also* Britain, Royal Government of; Stuart, John
Property, Personal, 10; European ideas of, 116, 120, 134; Indian ideas of, 116, 123–24, 125–26, 127, 134, 135–36; on paths, 116, 123–24, 127; and slavery, 116
Property, Private: and paths, 123–25; among Creeks, 5, 124, 165, 171, 177–78; and trading stores, 157–58, 169–70
Purcell, Joseph, 40, 44–45; manuscript map, 39–40, 26, 46

Rae, John (Boatman, Merchant-Trader), 78, 89, 90, 96, 104, 112, 128, 176; as boatman, 49, 65, 70, 76; career of, 49–50, 97–98; as slaveowner, 50, 75, 107–8; as rancher, 106; sells horses, 131. *See also* Barksdale, Isaac; Boatmen,

INDEX / 257

Indian Trade; Brown, Rae, and Company; Pettygrew, John
Rae, William, 78, 168–69. *See also* Barksdale, Isaac
Rae's Creek, 114
Regulators (South Carolina), 133, 135
Richmond County Academy Board of Trustees, 173, 195, 196; tasked with re-ordering Augusta, 173–74; and geographic education, 179–80
Rivers: unpredictability of, 6–7, 9, 61–64, 122; English ideas of, 8, 9, 54–56, 58, 62–63; Indian ideas of, 8, 24, 51–52; in England, 9, 54, 63; as map feature, 23; roles in colonization, 50; African ideas of, 71–72; and paths, 120, 122. *See also* Boatmen, Indian Trade; Savannah River
Roads: in England, 122; in Scotland and Ireland, 122–23; in Anglo-America, 126; in nineteenth-century Southeast, 194–95
Romans, Bernard, 47, 170, 182
Ross, John (Creek Trader), 78, 96, 125–26, 168–69
Ross, Thomas (Creek Trader), 121
Rum: in Trustee Georgia, 56–59; and travel, 121; and trade, 125, 134, 142; Indian complaints about, 136, 159. *See also* Indian Trade Goods

Salisbury, North Carolina, 91
Savannah (City), 1, 3, 20, 53, 56, 180, 196; place in Indian trade, 49; merchants of, 60–61; African American community at, 74; plan of, 79–80; walled city, 91; and American Revolution, 175
Savannah Indians, 31, 52, 127
Savannah River, 3, 17, 19, 134; as landscape, 1, 9, 51–52, 61–63, 68–69, 70; relationship with Augusta, 1, 50; relationship with Indian trade, 3, 49–51, 144, 171; European ideas of, 9, 50, 52, 53–56, 58–64, 68–69, 76; as boundary, 20, 45, 50, 52–53, 72, 76, 84–86; boatmen's ideas of, 50; Indian ideas of, 50–51, 53, 76; and slavery, 50, 69–70, 72–76; In nineteenth century, 196. *See also* Rivers
Schenectady, New York, 91

Scottish Enlightenment, 148–49
Settlers, 136, 175; and backcountry, 4–5, 90–91; influence on Indian trade, 47, 102–5; and American Revolution, 48, 175; and town formation, 90–91; in Georgia (State), 191–92, 194; relations with Creeks, 78, 102–5
Seven Years' War, 39, 41–43, 47, 78, 149, 159
Shawnees, 118
Shepherd, Peter (Boatman), 65, 68, 70; as slaveowner, 74
Silver Bluff, 62, 94, 150; and local economy of Augusta, 105–6; slavery at, 109–11, 139. *See also* Galphin, George
Slavery. *See* African Americans, Enslaved; Augusta; Boatmen; Creek Women; Creeks (General References); Indian Trade; Mylne, William; Packhorsemen; Property, Personal; Savannah River; Traders, Merchant; Traders, Village; Trading Boats; Trading Companies; Trading Compounds; Trading Stores
Sludders, William (Elder, Merchant-Trader), 88, 89, 96, 112, 128. *See also* Archibald McGillivray and Company; Brown, Parick; Brown, Rae, and Company; Clark, Daniel; Galphin, George; McGillivray, Lachlan; Rae, John
Sludders, William (Younger, Merchant-Trader), 128
Smith, Adam, 149
South Carolina, 3, 20, 24, 31, 51; diplomatic concerns of, 12, 14–18, 30; reforms Indian trade, 19, 42; relations with Creek Indians, 16–17, 52–53; conflicts with Georgia over Savannah River, 52–59; relations with Cherokees, 39, 41, 78
Spencer, John (Creek Trader), 164; defies British authority, 98, 157–58; personal relations with slaves, 109; trade with Fort Toulouse, 160–61
Spain. *See* Florida (Spanish)
Stephens, William, 65, 66, 68, 69, 74, 80, 81, 83–86, 89, 155. *See also* Oglethorpe, James; Trustees for Establishing the Colony of Georgia
Stewart, Mrs., 105–6

Stuart, John, 44, 48, 137, 145, 148, 150, 153; manuscript map, 26, 39–41, 43, 45–46, *46*, 121; attempts to regulate Indian trade, 39–46, 141, 156–57; and Enlightenment cartography, 40–41; opinion of traders, 42, 47, 147, 157. *See also* Britain, Royal Government of

Sturges, Daniel, 194–95

Surveyors, 43–44, 128

Sympathy, 149

Taitt, David (Surveyor), 44, 170

Telfair, Edward, 178, 184, 189

Towns, British: ideas of, 7, 8, 9, 80–86; settlement pattern in America, 90–91

Towns, Creek: idea of, 93; settlement patterns of, 51, 162; African Americans in, 137, 138–39. *See also* Creeks (General References); Creeks, Lower; Creeks, Upper

Towns, Indian, 3, 8, 10, 27; as map features, 30–34, 36–37, 45, 194–95; political independence of, 34–35; links to Augusta, 90–91, 93; links to paths, 116; number of, by confederacy, 130; relation to trading stores, 154, 159–60; effects of trade on, 171

Traders, Carolina: blamed for Yamasee War, 16, 20; conflict with Georgia Trustees, 21–21, 86–87, 147, 152–53; beliefs about Savannah River, 57–59;

Traders, Merchant, 2–3, 6, 103–104, 152, 195; and slavery, 8, 54, 61, 66, 70, 107–8, 109–11; claims to authority, 20, 46–47, 86–87, 94, 104–5, 118; dispossessed by American Revolution, 48, 173; relation to Savannah River, 50, 54, 57, 60, 61, 84–86, 122; influence over Augusta, 78, 79–81; 89, 97–98, 105–7; protected by Eastern Chickasaws, 92; conflict with settlement traders, 97, 102–5; leave Augusta, 98, 141–42, 173, 175–76; sociability among, 101–2, 113; and debts, 112–14; limits of authority, 132, 140–41. *See also* Augusta; Indian Trade; "New Purchase" of 1773; Proclamation of 1763; Traders, Village; Trading Companies

Traders, Village ("Sojourners"), 19, 32, 121, 171, 177, 196; movements of, 7, 8, 9, 22, 27, 43, 48, 121–24; conflict with British authorities, 16, 19–20, 32, 42, 132, 157, 167; marriage to Indian women, 19, 155, 161–62; 163–65; narrative mapping of, 28–29; claims to independence and authority, 29, 46–47, 121, 128–29, 132–33, 143, 155, 157–58; role as diplomats, 29, 30, 155–56; in Augusta, 49, 81, 83–84; relation to Indian authority, 87, 92, 152, 157–59, 161–62, 166–67; opportunities of, 119–20, 155; as employees of Augusta companies, 120–22, 124–25, 132, 134–35, 158, 170; and paths, 121–22; and horses, 128–32, 133–34; reliance on slave labor, 136, 177; competition with general-licensed traders, 144, 148–50; and idea of "civilization," 144, 146–50, 172; raise livestock, 149, 152, 177; disapprove of "beaver catchers," 155–56; violate Creek ideas of fair prices, 158–59, 166–67; trade with French, 160–61; adopt Indian cultural practices, 163–65; length of careers, 164; relations with children, 165, 171; relations with Creek headmen, 168–69; and slaves, 138, 169–70. *See also* Creek Men; Creek Women; Creeks (General References); Indian Trade; Traders, Merchants; Trading Stores

Trading Boats: description of, 1, 49–50, 64–66, 67; relation to Augusta, 1, 55–56, 60; regulated in Trustee Georgia, 21, 57–59; crews of, 49, 66–69, 70; and slave trade, 108

Trading Companies; influence in Augusta, 9, 78–79, 81, 86–89, 93–95, 97–102, 105–8; and slavery, 9, 107–08; as "houses," 29, 93–94, 96, 144–45; complaints about, 88, 97; personal connections within, 89, 93–96; rivalry with settlement traders, 102–5; effects of American Revolution on, 111–14; influence over village traders, 124–25; relocate to Gulf Coast, 142–143; partnerships with Creeks, 177. *See also* Traders, Merchant; Trading Licenses, Private

Trading Compounds, 9, 78, 89, 90, 94–95, 96–98, 152, 167, 195; fortified, 89–90, 92–95, 104–5; and slavery, 107–9

Trading Licenses, General, 143

Trading Licenses, Private, 19, 124, 143; held by Augusta trading companies, 124–25

Trading Stores, 10, 38, 47, 48, 60, 124, 141, 152, 155, 163, 170, 195; and housebreaking, 142, 152–53, 167–68; as symbols of authority, 142–43, 152; contested, 143, 152, 157–59, 162–63 167–69; European opinions of, 143, 152, 154–55; Indian opinions of, 143, 154, 155–56; appearance of, 152, 159–61, 166–68; as household, 152, 155, 156; British attempts to regulate, 156–57; as feature of Indian villages, 159–60; and Indian ownership, 159, 161–62; and neutrality, 160–61; Creek women's influence over, 162–65; cultural exchange at, 163–65; Creek men's influence over, 166–68; slavery at, 169–70. *See also* Towns, Creek; Traders, Merchant; Traders, Village

Treaty of Augusta, 1763, 137, 182

Treaty of New York, 1790, 181, 188–92

Treaty of Paris, 1763, 39, 142–43

Trewin, Sludders, and McGillivray, 97

Trewin, William (Merchant-Trader), 97, 98, 124–25

Trustees for Establishing the Colony of Georgia, 18, 49, 58, 80, 74, 147; conflict with Carolina traders, 21–21, 86–87, 147, 152–53; and rivers, 55–56, 57–59; reform Indian trade, 58, 79, 86–87; plans for Augusta, 79s–82, 84–86, 97–98. *See also* Georgia (Colony); Oglethorpe, James

United States: and Indians, 10, 151–52; relations with Creeks, 177, 179, 180, 187–88; relations with Georgia (State), 178, 186–91; relations with Spanish Florida, 184, 187

Velden, Vanden (Creek Trader), 147–48

Voyageurs, 129

Walton, George, 174, 184, 197

Washington, George, 172, 184, 189

Washington Administration: and "Plan for Civilization," 172, 187–88; policy towards Creeks, 187–88, 189; relation to Indian trade geography, 187–88; views of settlers, 190–91

West Indies, 72, 112, 163; Georgia Trustees' view of, 56–57

Westos, 52

Williams, Catherine, 99, 100

Williams, John Francis (Merchant-Trader), 95, 98, 100–1; illicit trade shielded from view, 98–99; leaves property to Barbadian family, 112. *See also* Mackay, Mary Chilcott; Mackay, Robert

Winchester, Virginia, 91

Wolf of Muccolasses (Upper Creek Headman), 119, 136, 139

Wright, James, 42, 48, 112–13, 150, 175

Yamacraws, 2

Yamasee War, 7, 16, 20, 42, 86, 185; blamed on traders; Influence on Southeast, 16–17, 19 32, 52, 61–62

Yamasees, 17, 118

Yazoo Land Sales, 114, 180, 181, 191

Yonge, Philip, 44

Yuchis, 2, 118 migration to Shenandoah Valley; 52; settlements on Savannah River, 61–62

Early American Places

On Slavery's Border: Missouri's Small Slaveholding Households, 1815–1865
by Diane Mutti Burke

Sounding America: Identity and the Music Culture of the Lower Mississippi River Valley, 1800–1860
by Ann Ostendorf

The Year of the Lash: Free People of Color in Cuba and the Nineteenth-Century Atlantic World
by Michele Reid-Vazquez

Ordinary Lives in the Early Caribbean: Religion, Colonial Competition, and the Politics Of Profit
by Kirsten Block

Creolization and Contraband: Curaçao in the Early Modern Atlantic World
by Linda M. Rupert

An Empire of Small Places: Mapping the Southeastern Anglo-Indian Trade, 1732–1795
by Robert Paulett

www.ingramcontent.com/pod-product-compliance
Lightning Source LLC
Chambersburg PA
CBHW011753220426
43672CB00017B/2946